Library of Congress Cataloging–in–Publication Data

Simonds, John Ormsbee.
    Landscape architecture : a manual of site planning and design /
John Ormsbee Simonds. — 3rd ed.
        p.   cm.
    Includes bibliographical references (p.   ) and index.
    ISBN 0–07–057709–9
    1. Landscape architecture.   2. Building sites—Planning.
I. Title.
SB472.S58   1997
712—dc21   97–16077
                                                    CIP

McGraw-Hill

A Division of The **McGraw·Hill** *Companies*

1 2 3 4 5 6 7 8 9 0   IIMP/IIMP   9 0 2 1 0 9 8 7

ISBN 0–07–057709–9

The sponsoring editor for this book was Wendy Lochner, the editing supervisor was Virginia Carroll, and the production supervisor was Clare Stanley. It was set in Nofret by North Market Street Graphics.

Printed and bound by Print Vision.

LANDSCAPE ARCHITECTURE

A Manual of Site Planning and Design

THIRD EDITION

Completely revised with emphasis on the shaping of a
better environment for living and the care of planet Earth

JOHN ORMSBEE SIMONDS

McGraw-Hill

New York   San Francisco   Washington, D.C.   Auckland   Bogotá
Caracas   Lisbon   London   Madrid   Mexico City   Milan
Montreal   New Delhi   San Juan   Singapore
Sydney   Tokyo   Toronto

LANDSCAPE ARCHITECTURE

This text is gratefully dedicated

To my teachers, whose gifts to all who would accept them were the open mind, the awakened curiosity, the discerning eye, and the compelling vision of that which is higher, wider, deeper, and greater—and worth the striving for...

To my students, who in thoughtful agreement or in lively dissent have proved a reverberating sounding board and provided a stimulating climate for discussion and research...

To my partners and colleagues in practice, for whom the planning of a better environment for living is a strong and vital compulsion...

And to my lovely wife, Marjorie, who has contributed much of time, thought, and inspiration in the writing of this book.

Contents

Foreword

Landscape Architecture has been written in response to the need for a book outlining the site-planning process in clear, simple, and practical terms.

It introduces us to an understanding of *nature* as the background and base for all human activities;

Describes the planning constraints imposed by the *forms, forces, and features of the natural and the built landscape;*

Instills a feeling for *climate* and its design implications;

Discusses *site selection* and *analysis;*

Instructs in the planning of workable and well-related *use areas;*

Considers the volumetric shaping of exterior *spaces;*

Explores the possibilities of *site-structure organization;*

Searches out the lessons of history and contemporary thought in the planning of expressive *human habitations* and *communities;* and

Provides guidance in the creation of more efficient and pleasant *living environments* within the context of the city and the region.

It is not proposed that the reader will become, per se, an expert land planner. As with training in other fields, proficiency comes with long years of study, travel, observation, and professional experience. The reader should, however, gain through this book a more keen and telling awareness of our physical surroundings. One should also gain much useful knowledge to be applied in the design of homes, schools, recreation areas, shopping malls, trafficways...or any other project to be fitted into, and planned in harmony with, the all-embracing landscape. This, at least, has been the express intent.

The work of the landscape architect
(architect of the landscape)
is to help bring people,
their structures, activities, and communities
into harmonious relationship
with the living earth—
with the "want–to–be" of the land.

The Hunter and the Philosopher

Once there was a hunter who spent his days tracking the wide prairies of North Dakota with his gun and dog and sometimes with a small boy who would beg to trot along. On this particular morning hunter and boy, far out on the prairie, sat watching intently a rise of ground ahead of them. It was pocked with gopher holes. From time to time a small striped gopher would whisk nervously from the mouth of his den to the cover of matted prairie grass, soon to reappear with cheek food pouches bulging.

"Smart little outfits, the gophers," the hunter observed. "I mean the way they have things figured out. Whenever you come upon a gopher village, you can be sure it will be near a patch of grain where they can get their food and close by a creek or slough for water. They'll not build their towns near willow clumps, for there's where the owls or hawks will be roosting. And you'll not be finding them near stony ledges or a pile of rocks where their enemies the snakes will be hiding ready to snatch them. When these wise little critters build their towns, they search out the southeast slope of a knoll that will catch the full sweep of the sun each day to keep their dens warm and cozy. The winter blizzards that pound out of the north and west to leave the windward slopes of the rises frozen solid will only drift loose powder snow on top of their homes.

"When they dig their dens," continued the hunter, "do you know what they do? They slant the runway steeply down for 2 or 3 feet and then double back up near the surface again where they level off a nice dry shelf. That's where they lie—close under the sod roots, out of the wind, warmed by the sun, near to their food and water, as far as they can get from their enemies, and surrounded by all their gopher friends. Yes, sir, they sure have it all planned out!"

"Is our town built on a southeast slope?" the small boy asked thoughtfully.

"No," said the hunter, "our town slopes down to the north, in the teeth of the bitter winter winds and cold as a frosty gun barrel." He frowned. "Even in summer the breezes work against us. When we built the new flax mill, the only mill for 40 miles, where do you think we put it? We built it right smack on the only spot where every breeze in the summertime can catch the smoke from its stack and pour it across our houses and into our open windows!"

"At least our town is near the river and water," said the boy defensively.

"Yes," replied the hunter. "But where near the river did we build our homes? On the low, flat land inside the river bend, that's where. And each spring when the snows melt on the prairie and the river swells, it floods out every cellar in our town."

"Gophers would plan things better than that," the small boy decided.

"Yes," said the hunter, "a gopher would be smarter."

"When gophers plan their homes and towns," the boy philosophized, "they seem to do it better than people do."

"Yes," mused the hunter, "and so do most of the animals I know. Sometimes I wonder why."

1
FUNDAMENTALS

PEOPLE ARE ANIMALS, too. We still retain, and are largely motivated by, our natural animal instincts. If we are to plan[1] intelligently, we must acknowledge and accommodate these instincts; the shortcomings of many a project can be traced to the failure of the planner to recognize this simple fact.

The Human Animal

Homo sapiens ("the wise one") is an animal (a superior type, we commonly assume, although neither history nor close observation altogether supports this assumption).

A human standing in the forest, with bare skin, weak teeth, thin arms, and knobby knees, would not look very impressive among the other creatures. As an *animal*, the bear with powerful jaws and raking claws would clearly seem superior. Even the turtle seems more cunningly contrived for both protection and attack, as do the dog, the skunk, and the lowly porcupine. All creatures of nature, upon reflection, seem superbly equipped for living their lives in their natural habitats and for meeting normal situations. All except the humans.

Lacking speed, strength, and other apparent natural attributes, we humans have long since learned that we can best attack a situation with our minds. Truth to tell, we have little other choice.

---

[1] The terms *plan*, *planning*, and *planner*, as used in this text, refer to the planning of our physical environment by architect, landscape architect, engineer, and urban or regional planner, working separately or, ideally, in close collaboration.

We alone of all the animals have the ability to weigh the factors of a problem and reason out a solution. We are able to learn not only from our own experiences but also from the disasters, the triumphs, and the lesser experiences of untold thousands of our fellows. We can borrow from and apply to the solution of any problem the accumulated wisdom of our species.

Our essential strength—the very reason for our survival and the key to all future achievement—is our unique power of perception and deduction. *Perception* (making oneself aware of all conditions and applicable factors) and *deduction* (deriving, through reason, an appropriate means of procedure) are the very essence of planning.

Down through the dim, chaotic ages, the force of the human mind has met and mastered situation after situation and has raised us (through this planning process) to a position of supremacy over all the other creatures of the earth.

Man makes his way with his mind.

We have in fact inherited the earth. This vast globe on which we dwell is ours, ours to develop further, as an agreeable living environment. Surely, we with our twinkling minds should by now have created for ourselves a paradise upon this earth.

Have we? What have we done with our superlative natural heritage?

We have plundered our forests.

We have ripped at our hills and laid them open to erosion and ever-deepening gullies.

We have befouled our rivers until even the fish and wildlife have often been killed or driven off by the stench and fumes.

Our trafficways are lined with brash commercial hodgepodge and crisscrossed with senseless friction points.

We have built our homes tight row on dreary row, with little thought for refreshing foliage, clean air, or sunlight.

Looking about us with a critical eye, we find much to disturb and shock us. Our cluttered highways, sprawling suburbs, and straining cities offend more often than they please.

We are the victims of our own building. We are trapped, body and soul, in the mechanistic surroundings we have constructed about ourselves. Somewhere in the complex process of evolving our living spaces, cities, and roadways, we have become so absorbed in the power of machines, so absorbed in the pursuit of new techniques of building, so absorbed with new materials that we have neglected our human needs. Our own deepest instincts are

> *Animals . . . live in the extensional world—they have no symbolic world to speak of. There would seem to be no more "order" in an animal's existence than the order of physical events as they impinge on its life.*
>
> S. I. Hayakawa

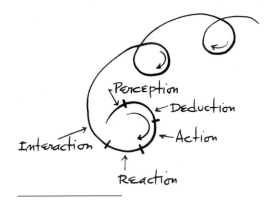

The thought processes of *perception-deduction* are in turn implemented by the physical processes of *action*, *reaction*, and *interaction*. These five dynamic drives form ever-repeating cycles and spin the intricate webbing of all human life.

> *And what is man? Amongst other things he is an organism endowed with a multiple organ, the brain, supported by the senses and the glands, in which the formative property of organic processes is applied to the memory records of experience. The brain orders its own records, and all mental processes express this basic activity. Art and science, philosophy and religion, engineering and medicine, indeed all cultural activities are based on the ordering of experience and the exploitation of the resulting design.*
>
> Lancelot Law Whyte

Ecology is the science of life or living matter in all its forms and phenomena interacting with the physical environment.

A consequence of the violation of nature.

White-tailed deer.

violated. Our basic human desires remain unsatisfied. Divorced from our natural habitat, we have almost forgotten the glow and exuberance of being healthy animals and feeling fully alive.

Many contemporary ailments—our hypertensions and neuroses—are no more than the physical evidence of rebellion against our physical surroundings and frustration at the widening gap between the environment we yearn for and the stifling, artificial one we planners have so far contrived.

Life itself is dictated by our moment-by-moment adjustment to our environment. Just as the bacterial culture in the petri dish must have its scientifically compounded medium for optimum development and the potted geranium cutting its proper and controlled conditions of growth to produce a thriving plant, so we—as complicated, hypersensitive human organisms—must have for our optimum development a highly specialized milieu. It is baffling that the nature of this ecological framework has been so little explored. Volumes have been written on the conditions under which rare types of orchids may best be grown; numerous manuals can be found on the proper raising and care of guinea pigs, white rats, goldfish, and parakeets, but little has been written about the nature of the physical environment best suited to human culture. Here is a challenging field of research.

The naturalist tells us that if a fox or a rabbit is snared in a field and then kept in a cage, the animal's clear eyes will soon become dull, its coat will lose its luster, and its spirit will flag. So it is with humans too long or too far removed from nature. For we are, first of all, animals. We are creatures of the meadow, the forest, the sea, and the plain. We are born with a love of fresh air in our lungs, dry paths under our feet, and the penetrating heat of the sun on our skin. We are born with a love for the feel and smell of rich, warm earth, the taste and sparkle of clear water, the refreshing coolness of foliage overhead, and the spacious blue dome of the sky. Deep down inside we have for these things a longing, a desire sometimes compelling, sometimes quiescent—but always it is there.

It has been proposed by many sages that, other things being equal, the happiest person is one who lives in closest, fullest harmony with nature. It might then be reasoned: Why not restore humans to the woods? Let them have their water and earth and

We are trapped in the fuming workings of our own machinery.

sky, and plenty of it. But is the primeval forest—preserved, un-touched, or simulated—our ideal environment? Hardly. For the story of the human race is the story of an unending struggle to ameliorate the forces of nature. Gradually, laboriously, we have improved our shelters, secured a more sustained and varied supply of food, and extended control over the elements to improve our way of living.

What alternatives, then, are left? Is it possible that we can devise a wholly artificial environment in which to better fulfill our potential and more happily work out our destiny? This prospect seems extremely doubtful. A perceptive analysis of our most successful ventures in planning would reveal that we have effected the greatest improvements not by striving to subjugate nature wholly, not by ignoring the natural condition or by the thoughtless replacement of the natural features, contours, and covers with our constructions, but rather by consciously seeking a harmonious *integration*. This can be achieved by modulating ground and structural forms with those of nature, by bringing hills, ravines, sunlight, water, plants, and air into our areas of planning concentration, and by thoughtfully and sympathetically spacing our structures among the hills, along the rivers and valleys, and out into the landscape.

We are perhaps unique among the animals in our yearning for order and beauty. It is doubtful whether any other animal enjoys a "view," contemplates the magnificence of a venerable oak, or delights in tracing the undulations of a shoreline. We instinctively seek harmony; we are repelled by disorder, friction, ugliness, and the illogical. Can we be content while our towns and cities are still oriented to crowded streets rather than to open parks? While highways slice through our communities? While freight trucks rumble past our churches and our homes? Can we be satisfied while our children on their way to school must cross and recross murderous trafficways? While traffic itself must jam in

There is that stupendous whole of a constructed environment, which, like fate, envelops civilized life. It must not be allowed to conflict seriously with . . . natural laws. . . .

We are convinced that patient research, starting from the elementary and progressing to the complex, can indeed gradually remodel the constructed world about us, to reach new levels of organic wholesomeness. . . .

The ancient idea of a world wisely ordered to function affords an emotional gratification that has shown eminent and long-tested survival value. It is the inspiration for all planning and designing.

Richard J. Neutra

In all, let Nature never be forgot.

. . . .

Consult the Genius of the Place in all.
Alexander Pope

The basic premise of science is that the physical world is governed by certain predictable rules.

Genius of place symbolizes the living ecological relationship between a particular location and the persons who have derived from it and added to it the various aspects of their humanness. No landscape, however grandiose or fertile, can express its full potential richness until it has been given its myth by the love, works, and arts of human beings.

René Dubos

and out of the city, morning and evening, through clogged and noisy valley floors, although these valley routes should, by all rights, be green free-flowing parkways leading into spacious settlements and the open countryside beyond?

We of contemporary times must face this disturbing fact: our urban, suburban, and rural diagrams are for the most part ill-conceived. Our community and highway patterns bear little logical relationship to one another and to our topographical, climatological, physiological, and ecological base. We have grown, and often continue to grow, piecemeal, haphazardly, without reason. We are dissatisfied and puzzled. We are frustrated. Somewhere in the planning process we have failed.

Sound planning, we can learn from observation, is not achieved problem by problem or site by site. Masterful planning examines each project in the light of an inspired and inspiring vision, solves each problem as a part of a total and compelling concept which, upon consideration, should be self-evident. Stated simply, a central objective of all physical planning is to create a more salubrious living environment—a more secure, effective, pleasant, rewarding way of life. Clearly, if we are the products of environment as well as of heredity, the nature of this environment must be a vital concern. Ideally it will be one in which tensions and frictions have been in the main eliminated, where we can achieve our full potential, and where, as the planners of old Peking envisioned, man can live and grow and develop "in harmony with nature, God, and with his fellow man."[2]

Such an environment can never be created whole; once created, it could never be maintained in static form. By its very definition it must be dynamic and expanding, changing as our requirements change. It will never, in all probability, be achieved.

[2] Translation from a manuscript in the possession of H. H. Li, descendant of architects of the imperial family.

The visual clutter of strip roadside development.

But striving *toward* the creation of this ideal environment must be, in all landscape design, at once the major problem, the science, and the goal.

All planning must, by reason, meet the measure of our physical dimensions. It must meet the test of our senses: sight, taste, hearing, scent, and touch. It must also consider our habits, responses, and impulses. Yet it is not enough to satisfy the instincts of the physical animal alone. One must satisfy also the broader requirements of the complete being.

As planners, we deal not only with areas, spaces, and materials, not only with instincts and feeling, but also with ideas, the stuff of the mind. Our designs must appeal to the intellect. They must fulfill hopes and yearnings. By empathetic planning, one may be brought to one's knees in an attitude of prayer, or urged to march, or even elevated to a high plane of idealism. It is not enough to accommodate. Good design must delight and inspire.

Aristotle, in teaching the art and science of persuasion, held that to appeal to any person an orator must first understand and *know* that person. He described in detail the characteristics of men and women of various ages, stations, and circumstances and proposed that not only each person but also the characteristics of each person be considered and addressed. A planner must also know and understand. Planning in all ages has been an attempt to improve the human condition. It has not only mirrored but actively shaped our thinking and civilization.

With our prodigious store of knowledge, we have it within our power to create on this earth a veritable garden paradise. But we are failing. And we *will* fail as long as our plans are conceived in heavy-handed violation of nature and nature's principles. The

Rape by the carryall.

> There is a creature native to Kenya called the flattid bug, and I was introduced to it in Nairobi, some years ago, by the great Dr. L. S. B. Leakey. What Dr. Leakey introduced me to was a coral-coloured flower of a raceme sort, made up of many small blossoms like the aloe or hyacinth. Each blossom was of oblong shape, perhaps a centimetre long, which on close inspection turned out to be the wing of an insect. The colony clinging to a dead twig comprised the whole of a flower so real in its seeming that one could only expect from it the scent of spring....
>
> The coral flower that the flattid bug imitates does not exist in nature. The flattid bug has created the form ... from each batch of eggs that the female lays there will always be at least one producing a creature with green wings, not coral, and several with wings of in-between shades.
>
> I looked closely. At the tip of the insect flower was a single green bud. Behind it were a half dozen partially matured blossoms showing only strains of coral. Behind these on the twig crouched the full strength of flattid bug society, all with wings of purest coral to complete the colony's creation and deceive the eyes of the hungriest of birds.
>
> Leakey shook the stick. The startled colony rose from its twig and filled the air with fluttering flattid bugs. They seemed no different in flight than any other swarm of moths that one encounters in the African bush. Then they returned to their twig. They alighted in no particular order and for an instant the twig was alive with the little creatures climbing over each other's shoulders in what seemed to be random movement. But the movement was not random. Shortly the twig was still and one beheld again the flower. The green leader had resumed his bud-like position with his vari-coloured companions just behind. The full-blown rank-and-file had resumed its accustomed places. A lovely coral flower that does not exist in nature had been created before my eyes.
>
> Robert Ardrey

most significant feature of our current society is not the scale of our developments but rather our utter disdain of nature and our seeming contempt for topography, topsoil, air currents, watersheds, and our forests and vegetal mantle. We think with our bulldozers, plan with our 30-yard carryalls. Thousands upon thousands of acres of well-watered, wooded, rolling ground are being blithely plowed under and leveled for roads, homesites, shopping centers, and factories. Small wonder that so many of our cities are (climatologically speaking) barren deserts of asphalt, masonry, glass, and steel.

For the moment, it seems, we have lost touch. Perhaps, before we can progress, we must look back. We must regain the old instincts, relearn the old truths. We must return to the fundamental wisdom of the gopher building a home and village and the beaver engineering a dam. We must apply the planning approach of the farmer working from day to day in the fields, fully aware of nature's forces, forms, and features, respecting and responding to them, adapting them to a purpose. We must develop a deeper understanding of our physical and spiritual ties to the earth. We must rediscover nature.

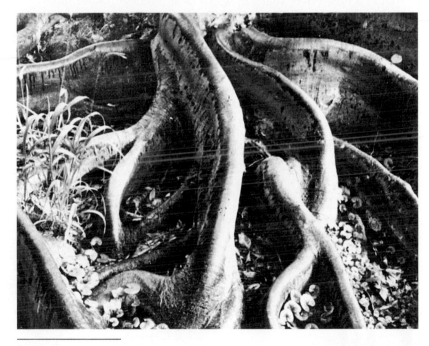

Roots.

Nature

Nature reveals itself to each of us according to our interests. To the naturalist, nature unfolds a wonderland of spiderweb, egg mass, and fern frond. To the miner, nature is the tenacious yet prodigious source of minerals—coal, copper, tungsten, lead, silver. To the hydroelectric engineer, nature is an abundant reservoir of power. To the structural engineer, nature in every guise is an eloquent demonstration of the universal principles of form creation to be understood and applied.

To the physical planner, nature reveals itself as the eternal, living, formidable, yet beneficent setting for every project and plan. It is essential to the success of our efforts that we come to know and understand nature. Just as a hunter is at home with nature—drinks of the springs, uses the cover, hunts into the prevailing winds, knows when the game will be feeding on the beechnuts and acorns of the ridges and when on the berries in the hollows; just as he senses the coming of a storm and instinctively seeks out shelter; and just as a sailor is at home on the sea, reads the shoal, senses the sandbar, interprets the sky, and observes the changing conformation of the ocean bottom—just so must planners be conversant with all facets of nature, until, for any major tract of land, local building site, or landscape area, we can instinctively recognize the natural characteristics, limitations, and fullest possibilities. Only by being thus aware can we develop a system of compatible relationships.

History shows us inspiring examples of humanized landscape planned in harmony with nature. One such example was the breathtakingly beautiful preindustrial city of Kyoto as it existed at the turn of the twentieth century.[3] Until only recently it could be said:

> Set amidst a national forest of pine and maple trees, Kyoto overlooks a broad river valley in which clear mountain water slides and splashes between great mossy boulders. Here in ordered arrangement are terraced the stone, timber, and paper buildings of the city, each structure planned to the total site and fitted with great artistry to the ground on which it stands. In this remarkable landscape, each owner considers his land a trust. Each tree, rock and spring is considered a special blessing from his gods, to be preserved and developed, to the best of his ability, for the benefit of city, neighbors, and friends. Here, as one overlooks the wooded city or moves through its pleasant streets, one realizes the fullest meaning of the phrase "the stewardship of land."

Civilizations have risen and fallen without apparently perceiving the full import of their relations with the earth.

Lewis Mumford

From the dawn of China's primitive folk religion, the relationship between man and nature has been conceived as a deep, reciprocal involvement in which each can affect the other. As the forces of nature can bring prosperity or disaster to man, so can man disrupt the delicate balance of nature by his misdeeds, for Heaven, Earth and man constitute a single, indivisible unity, which is governed by cosmic law (tao)....

No boundaries may be drawn between the supernatural world, the domain of nature, and that of man. Hence, if this sensitive organism is to function easily, man must do his part; when he conforms to natural law, society enjoys peace and tranquility; when he transgresses it, both Heaven and nature are disturbed, the intricate machinery of the cosmos breaks down, and calamities ensue.

The World's Great Religions

---

[3] With the rapid industrialization of Japan, many philosophic tenets developed over 3000 years of unbroken cultural evolution, which had guided all lives, thought, and land planning, have been tragically abrogated. Even Kyoto, the nation's cultural capital, while still one of the loveliest cities of the world, has felt the disruptive impacts.

A plant.

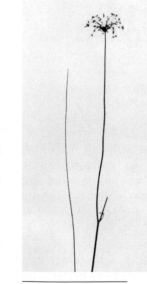

Weeds in snow.

Diatoms.

Kyoto, as an illustrious example of oriental land planning, was laid out in accordance with the precepts of geomancy. These deal with the location and design of land use patterns and structural forms in response to, and in harmony with, the paths of energy flow through the earth and the atmosphere.

To the western mind this practice may seem dubious. In the more mature cultures its efficacy is unquestioned. Unfortunately its principles have been veiled in religious mysticism and never clearly defined in technological terms.

Let it be said only that historically architects, planners, and engineers have expressed in their constructions an intuitive feeling for those geologic conditions and natural forces which have shaped and continue to govern the physical landscape and which have a powerful influence on all elements introduced. Such pervasive conditions include surface and subsurface rock formations, strata, cleavages, fissures, drainageways, aquifers, mineral seams and deposits, and lines and upwellings of electrical energy flow. They include also the air currents, tides, variations in temperature, solar radiation, and the earth's magnetic field.

The contemporary planner can only bring to bear a diversified training in such related fields as geology, chemistry, physics, astronomy, and hydrology and hope in time to develop a fuller understanding of cause, effect, and relationships.

66 *Kyoto,*
Mountain green,
And water clean.

Sanyō Rai

66 *Nature is more than a bank of resources to draw on: it is the best model we have for all the design problems we face.*

Sim Van der Ryn

Stuart Cowan

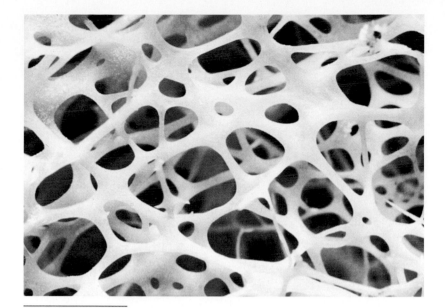

Bone cell structure.

Kyoto is a city of great harmonies, great order, and great beauty, because from broadest concept to smallest detail *it was planned that way.*[4]

The Ecological Basis

From the time of earth's beginnings there has evolved an interacting, counterbalancing framework for all life. This life matrix, or *biosphere*, born of earth, air, fire, and water, comprises the whole of our living environment.

It is as vast as the space between the basalt floor of the deepest ocean bed and the highest rarefied reaches of the outer ionosphere.

It is as awesome as the towering thunderheads, the roaring hurricane, and the crashing surf.

It is as tough as the granite hulk of a mountain.

It is "as fragile as frost at dawn."[5]

The biosphere, so fearfully and wonderfully contrived, is home to countless plant and animal communities that range in type and size from the invisible virus cluster to the roaming elephant herd or the pod of sounding whales. The biosphere is home as well to all members of the human race. As yet we have no other.

We are just beginning to learn the extent to which all organisms are interrelated and interdependent and the sometimes critical effects of almost imperceptible changes in the temperature, chemistry, moisture content, soil structure, air movements, and water currents on our habitat. The slightest change in the delicate web of life may have repercussions throughout the whole of a

---

[4] First edition of *Landscape Architecture* (McGraw-Hill, New York, 1961), p. 14.
[5] Ernest Braun and David E. Cavagnaro, *Living Water.*

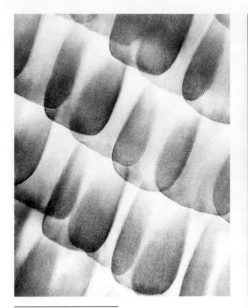

Wing scales of a butterfly.

Marine plant forms.

natural system such as that of a marsh, pond, watershed, or receiving ocean basin.

While soil and adequate water supply are essential to all living matter, their life–giving, life–sustaining energy is ultimately de-rived from the sun. This is received and transmitted through many life–supporting processes, such as evapotranspiration, osmosis, capillary action, fermentation, and oxidation. But it can be said that the underlying basis of all higher forms of life is the process of *photosynthesis*, which takes place in the chlorophyll cells of water–borne phytoplankton and land–based plants. Here, carbon dioxide is consumed in the presence of air, sunlight, and water, producing carbohydrates and free oxygen. These two component products are essential to life.

As living, breathing human beings, inextricably related to all other organisms and creatures, we are utterly dependent upon

Nature's ingenious process of pollination. As the honeybee lands and presses into the blossom after nectar, it triggers the flower stamen, forcing it down in an arc to make contact with and deposit pollen on the bee's body. Bee, flower, mechanism—what have we humans made to compare?

Shoals off Mozambique, from 20,000 feet.

the life-giving productivity of the remaining un-built-upon landscape areas of the earth. Should their life-support functions be diminished or disrupted to the point that they fail, we would then cease to exist. Only very recently, in the face of burgeoning population growth, rising indices of pollution, and the rapid depletion of our land and water reserves, has such a catastrophe seemed a remote possibility. Today, however, those scientists best able to assess trends and conditions have this very much on their minds.

What does all this mean to the planner, the designer of communities, the highway engineer, or the builder of home and garden? Simply that the integrity of the natural or cultivated landscape and the quality of the water within it and the air above it are to be in all ways protected. Land areas can no longer be treated as little more than pictorial stage sets of forest, billowing grass, limpid water, or lavender hills in profile, amid which constructions can be blithely aligned or indiscriminately plunked. It is no longer acceptable that any land area be considered an isolated private domain, to be shaped at will to the heart's desire or carved up unfeelingly into cold geometric patterns. No smallest parcel can any longer be considered apart from all other contiguous land and water areas. For it is now well recognized that each draws upon the other and in turn affects them. Ecologically, all land and water areas are interconnected and interrelated.

It is fundamental to intelligent land and resource planning that the natural systems which protect our health and well-being be understood and sustained.

That those most sensitive and productive, together with nature's superlatives, may be *preserved* in their natural condition;

Pond lilies.

Biosphere.

That protective support and buffer areas be *conserved* and devoted to limited and compatible uses;

That the less critical areas selected for *development* be so planned as to do no significant harm to their environs;

and that all land use plans be so conceived as to bring people into the best possible relationships with each other and with the living landscape.

The Earthscape

We have come to learn through the centuries that the spinning orb on which we live is a minor planet suspended in limitless space—an infinitesimal speck of matter in the universal scheme of things. Yet it is our world—vast, imponderable, and wonderful to us, a world of marvelous order and boundless energy. It is illumined and warmed in rhythmic cycles by the heat of our sun, bathed in a swirling atmosphere of air and moisture. Its white–hot core is a seething mass of molten rock; its thin, cool crust, pocked and creased with hollows and ridged with hills, mountain ranges, and towering peaks. The greater part of its area is immersed in saltwater seas, which ebb and flow with heaving tides and are swept to their depths by immense and intricate patterns of current.

From the ice-sheathed poles to the blazing equator, the earthscape varies endlessly. Wandering over it for something close to a million years, the human earth dwellers have learned

The biosphere of the planet Earth is divided into several major habitats: the aquatic, the terrestrial, the subterranean, and the aerial.

first to survive and later to thrive through a process of adaptation. This process, if wisely continued, should gain for us an ever-improving way of life. The study of the human–nature relationship is as old as humans themselves. In long-range perspective it is probably still a very young science, but, everything considered, it is the most basic science of all.

In our lifetime, we have for the first time scaled earth's highest peak, plumbed its deepest ocean trench, and penetrated outer space. We are tempted to believe that we have conquered nature. There are those who hold that in the years ahead we will finally subject nature to our control. Let us not delude ourselves. Nature is not soon to be conquered by puny human beings.

Conquer nature! How can we conquer nature? We are—blood, bone, fiber, and soul—a very part of nature. We are spawned of nature, rooted in nature, nourished by nature. Our every heartbeat, every neural impulse, and every thought wave, our every act and effort are governed by nature's all-pervading law. Conquer nature! We are but fleeting traces of life in nature's eternal process of evolving life and growth. Conquer nature! It is far better that we turn again to nature's way to search out and develop an order consonant with the universal systems, that our living may tap the vital nature forces, that our cultural development may have orientation, that our form building, form organizing, and form ordering may have meaning, that we may know again the rich, pulsing harmonies of life at one with nature.

The history of our progress on this earth is the history of an increasing understanding of nature's vitalities and powers. The wisdom of the wisest among us is no more than a comprehension of the simplest natural principles. The knowledge of our most perceptive scientists is gained through a faint insight into the wonder of natural phenomena. Our labored development is the development of those sciences that reveal to us a way of life more closely *attuned to nature's immutable way.*

Those of the forests, jungles, and sea are keenly sensitive to their natural surroundings and instinctively shape their living patterns to comply with nature's rhythms and cycles. They have learned that to do otherwise is to court inevitable disaster.

Years ago the urge to wander to strange new lands led the author to live for some months in lonely, exotic British North Borneo (Sabah). There he came to be profoundly impressed by the tremendous joy of the people in simply being alive—exultantly healthy and happy sons and daughters of nature. On the islands all live not only close to nature but *by* nature. Their whole life is guided day by day and hour by hour by the sun, the storms, the surf, the stars, the tides, the seasons. A full moon and an ebbing tide give promise of successful milkfish spearing on the shoal. The wheeling and screeching of the birds give warning of an approaching storm. In the quiet freshness of early morning a hunter may draw his little daughter to his side and, crouching, point a long brown finger to the peak of Mount Kinabalu looming high above the palm fringe. "Tiba, little Tiba," he may caution. "Look now at the clouds on the mountaintop. Soon it will be blowing and raining there, and the streams will be rushing full. So stay away from the banks today and play at home with your mama."

On the islands, clearly, the closer one's life is adapted to nature, the happier one's life will be. But not only on the islands.

Wildlife management area. (Kaneohe Bay, HI)

Of wide-reaching interest is an innovative schoolyard design program that features a working ecosystem. Its mentor, a professor of landscape architecture at the University of Florida, has shown hundreds of teachers how to work with their students in installing a habitat garden.

Life-support systems are those functions of nature which must be maintained in order to support human (and other) life. The primary functions include the production of carbohydrates through the process of photosynthesis and the provision of available water through the workings of the hydrologic cycle.

The hydrologic cycle is the continuous process in which water moves by evaporation and transpiration to the atmosphere, falls to the land as precipitation, and flows toward the receiving water bodies, principally the oceans.

This observation is fully as true of our life on our farms and in our suburbs and cities. Sometimes we tend to forget this salient fact as we go about our living and planning for living. And often this forgetting is the root of much distress.

The city of Toronto, for example, is surging northward into an area many miles from its harbor on Lake Ontario. Aside from the convenience of the lakeshore, the summer temperature there is often 20° cooler and the winter temperature 30° warmer than in the districts of new building concentration.

A popular ski resort in Pennsylvania was laid out with the major runs facing south and southwest, directly exposed to the melting winter sun. On the same property, undeveloped northerly slopes have excellent snow on two days for every day on which the planned slopes are usable.

In many cities along the Ohio, Missouri, and Mississippi rivers from 10 to 25 percent of the developed land area is inundated at least once every 35 years.

A perceptive architect has noted that not 1 percent of all the buildings in his contemporary city give evidence of having been planned with any regard for prevailing winds, solar radiation, or natural thermodynamics. The meanest thatched hut in Borneo is planned in well-considered relation to all three. It is a jolting experience to reflect on the natural-landscape potential of the site on which our city is built and to realize the pathetic results of our city-building efforts.

An ecologically sound community is one in which the plan layout, structures, and the daily lives of the inhabitants are responsive to place and to nature's processes.

" *Perceptions of nature form the framework of our lives. Shared beliefs about it are the deep structure of society.*

Since the dawn of civilization people have embraced the axiom that their social institutions must be in harmony with the earth. They have viewed nature as the objective reservoir of value . . . to shape and justify their law, economy, art, religion, educational system and family mores.

Alston Chase

Natural law guides and undergirds all sound planning considerations.

" *No myth, no religious miracle, no human invention begins to compare with nature.*

Ian L. McHarg

> *Tao, the Way—the basic Chinese belief in an order and harmony in nature. This grand concept originated in remote times, from observation of the heavens and of nature—the rising and setting of the sun, moon, and stars, the cycle of day and night, and the rotation of the seasons—suggesting the existence of laws of nature, a sort of divine legislation that regulated the pattern in the heavens and on earth. It is worth noting that the original purpose of ritual was to order the life of the community in harmony with the forces of nature (tao), on which subsistence and well-being depended.*
>
> *Mai-mai Sze*

> *The first chart of the Gulf Stream was prepared about 1769 under the direction of Benjamin Franklin while he was deputy postmaster general of the colonies. The board of customs in Boston had complained that the mail packets coming from England took two weeks longer to make the westward crossing than did the Rhode Island merchant ships. Franklin, perplexed, took the problem to a Nantucket sea captain, Timothy Folger, who told him this might very well be true because the Rhode Island captains were well acquainted with the Gulf Stream and avoided it on the westward crossing, whereas the English captains were not. Folger and other Nantucket whalers were personally familiar with the stream because, he explained, "In our pursuit of whales, which keep to the sides of it but are not met within it, we run along the side and frequently cross it to change our side, and in crossing it have sometimes met and spoke with those packets who were in the middle of it and stemming it. We have informed them that they were stemming a current that was against them to the value of three miles an hour and advised them to cross it, but they were too wise to be counselled by simple American fishermen."*
>
> *Rachel Carson*

Cone nebula, 2000 light-years away.

If our planning is basically a studied attempt to improve our living environment, it would seem only logical to proceed in full awareness of the sweep of the sun, the air currents, the peaks and hollows of the earth, rock and soil strata, vegetation, lakes and streams, watersheds, and natural drainageways. If we disregard them, we will engender countless unnecessary frictions and costs and preclude those experiences of fitness and compatibility that can bring so much pleasure and satisfaction to our lives.

We have learned to unleash the awesome power contained within the atom. Now we must learn the means by which to control it.

2
CLIMATE

IF A CENTRAL PURPOSE of planning is to create for any person or group of persons an environment suited to their needs, then *climate* must be a first consideration. It is fundamental, first, in the selection of an appropriate region for the proposed activities and then, within that region, in the selection of the most appropriate property. Once a site has been chosen, two new considerations suggest themselves. How do we best respond to the climatic givens in terms of site and structural design, and by what means can we modify the effects of climate to improve the situation?

The Planetary Framework

As an introduction to a better understanding of climate, it would be well to pause for a moment to contemplate the immensity of the universal framework that governs climatic and weather cycles.

The larger dimensions of world climate are determined and continually influenced by a number of imponderable factors, chief among which is the amount of solar radiation that the earth receives from the sun. This is the source of all terrestrial energy. It sets into motion and controls the thermal currents that sweep the oceans to their depths. It activates and determines the intensity of the sometimes mild, sometimes raging air currents of the troposphere. It sets the ponderous rhythm of glacial advances and retreats. Such phenomena are unalterable. We can only recognize the certainty of cause and effect and adapt our thinking accordingly.

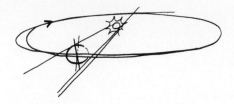

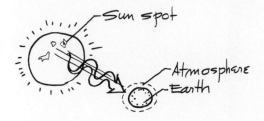

The planet Earth, with tilted axis, moves in its yearly loop around the sun. The incidence of the sun's radiation is a function both of our sphere's elliptical orbit and of its oscillating axial tilt. This variance in radiation accounts for climatic differentials and seasonal temperature change.

All terrestrial heat (energy) derives from the sun. The *amount* of energy received is related to the position of the earth in its elliptical orbit and in some yet inexplicable way to variations in the pattern of sunspots. In a lesser way energy reception is affected by conditions pertaining within the earth's intervening atmosphere.

Physical characteristics

Perhaps the most obvious facts of climate are the annual, seasonal, and daily ranges of temperature. These will vary with changing conditions of latitude, longitude, altitude, exposure, vegetation, and proximity to such weather modifiers as the Gulf Stream, water bodies, ice masses, or desert.

The amount of precipitation in the form of dew, rainfall, frost, or snow is to be recorded, as well as seasonal variations in humidity. The duration of sunlight in hours per day is of planning and design significance, as are the angles of incidence at prescribed times of day and year and the intensity of solar radiation. The direction and velocity of the winds and the date and path of violent storms are to be charted. The availability, quantity, and quality of potable water are to be noted, together with the depths at which it occurs. The geologic structure is to be described, together with soil types and depths and the existing vegetation and wildlife. Finally, the working together of all the physical elements as an ecological system is described to complete the story of regional climate.

The cyclic buildup and melt of polar ice are unpredictable. The periodic advance and retreat of the polar caps as they respond to solar forces in turn exert a massive influence on world weather conditions.

Social characteristics

The physical well–being and attitudes of people are directly affected by climate, and these in turn prescribe the planning needs. It is well, therefore, in the study of climatic regions to note behavioral reactions and patterns of community organization that are unique and attributable to the climate or the weather. The special foods and dishes, the manner of dress, and the traditional customs are indicative. And so it is with the favored types of recreation, the level of education, and cultural pursuits. Economic factors such as agricultural yields and the production of goods are to be noted. The forms of government and political trends are analyzed, as are the general state of public health and the incidence of particular health hazards and types of disease. A person's height, weight, circulation, respiration, perspiration, and dehydration have a direct relationship to climate, as do the factors of hardiness and acclimatization. It is no happenstance that the birdlike form of the maidens of the high Andes, with their thin ankles and capacious chests, differs from the squat and heavy build of Eskimo women. There are sound climatological reasons. In short, what one eats, drinks, believes, and *is*, is climate–induced and characteristic of the region.

Literature, art, and music all give illuminating insights into the character of the various regions and their inhabitants. Travel

The ocean currents help to distribute the solar energy input to all areas of the globe. The thermal currents of the ocean, like the currents of the troposphere, are solar-generated. They sweep in counterrotary patterns and help to distribute the earth's store of sun-emitted heat.

and direct observation give even more vivid impressions, and if one is to work and plan for the people of any area, detailed on-site research is essential.

Climate and Response

There is little to be done about the world climate except to adjust to it. The most direct form of adjustment is to move to that region which has a climate best suited to one's needs or desires. Such migrations or attempted migrations are the basis of much of human history. The alternative approach, barring admission to a climatological Shangri-la, is to make the best of existing conditions wherever one may be.

In broad terms, the climatic regions of the earth are four: the *cold*, the *cool-temperate*, the *warm-humid*, and the *hot-dry*. North America provides examples of all four. While the boundaries of these regions or zones cannot be defined precisely and while there are within them considerable variations, each has its distinctive characteristics and its strong influences upon any site development or structures to be planned.

As in the two-dimensional plan layout of farm, home, and community, so it is with the three-dimensional design of sites and structures within a region. Just as the use area or trafficway is oriented "into the breeze," "away from the wind," or "toward the sun" in some instances, so are site and architectural *volumes* shaped to afford exposure to the sun's warmth and light summer airs or protection from glare, oppressive heat, or fierce winter winds. All site and architectural spaces of excellence are weather-responsive; their form, materials of construction, and even colors are all climate-related. A postcard received from any part of the world depicting people, their dress, or their buildings will convey at a glance an informative story of *region*.

It is proposed that within each region there is, for a given climatological *condition*, a logical *planning-design response*. The accompanying examples show for various conditions an appropriate accommodation in the shaping of community patterns, site plans, or building designs.

Climate defines the type and range of human activities.

The Cold Region

Timberline and above.

Condition

1. Extreme winter cold.
2. Deep snow.
3. Strong winds.
4. High windchill factor.
5. Deep frost.
6. Scrub forest cover.
7. Short winter days.
8. Long winters.
9. Alternating freeze and thaw.
10. Rapid spring melt.

The Cool–Temperate Region

Mild winters, agreeable summers.

Condition

1. Variable temperatures, ranging from warm to hot in the summer, cold in winter, and moderate in spring and fall.
2. Marked seasonal change.
3. Changing wind directions and velocities.
4. Violent storms occur infrequently.
5. Periods of drought, light to heavy rain and frost and snow may be expected.
6. Soils are generally well drained and fertile.
7. Many streams, rivers, and freshwater lakes.
8. An abundant supply of water.
9. Land cover varies from open to forests with rich vegetative variety.
10. Topographically scenic, including marine, plain, plateau, and mountainous areas.

Community

1. Orientation to warming sun.
2. Provision for snowplowing and snow storage.
3. Utilization of all protective ground forms and covers as windscreens and soil stabilizers.
4. Crosswind alignment of trafficways and linear site use areas.
5. Reduction in size of plan areas to minimize costly excavation and frostproof construction.
6. Preservation of all possible vegetation, with the strong wind-resistant edges left intact.
7. Grouping of activity areas to reduce travel time.
8. Provision of community recreation and cultural centers within or near concentrations of dwellings.
9. Alignment of trafficways to fall within shadow bands to preclude ice buildup.
10. Avoidance of low ground, natural drainageways, and floodplains.

Site

1. Creation of enclosed courts and sun traps; use of textured construction materials and warm, "primitive" colors.
2. Use of short accessways, grouped entries, raised platforms, and covered walks.
3. Preservation or planting of windscreens; installation of snow fencing; use of low, strong vertical enclosure to brace for the gale.
4. Provision of intermediate points of shelter on a long traverse; placement of structures to block or sideslip the wind.
5. Use of post, beam, and platform construction to avoid the need for extensive excavation and foundations. Move with the ground surface by the use of stepped horizontal planes.
6. Clearing of small and clustered use areas, or "rooms," and meandering paths of interconnection *within* the scrub and tree growth. Developed areas should be limited in size to leave natural growth undisturbed insofar as possible.
7. Maximum utilization of daylight; orientation of buildings toward sunlit spaces with views to the sky and sunlit hills.
8. Utilization of the clustered-compound plan approach, which tends to engender pleasant community life and close social ties.
9. Use of decks, raised walkways, and flexible ground surfacings to preclude frost heave and keep people out of the slush and mud.
10. Provision of positive surface drainage to the natural lines of storm-water flow, with the soils, grasses, and other covers left undisturbed to prevent soil erosion.

Building

1. Design of massive, low-profile, well-insulated structures, with maximum exposure of walls and roof areas to the sun and minimum exposure to the wind; heat loss to be reduced in all ways possible, including limitation of the window area.
2. Protection of approaches from snow drift; the raising of entrance platforms above anticipated levels. The hazard of roof collapse may be reduced by steep-roof-and-storage-loft architecture.
3. Placement of windows away from prevailing winds; orientation of the long building axis into the wind and utilization of all possible topographic shielding and tree screens.
4. Location of entrances in the lee of the structure, with short protected passageways to limit the time of exposure.
5. Reduction of building perimeter and ground contact to reduce foundation problems and heat loss.
6. Forest cover preserved and buildings nestled against the protective slopes and tree masses.
7. Design of windows and living areas to exact the full contribution of the sun.
8. Attention lavished on comfort, architectural interest, and detail. In frigid climates particularly the "home is a castle."
9. With condensation and ice formation a problem, elimination of vulnerable joints and hazardous surfaces insofar as possible.
10. Use of steep roof pitches, deep overhangs, and exaggerated storm drainage gradients and capacities to facilitate rapid runoff.

Community

1. Definition of land use and trafficway patterns to reflect local temperature ranges and other climatic conditions. Extremes suggest compact plan arrangements; more moderate conditions permit dispersal.
2. Accommodation. Community plans must stand the test of function in all seasons.
3. Alignment of streets and open spaces to block cold winter winds and admit welcome summer breezes.
4. Design of streets, utility systems, and drainage channels to meet extreme conditions.
5. Consideration of high winds, flooding, and occasional snowstorms as important design factors.
6. Provision of extensive park and open-space systems as distinguishing attributes.
7. Incorporation of the natural waterways into the community plan for the use and enjoyment of the public.
8. Widespread installation of private and public gardens as regional features.
9. Preservation of indigenous vegetation within the open-space framework.
10. Planning of each community as a unique expression of its setting.

Site

1. Possibility of, and necessity for, wide variety in the type and size of outdoor activity areas.
2. Dramatization of the seasonal variations; consideration of spaces for winter, spring, summer, and fall activities.
3. Design recognition of the prevailing wind and breeze patterns.
4. Construction to withstand the worst of the storms.
5. Provision for all-weather durability and maintenance.
6. Protection of prime regional forest and agricultural lands.
7. Sensitive planning and zoning of all water-related lands to preserve their scenic and ecological values.
8. Use of pools and fountains to enhance community parks and gathering places.
9. Adaptation of community plan forms to provide the best possible integration with the natural-landscape features.
10. Full utilization of scenic possibilities.

Building

1. Elimination, by design, of extremes of demands for cooling, heating, and ventilating.
2. Consideration of the special design requirements and possibilities suggested by each season in turn.
3. Architectural plan organization and detailing in response to the cooling and chilling effects of local breezes and winds.
4. Structural design to meet the most severe storm conditions.
5. Consideration of shrinkage, swelling, condensation, freezing, and snow loadings.
6. Expansion and extension of plan forms when desirable, since excavation and foundation construction are not generally a problem.
7. Full utilization of the recreation values of each site.
8. Water catchment and storage is not a prime consideration.
9. Design of building areas and form in response to the topography.
10. Treatment of each building site to realize the full landscape potential.

The Warm–Humid Region

High temperatures and humidity.

Condition

1. Temperatures high and relatively constant.
2. High humidity.
3. Torrential rainfall.
4. Storm winds of typhoon and hurricane force.
5. Breeze often constant in the daylight hours.
6. Vegetative covers from sparse to luxuriant and sometimes junglelike.
7. The sun's heat is enervating.
8. Sky glare and sea glare can be distressing.
9. Climatic conditions breed insects in profusion.
10. Fungi are a persistent problem.

The Hot–Dry (Desertlike) Region

Desert.

Condition

1. Intense heat in the daytime.
2. Often intense cold at night.
3. Expanses are vast.
4. Sunlight and glare are penetrating.
5. Drying winds are prevalent and often raise devastating dust storms.
6. Annual rainfall is minimal. Vegetation is sparse to nonexistent except along watercourses.
7. Spring rains come as a cloudburst, with rapid runoff and heavy erosion.
8. Water supply is extremely limited.
9. Limited agricultural productivity necessitates the importation of food and other goods.
10. Irrigation is a fact of life.

Community

1. Spacing of habitations in the dispersed "hunter" tradition.
2. Adjustment of community patterns to channels or areas of air movement.
3. Avoidance of floodplains and drainageways. Disturbed areas are subject to heavy erosion.
4. Location of settlements in the lee of protective land masses and forest and above the level of storm-driven tides.
5. Alignment of streets and placement of gathering places to capture all possible air currents.
6. Avoidance of natural growth insofar as feasible. Disturbance of the ground-cover subjects soils to erosion.
7. Use of existing tree masses and promontories to provide a sunscreen to public ways and places. Supplementary planting of shade trees is often desirable.
8. Planned location of settlements with the arc of the sun to the *rear*, not *seaward*, of the building sites.
9. Location of settlements upwind of insect-breeding areas.
10. Admittance of sun and breeze to building areas to reduce fungi and mildew.

Site

1. Design of site spaces to provide shade, ventilation, and the cooling effects of foliage and water.
2. Provision for air circulation and evaporation.
3. Protection against driving rains and adequate runoff capacity.
4. Location of critical-use areas and routes in unexposed places, above the reach of tides and flooding.
5. Maximization, by exposure, channeling, and funneling, of the favorable effects of the breeze.
6. Use of lush foliage masses and specimen plants as backdrop and enframement and for the interest of form, foliage, or floral display.
7. Planning of outdoor activity areas for use in the cooler morning and evening hours. Heat-of-the-day gathering places should be roofed or tree-shaded.
8. Reduction or elimination of glare by plan location and well-placed tree plantings.
9. Elevation of use areas and walkways by deck and platform construction to open them to the breeze and reduce annoyance by insects.
10. Use of stone, concrete, metals, and treated wood only in contact with the ground.

Building

1. Induction of cooling by all feasible means, including the use of open building plans, high ceilings, broad overhangs, louvered openings, and air conditioning of local areas.
2. Provision of air circulation; periodic exposure to sunlight and artificial drying where required.
3. Architectural use of the colonnade, arcade, pavilion, covered passageway, and veranda; orientation of entranceways and windows away from the path of the storm track.
4. Design of wind-resistant structures or lighter temporary and expendable shelters.
5. Design of rooms, corridors, balconies, and patios as an interconnected system of breezeways.
6. Utilization, indoors and out, of indigenous plant materials for the cooling effect of their foliage.
7. Provision of shade, shade, shade.
8. Positioning of viewing points away from the glare and provision of well-designed screening.
9. Elevation of structures above the ground, facing into the breeze, and insectproofing of critical points and areas.
10. Provision of open, well-ventilated storage areas; use of fungus-resistant materials and drying devices as needed.

Community

1. Creation of cool and refreshing islands of use within the parched surroundings.
2. Provision of opportunities for group activity. Chill evenings in the desert, as on the tundra, suggest the need.
3. Adaptation of "outpost," "fort," and "ranch" plan patterns.
4. Within the dispersed compounds the planning of compact spaces with narrow passageways and colonnades to provide relief from the sun.
5. Location of homesteads and trade centers in areas of established ground covers; use of shelterbelt tree plantations.
6. Protection of all possible natural growth surrounding the development.
7. Avoidance of flood-prone areas. Those who have experienced desert freshets will keep well out of their way.
8. Minimization of irrigation requirements by compact planning and multiple use of planted and seeded spaces.
9. Location of settlements and community centers close to transportation and distribution nodes.
10. Coordination of land use and traffic patterns with existing and projected irrigation canal routes and reservoir locations.

Site

1. Amelioration of heat and glare by orientation away from the sun, by shading, by screening, and by the cast-shadow patterns of well-placed building components.
2. Adoption of the corral-compound (herder) arrangement of homesteads and neighborhood clusters.
3. Recognition of the automobile as the crucial means of daily transport and a dominant site-planning factor.
4. Screening of use areas and paths of movement from the direct blast of the sun.
5. Protection of outdoor activity spaces from exposure.
6. Preservation of native plant materials as self-sustaining and handsome components of the desert landscape.
7. Avoidance of arroyos and floodplains as development routes and sites.
8. Limitation in the size of parks, gardens, and seeded areas.
9. Use of tubbed and container grown plants, drip irrigation, and hydroponic gardening.
10. Incorporation of irrigation canals, ponds, and structures as attractive site features.

Building

1. Architectural use of thick walls, high ceilings, wide roof overhangs, limited fenestration, light reflective colors, and a precise design response to the angles and arcs of the sun.
2. Exclusion of the chill night air by insulation, reduction of heat loss, and use of localized radiant heat. The open fireplace is a desert tradition for good reason.
3. Low ranch-type spreads are a logical architectural expression of the hot–dry climate and desert topography.
4. Provision of cool, compact, and dim interior spaces in contrast to the stifling heat and brilliance of the great outdoors.
5. Sealing of all buildings against dust and wind. Airtight openings and skillful architectural detailing are required.
6. Grouping of rooms or structures around planted and irrigated courts and patios.
7. Provision of spring rainfall catchment and storage. Water from roofs, courts, and paved areas can be directed to cisterns.
8. Recycling of wastewater is prescribed. The type of use will determine the degree of treatment and purification required.
9. The provision of food and fodder storage is an important consideration in desert building design.
10. Adaptation of irrigation to interior courts and garden spaces. The evaporation of moisture from paved surfaces, fountains, spray heads, mulches, or foliage provides welcome relief from the heat.

Planning considerations

Clearly, architectural or landscape planning for the well-being of a cultural group demands an understanding not only of the physical nature of the region and site but of the people as well. Then, given a specific location within the region and a well-defined program of needs, the two-dimensional plan forms can be developed to achieve a pattern of appropriate, functional, and agreeable relationships.

The plan layout of farms and homesteads within any region is a telling statement about the climate and the people's accommodation to it. Community plan organization, too, and the patterns of urban form respond directly to heat and cold, wind direction, the frequency and intensity of storms, the annual fall of snow and rain, the availability of fresh water, or the need for irrigation. Modes and routes of transportation and even trip lengths are functions of weather and climate also.

Sometimes the most important consideration in site selection or planning is a realization of the need and benefits of protecting the natural environment. Native Americans well understood that to preserve the integrity of their hunting grounds their nomadic villages must be widely dispersed and clustered. Contemporary Americans have yet to understand the timeliness and wisdom of this lesson.

Microclimatology

Microclimatology is the study of climatic conditions within a limited area. It is sometimes referred to as the "science of small-scale weather." It may be inferred that the purpose of the scientific study is to discover facts and principles which may be applied to improve the human condition. This is precisely the case.

An example

As a hypothetical example let us consider a small walled courtyard in a hot-dry (desert) setting. It is proposed that, by the application of well-known principles of microclimatic design, an ambient air temperature at a point three feet above the ground surface could be reduced by as much as 30 to 40°F. This could well improve the existing condition from an intolerable situation to one of comfort and delight—all in all a worthy enterprise.

As a base condition, let us assume the worst. Let us assume that the enclosing walls are solid, admit no breeze, are high enough to provide an extensive sun-receiving, heat-radiating area, and are black in color to maximize their heat absorption. Let us then compound the disaster by flooring the empty courtyard space with solid concrete, thick enough for massive heat buildup and radiation and colored in a dark-red hue. To complete our experimental volume, let us imagine the courtyard to be so oriented as to receive the full force of the burning midday sun. It can be seen that a subject seated on a metal chair in the center of this unfortunate cube would be properly grilled, and that shortly.

In contrast, wishing to create a cool and refreshing courtyard in the same locality, let us "wing out" the side walls to catch the slightest breeze that might be channeled through the space. The walls themselves could be formed of light-gray textured concrete or stone rough enough to be heat-refractive and to receive several

clumps of vines. A pool, a brimming basin, or a splashing fountain installed on the base plane would introduce water. Water would also be used as a spray to moisten low mounded beds of planting edged with gravel mulch for rapid evaporation. From the irrigated planting bed a multistemmed shade tree might support a canopy of foliage and flowers, to cast patterns of shadow across the walls and paving. Additional shade could be provided on the overhead plane by light sails or panels of cool-colored nylon fabric. Tubbed and potted plants would add green relief and decorative interest. With webbed rattan furniture, iced drinks, and the sound of wafting music, the oasis would be complete.

The example is extreme, but it serves to illustrate the possibilities of small-scale climate improvement.

Guidelines

Whatever the climate or weather, when it comes to planning an agreeable living environment there are many microclimatic principles that can be applied to advantage. Among them are these:

Eliminate the extremes of heat, cold, humidity, air movement, and exposure. This can be achieved by intelligent site selection, plan layout, building orientation, and the creation of climate-responsive spaces.

Provide direct structural protection against the discomfort of solar radiation, precipitation, wind, storm, and cold.

Respond to the seasons. Each presents its problems; each provides its opportunities for adaptation and enjoyment.

Adjust community, site, and building plans to the movement of the sun. The design of living areas, indoors and out, should ensure that the favored type and amount of light are received at the favored time.

Use the sun's radiation and solar panels to provide supplementary heat and energy for cooling.

Consider the wind also as a time-tested source of energy.

Utilize the evaporation of moisture as a primary method of cooling. Air moving across any moist surface, be it masonry, fabric, or foliage, is thereby made cooler.

Maximize the beneficial effects of adjacent water bodies. These temper the atmosphere of the warmer or cooler adjacent lands.

Introduce water. The presence of water in any form, from film to waterfall, has a cooling effect, both physically and psychologically.

Preserve the existing vegetative cover. It ameliorates climatic problems in many ways.:

It shades the ground surface.

It retains the cooling moisture of precipitation.

It protects the soils and environs from the freezing winds.

It cools and refreshes heated air by evapotranspiration.

It provides sunscreen, shade, and shadow.

It helps to prevent rapid runoff and recharge the water-bearing soil strata.

It checks the wind.

Install new plantings where needed. They may be utilized for various types of climate control. Windscreens, shade trees, and heat-absorptive ground covers are examples.

The cooling effects of lawn, shade, foliage, moist soil, gravel, and water all modify the microclimate.

Consider the effects of altitude. The higher the altitude and latitude (in the northern hemisphere), the cooler or colder the climate.

Reduce the humidity. Generally speaking, a decrease in the humidity effects an increase in bodily comfort. Dry cold is less chilling than wet cold. Dry heat is less enervating than wet heat. Humidity can be decreased by induced air circulation and the drying effects of the sun.

Avoid undrained air catchment areas and frost pockets.

Avoid winter winds, floods, and the paths of crippling storms. All can be charted.

Explore and apply all natural forms of heating and cooling before turning to mechanical (energy-consuming) devices.

Reduction of heat loss

- Avoid exposure to prevailing winds and cold downdrafts from upper slopes.
- Avoid extremes in elevation.
- Avoid also site areas with wet, impervious soils, dead-air basins, and frost pockets.
- Provide wind shielding by ground forms and existing tree cover (preferably evergreen).
- If exposure cannot be precluded, plan compactly and for a slipstream effect, with narrow and solid building walls facing into the winter winds.
- Protect the dwelling entrances.
- Orient building facades to the east, southeast, and south and to the high arc of the sun.
- In cold climates locate use areas and structures in the lee of windbreaks to utilize snow outfall for ground and building insulation.
- Provide open space around buildings for air circulation and the play of the winter sun.
- Deciduous tree cover provides summer shade and casts shadows while admitting winter sunlight.
- Dig in. Partially buried structures receive insulation from the earth and present a lower profile.
- Select construction materials, surface treatments, and colors that absorb and radiate solar heat.

Reduction of cooling requirements

- Face use areas and buildings into the natural airstreams.
- Provide an overhead tree canopy.
- Utilize structural sun shields. Colonnades, arbors, wide overhangs, and recessed openings are familiar in hot climates.
- Compose buildings, ground forms, walls, fencing, and planting to channelize summer breezes through exterior and interior spaces. A broad, dispersed plan arrangement is indicated.
- Excavate for foundations. Structures built into well-drained slopes are warmer in winter and cooler in the summertime.
- Reach for the breeze. Utilize open planning, flying decks, and balconies.
- Promote ventilation by the use of breezeways, screened patios, louvered walls, and fans.
- Feature the use of water for its cooling effects.
- Utilize porous soils, mulches, ground covers, and irrigation to promote evapotranspiration.
- Use heat-reflective materials, rough textures, and cool colors.

Utilization of natural thermodynamics

- Consider energy generation by such sources as wind power, falling and flowing water, and solar panels.
- Maximize the warming effects of the sun and the cooling effects of shade, air currents, and moisture.

Site planning for energy conservation includes the above possibilities.

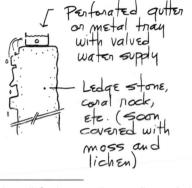

Trickle wall, for hot-weather cooling and plant irrigation.

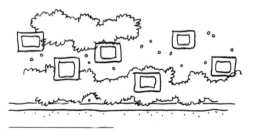

Pattern of stone, concrete, or metal pans, with spray heads, set in planting border or mulch and allowed to overflow, for cooling and irrigation.

MICROCLIMATOLOGY

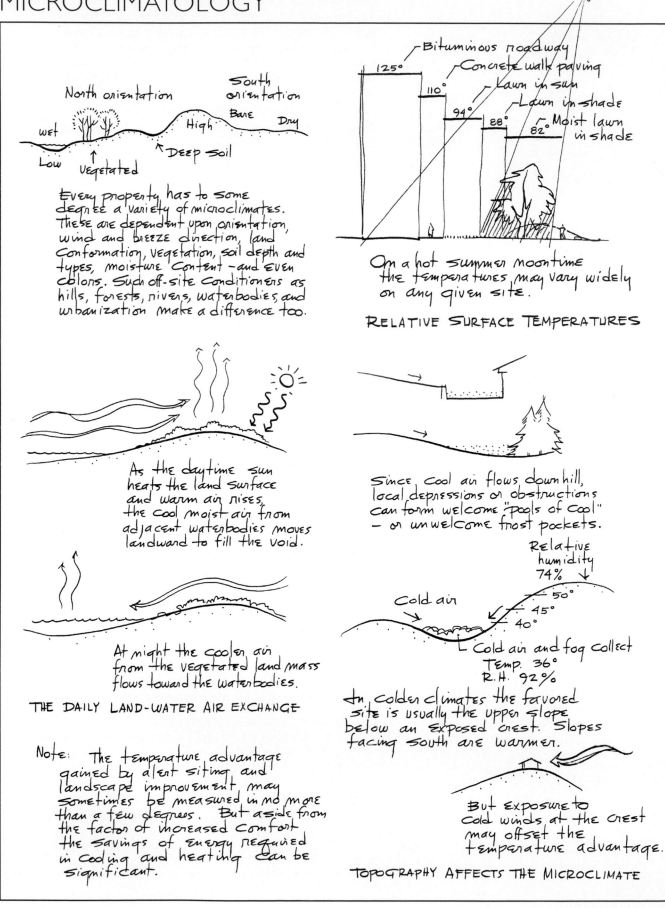

North orientation — South orientation

Wet — High — Bare — Dry

Low — Vegetated — Deep Soil

Every property has to some degree a variety of microclimates. These are dependent upon orientation, wind and breeze direction, land conformation, vegetation, soil depth and types, moisture content — and even colors. Such off-site conditioners as hills, forests, rivers, waterbodies, and urbanization make a difference too.

Bituminous roadway — 125°
Concrete walk paving — 110°
Lawn in sun — 94°
Lawn in shade — 88°
Moist lawn in shade — 82°

On a hot summer noontime the temperatures may vary widely on any given site.

RELATIVE SURFACE TEMPERATURES

As the daytime sun heats the land surface and warm air rises, the cool moist air from adjacent waterbodies moves landward to fill the void.

Since cool air flows downhill, local depressions or obstructions can form welcome "pools of cool" — or unwelcome frost pockets.

At night the cooler air from the vegetated land mass flows toward the waterbodies.

THE DAILY LAND-WATER AIR EXCHANGE

Note: The temperature advantage gained by alert siting and landscape improvement may sometimes be measured in no more than a few degrees. But aside from the factor of increased comfort the savings of energy required in cooling and heating can be significant.

Relative humidity 74%
Cold air
50°
45°
40°
Cold air and fog collect
Temp. 36°
R.H. 92%

In colder climates the favored site is usually the upper slope below an exposed crest. Slopes facing south are warmer.

But exposure to cold winds at the crest may offset the temperature advantage.

TOPOGRAPHY AFFECTS THE MICROCLIMATE

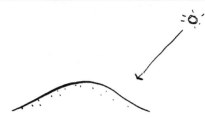

Slopes with southerly exposure receive the most hours and greatest intensity of solar heat each day. Spring can come weeks earlier on the sunny side of a hill.

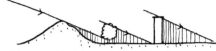

Topographical forms, tall buildings, trees, or other objects may reduce the total hours of daylight. Depending upon the climatic situation, full sun all day may or may not be desirable.

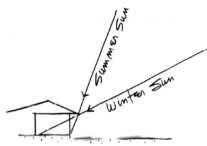

The sun's orbit and angle of incidence vary with the seasons. By orientation, screening, and overhang the amount of sunlight admitted to the interior can be precisely controlled.

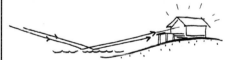

The glare from water, sand, or other reflective surfaces can increase heat loads.

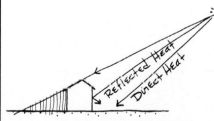

Buildings are temperature modifiers. By their positioning as well as by their form and character they suggest related uses.

Abrupt forms cause unpleasant air turbulence.

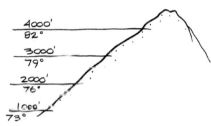

Smooth forms induce the smooth flow of air.

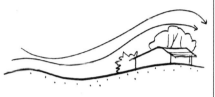

Temperatures vary with elevation—by about 3°F for each 1000 feet in the daytime. Nighttime differentials are greater.

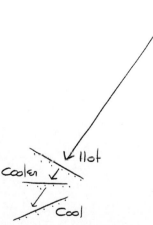

The more perpendicular a slope to the rays of the sun, the warmer the surface temperature.

A mild summer breeze can be amplified by the venturi effect of well-placed buildings, walls, hedges, or mass plantings.

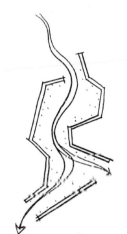

A breeze may be channeled and directed from space to space.

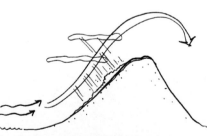

An air mass cools as it is driven up a mountain slope by prevailing winds, often to the point of precipitating its moisture content before reaching the crest. The windward slopes therefore tend to be humid and heavily vegetated, while the lee slopes, robbed of rainfall and subjected to the downdraft that warms as it falls, tend to be hot and arid. To a lesser extent any landform, such as a hill, island, or forest, can have the same effect.

LAND AS HERITAGE

By advanced land and resource planning, Virginia has shown that a state's ecologic, scenic, and historic superlatives can be conserved for the use and enjoyment of all now and future citizens and their visitors.

Hiking/camping

Hunting

Riding

Scenic

Trails

Historic

Water sports

Topsoil washed from the uplands to become the silt of the rivers.

A *natural system* is a co-related assemblage of topographic, climatic, or ecologic elements interacting in accordance with natural law.

Watersheds, wetlands, coral reefs, meadows, and anthills are examples.

of vegetation and animal life vary endlessly from patch to patch and from region to region. It is only recently that we have come to understand how closely all are interrelated.

When any area of land is disturbed, the delicate balances are shifted and the repercussions of change may be felt many miles away. This is not to imply that all natural or cultivated food–yielding land should be left unmodified. Often, with husbandry, its nutrient yield may be increased, and for many types of terrain there may be more important uses. It is rather proposed that in land planning and utilization the most productive areas are to be defined and protected. This is fully as true in the layout of a residential property as in the comprehensive planning of a state.

Habitat

The land is our terrestrial home not only for the human species but for all living organisms, which together comprise the biomass of the planet Earth.

Ecology has taught us that all organisms and creatures are interacting and interdependent; that all are contributors and have their necessary functions in the biologic scheme of things; that the mountains, forests, marshes, and rivers together form a *community* without definable limits; and that the integrity of the component natural systems must somehow be preserved.

While each living plant or animal can be seen to lay claim to its necessary living space, such patterns of use have been fluid, transient, and intermittent, changing as environmental conditions change. In the past, such adaptive plant and animal communities have formed spontaneously across the land–water surface of our planet, leaving the Good Earth time to heal between uses in preparation for new and often higher forms of life.

All organisms turn energy and food into living matter while producing waste materials of various kinds. This waste matter becomes food for legions of saprophytes, literally "decay eaters." These decomposers, which outnumber species of all other kinds, include beetles, fungi, nematodes, and bacteria. Through their complementary metabolic pathways, they return both essential nutrients and trace minerals to active circulation.

Sim Van der Ryn

Stuart Cowan

It is only within very recent times that members of the human race have seen fit to claim sole rights in land. This newly acquired compulsion to *own* land and take a permanent *fix* has become epidemic. Today, whole regions of the earthscape have been marked off by boundary posts and line fences, only to be further divided and subdivided, again and yet again.

Most such property ownership demarcations have been made on a wholly haphazard, geometric basis, without regard for topographic conformation.

Egret in natural habitat. Those who fail to understand the oneness of the natural systems are in many ways impoverished.

Reason would tell us that if land *must* be parceled and subdivided (our entire culture seems now to be operating on this premise), new lines of ownership should be brought into consonance with the boundaries of functioning land and water systems. It would seem obvious that neither property lines nor development patterns should transect or disrupt the crest of a ridge, the continuity of a flowing stream, or the organic unity of a tidal estuary.

Not only should our remaining undisturbed land be so apportioned as to express and accommodate the natural form order, but the presently fragmented landholdings must in many cases be reassembled and more logically defined. Over the ensuing years, through the emerging techniques of land use planning, zoning, redevelopment, reclamation, and resource management, the mutilated landscape may be restored to fairer form and to a healthful wholeness. This is not implausible. Nature is slow but inexorable in its progressions, leveling constructions that are artificial, erasing lines that are arbitrary. Nature is patient and has immense powers of recuperation and regeneration. Once we gain fuller understanding of its processes and laws and recommit our society to a supportive nature–human relationship, we can literally recreate the landscape as a more bountiful earthly habitat.

Land Grants

In the United States, rights in land have flowed to individuals, corporations, and agencies mainly from government—from colonial powers in earlier times and later by acts of Congress.

Through the century following the Louisiana Purchase in 1803, the United States disposed of almost 1 billion acres of land held in the public domain. At first, the more important dispositions were those made to the states in support of public schools and the land–grant colleges. Then followed allotments for wagon roads, canals, and the building of railroads. In the last–named case the entrepreneurs were usually given alternate sections within a broad swath contiguous to the railroad right–of–way. The price of the remaining sections was then doubled to provide the government as much revenue as it otherwise would have received and to reflect the fact that the presence of transportation increased the raw–land values. The Homestead Act of 1862 extended rights in land to settlers, who by five years of homesteading and making of certain improvements could obtain a clear title at the going rate of $1.25 per acre. Military bounties, Indian rights, and grants to encourage such activities as timber culture, mining, irrigation, and reclamation were to swell the dispositions to date to almost half of the total land area of fifty states, which is, in the aggregate, about 2.3 billion acres.

In Alaska today, the land–grant saga continues. From the time of the Alaska Purchase in 1867 until the Alaska Statehood Act of 1958, the federal government owned almost the whole of the territory, which is approximately one-fifth as large as all the contiguous states put together. In the act, Congress promised to transfer to the state of Alaska ownership in 103 million acres of the 375 million total. Another 40 million acres (plus a $1 billion bonus) have since been awarded in settlement to Inuit, Indians, and Aleuts who successfully pressed their claim of prior occupancy. Yet other vast tracts of Alaskan wilderness are being considered as new national parks and national monuments.

It can be seen that from our country's beginnings to the present time the dynamics of land transfer, ownership, and use have had profound political, social, and economic implications. The story of land exploration, land hunger, land transactions, regulation, and use (and too often *abuse*) is the story of America. Land is our ultimate resource. We must plan for its conservation, regulation, and development on a more scientific basis. We must learn to use it more wisely.

Land Rights

Once in private ownership, land can be readily used or sold as a valued commodity. A factor of use or sale is, of course, the ability to define and prove rights of ownership by clear title to the property. Such proof presupposes a survey and the establishment on the ground of stakes, monuments, or other markings by which the property boundaries can be identified. Further, there must be a means by which a lot or parcel may be so described as to dif-

66 *The [Anchorage] bowl has about a hundred and eighty thousand people now, or almost half of human Alaska. There are some . . . who would like to see Anchorage grow to seven hundred thousand.*

Idealists here in town see a need for a park in every housing development. They want to bury utility lines, reserve green belts, build bicycle paths. With these things the bowl could only contain three hundred and fifty thousand. They are making it very difficult for man, these people. They favor animals, trees, water and flowers. Who ever makes a plan for man?

A promoter, as quoted by John McPhee

66 *Conservation is a way of life which deals wisely with all natural resources, recognizing them to be . . . irreplaceable and essential to the welfare of mankind.*

Warner S. Goshorn

An analogy: that in its land and resource planning each state be considered as a developing farmstead. An astute farmer would study the lay of the land until he or she came to understand it—its nature, constraints, and possibilities. The farmer would then so lay out (and continually adjust) the working components—living quarters, barn, pens, fields, orchard, and lines of connection—as to bring them into best relationship to each other and to the land–water holding. The farmer would plan the whole and each new element in such a way as to conserve and take full advantage of the land's best features: the ground forms, the woodlot, the spring, the drainageways, the soil, and the natural covers.

Not only is such a farm (state) more productive,

Not only is it more efficient,

Not only is it more agreeable as a place to live and work,

It is also the best possible investment for the farmer, the farmer's spouse, and their heirs.

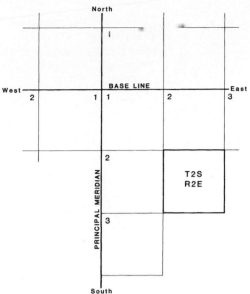

Within each region of the U.S. an east-west <u>base line</u> and north-south <u>principal meridian</u> have been established, and to these all subsequent land subdivision and title descriptions are related.
<u>Townships</u> are numbered north and south of the base line, and <u>ranges</u> east and west of the principal meridian.

The principal units of land within counties are <u>townships</u>, six miles on a side, comprised of 36 <u>sections</u>, each approximately 1 mile square.

6	5	4	3	2	1
7	8	9	10	11	12
18	17	16	15	14	13
19	20	21	22	23	24
30	29	28	27	26	25
31	32	33	34	35	36

TOWNSHIP 2 SOUTH
RANGE 2 EAST

<u>Sections</u> are further subdivided as shown. Lots or parcels are described by bearings and distances or "metes and bounds" from stated reference points within a given area of the survey grid.

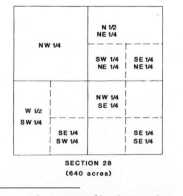

SECTION 28
(640 acres)

Diagrammatic system of land surveying.

rerentiate it from and relate it to all other landholdings. Finally, there is need for a systematic and orderly means of recording land descriptions and titles.

In the United States, by comparison, we are fortunate in our system. In many Latin American countries, for instance, few of these conditions pertain. There, accurate surveys seldom exist; rights in land are often clouded and in dispute, and the systematic recording of titles is not yet a fact of life. Much land has been preempted by squatters, now backed by traditional sentiment in favor of the pioneer and against those who own or believe they own superseding rights to the land. Such vague and chaotic conditions of property ownership lead to a lack of commitment, investment, and improvement by those not certain of established rights and give force to a growing movement toward massive land reform.

Land Surveying

The original land survey has left an indelible mark upon those parts of the United States to which it was applied. As Marion Clawson has noted, we are a rectilinear country, divided into squares and oblongs like a haphazard checkerboard, with the lines running directly north-south and east-west.

Roads typically follow the surveyed section lines even though this means going up and down hills instead of around them. Farmers tend to lay out their fields parallel to the boundaries of their land even though this may mean cultivating up and down the slope rather than along the contours. Much erosion has been caused or accelerated in this way. Some land experts, observing these types of bad land use, have been highly critical of the rectilinear land survey and argue for modification.

Land definition by transit and rod.

Perhaps the time has now come. The crude surveying instruments and need for range lines cleared through forest and swamps made the mechanical grid quite reasonable in its time. But now with the advent of photogrammetry, laser sighting, computer techniques, and electronic traverse computation it is time for a whole fresh look at the process of land description and measurement. A gradual land *resurvey* to follow and respond to natural topographical conformation is clearly in order. Governmental regulation could now require that future land surveys and dispositions be based, as appropriate, on more logical parcel boundaries to meet sound land use criteria.

Land Use

We Americans, with a seemingly inexhaustible land reserve, have been extremely wasteful. We have claimed, cleared, and too often exploited, then moved on, to do it all over again. It is only now, with open land at a premium, that we have begun to understand the need for husbandry.

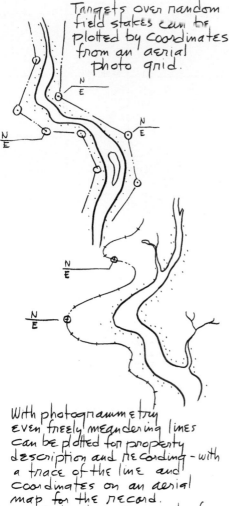

Tangets over random field stakes can be plotted by coordinates from an aerial photo grid.

With photogrammetry even freely meandering lines can be plotted for property description and recording - with a trace of the line and coordinates on an aerial map for the record.

Only when all or part of the boundary line needs be staked or monumented is a field crew needed.

Meandering property lines are easily established.

Cherry orchards in Michigan: preservation, conservation, and sound development.

There are many examples of land well used—among them New England villages fitted to the topography, the Amish farmsteads of Pennsylvania, Florida citrus groves, Wisconsin dairy farms, wheat and corn fields of the prairies, ranch lands of the plains, and bean fields, vineyards, and orchards along the west coast—and across the breadth of the land, well-tended homesites and gardens.

In the good examples we may perceive these simple precepts of sound land management:

* *Learn to read the landscape,*
    to comprehend the grandeur of its geologic framework,

> In the past decade we have lost farmlands equivalent to the combined areas of Vermont, New Hampshire, Massachusetts, Rhode Island, Connecticut, New Jersey and Delaware.
> Peter J. Ognibene

The *carrying capacity* of a land–water area is the population or level of activity that can be sustained for a given length of time without depletion of the resources or breakdown of the biological (natural) systems.

Adapt to the landforms:

To diminish landscape disruption

To reduce the costs of earthwork

To prevent the wasting of topsoil

To preclude the need for erosion control and replanting

To make use of existing drainageways

To blend into the natural scene

By means of site reconnaissance and soil surveys the most productive land can be designated for lawns, gardens, or crop production or be preserved in its natural state. Areas of thin soil, poor or excessive drainage, or underlying rock are prime candidates for projected development.

Homes, roadways, and cities belong on areas of low productivity.

The natural ground forms are best accepted as givens. They are the resolution of myriad forces at work over a long span of time. To adapt to them is to harmonize with the forces and conditions by which they have evolved.

to understand the vital workings and interdependence of the land and water systems,

to discern in each form and feature the unique expression of nature's creative process.

• *Let the land's nature determine its use. And so address each measure of the landscape as to evoke, through our planning, use, and treatment, its highest qualities and potential.*

Land use implications

When land passes from one ownership to another, certain legal rights are transferred with the property. Unless otherwise specified in the deed or governing regulations, these include the right to use, cultivate, mine, perform earthwork, remove the soil or vegetation from the land, or build upon it.

Running with the land are also certain responsibilities, many firmly established by our land law tradition. It is unlawful, for instance, to cause damage by directing an increased flow of storm–water runoff onto a neighbor's property. It is not lawful to alter grades significantly along a property line, or to create off–site earth slippage, erosion, or siltation, or to generate undue air, water, noise, or visual pollution. Other more recent restrictions dealing with such matters as wetland protection, beach access, erosion control, and unregulated grading are still to be fully tested in the courts.

Since most sites were acquired in the first place because they were attractive or had other positive qualities, it might well be proposed as a general rule that *the less modification, the better.* A fundamental principle of landscape design is to "plan to the site," letting the natural contours, conditions, and covers dictate the building and landscape forms.

Where for one reason or another it may be desirable to alter the grades, as to provide required use areas or to dispose of excavated foundation materials, the topsoil on disturbed areas should first be stripped and stockpiled. The revised contours will then be reshaped to accommodate the proposed uses, to express the meld of natural and constructed elements, and to enhance the building–site composition.

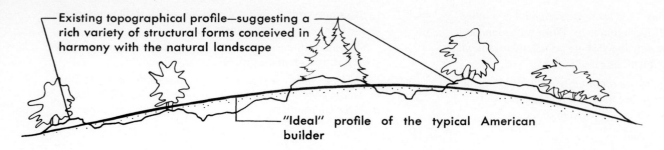

Existing topographical profile—suggesting a rich variety of structural forms conceived in harmony with the natural landscape

"Ideal" profile of the typical American builder

The code of the American subdivider and homebuilder (as it would seem to the casual observer)

Axiom 1. Clear the land.

Axiom 2. Strip the topsoil (or bury it and haul in new if this saves one operation).

Axiom 3. Provide a "workable" land profile (that is, as flat as possible).

Axiom 4. Conduct all water to storm sewers (or else to the edge of the lot).

Axiom 5. Build a good wide road—inexpensive but wide.

Axiom 6. Set the house well back for a big front yard.

Axiom 7. Keep the fronts even (this looks neat).

Axiom 8. Hold to a minimum side yard.

Axiom 9. Throw on some lawn seed.

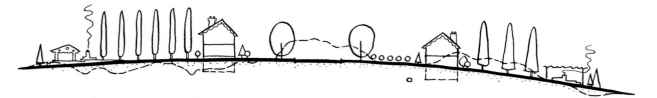

The American suburbanite dream (as seemingly interpreted by the suburban builder and by our present building restrictions)

A revised topography by courtesy of the bulldozer and carryall. The boulders are buried, the natural cover stripped, the brook "contained" in storm sewer or culvert. The topsoil is redistributed as a 4-inch skin over sand, clay, or rock. There sprouts a new artificial fauna of exotic nursery stock.

This is our constructed paradise.

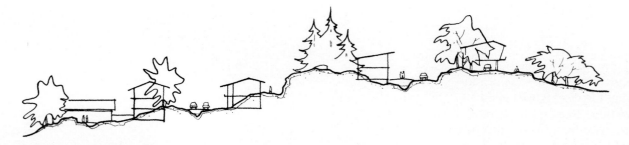

A better way is building *with* nature and in compression, which provides the human scale and charm we find so appealing in the older cultures, in which economy of materials and space dictated a close relationship of structure and landscape form.

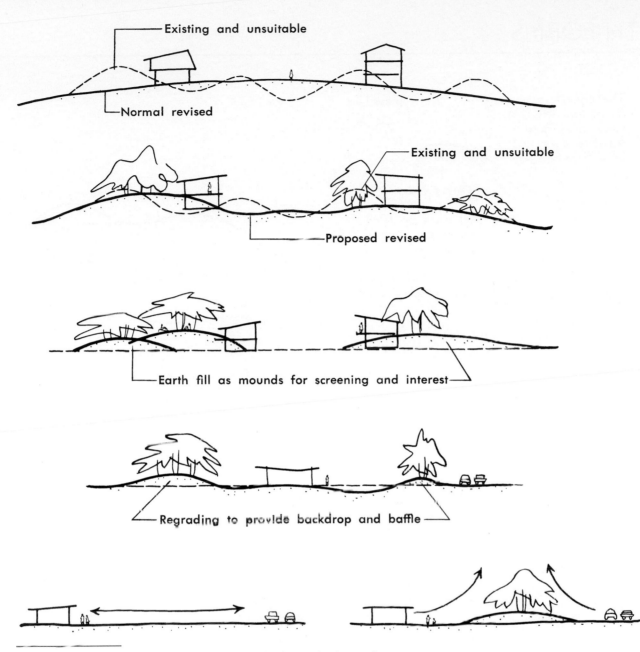

Existing and unsuitable

Normal revised

Existing and unsuitable

Proposed revised

Earth fill as mounds for screening and interest

Regrading to provide backdrop and baffle

If we must use our earthmovers to create a new landscape (and sometimes we must), let us use them to create a landscape of topographical interest and pleasant and useful forms.

EARTH FORMS

Protected,
Uncertain bearing,
Rich, deep soil,
Moist to wet,
Often flood-prone.

Prevailing wind

Thin soil,
Rocky base,
Exposure to sun,
breeze, and
storms.

Earth forms are eloquent statements
of the constraints and possibilities

New land shapes may create
a sculptural quality often lacking
in the existing topography.

The significant rise or depression
is a limit of visual space.

Cut and fill
in balance

Cut slopes - blended out -
add interest to a roadway

or home site.

Engineered

Naturalized

Landscape
Curve

Embankment

Shaped
Slope

Gully

Swales

Ditch

Mound

Knoll

Blending or simulation of
natural ground forms

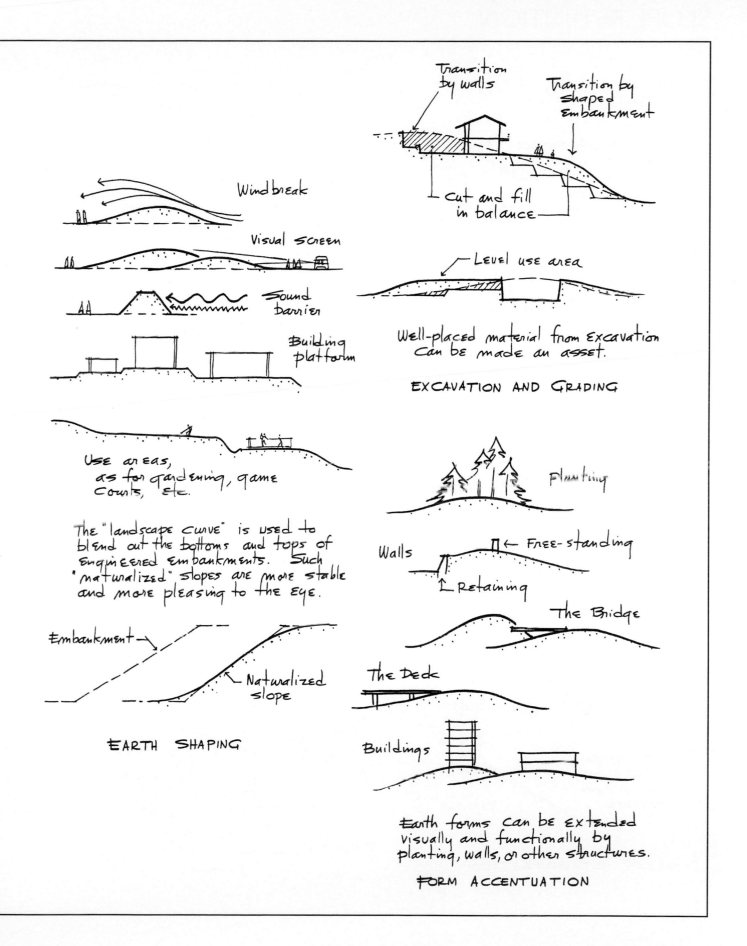

Transition by walls

Transition by shaped Embankment

Cut and fill in balance

Windbreak

Visual Screen

Sound Barrier

Building platform

Level use area

Well-placed material from excavation Can be made an asset.

EXCAVATION AND GRADING

Use areas, as for gardening, game Courts, etc.

Planting

Walls ← Free-standing

Retaining

The "landscape curve" is used to blend out the bottoms and tops of Engineered Embankments. Such "naturalized" slopes are more stable and more pleasing to the eye.

Embankment →

Naturalized slope

EARTH SHAPING

The Bridge

The Deck

Buildings

Earth forms can be extended visually and functionally by planting, walls, or other structures.

FORM ACCENTUATION

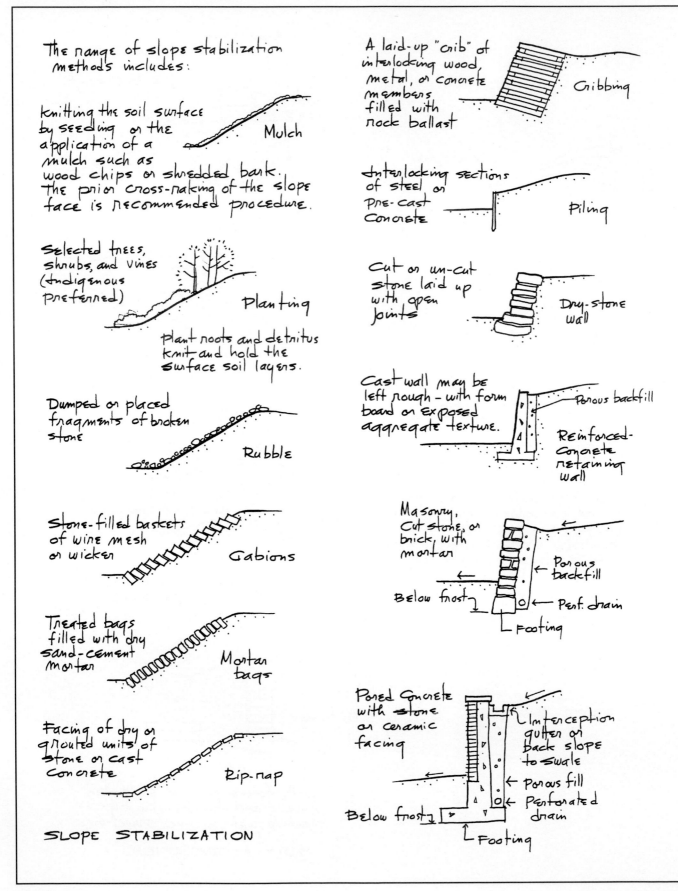

The range of slope stabilization methods includes:

knitting the soil surface by seeding or the application of a mulch such as wood chips or shredded bark. The prior cross-raking of the slope face is recommended procedure.

Mulch

Selected trees, shrubs, and vines (indigenous preferred)

Planting

Plant roots and detritus knit and hold the surface soil layers.

Dumped or placed fragments of broken stone

Rubble

Stone-filled baskets of wire mesh or wicker

Gabions

Treated bags filled with dry sand-cement mortar

Mortar bags

Facing of dry or grouted units of stone or cast concrete

Rip-rap

SLOPE STABILIZATION

A laid-up "crib" of interlocking wood, metal, or concrete members filled with rock ballast

Cribbing

Interlocking sections of steel or pre-cast concrete

Piling

Cut or un-cut stone laid up with open joints

Dry-stone wall

Cast wall may be left rough - with form board or exposed aggregate texture.

Porous backfill

Reinforced-concrete retaining wall

Masonry, cut stone, or brick, with mortar

Porous backfill

Below frost

Perf. drain

Footing

Poured concrete with stone or ceramic facing

Interception gutter on back slope to swale

Porous fill

Below frost

Perforated drain

Footing

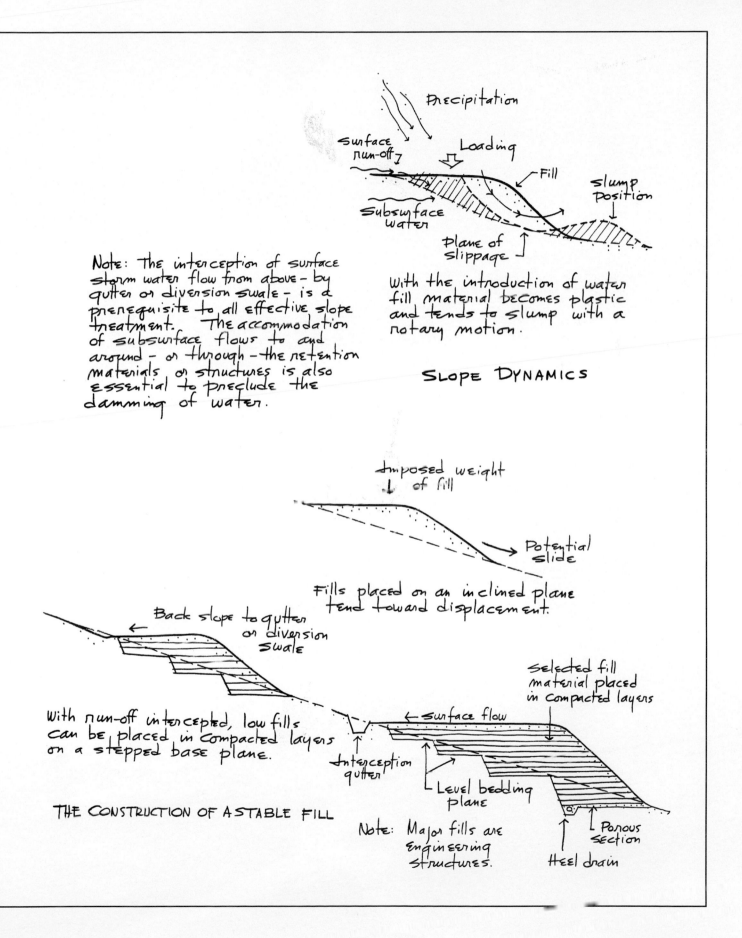

Precipitation

Surface run-off

Loading

Fill

Slump Position

Subsurface water

Plane of slippage

Note: The interception of surface storm water flow from above – by gutter or diversion swale – is a prerequisite to all effective slope treatment. The accommodation of subsurface flows to and around – or through – the retention materials or structures is also essential to preclude the damming of water.

With the introduction of water fill material becomes plastic and tends to slump with a rotary motion.

SLOPE DYNAMICS

Imposed weight of fill

Potential slide

Fills placed on an inclined plane tend toward displacement.

Back slope to gutter or diversion swale

Selected fill material placed in Compacted layers

Surface flow

With run-off intercepted, low fills can be placed in Compacted layers on a stepped base plane.

Interception gutter

Level bedding plane

THE CONSTRUCTION OF A STABLE FILL

Note: Major fills are Engineering Structures.

Porous Section

Heel drain

4
WATER

Free water is the shining splendor of the natural landscape. From the bubbling spring and upland pool to the splashing stream, rushing rapids, waterfall, freshwater lake, and brackish estuary, and finally to the saltwater sea, water has held for all creatures an irresistible appeal. To some degree we humans still seem to share with our earliest predecessors the urgent and instinctive sense that drew them to the water's edge.

Perhaps at first they were drawn only for drink, to lave hot and dust-streaked bodies, or to gather the bounty of mollusk and fish. Later, water for the cooking pots would be dipped and carried in gourds, skins, hollow sections of bamboo, and jars of shaped, fire-baked clay. Perhaps our affinity for water has increased with the discovery of its value in gardens and irrigation and with the knowledge that only with moisture present can plants flourish and animals thrive. It may be because in the deep, moist soils of the bottomlands the grasses are richer, the foliage more lush, and the berries larger and sweeter. Here too the refreshing breeze seems more cool, and even the song of the birds more melodious.

As Resource

In planning the use of land areas in relation to waterways and water bodies, a reasonable goal would be to take full advantage of the benefits of proximity. These benefits would seem to fall within the following categories.

Water supply, irrigation, and drainage

When these are important considerations, the area of more intensive use will be located near the sources. Those site functions requiring the most moisture in the soil or air will be given location priority. The efficiency of pumping and gravity flow will have much to do with the plan layout.

Irrigated fields will be established below points of inlet where possible and be so arranged that lines or planes of flow will slope gently across the contours to achieve maximum percolation and continuity.

Drainage will be maintained whenever possible along existing lines of flow, with the natural vegetation left undisturbed. It would be hard to devise a more efficient and economical system of storm drainage than that which nature provides. Runoff from fertilized fields or turf will be directed to on-site retention swales or ponds so that the water may be filtered and purified before reentering the source or percolating into the soil to recharge the water table.

Use in processing

When drawn from surface streams or water bodies for use in cooling, washing, or other processes, water of equal quantity and quality is to be returned to the source. Makeup water may be supplied from wells or public water supply systems.

Transportation

When waterways, lakes, or abutting ocean are to be used for the transport of people or goods, the docking installations and vessels are to be so designed and operated that the functional and visual quality of the water is at all times assured.

Microclimate moderation

The extremes of temperature are tempered by the presence of moisture and by the resulting vegetation. This advantage may be augmented by the favorable placement of plan areas and structures in relation to open water, irrigated surfaces, or water-cooled breeze.

Habitat

Lakeshores, stream edges, and wetlands together form a natural food source and habitat for birds and animals. When flora and fauna are to be protected, the indigenous vegetation is to be allowed to remain standing whenever feasible, and continuous swaths of cover are to be left intact to permit wildlife to move from place to place unmolested. The denser growth is usually concentrated along water edges and converging swales.

Recreational use

Our streams and water bodies have long provided our most popular types of outdoor recreation such as boating, fishing, and swimming. Along their banks and shores is found the accretion of cottages, mobile home parks, and campsites that attest to our love

More than two-thirds of the earth's surface is submerged in saltwater. The balance of surface area is generally underlaid with fresh water that fluctuates slowly in elevation and flows imperceptibly through the porous aquifers toward the waiting sea.

66 *If there is magic on the planet, it is contained in water . . . its substance reaches everywhere; it touches the past and prepares the future; it moves under the poles and wanders thinly in the heights or air. It can assume forms of exquisite perfection in a snowflake, or strip the living to a single shining bone cast up by the sea.*

Loren Eiseley

In Florida at least 65 percent of all marine organisms, including shrimp, lobsters, oysters, and commercial and game fish, spend part of their life cycle in the brackish waters of tidal estuaries and coastal wetlands.

Within the past century, over half of the state's wetlands have been dredged, filled, or drained.

The only way to protect fish and wildlife is to protect their habitat.

Water edges have universal appeal.

The qualities of water are infinite in their variety.

In depth, water may range from deep to no more than a film of surface moisture.

In motion, from rush to gush, plummet, spurt, spout, spill, spray, or seep.

In sound, from tumultuous roar to murmur.

Each attribute suggests a particular use and application in landscape design.

of water. It is proposed that in long-range planning, with few exceptions, all water areas and edges to the limits of a 50-year flood would be acquired and made part of the public domain. Sheathed in green and incorporated within the regional open-space network, such landscape features would provide a recreational environment second to none.

Scenic values

For most people, the glimmer of sunlight on open water is sure to elicit an exclamation of discovery and delight. The feelings may be expressed as a shout of triumph or as a silent upsurge of the

The sight and sound of moving water. (Missouri Botanical Garden, St. Louis, Missouri)

spirits. Not only the *sight*, but as well the *sounds* of water evoke a sense of pleasure. It would seem that we are so acutely attuned to the language of water—the trickle and gurgle of ice melt, the splash of the stream, the lapping of water on lakeshore, the surf crash, even the cry of shorebirds—that we can almost see with our ears.

A glimpse, a view, an unfolding panorama of the aquatic landscape is a scenic superlative. Streams and water bodies are the punctuation marks in reading the landscape. They translate for us the landforms and the story of their geologic formation. They set the mood; they articulate; they intensify. They give the essential meaning. What is a prairie without its sloughs? A meadow without its meandering brook? A mountainside without its cascade? A valley without its river?

Site amenity

Fortunate is the landowner whose property includes or borders upon an attractive stretch of water or affords even a distant view. In landscape and architectural planning, a chief endeavor will be the devising of relationships that exact the full visual and use possibilities.

Water as landscape feature

Most attributes of nature—the hills, the trees, the starlit sky—are usually taken for granted, but the value of free water is not. Where it exists, as in the form of pond, stream, lake, or ocean, the adjacent landholdings are eagerly sought. They are prized as sites for parks and parkways, for homes, institutions, resort hotels, and other commercial ventures. It could almost be stated as a law of land economics that "the closer a site to open water, the higher its value as real estate."

In the shaping of water bodies it is desirable that the outline be curvilinear, rather than angular, to reflect the undulating nature of water.

Often, to provide more efficient use of the bordering land, the pond or lake is first excavated along straight lines, which are then softened by curvature and by rounding the intersections.

Since in most methods of excavation, as by dragline or pans, straight, deep cuts are more economical, the central body of a lake is often a rectangle or a polyhedron in shape, with a widened perimeter shelf sloped to the deeper excavation pit and trimmed to more natural form.

From no point along the shore should the expanse of the water surface be seen in its entirety. If possible, the shoreline should be made to dip out of sight at several points to add interest and to set free the observer's imagination. By this design device not only is the water body made more appealing, but its apparent size is increased.

Natural Systems

In the past, fresh water in all its forms has been used, and too often misused or wasted, as if these were God-given privileges. Except in irrigated lands, where water rights and supply are jealously guarded, there has been little concern for what is happening upstream or downstream unless the flow should be cut off or increased to the point of flooding.

Water *flows*, inevitably, from source to receiving ocean basin. This continuity of rivulets, streams, and rivers can be readily observed. Not so obvious are the sequential and interacting relationships of the ponds, lakes, and wetlands. These too are links in the chain of flow. They are affected not only by the things that happen at their sides but by all that transpires within the upper watersheds or the subsurface aquifers that feed and help sustain them. These same subsurface water-bearing, water-transporting, water-yielding strata provide, also, the groundwater essential to farmland, meadow, and forest and to maintaining the level of the well fields from which our water supplies are drawn.

Water and water areas well used can benefit all who live within their sphere of influence. If, however, they are unwisely used, contaminated, or wasted, dependent life is thereby threatened, sometimes with minor loss or inconvenience, sometimes

The subsurface reservoir of fresh water may be tapped and used freely as long as the local supply is not thereby depleted. Depletion is caused not only by overuse but also, and more often, by destruction of the natural ground covers and vegetation, which would otherwise retain precipitation for filtration to the aquifer.

NATURE'S WATERWAYS

Snow trickle or other precipitation from the upper watersheds eventually makes its way to the sea.

Upland source

Freshwater stream

Bay

Ocean

Descending streams form riffles, rapids, cascades, and, often, plunging waterfalls.

Pools

Falls

Cascades

Lake

Marsh

Along the way are ponds, lakes, wetlands, and, finally, the teem-ing estuaries

Estuary

with major disaster, as by devastating drought or overwhelming flood.

It is only recently that entire river basins have come to be studied as unified and interrelated systems. Such a rational approach increases rather than limits the possibilities of fuller use and enjoyment and sets a workable framework within which all subareas may then be better planned.

Any consideration of the flow of surface or subsurface water leads one to the obvious conclusion that only comprehensive watershed management makes any sense at all. A parcel–by–parcel approach to the use of river-basin lands can only fracture the contiguous water–related matrix and disrupt the natural systems.

Problems

The problems to be precluded are those of rapid runoff, erosion, siltation, flooding, induced drought, and contamination. Simply stated, *any use that causes one or more of these abuses to any significant degree is improper and should not be condoned.* It can be left to biologists and legal experts to define a *significant* impact. But it can no longer be left to individuals or groups to determine whether their activities may cause harm to their neighbors, no matter if the "neighbors" live next door or at the river mouth 1000 miles downstream.

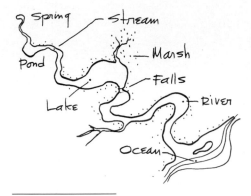

From upland spring to ocean outfall the river basin, river, and all its tributaries are part of a unified system.

Corruption.

What happens in the wheat fields of North Dakota can have a telling effect on the working of the lower Missouri and Mississippi rivers. What happens or doesn't happen on the forest slopes of the upper James River may decimate the wildfowl yield of the distant salt marsh or contaminate the oyster beds of the Chesapeake Bay. In Florida a cloud of spawning shrimp may die where the Apalachicola River debouches, because of an oil spill on a tributary two states away.

Present liability; potential community asset.

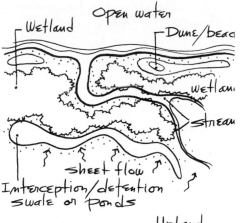

Ten Axioms of Water Resource Management

Within each rationally defined hydrographic region:

- Protect the watersheds, wetlands, and the banks and shores of all streams and water bodies.

- Minimize pollution in any and all forms and initiate a program of decontamination.

- Gear land use allocation and development capacities to the available water supply, rather than vice versa.

- Return to the underlying aquifer water of quantity and quality equal to that withdrawn.

- Limit use to such quantities as will sustain the local fresh-water reserves.

- Conduct surface runoff by natural drainageways insofar as feasible rather than by constructed storm sewer systems.

- Utilize ecologically designed wetlands for wastewater treatment, detoxification, and groundwater recharge.

- Promote dual systems of water supply and distribution, with differentiated rates for potable water and that used for irrigation or industrial purposes.

- Reclaim, restore, and regenerate abused land and water areas to their natural healthful condition.

- Work to advance the technology of water supply, use, processing, recycling, and recharge.

Possibilities

If there may be *problems,* there are *possibilities* also. These include the *preservation* of those areas of wilderness or wild river yet unspoiled. They include the *conservation* and compatible uses of those river-related areas which are rich in soils, cover, or scenic quality and which in their natural or existing state are important contributors to our ecological well-being. The possibilities include the *restoration* of depleted farmlands and dilapidated urban wastelands to productive use by regrading, soil stabilization, and replanting of eroded slopes and slashings. Well-planned agricultural districts, recreation lands, towns, and cities could then be clustered within a green-blue surrounding of field, forest, and clean water, linked with parklike transportation ways. Far more than many may realize, we are already well on our way to such a concept, and ethic, of land and water management.

San Antonio River. This once trash-littered stream has been converted to a delightful urban blueway.

Proficient land and site planning at any scale will help solve the water-related *problems* and ensure that the *possibilities* are fully realized. The level of performance should be continually improved in the light of increasing public support and advancing technology. It is quite possible that, within the span of our lifetimes, wide reaches of our land and waterways may be restored to the fairer form that our naturalist friends Henry David Thoreau, John Muir, and Aldo Leopold once found so exhilarating.

Management

In considering the site development of any landscape area, a first concern is the protection of the surface and subsurface waters both as to quality and as to quantity. *Quality* is maintained by precluding contamination in any form, as by the flow or seepage of pollutants, by groundwater runoff charged with chemicals or nutrients, by siltation, or by the introduction of solid wastes. The assurance of acceptable water *quantity* is largely a matter of retaining surface runoff in swales, ponds, or wetlands to prevent the flooding of streams or water bodies, to sustain the level of the underlying water table, and to replenish the deep-flowing aquifers.

Utilize

Since propinquity to water is so highly desirable, since there is only so much water area and frontage to go round, and since the protection of our water and edges has become so critical in our environmental planning, it would seem reasonable that all water-oriented land areas should be planned in such a way as to reap the maximum benefits of the water feature while protecting its integrity. This goal often resolves itself into the simple device of expanding the actual and visual limits of water-related land to the reasonable maximum. This is not as difficult as it might seem.

In practice, the rim of frontage is extended landward from the water edge in such a manner as to define an ample protective sheath. This variform vegetated band, at best following the lines of drainage flow and responding to the subtle persuasions of the topography, will provide frontage for compatible development and serve as access to the water. The possible variations are limitless, but the principle remains always the same.

Each variable diagram must stand the test of these three underlying conditions:

1. All related uses are to be compatible with the water resource and landscape.
2. The intensity of the introduced uses must not exceed the carrying capacity or biologic tolerance of the land and water areas.
3. The continuity of the natural and built systems is to be assured.

If these three principles are adhered to, it can be seen that all land–water areas, from homesite to region, can be planned and developed in such a way that both the scenic quality and ecologic functions can be maintained.

Open water is fast disappearing from the American scene. Expanding agricultural lands and development continue to follow the drainage ditches and tile fields across prairie wetlands and

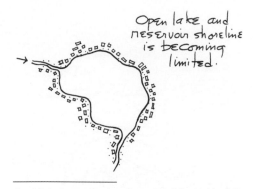

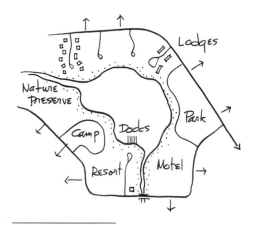

Avoid the water-edge ring of roads and buildings that seal off water bodies and limit their use.

By expanding the traffic-free lake environs to include park, wildlife preserve, and public areas as well as private cottages and resorts, the use and enjoyment of the lake (and surrounding real estate values) are enhanced.

Here wastewater is scientifically treated by interaction with selected introduced plants. It is then used to irrigate the nearby Koele Golf Course. (Lanai Auxiliary Wastewater Treatment Facility, Lanai, Hawaii)

> *Anyone who can solve the problem of water will be worthy of two Nobel prizes—one for peace and one for science.*
> John F. Kennedy

Ecologically managed wetlands are rapidly becoming an important alternative to conventional wastewater treatment systems.

As a breakthrough in the treatment of wastewater and toxic effluents it has been discovered that ecologically engineered wetlands can be devised to extract and retain the contaminants while storing the clarified water and providing habitat.

everglades. The urgent compulsion to dredge and fill, while slowed by recent conservation legislation, continues to "reclaim" the marsh, the cedar bog, and the mangrove strands. Rivers, lakes, and oceanfront are being hidden from public view and shielded from public access by a rising wall of apartments and office towers.

Is it not too late?

It is not too late!

Protect

Where water features exist, protect them. Work to preserve not only the open water but the supporting watershed covers, the natural holding ponds, the swampland, the floodplain, the feeding streams, and the green sheath along their banks. To be protected as well are the coastal wetlands, the landward dunes, and the outward reefs or sandbars.

In the planning of every water-related project site there is an opportunity to demonstrate sound management principles. Each well-designed example not only serves the interest of the client but also stands as a lesson to others.

Rediscover

Many water features of great potential landscape value have been bypassed in the process of building or roadway construction. They remain "out back" or "yonder," often in their natural state,

(Koele Golf Course, Lanai, Hawaii)

more often as silted or polluted drainage sumps or dump sites. They are waiting to be reclaimed by the community as parkland or open-space preserves. Preserved or modified, they may be rediscovered and featured in new public or private landscape development.

Restore

Again, a spring, a pond, or a section of stream may have been enclosed in a culvert and buried in fill. Or it may have been used as a dumping ground and covered with brush and trash. Sometimes, to add to the disgrace, such water features have been shamefully polluted with oils and chemicals and are coated with scum. In most urban and suburban precincts and often in the open countryside, there are to be found such unrecognized landscape treasures waiting to be reclaimed.

Conserve

The alarming drawdown and depletion of our freshwater reserves underscores the need for new attitudes toward water use and resource management. Even in times of moderate drought many city reservoirs are emptied. While in most parts of the world water is considered a precious commodity and used sparingly, in the United States it is squandered as though the supply were unlimited. It is not.

To conserve our diminishing supply in the face of ever-increasing demands, several courses of action are proposed:

- *Limit consumption.* Regulate household use by sharply escalating the rates on a sliding scale for use above a basic norm.
- *Preclude use of well water for irrigation.*
- *Recycle wastewater.* In urban areas this suggests a dual system of water supply—one for drinking, cooking, and bathing; the

Xeriscape landscape construction, planting, and gardening is that requiring a minimum of irrigation.

Only in America with its abundance of buildable land and fresh water has it been the fashion to surround single-family homes and apartments with irrigated lawn. With land and water supplies in short supply it will no longer be affordable or acceptable.

" *Lawns cover over fifty thousand square miles of the surface of the United States—an area roughly equal to Pennsylvania, and larger than that occupied by any agricultural crop.*
Wade Graham

Water edge cover.

Homes grouped around a preplanned excavation site: Miami Lakes, Florida.

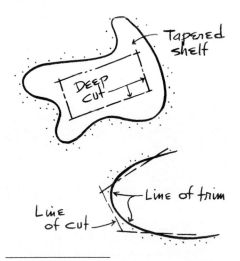

For safety, a beach should slope to a depth exceeding a swimmer's height (6 feet plus) before reaching a deep-cut line.

Rectilinear excavation pits can be reshaped by supplementary grading to create free-form lakes.

other for all other purposes. Treated and sanitized wastewater (at a much lower unit cost) is to be used exclusively for irrigation, air conditioning, street washing, and industrial processing.

Replenish

In undisturbed nature the subsurface water reserves are sustained automatically—by the retention and soil filtration of precipitation. When trees, grasses, and other vegetative covers are removed—and especially when replaced by paving or construction—the water tables are thereby lowered.

Three feasible remedies are suggested:

- *Protect and replant* the upland watersheds.
- *Restore* the natural drainageways (to the 50-year flood stage) to the public domain or restricted private use, and sheathe them in vegetation.
- *Require* of all new development that the storm-water runoff be retained in catchment basins, swales, or ponds, for percolation and aquifer recharge.

Preplan

Sometimes in the necessary process of mining or in the excavation of open extraction pits, there exists the need to create new water areas. From the air in some regions these can be seen to dot the landscape, usually in the form of dull, rectilinear dragline creations. Each may now be recognized as a lost opportunity. With advanced planning and sometimes little additional cost, these pits and the bordering property area could have been, and yet can be, shaped into new and attractive waterscapes, with free-form lakes, grassy slopes, and tree-covered mounds. This reasonable preplanning approach, as a condition of obtaining excavation permits and combined with soil conservation and afforestation, provides the opportunity to preclude new scars on the countryside and, instead, to create new landscapes from the old. With enterprise, many existing extraction pits could be acquired, reshaped, and transformed into highly attractive and valuable real estate.

Water-related Site Design

In the development of land-water holdings, special care is required in the delineation of use areas, in the location of paths of vehicular and pedestrian movement, and in site and building design.

Natural streams and water bodies

Where these exist, they represent the resolution of many dynamic forces at work—precipitation, surface runoff, sedimentation, clarification, currents, wave action, and so forth. It can be seen that to alter a natural stream, pond, or lake will set in motion a whole chain of actions and interactions that must then be restored to equilibrium. It is soon learned, therefore, that a first consideration in the site planning of water-related areas is to leave the natural conditions undisturbed and build up to and around them.

In their existing state the banks of streams and rivers are lined by a fringe of grasses, shrubs, and trees that stabilize soils and check the sheet inflow of surface storm-water drainage. The bank faces are held in place by stones, logs, roots, and trailing plants that resist currents and erosion.

Beach bonfire, Lake Michigan shoreline.

Lakeshores and beaches, armored with wave-resistant rock or protected by their sloping edges of sand or gravel, are ideally shaped to withstand the force and wash of wind-driven waves. Even the quiet pond or lagoon is edged with reeds or lily pads, which serve a similar purpose.

Where a water feature such as a spring, pond, lake, or tidal marsh occurs in nature, it is usually a distillate of the surrounding landscape and a rich contributor to its ecologic workings and the scene. Such superlatives are to be in all ways protected. This is not to preclude their use and enjoyment, for the purpose of sensitive planning is to ensure protection while facilitating the highest and best *use* of the landscape feature.

Canals and impoundments

Parts of the American landscape are laced and interlaced with networks of canals. Some have been in operation since colonial times. Many have been long abandoned. When "rediscovered" and reactivated in rural or urban settings, these waterways, with hiking or biking trails alongside, become treasured community features. All are to be preserved and protected.

At a miniscale, a trickling rivulet can be impeded by a few well-placed stones to increase its size and depth. By the construction of a proper dam, larger and deeper pools can be created for fishing, swimming, or boating or as landscape features.

At a greater scale, huge reservoirs or lakes may be impounded for water storage, flood control, or the provision of hydroelectric energy. Provided the drawdowns are not too severe or frequent, such large impoundments offer the opportunity for many forms of water-related recreation and often become the focal attraction for extensive regional development. To assure their maximum contribution and benefits, all major reservoirs and the contiguous

> *Ocean beaches are built and rebuilt by the forces of currents, storms, and tides. They are essentially temporary, since the forces that built them can also alter them beyond recognition—sometimes during a single great storm. Even the most costly stabilization projects have proven ineffective against ... beach evolution.*
>
> Albert R. Veri et al.

Often, and particularly in large parks and nature preserves, the migratory aspect of beaches and shores is acknowledged, and they are allowed full freedom to assume and constantly adjust their natural conformation. This eminently sound approach deserves far wider application.

The Springs, Longwood, Florida. Here upwellings of crystal-clear water have been featured as the crown jewels of a planned community.

(Cascades Commercial Place, Norfolk, Virginia)

The water in many city reservoirs is hidden from public view. In its storage and processing it could be used to refresh and beautify urban surroundings.

lands around them should be preplanned before construction permits are issued, with dedication provided for necessary rights-of-way and for appropriate public and private uses.

From the smallest dam to the largest, the location must be well selected to assure its stability, for a failure and surging washout can bring serious problems downstream. Water levels are to be studied in relation to topographical forms so that the edges of the pond or lake may create a pleasing shape well suited to adjacent paths of movement, use areas, and structures.

Where the feeding streams are silt-laden or subject to periodic flooding, upstream settling basins with weirs and a gated bypass channel will be required.

Paths, bridges, and decks

People are attracted to water. It is a natural tendency to wish to walk or ride along the edge of a stream or lake, to rest beside it enjoying the sights and sounds, or, in the case of streams, to cross to the other side.

These desires are to be accommodated in site planning. Routes of movement will be aligned to provide a variety of views and will, in effect, combine to afford a visual exploration of the lake or waterway. It is fitting that water-edge paths or drives be undulating in their horizontal and vertical curvature and constructed of materials that blend into the natural scene. At points where water-oriented uses are intensified or where the meeting of land and water is to be given more architectural treatment, the shapes and materials of the pathways and use areas will become more structural, too.

FORMED POOLS AND FOUNTAINS

Water features at garden scale can be
of infinite variety.

Still surface with dark basin for reflection

A shallow pool with stone spout and recirculation

The contrast of fluid, sparkling water and geometric forms

Tiered trays make music of falling water

Pools, ponds, and lakes in many forms enhance planned communities.

(Pershing S

(Greenacr

(Fisher Island, Florida)

(Amelia Island plantation)

(Fisher Island)

5
VEGETATION

NOT MANY CENTURIES AGO, except for the water bodies and windswept deserts, the whole of planet Earth above the level of the sea was covered with vegetation. From the lichens, mosses, and sedges at the water's edge to the billowing grass of the prairies and plains. From the lush foliage of the swamp and marsh to the sparse fringe at the mountain timberline. In between, the dunes, rolling hills, and upland slopes were for the most part clothed with a dense growth of deciduous shrubs and trees or needled conifers.

In the Americas, until the migrations across the land bridge of the Bering Sea (the latest some 10,000 years ago), there were no living humans on either the North or South American continents to disturb or destroy this vegetative cover. As long as it remained intact, the fertile topsoil mantle, laid down by the ages, was secure and protected. This rich and loamy topsoil substance which overlays the weathered subsoils and granite earth crust is the wealth of every nation, for only where it remains in place can food, fiber, or timber be produced. Where the vegetative growth has been destroyed by overgrazing, by unsound tillage, or by the clearing or burning of timberlands, the vital topsoil is soon washed or blown away to leave the vulnerable substrata or naked rock exposed. This is the case in large areas of such lands as Greece, Syria, Iran, Iraq, Saudi Arabia, and Spain—where much of the once forested, but now parched land resembles a deeply eroded moonscape.

In the United States we've not been immune to such wanton and destructive practices. Within the past century, with our power saws, earthmoving equipment, careless farming, and lax developmental regulations we have lost a third or more of our topsoil heritage to the wind and storm-water erosion.

Bromeliads.

Aside from its protective function, the vegetation of the earth serves to catch and retain precipitation. Its foliage and roots absorb and transpire but a fraction of the falling snow or rain, the dew or drifting mist. Much of the rest is detained to filter through the soils to replenish the underlying freshwater tables or aquifer reservoirs.

Plants in Nature

The vegetal growth that covers most of our globe occurs in myriad forms that range from the towering redwoods of the Pacific coastal forest to the microscopic forms of algae and plant diatoms of our streams, freshwater bodies, and teeming saltwater seas. This wonder world of vegetation provides the habitat and basic food supply of all living creatures.

Food chain

In the green chlorophyll cells of plants, and only there, the energy of the sun is transformed into the simple starches at the base of the biologic food chain. In this process of photosynthesis, plants draw moisture from the air and soil and in the presence of sunlight convert carbon dioxide into free oxygen and carbohydrates. It is in this vital miracle of chemistry that both the oxygen we breathe and the simple starches and sugars upon which all life depends are produced and replenished.

Some carbohydrates are consumed directly by humans, as in vegetables and fruits. Most reach our tables, however, through a complex spiral that begins with the lower forms of grazing organisms of land and sea and moves through a succession of increasingly larger and more complex herbivores and carnivores. Finally they become our fare as fish, game, butchered livestock, or animal products. It can be seen that as plant life is diminished, life in all its varieties is thereby diminished, too.

Transpiration

It is not only the free oxygen produced by plants that refreshes the air. Water drawn by the plants from the soil and water table is given off by foliage as vapor through evapotranspiration. This cooling and moisturizing function contributes to the growing conditions for other plants and to creature comfort as well. Where it is lacking, arid desert conditions exist.

Climate control

Plants ameliorate the climate in other ways also. They serve as buffers against a storm. Their foliage and mat of fallen leaves protect the soil against drying winds and sun. Even in wintertime their branches, twigs, and stems form a mesh to receive and transmit solar heat and help protect soils from freezing temperatures.

Water retention

Plants store the moisture that falls as precipitation—as droplets of dew or rain on their leaves, in the crevices of their bark, in the fountain of woody yet aqueous cells that constitute their internal structure, and in the fibrous mat of detritus and roots that cover and penetrate the earth. Water retained is water allowed to cleanse the air or seep into the topsoil and subsurface aquifers. Runoff unchecked is erosion in the making, with siltation as a result.

Soil building

In the cycle of living and dying, plants return to the earth their decaying fibers and cells to provide humus and deepen the film of topsoil. This slowly accreting and vital substance, if protected from erosion, increases available nutrients and moisture and the earth's fecundity.

Detritus

The fallen leaves, fruits, stems, and rotting wood that are not retained by the soil as humus are washed away in the stream and river systems to enrich the broth of the tidal estuaries. This organic material in turn becomes food for new aquatic plants and for oysters and spawning shell- and finfish.

Productivity

Long before our progenitors gathered their first handfuls of berries or dragged in the first game to their campfires, the forest, prairies, and waters had provided provender for a vast and voracious domain of insects, fish, reptiles, soaring birds, and roving animals. Today, natural conditions would be much the same as they were a million years ago were it not for the ascendancy of humankind. Human hands first stripped and stored nature's bounty, then harvested the grass, grain, and timber, and finally pushed back and destroyed the indigenous covers to make room for garden patches, fields, and settlements. Too often, we humans have gained our abundance at the expense of the earth's other inhabitants, until the destruction of vegetative cover and wildlife has now reached devastating proportions. It is only within very recent times that we have paused to consider the consequences. More recently we have begun to understand the direct and fragile relationships that exist between the whole biologic realm of animals and plants.

Plant Identification

To work with plants one must come to recognize them and be able to describe them in terms that others can comprehend.

Classification

Botany, as a field of scientific inquiry, has grown from the early classification of plants and their systematic study. Linnaeus,[1] sensing a need to better understand the relationships, established the botanical orders and introduced the concept of standardized nomenclature. With over 250,000 plant species now known to exist, it is doubtful that more than a few thousand yet remain unclassified.

Naming

All plants (and other organisms) are given two scientific (Latin) names. One is for the group or *genus*; the second is for the *species*. The scientific names are generally descriptive of the plant characteristics or botanic significance. Latin is used because the meaning of Latin words is unchanging and universal. Were it not for scientific classification it would be impossible to identify a plant or describe it to others since the "common name" or name commonly used in a given locality may differ from place to place— even within limited regions of the same country. In view of the international scope of plant study and use, it can be seen that standardized plant names are a great boon, even if they *are* in Latin.

Plant Culture

Collection

The rambling sorties of the first botanists have given way to well-organized expeditions. In more recent times plant explorers such as E. H. Wilson and David Fairchild have ranged the world, from the jungles of Africa to the Mongolian deserts and the peaks of the lofty Himalayas, in search of specimens for herbaria and botanic garden collections and for introduction to our gardens and farms.

Breeding

Early attempts at selective plant breeding and cross-pollination have led to more sophisticated techniques of hybridization. The pioneering feats of the plant breeder Luther Burbank excited

---

[1] Carolus Linnaeus, Swedish botanist, 1707–1778. The first naturalist to classify the plants of the earth in an orderly arrangement.

enthusiastic interest and produced a tantalizing array of new and superior roses, potatoes, oranges, plums, and other improved plant varieties. Today, plant selection, plant crossing, and seed radiation are creating a veritable cornucopia of hardier, more disease-resistant grains, more luscious fruits, more nutritious vegetables, and more attractive ornamental plants.

Horticulture

The science of horticulture holds great promise. Yet, in our exuberant pursuit of new and improved plant varieties we tend to ignore the vast and marvelous store of indigenous plants that surround us. They have evolved over countless centuries in nature's selective scheme of things. Each is a miracle of evolutionary adaptation and survival—the resultant of all natural forces. Each, where and as it stands, represents the highest form of plant life that the given situation can produce and, for the time being, sustain. We are only beginning to understand the essential functions of plants in our biosphere or the full extent of their contributions to the environment in which we work and live.

A Sunday afternoon visit to the botanical garden is usually sufficient to awaken an interest in plants. As a start in attaining a broader knowledge it is well to learn to identify those plants within view of your residence windows—by their form, bark, twigging, buds, foliage, flower, and fruit. The range can then be extended to

(Missouri Botanical Garden, St. Louis, Missouri)

yard and to neighborhood. Beyond the town or city limits, in the field or woodland, lies a wealth of plants to be recognized and admired in all seasons of the year. Finally, for many enthusiasts the quest will eventually lead out along the streams and rivers and into the wilderness. There, in undisturbed nature, is to be found the realm of plants as they were created. For those who understand what they see, it is a profoundly moving experience.

For the initiate, the simplest plant guide will suffice as a start on the trail of exploration, but think twice before scanning the pages; they may lead you a very long way.

Introduced Plantations

Who could it have been, in the dim and distant beginnings of human development, that on some daily food–gathering round first thought to dig and transplant a tuber? Or who consciously gathered and sowed the first seeds, to watch with impatience and then exclaim at the wonder of their sprouting? Whoever, when-ever, these acts were the start of agriculture and, together with fire and toolmaking, the start of civilization. From that time, the culture of plants has become, in one way or another, an almost universal enterprise.

The propagation and cultivation of plants for food and fiber is a logical extension of the nomadic way of life. Nature's yield of forage, cereals, vegetables, nuts, and fruits was often sporadic and scattered. The farm field, orchard, and vineyard have increased the bounty manyfold, while barns, silos, storage cellars, and bins have sustained the supply.

The pioneer farms of the early settlers—those of the rail–splitter and horse–drawn plow—were fitted to the lay of the land. Streams, wetlands, and the surrounding forest were left undisturbed. As homesteading increased and the covered wagons rolled westward, the landscape changed with the impact—with rutted trails, line fences, cleared woodlands, plowed fields, and settlements. But the underlying topography remained intact. The air was clean, and the streams ran clear to debouche into pristine lakes.

As centers of trade were established to serve the farmlands, as ports and harbors were built, as first meandering rural roads, then sweeping highways and transcontinental railways traced their paths across America and cities formed at their crossings, the land-scape of nature gave way. It was a rapid and disheartening retreat.

It is disturbing to look about us at most of our develop-ments—at the extent of the destruction of vegetation and the earth conformation, the degradation of lakes and waterways, the pollu-tion of air and countryside. It is saddening to envision the land-scape that once existed and to realize the superbly agreeable communities that, with intelligent planning, might have been brought into being.

It is mainly in nineteenth– and twentieth–century America, with our mechanized equipment and our pioneering "Clear the land! Drain the marsh!" complex that we have wrought so much damage to the natural landscape and ecological matrix. It need not be so. In the rural areas of Germany, England, and Scandi-navia, we find instructive examples of agriculture, villages, and nature in symbiotic balance—with towns and cities contained, farmland intact, forests well tended, and much of the wilderness preserved.

Good husbandry increases nature's yield.

Vanishing Vegetation

A new American landscape is taking form. There are encouraging signs. We find in our rural, suburban, and urban areas many examples of land well used and natural features preserved. Many farmsteads, homes, and communities have been planned in sympathetic response to their topographical settings, and extensive areas of open space have been acquired to conserve scenic mountain slopes, riverbanks, and shores. Unfortunately, however, the good examples are far outnumbered by the bad.

It is not a lost cause—far from it. We have learned that the wanton destruction of our earthscape can be precluded, that defilement and pollution can be stopped, that eroded land can be restored, that towns and cities can in time be rebuilt, and that the natural vegetation can be restored. Moreover, we are learning much about our ecology, we are developing a whole new science of resource management, and we are constantly increasing our knowledge of community and landscape planning. Within the next few decades it will be well within our capacity to preserve our natural systems and reshape our constructed environment more responsibly. In this endeavor the preservation and creative use of plants will play an essential role.

Reestablishment

Many of those who have witnessed the slow degradation of the American landscape and the destruction of the vegetative covers have taken steps to reverse the trend.

Concern for the vanishing upland meadows, mountain and riverine forests, prairies and coastal wetlands has resulted in the setting aside of millions of acres of state and national preserves. In addition, vast areas of cutover forest have been reestablished, and new plantations of trees (afforestation) have been installed on depleted or eroded lands as watershed protection, wildlife management preserves, and shelterbelt windscreens and for timber and grain production. These commendable programs have received and deserve wide public support and are to be expanded.

(Point Lobos State Park, California)

6
LANDSCAPE CHARACTER

Looking down at the surface of our globe or moving in any direction across it, we find areas where there is an apparent harmony or unity among all the natural elements—ground forms, rock formations, vegetation, and even animal life. We may say of these areas that they possess a naturally produced *landscape character*. The more complete and obvious this unity, the stronger the landscape character.

The Natural Landscape

Let us imagine that we have been dropped into the uplands of Utah's great spruce forest. All about us rise wild and rugged slopes of rock bristling with tall evergreen spires that tower against the sky. The deep, shadowy ravines are choked with great boulders and fallen trees. Melting snow drips or trickles from the crevices or foams from high ledge to chasm, cascading toward the stillness of a mountain lake that lies below, deep blue at its center, shading to pale green along its gravelly edges. Here all is in harmony, all is complete. Even the brown bear lumbering close to shore is clearly native to this place. The leaping trout, the wading tern, the caw-caw of the flapping crow are part of this scene, part of its *landscape character*.

The blazing desert, the fetid mangrove forest, the rockbound California coast—each has its own distinctive landscape character, and each evokes in the observer a strong and distinctive emotional response. No matter what the natural landscape character of an area and no matter what the mood it produces in us—exhilaration, sadness, eeriness, or awe—we experience a very real plea-

(Death Valley, California)

sure in sensing the unity and harmony of the total scene. The more nearly complete this "oneness" and "wholeness," the greater the pleasure of the observer.

The degree of evident harmony of the various elements of a landscape area is a measure not only of the pleasure induced in us but also of the quality we call *beauty*. For beauty by definition is "the evident harmonious relationship of all the sensed components."

Natural landscape beauty is of many varying qualities, which include:

The picturesque	The bizarre	The delicate
The stark	The majestic	The ethereal
The idyllic	The graceful	The serene

Natural landscape character, too, is of many categories, including:

Mountain	Lake	Canyon	Pond	Dune
Sea	Forest	Desert	Prairie	Stream
River	Plain	Swamp	Hill	Valley

Each of these and other types may be further subdivided. A *forest* landscape character, for instance, might be one of the following subtypes:

White oak	Larch	Cypress
Scarlet oak	Spruce	Sabal palm
Beech	Hemlock	Mangrove
Ash	White pine	New Jersey coastal
Maple	Red pine	New Jersey river
Aspen	Jack pine	New Jersey barrens
Cottonwood	Loblolly pine	Rocky Mountain
Redwood	Piñon pine	Douglas fir
Eucalyptus	Live oak	Mixed hardwood

Mangrove forest.

Pacific Coast.

An area of land that has common distinguishing visual characteristics of landform, rock formations, water forms, and vegetative patterns is termed a *landscape type*. When the major type is broad or diversified, there may be defined within it *landscape subtypes* of significant differentiation.

Each of the myriad examples that come to mind is in itself distinctive. For each, the more closely an area or any object within it approaches the ideal (or has the most of those qualities that we associate with perfection in a given type), the more intense is our pleasure.

The opposite of beauty we call *ugliness*. Ugliness results from a sensed lack of unity among the components or the presence of one or more incongruous elements. Since that which is beautiful tends to please and that which is ugly tends to disturb, it follows that a visual harmony of all parts of a landscape is desirable.

With only the visual aspects of site character in mind, it would seem that in developing a natural area we should do all that we can to preserve and intensify its inherent landscape quality. We should therefore eliminate objects that are out of keeping, and we may even introduce objects to increase or accentuate this native character.

(Florida Gulf)

Elimination of incongruous elements

In all planning, as in life, the elimination of an incongruous element usually effects an improvement.

Let us suppose, for example, that we have wandered into a giant sequoia forest and stand in silent awe of the tremendous upward thrust of the redwood boles and their imposing timeless grandeur. And then suppose that on the forest floor we should happen to notice a neatly cultivated bed of pink petunias. The same petunias in a suburban garden bed might make quite a pleasant splash. But to find them here in the redwood forest would first surprise and then annoy us. They would annoy us because our experience would tell us that in this natural redwood grove petunias are not in keeping. They would set up unpleasant visual and mental tensions, and should we come often enough to this place, it is possible, even probable, that we would ultimately root them out with the toe of our boot. We would be eliminating an element that was in conflict with the natural landscape character.

An incident from the author's own experience further illustrates this point. As a small boy he spent summers in a camp on Lake George in the backwoods of Michigan. At the lower end of this lake he found a spot that he came to consider his private bullfrog pond. It was a clearing in the cattails, jammed with mossy logs and stumps and closed almost tight with the pads of water lilies. When he waded quietly through the cattails, he would spy huge green–black bullfrogs floating among the pads or squatting dreamily on the logs. These he hunted for their saddles, which were most welcome at the family table. Every day he visited his pond, lying hour after hour on a log, motionless, with a whittled birch rod poised ready for a frog to surface. It was an idyllic world of cedar smell, sunlight, patrolling dragonflies, lapping water, and contentment.

One morning he found that a battered yellow oil drum had been washed into his frog pond by a storm. He pushed it outside the cattails. Next morning it was back. Again he pushed it from the pond, farther this time but not far enough. Finding it once again floating jauntily among the lily pads, he shoved it out and went for a rowboat. With the anchor rope he towed the drum to the deepest part of the lake, bashed a jagged hole in its top with a hatchet and scuttled it. As he watched it slowly founder, he wondered why he had felt such anger at an old, rusty metal barrel. Years later, when the author recollected the pond in terms of its landscape character, he realized at last why the drum had to go. It was a disturbing, inharmonious element in the minilandscape, and it had to be removed. (Note: In later years he also came to realize that the lake bottom was no place to leave a barrel.)

The elimination of an incongruous element will usually effect an improvement.

Introduction of accentuating elements

If it is true that the elimination of certain elements from an area can improve its landscape quality, it follows that other elements might be *introduced* with the same result. To accentuate the landscape quality of a site within or abutting a cactus desert, for instance, we might remove an old tire that had been tossed there and replace it with a clump of fine native cactus plants gathered from the surrounding sandy draws. Or we might plant a single picturesque Joshua tree that would reflect and articulate the area's mood or landscape expression.

To sum up, then, the landscape character of any area may be developed or intensified by eliminating any negative elements and by accentuating its positive qualities.

To improve a landscape or land area intelligently we must not only recognize its essential natural character but also possess knowledge that will enable us to achieve the optimum development of that character.

During the Ming dynasty in China this art was so highly refined that within a single garden of a few acres one might experience lofty mountain scenery, a misty lakeshore, a bamboo grove at the edge of a quiet pond, a pine–sheltered forest overlook, and a cascading waterfall. And, through the skill of the designer, the transition areas between viewing points were so masterfully con-

The Red Rocks Amphitheater, Denver, Colorado. This magnificent outdoor space has been conceived in studied harmony with the existing terrain.

> Gravity is one of man's greatest enemies. It has shaped man himself, conditioned his body as well as his thoughts, and put its unmistakable stamp upon his cities. Thus in the narrow winding valleys of the world, life is a continual battle with gravity. One must live on the valley's bottom, or "fight the slope" until his dying days.
>
> Grady Clay

trived as to be fully as pleasant and dramatic as the major views themselves.

Major landscape features

There are dominant natural landscape forms, features, and forces that we can alter little, if at all. We must accept them and adapt ourselves and our planning to them. These unchangeable elements include such topographical forms as mountain ranges, river valleys, and coastal plains; such features as precipitation, frost, fog, the water table, and seasonal temperatures; and such forces as winds, tides, sea and air currents, the process of growth, solar radiation, and gravity.

These we analyze to the extent necessary to make an accurate assessment of their influence and effects. Then, if wise, we will shape our plans in full awareness of, and response to, the constraints and possibilities. Such considerations are fundamental to the placing of cities, the zoning of a community, the projected alignment of highways, the siting of industries, or the orientation and layout of a single home or garden.

The notable planning projects of any age demonstrate with clarity the adaptation of a structure or activity area to the landscape in such a way that the best qualities of each were made to complement the other. In such works not only the constructed elements but the natural elements as well appear to have been designed by the planner, as in one sense they were, for all were considered together as integral parts of the total conceptual plan.

Minor landscape features

Taking a hill as an example, its landscape character may be such that its optimum yield or use is realized if it is carefully preserved

ing placidly out at "the hill." For our purpose, we have eliminated the negative aspects of our hill and accentuated its positive qualities.

Any area of the natural landscape—pond, island, hillside, or bay—can be developed in this manner.

Early in his career the author was engaged by the Michigan State Department of Parks in the planning of several campgrounds. His first assignment was to develop a site in northernmost Michigan as a state park for tourists, who would come to experience the joys of "wilderness living." Upon arrival at the park site, he found a large white "Public Park" sign at the entrance of a farm road that led in through a flat field of wild carrots to a trailer parking lot beside a muddy pond—not much of a wilderness campsite.

The planner's first step was to spend several weeks exploring the tract to become acquainted with all its natural features, good and bad. His aim was to utilize these features to the utmost. He proposed, in short, to intensify the native landscape quality of the site.

As a first step in the improvement program, the entrance road was moved from the open field to the thickest stand of balsam. Here a rough trail was carved through the rock and snaked up a ridge between the tree trunks, so that a camper's car or trailer could just squeeze through. The caretaker's sagging clapboard cottage with its red-and-white-painted window boxes was demolished and replaced with a rough-sawn slab cabin near the base of a towering pine. This change was made because the camper's first impression of the campsite would be of this venerable tree and the cabin in its shadow, and first impressions are usually the most lasting.

The site's main attraction, a spring-fed pond, was drained, scooped out, and developed as a natural swimming pool with a clean sand and gravel bottom. Above it, a large area of water was impounded to form a settling basin, and here the marsh birds, muskrats, and other wildlife could be seen from a timber bridge that was arched across the dam. At the lower end of the swimming pool a second bridge was built across the waterfall and spillway, where large speckled trout rolled and swam in the sparkling water of the pool below.

Trails were slashed through the densest cover and between the most jagged ledges. Every point of interest was strung on the new trail system like an offset bead.

In one of the more remote areas, a colony of beavers inhabited a stream, where they had built a dam. Much thought was given to the best way of displaying these shy creatures, a prize in any park. It was decided that to view them the hikers must find their way along an unmarked game trail as it threaded tenuously through a deep cedar swamp until, from the sloping trunk of a great fallen tree that overhung the pond, the hikers could look down to "discover" the beaver workings below them.

In the development of any land or water area, the landscape designer will focus on the essential effect to be conveyed (one inherent in the site). By emphasis, by articulation, and by the creation of progressive sequences of revealment, the observer will be led to discover the positive features of the locale and thus exact its full pleasurable impact.

Big South Fork National River and Recreation Area, Tennessee and Kentucky.

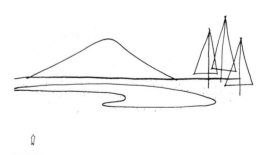

In the natural landscape a human being is an intruder.

These Japanese homes of hewn timber seem completely in character with the ancient grove that is their site.

The Built Environment

Up to this point we have considered the natural landscape as something to be observed, as in some of our larger parks, for example, or along scenic parkways, or at the better resort hotels. In such cases a person becomes a microvisitor, permitted only to enter an area inconspicuously, observe respectfully, and leave unobtrusively. But there are relatively few areas that can be reserved in their pristine state or developed solely for the display of their natural beauty.

Use as a landscape factor

We generally consider land in terms of use. At this point, one is quite likely to ask: "What's all this talk about beauty and landscape character? What I want to know is, how can this property be *used?*"

But the hard, cold fact of the matter is that the most important factor in considering the use of land is a thorough understanding of its landscape character in the broadest sense. For the planner must first comprehend the physical nature of the site and its extensional environment before it is possible to:

- *Recognize* those uses for which the site is suited and which will utilize its full potential.
- *Introduce* into the area only those uses which are appropriate.
- *Apply and develop* such uses in studied relationship to the landscape features.
- *Ensure* that these applied uses are integrated to produce a modified landscape that is functionally efficient and visually attractive.
- *Determine* whether a project is *unsuited* and would be incongruous not only on the immediate site but in the surrounding environs as well and thus appear to be misplaced, unfit, and (by definition) ugly. Such an improper use would be disturbing not only aesthetically but practically, for an unsuitable use forced upon an unreceptive parcel of land generates frictions that may not only destroy the most desirable qualities of the landscape area but preclude proper function as well.

Suitability

Since we are repelled by disorder, the discordant, and that which is ugly; since we are instinctively drawn to that which is harmonious and well formed; and since most artifacts and developments are designed to please, it follows that resultant beauty is a highly desirable attribute.

It is compatible; it seems well suited to its place. *It works well;* there is an efficient arrangement of all the parts. *It looks good:* it is beautiful; *I like it.*

Anything planned in the landscape affects the landscape. Each new plan application sets up a series of reactions and counterreactions not only about the immediate site but upon its extensional environment as well. This environment may extend a great distance in any direction and may include many square miles.

A compatible use and sensitive siting. (Santa Cruz Quarry Theater, University of California)

Esthetic impacts influence us at all moments. Consciously, or in most cases subconsciously, they provoke friendly or hostile reactions.... Their impacts on ... decisions reach even into the most practical problems, into the shaping of things of daily use—cars, bridges—and above all, of our human environment.
Siegfried Giedion

In considering the development of any area of the earth's surface we must realize that this surface is a continuous plane. A project applied to this plane affects not only the specific site but all flow past it. Each addition or change, however minute, imposes upon the land certain new physical properties and visual qualities. It can thus be seen that the planner is engaged in a continuing process of landscape modification.

Harmony

The untouched landscape is in repose, a repose of equilibrium. It has its own cohesive, harmonious order in which all forms are an expression of geologic structure, climate, growth, and other natural forces. In the primeval forest or upon the open plain, the human is an intruder. If one penetrates the wilderness by trail or road, one may either roll with the topography and develop expressive harmonies or buck the terrain and generate destructive frictions. As human activity in an area increases, the landscape becomes more and more organized; agreeably, if the organization is one of fitting relationships, disagreeably, if the relationships are chaotic or illogical. The development of any area may entail a concentration of its natural landscape character, an integration of nature and construction, or the creation of a wholly built complex of spaces and forms. In any case, the commendable plans are those that effect a resolution of all elements and forces and create a newly unified landscape of dynamic equilibrium.

We are all familiar with humanized landscape areas in which everything seems to be working well together. We recall pleasant stretches of New England farmland, western ranch territory, or Virginia plantation country. In or near such areas, we experience a sense of well-being and pleasure. We say that a certain town or region is quaint, delightful, or picturesque. What we probably mean is that we subconsciously sense certain qualities of compatibility that appeal to us. These we like. Other places of disorder, confusion, pollution, "bad taste," or "poor planning" are disagreeable and bother us. If we were traveling, these would be bypassed. We would prefer not to live in or near them.

Mont Saint-Michel, France, surrounded by its rushing tides and reached only by causeway—an ingenious and powerful adaptation of structure to natural forces and forms.

A community planned into the landscape. Note scars from clear-cutting of forest beyond. (Proposed new community, State of Washington)

> *Is it not yet conceivable that a well-designed and well-placed building, a bridge or road, can be an addition rather than a menace to the countryside?*
>
> Christopher Tunnard

The negative qualities of such places are those we would attempt to eliminate in any replanning process; the positive qualities are those we would strive to retain and accentuate. It would seem to follow as a guiding principle that *to preserve or create a pleasing site character, all the various elements or parts must be brought into harmony.*

We make much of this word *harmony.* Do we mean to imply that everything should blend with or get lost in the landscape as through protective coloration or camouflage? No, but rather that the planner, in addressing a land–water holding, from small plot to vast acreage, will so integrate the structural and topographical forms as to produce the best possible fit. If the completed project seems to blend with the landscape, it is the happy result of an inspired design rather than the mistaken aim of an uninspired designer.

Fitting relationships. (Keehi Lagoon Canoe Complex, Honolulu, Hawaii)

The Rinshun Pavilion. In the Japanese tradition structures and site are wholly complementary.

To me the quest of harmony seems the noblest of human passions. Boundless as is the goal, for it is vast enough to embrace everything, it yet remains a definite one.

Le Corbusier

Contrast

It is known that the form, color, or texture of a handsome object can be emphasized through contrast. This principle applies as well to planning in the landscape and is exemplified by the bridges of the brilliant Swiss engineer Robert Maillart. All who have seen them marvel at the lightness and grace of the white reinforced-concrete arches that span the wild mountain gorges in Switzerland and Bavaria. Surely the lines and materials of these structures are foreign to the natural character of the craggy mountain background. Are they *right* for such a location? Or would the bridges have been more suitable if constructed of native timbers and stone?

In our national parks, bridges have usually been built of indigenous materials. Although some may quarrel with this policy, it has produced many bridges of high design quality and spared the park-using public from more of the typical fluted and fruited cast-metal or balustraded cast-stone monstrosities that clutter up so many of our American river crossings.

In his bridge design, however, Maillart has simply and forthrightly imposed a necessary function—a highway crossing—on the natural landscape. He has expressed with logical materials and refreshing clarity the force diagram of his structures. Moreover, by sharply contrasting his elegantly dynamic bridges and the rugged mountain forest, he has dramatized the highest qualities of each. The gorges seem more wild, the bridges more precise, more eloquent.

The Salginatobel Bridge, Switzerland, leaps the wild chasm as lightly and surely as a native stag.

The precise lines of this residence and the rough character of the rocky slope are both enhanced by their well-planned juxtaposition.

As another application of the principle of contrast, we may recall in color theory that to produce an area of greenest green a fleck of scarlet may be brought into juxtaposition. To make a spot of scarlet glow with fire, an artist brings it into contrast with the greenest possible background.

It follows that before introducing contrasting elements into a landscape it would be well to understand the nature of the features to be accentuated. The contrasting elements will then be contrived to strengthen and enrich the visual impact of these natural features. Conversely, to emphasize certain qualities of the structure or component introduced, one will search the landscape and bring into contrasting relationship those features that will effect the desired contrast.

A further principle in the use of contrast, as illustrated by the work of Maillart, is that of two contrasting elements one must dominate. One is the feature; the other, the supporting and contributing backdrop. Otherwise, with two contrasting elements of equal power, visual tensions are generated that weaken or destroy, rather than heighten, the pleasurable impact of the viewing experience.

We have said that to create a pleasing character for an area, all components must work together in harmony. We find striking examples that seem to violate this precept; Maillart's bridges, for instance, and Frank Lloyd Wright's Fallingwater at Bear Run, Pennsylvania. At first appraisal these structures would seem to be completely alien to their surroundings. Yet, with study, one senses in each a quality of fitness—of spirit, purpose, material, and form.

Construction

We have considered natural landscape elements and their importance in the planning process. Constructed forms, features, and lines of force are major planning factors, too.

As we look at any road map, we find it crisscrossed with lines of various kinds and colors that we recognize as highways, minor roads, streets, railroads, ferryboat routes, and even subways. These lines seem innocuous enough on paper. But those of us who have zoomed along with the streaming traffic of a turnpike, or stood by the tracks as the *Limited* roared by, or tried to maneuver a catboat through the churning wake of a ferry will agree that the map lines tracing their paths indicate powerful lines of force. Such lines are essential to the movement of people and goods, but, unfortunately, they may also be disruptive, and sometimes lethal. Every few minutes someone in the United States is killed by a moving vehicle, and the incidence of serious injury is much higher. It must occur to us, if we ponder these facts, that we planners have as yet failed to treat transportation routes with the proper respect, or else we have not yet learned to design them with foresight and imagination.

There are countless other features of the built environment that, if perhaps less dominant, still have great effect on our planning. To understand their importance we might list a few that deserve investigation in project siting. For openers the list will include:

Peripheral streets

Walkway access

Adjacent structures to remain

Structures to be demolished

Subsurface construction

Energy sources and supply

Utility leads and capacities

Applicable zoning

Building code and regulations

Easements

Deed restrictions

This sampling may in itself seem formidable, but it does not include such additional considerations as neighborhood character, general site aspects, mineral rights, amenities, and public services. Any one of these features might well spell the failure or success of an enterprise. The list will differ considerably, of course, with projects of such varying types as a residence, school, shopping mall, or marina.

If our plans are to respond to a wide variety of contrived and natural givens, how do we proceed? It is proposed that, starting down the list, each item in turn will be studied as to where the problems and possibilities lie. We will then maximize all possible benefits and reduce or eliminate, insofar as feasible, any negative aspects. An ingenious solution has often converted liabilities into assets.

The changing landscape

The most constant quality of the landscape is the quality of change. Aside from the processes of growth and the changing seasons, we are forever tugging and hauling at the land, sometimes senselessly, destroying the positive values, and sometimes intelligently, developing a union of function and site with such sensitivity as to effect an improvement. Whenever constructions are imposed on a site, its character is thereby modified.

Landscape evolution is a continuing process. At its best it is an ongoing exercise by which compatible uses are brought into harmonious interaction with our natural and built environs.

66 *The ultimate principle of landscape architecture is merely the application and adjustment of one system to another, where contrasting subjects are brought into harmonious relationship resulting in a superior unity called "order."*
Stanley White

The precision and lightness of the concrete forms contrast boldly with the natural forms, colors, and textures of the site. Yet the structure seems at home here. Why? Perhaps because the massive cantilevered decks recall the massive cantilevered ledge rock. Perhaps because the masonry walls that spring from the rock are the same rock tooled to a higher degree of refinement. Perhaps because the dynamic spirit of the building is in keeping with the spirit of the wild and rugged woodland. And perhaps because each contrasting element was consciously planned to evoke, through its precise kind and degree of contrast, the highest qualities of the natural landscape. (Fallingwater, Bear Run, Pennsylvania)

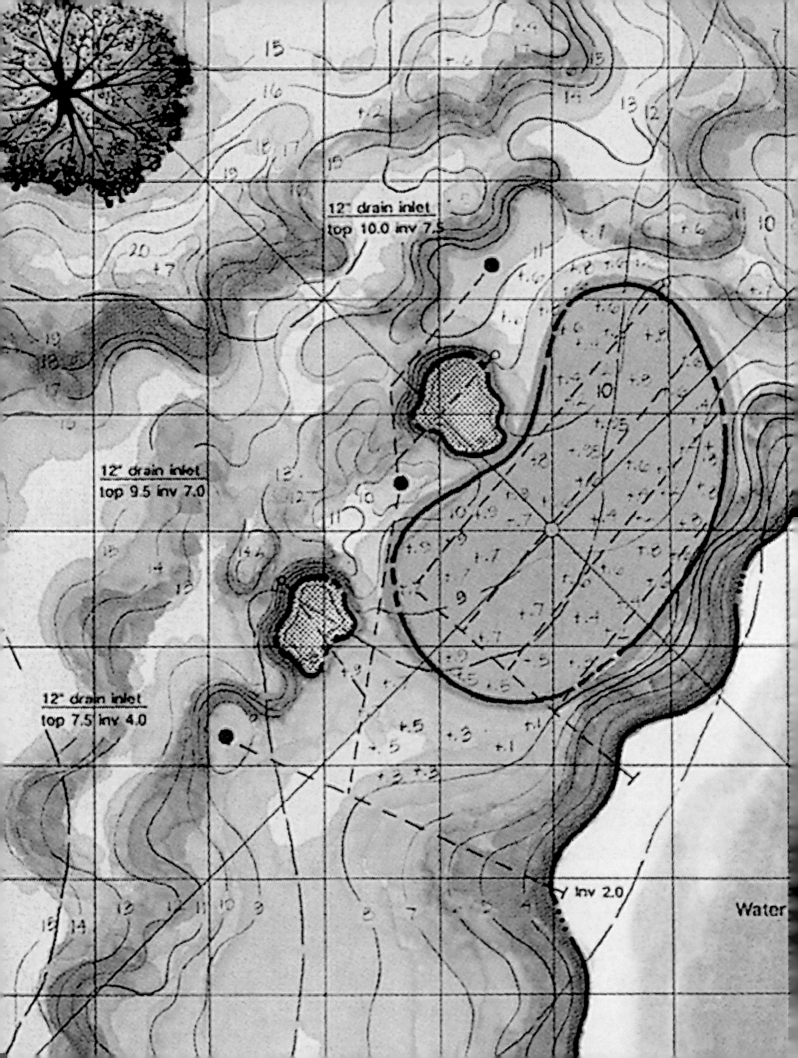

12" drain inlet
top 10.0 inv 7.5

12" drain inlet
top 9.5 inv 7.0

12" drain inlet
top 7.5 inv 4.0

Inv 2.0

Water

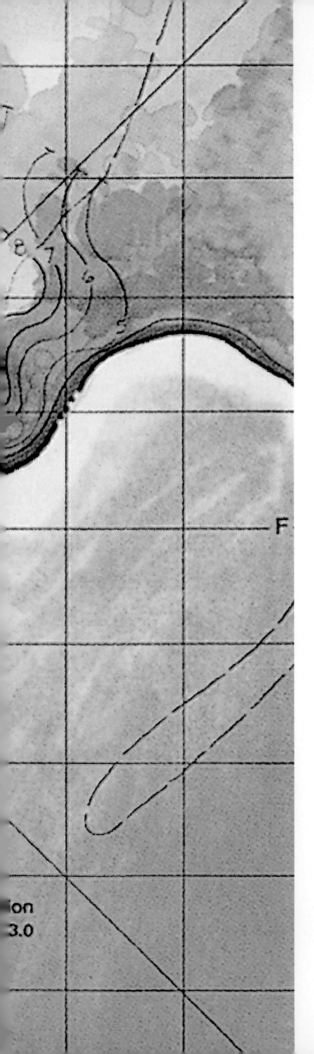

7 TOPOGRAPHY

Land areas and the bottoms of water bodies are seldom level. They slope up or down; they undulate; they sometimes pitch precipitously to great heights or depths, and are often creased with stream beds, ravines, or seismic faults.

Contours

The shape, or *relief,* of the ground surface can be indicated by contours. These are lines of equal height above a fixed reference point or *benchmark* of known or assumed elevation. For some engineering projects of exceptional scope or precision, the benchmark will be a permanent monument with machined brass cap—its elevation recorded in hundredths of feet above mean sea level. Again, for a project of lesser scope, the B.M. may be no more than the top of a rock or a driven pipe, assigned an arbitrary elevation of say, 100.0 feet.

Where the land gradient is mild, the contour interval or height differential may be reduced. Where the land is rugged, as in mountainous country, the interval may be increased to 10 feet, 100 feet, or more, depending upon the need.

It can be seen that by contours alone the modulations of the earth's surface can be graphically portrayed. In architectural or landscape planning, a site plan prepared with a contour map as a base gives an invaluable "feel for the land."

Sections

As a further aid, the contour map provides the opportunity to plot sections wherever an accurate land profile is needed. In Fig-

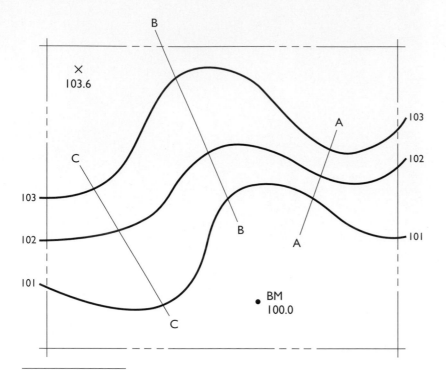

Figure 1 is the plan of a small land area. The dot represents a stone or stake, the top of which has an assumed elevation of 100.0 feet. The curving contours are lines of equal height at 1-foot intervals above the top of the benchmark (B.M.). The closer together the contours (as along section A-A), the steeper the slope as compared with B-B (a valley) or C-C (a ridge).

ure 2, for example, if section lines are drawn through any area of the map—as at lines A–A or B–B, a profile can be plotted, and enlarged or reduced to any useful scale.

Models

Even more graphic than plans or sections is a model prepared by cutting and superimposing sheets of matboard, plywood, or plastic of the appropriate thickness along the contour lines. By means of such an exhibit, the surface conformation or modeling of the entire property can be perceived at a glance.

Aerial or perspective views of the model in photographic form are often used for ready reference.

Surveys

It is well to understand that surveying methods and maps are of many types and must be suited to their purpose. As to methods, the compass and chain is good enough for plotting logging roads but hardly suited to precision mapping. The *plane table* survey may be adequate for a limited site where accurate property line descriptions and elevations are not needed. The *stadia* survey has long been the standard for accurate topographic mapping, but has recently been superseded by the laser transit. For larger area coverage a photogrammetric survey is usually prescribed. This involves the piecing together of overlapping aerial mosaics and

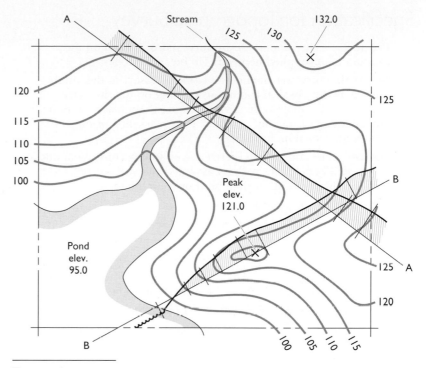

Topography

Although Figure 2 shows a larger land area of more topographic diversity, the principle is the same as in Figure 1.

A vertical measurement from the intersection of each contour with the base line gives a series of points which, when connected, show the land profile at lines A-A and B-B.

the plotting of surface features by stereoptic projection. Commonly used in military reconnaissance, it yields a high degree of precision.

To utilize land for most purposes, a topographic survey is needed. Such a map will show not only the surface *conformation* by contours and spot elevations, it will indicate also the lines of *property ownership, surface and subsurface features,* and such other *supplemental information* as may be specified.

Some surveys give no more information than a description in bearings and distances (metes and bounds) of the property perimeter. Often this is all that is required. If contouring and spot elevations are needed, they must be requested. With detailed site planning to be accomplished, the topographic survey specification may be expanded to include the location and description of specific surface and subsurface features. Core borings or test pits may be required and such elements as the adjacent roadway or the nearest off-site utility leads and projected capacities.

When a topographic survey is needed, it is well to meet with the surveyor and review the requirements in detail. A specification and work order can then be drafted for execution. For an extensive or complicated development project, the survey specification may be many pages in length. For a typical residential homesite, however, the following sample specification should normally suffice.

Specification for Topographic Survey

Property: The property to be surveyed is marked on the location map supplied herewith. (To be appended).

General: Surveyor shall do all work necessary to determine accurately the physical conditions existing on the site. Surveyor shall prepare a map of the given area in ink on plastic drafting film at scale of 1 inch to _____ feet. Four black-line prints of the survey map shall be furnished.

Datum: Elevations shall be referenced to any convenient and permanent benchmark with an assumed elevation of 100.0 feet. The benchmark location shall be shown on the map.

Information required:

1. Title of survey, property location, scale, north point, certification, and date.

2. Tract boundary lines, courses, distances, and coordinates. Calculate and show acreage.

3. Building setback lines, easements, and rights-of-way.

4. Names of on-site and abutting parcel owners.

5. Names and locations of existing streets on or abutting the tract. Show right-of-way, type, location, width of surfacing, and centerline of gutters.

6. Position of buildings and other structures, including foundations, piers, bridges, culverts, wells, and cisterns.

7. Location of all site construction, including walls, fences, roads, drives, curbs, gutters, steps, walks, trails, paved areas, etc., indicating types of materials or surfacing.

8. Locations, types, sizes, and direction of flow of existing storm and sanitary sewers on or contiguous to the tract, giving top and invert elevations of manholes and inlet and invert elevations of other drainage structures; location, ownership, type, and size of water and gas mains, manholes, valve boxes, meter boxes, hydrants, and other appurtenances. Locations of utility poles and telephone lines and fire-alarm boxes are to be indicated. For utilities not traversing the site show, by key plan if necessary, the nearest off-site leads, giving all pertinent information on types, sizes, inverts, and ownership.

9. Location of water bodies, streams, springs, swamps or boggy areas, and drainage ditches or swales.

10. Outline of wooded areas. Within areas so noted, show all trees that have a trunk diameter of 4 inches or greater at waist height, giving approximate trunk diameters and common names of the trees.

11. Road elevation. Elevations shall be taken at 50-foot intervals and at high or low points along centerlines of roads, flow line of gutter on property side, and tops and bottoms of curbs. The pertinent grades of abutting street and road intersections shall also be indicated.

12. Ground surface elevations shall be taken and shown on a 50-foot grid system as well as at the top and bottom of all considerable breaks in grade, whether vertical as in walls or sloping as in banks. Show all floor elevations for buildings. Spot elevations shall also be indicated at the finished grade of building corners, building entrance platforms, and all walk intersections. In addition to the elevations required, the map shall show contours at _____ foot vertical intervals. All elevations shall be to

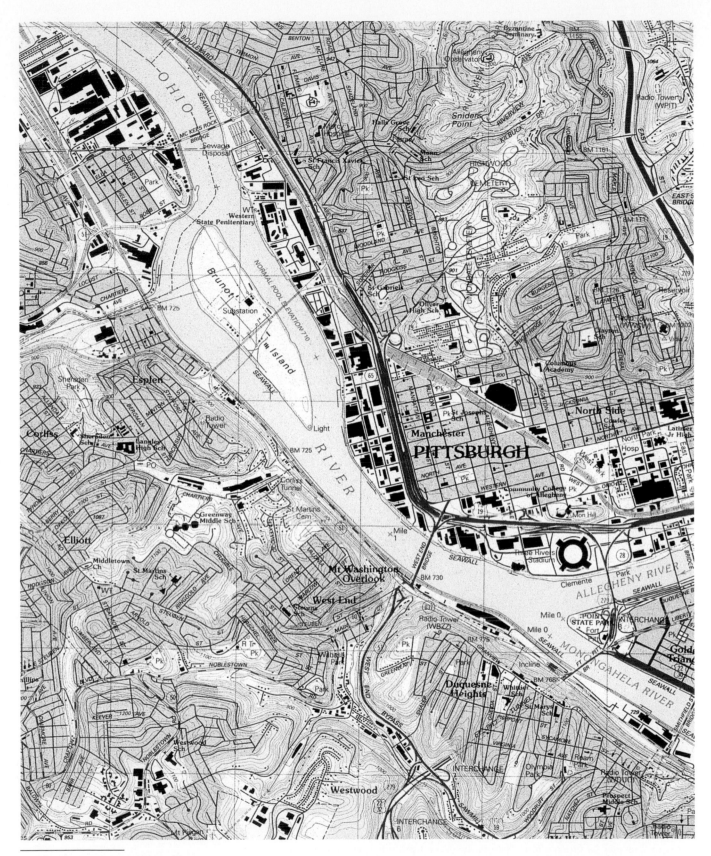

U.S. Geological Survey (Figure 3).

the nearest tenth of a foot. Permissible tolerance shall be 0.1 foot for spot elevations and one–half of the contour interval for contours.

Supplementary Data

Aside from the basic topographic, or "topo," survey prepared by a professional surveyor or civil engineer and needed for most project design and construction, there are other sources of useful maps and reports available at nominal cost. Of these, the U.S. Geological Survey (USGS) maps warrant special mention.[1] Several series are available, at different scales, but the one most often useful to the planner is the 7.5–minute series, in which each map (or *quadrangle*, as it is called) covers an area of about 60 square miles at a scale of 1 inch to 2000 feet. These survey maps show most of the pertinent topography of the area, including relief, wooded areas, all bodies of water, transportation routes, and major buildings. A section of typical coverage is illustrated in Figure 3.

For many counties the *Natural Resources Conservation Service* (formerly the U.S. Soil Conservation Service) has available Published Soil Survey Reports, which include 11– × 14–inch field sheets of aerial photos on which soil types are delineated. These may be purchased at the nearest field office. For the areas covered, they can be most useful. Then there are the various types of coverage by satellite mapping and photography, which for certain localities show surface conditions with startling detail and accuracy.

Planning agencies and highway departments are often able and willing to provide survey information and reports for extensive metropolitan areas. This is especially useful in large–scale comprehensive planning, as for a campus, community, river basin, or park and open space systems.

Other public agencies also can help with overall background mapping and data which may be sufficient for site selection and preliminary land use diagrams. When it comes time, however, for detailed site planning and recording there is need for a certified *topographic survey.*

---

[1] U.S. Geological Survey maps may often be purchased locally at map or stationery stores, or they may be ordered directly from the main distribution center at

U.S.G.S. Information Services
Box 25286
Denver, CO 80225

If requested, an index map shows for each state the quadrangle to be ordered for a particular location.

Topographical splendor. The sensitive modeling of the earth's surface is fundamental
to superior landscape design. (The Golf Club of Georgia. Atlanta, Georgia)

8
SITE PLANNING

F*OR EVERY SITE*, there is an ideal use. For every use, there is an ideal site.

Program Development

A first step in the design of any architectural, landscape architectural, or engineering project is to have a clear understanding of just what is being designed.

Many a completed installation functions poorly or actually precludes the very uses for which it was planned. Perhaps it was doomed because it was forced upon an unsuitable site or because it was not well designed, not clearly expressive of its purpose. Or its operation may be hampered by the frictions it generates. Most often, however, the root of failure lies in the fact that a program was never fully considered; the complete project with all its essential relationships and impacts was never envisioned or thoughtfully conceived.

It is our tacit responsibility as planners to help carry each work to successful conclusion. To accomplish this aim, to plan a project intelligently, we must first understand its nature. It is essential that we develop a comprehensive *program*. By research and investigation we must organize a precise and detailed listing of requirements on which we can base our design. To this end we might well consult with all interested persons and draw freely upon their knowledge and views—with the owners, with potential users, with maintenance personnel, with planners of similar undertakings, with our collaborators, with anyone who can contribute constructive thought. We will look to history for applicable examples. We will look ahead to envision possible improvements based on

Facing page: Sentosa Resort, Singapore

newly developing techniques, new materials, and new concepts of planning. We will try to combine the best of the old with the best of the new. Since the completed work will be the physical manifestation of this program, the program itself must be designed thoroughly, imaginatively, and completely.

Site Selection

If we as planners are concerned with wedding a proposed function to a site, let us first be sure that the parties are compatible. We have all seen buildings or groups of buildings that seem foreign to their locations. No matter how excellent these structures or how well contrived their plan, the total result is disturbing.

It would seem obviously foolish, for instance, to situate:

A school fronting on an arterial trafficway

A roadside restaurant with zero approach–sight distance

A shopping center without adequate parking space

A farm without a source of potable water

A tavern near a city church

A fabricating plant with room for neither storage yard nor expansion

A new home at the end of a jet landing strip

A meat–packing plant upwind of a suburb

An apartment building 30 feet above a mined–out seam of coal

Each would seem, on the face of it, doomed to failure. Yet each, to the author's knowledge, has been attempted. It is reassuring to those of logical mind to note that in the due course of events each enterprise has been subjected to disrupting strains, scathing antipathies, bankruptcy, or collapse—all rooted in the choice of an inappropriate site for the given use.

In far too many cases, a project has started with the unquestioned acceptance of an unsuitable location. This is a cardinal planning error. An important, if not the most important, function of a planner is the sometimes delicate, sometimes forceful task of guiding an entrepreneur to the selection of the best possible location.

Alternative sites

As advisers, we should be capable of determining the requisite site requirements for any given venture and be able to weigh the relative merits of alternative situations. First we must know what we are looking for. We must thoughtfully, perhaps even tediously, list those site features that we consider necessary or useful for the proposed project, be it a power dam, a new town, or a frozen yogurt stand. Next we should reconnoiter and scout out the territory for likely locations. For this task we have a number of helpful tools, such as U.S. Geological Survey (USGS) maps, aerial and remote–sensing photography, road maps, transportation maps, planning commission data, zoning maps, chamber of commerce publications, plat books, and city, county, township, and borough plans.

With maps or other materials as a guide, we will visit the most likely places and explore them. Such scouting parties may be

In defining the program for a project we are at this point less concerned about *what it will look like* and more concerned about *what it will be.*

To dream soaring dreams is not enough. To have value, dreams and ideas must be translated into the hard reality of feasible proposals.

Design as a form–giving process is the creation of places, spaces, or artifacts to serve a predetermined purpose.

In every area of human endeavor, the most successful projects are those best planned and designed.

The responsibility of the planner is to guide those involved to the best solution and to help ensure in all ways possible the project's success.

66 *Any plan is essentially the scheduling of specific means to definite ends. . . .*
Any kind of planning implies conscious purpose. . . .
Catherine Bauer

66 *Planning is that conceiving faculty which must recommend ways and means of transmuting the possibilities and impossibilities of today into the realities of tomorrow.*
Eliel Saarinen

66 *For planning of any sort our knowledge must go beyond the state of affairs that actually prevails. To plan we must know what has gone on in the past and what is coming in the future. This is not an invitation to prophecy but a demand for a universal outlook upon the world.*
Siegfried Giedion

LOCATION APPRAISAL CHECKLIST

A Comparative Analysis of Alternative Residential Sites

Legend:
- ■ Severe limitation
- □ Moderate constraint
- ○ Condition good
- ● Condition excellent

Suggested procedure:

A visit to each site and locale is essential. Photographs help – as do notes describing in more detail the key features rated by symbol on the appraisal checksheet.

Note:
By substituting numbers for symbols (from 10 to 1 for positive values and from −1 to −10 for negative values) the arithmetic sum for each column would give a general indication of its relative overall rating. It is to be realized, however, that in some cases a single severe constraint or superlative feature might well overwhelm the statistics and become the deciding factor.

(1) Social mix and concerns
Architectural quality
Level of maintenance
Freedom from pollution
Parks, recreation and open space
Landmarks
General tone

CRITERIA	1	2	3	4	5
REGIONAL					
Climate (Temperature, rainfall, storms, etc.)	■	○	○	□	○
Soils (Stability, fertility, depths)	○	●	□	■	○
Water supply and quality	□	●	□	■	○
Economy (Rising, stable, declining)	○	○	□	□	○
Transportation (Highways and transit)	■	○	○	■	●
Energy (Availability and relative cost)	□	○	○	□	○
Landscape character	●	●	○	□	○
Cultural opportunities	○	○	○	□	□
Recreational opportunities	●	●	○	○	●
Employment opportunities	□	□	■	□	○
Health care facilities	○	□	□	○	□
Major detractions (List and describe)	□	○	○	■	○
Exceptional features (List and describe)	□	●	●	□	●
COMMUNITY					
Travel (Time-distance to work, shopping, etc.)	■	□	○	○	■
Travel experience (Pleasant or unpleasant)	○	○	○	□	○
Community ambience(1)	○	●	□	■	○
Schools	○	○	□	□	○
Shopping	○	●	○	□	○
Churches	○	○	○	□	○
Cultural opportunities (Library, auditorium)	○	○	○	□	○
Public services (Fire, police, etc.)	○	○	■	□	○
Safety and security	■	○	○	■	○
Medical facilities	○	□	■	□	○
Governance	○	○	○	■	□
Taxes	○	□	○	○	○
Major detractions (List and describe)	○	○	□	□	○
Exceptional features (List and describe)	○	●	○	□	○
NEIGHBORHOOD					
Landscape character	○	●	●	□	○
Life style	□	●	○	■	○
Compatibility of proposed uses	○	●	○	■	●
Trafficways (Access, hazard, attractiveness)	○	○	○	□	○
Schools	□	○	○	□	□
Conveniences (Schools, service, etc.)	□	○	□	□	●

CRITERIA	1	2	3	4	5
Parks, recreation and open space	○	●	○	□	○
Exposure (sun, wind, storms, flooding)	○	○	□	■	○
Freedom from noise, fumes, etc.	○	●	○	□	○
Utilities (Availability and cost)	■	○	■	■	●
Major detractions (List and describe)	○	○	○	□	□
Exceptional features (List and describe)	○	●	○	□	○
PROPERTY					
Size and shape (suitability)	○	●	○	■	○
Aspect from approaches	□	●	○	○	○
Safe entrance and egress	□	○	○	□	●
On-site "feel"	○	●	●	□	●
Permanent trees and cover	○	●	○	■	○
Need for clearing, weed eradication	○	■	○	●	○
Ground forms and gradients	○	○	○	●	○
Soils (Quality and depth)	○	○	□	○	○
Relative cost of earthwork and foundations	□	□	■	□	○
Site drainage	□	●	○	●	○
Adjacent structures (or lack of)	○	●	○	○	○
Neighbors	○	○	□	■	○
Relationship to circulation patterns	□	●	■	□	○
Relative cost of land and development	●	□	○	○	○
Major detractions (List and describe)	○	○	○	■	○
Exceptional features (List and describe	○	●	○	■	○
BUILDING SITE					
Topographic "fit" of programmed uses	○	○	○	□	○
Gradient of approaches	○	○	□	□	□
Sight distance at entrance drive	■	○	□	■	○
Orientation to sun, wind and breeze	○	●	○	□	○
Views	○	●	○	□	●
Privacy	○	●	○	○	○
Freedom from noise and glare	●	●	□	○	□
Visual impact of neighboring uses	○	○	□	□	○
Visual impact upon neighboring uses	●	●	○	○	○
Proximity to utility leads	○	○	□	■	●

> *The purpose of the game is to improve the environment whenever you do anything to change it.*
> *Garrett Eckbo*

If a client makes the wrong planning decision in site acquisition or otherwise, and has first advised the planner, the fault lies not so much with the client as with the planner, who has failed to present a persuasive case.

Given the facts and a full understanding of the alternatives, reason tends to prevail.

launched by automobile or plane or, even better, by helicopter. The last-named method not only makes one immune to barbed-wire fences, cockleburs, and no-trespassing signs but also gives an ideal overall perspective of likely properties. Much can be noted from an automobile, especially the relation of proposed sites to adjacent development patterns and approaches. But sooner or later, to be effective, we must get up off the seat cushions and cruise about the property on foot.

Having narrowed our choice to several alternative tracts of land, we will then analyze them in detail. The favorable and unfavorable aspects of each will be carefully noted and assayed. Sometimes we will informally discuss with the client the comparative analysis of the various parcels. Again, we may prepare a well-documented report for presentation, as to a board of directors, an authority, or a city council. Such a report, oral or graphic, may list the sites in order of suitability. Often, however, it is better to present only the relative merits of the alternative sites, in clear, concise terms, and leave to the decision makers the business of discussing pros and cons and making the selection.

The ideal site

We all know planned developments that seem to be natural out-growths of their sites: a home terraced down to a fronting beach; a subdivision artfully fitted to the contours, vegetation, and other topographical features of a pleasant valley; a school with its playground in a parklike setting placed at the community center and approached along safe and inviting pedestrian paths; a factory with ordered production units, tanks, storage areas, and shaded parking space all planned in admirable relationship to approach roads, trackage, or piers.

We must determine those landscape features, natural and built, best suited to our needs and then search for a site that provides them. The ideal situation is the one that, with least modification, most fully meets the project requirements.

(Miami Lakes, Florida)

Compatible siting.

Our primary work as planners is to help fit human activities to the "want to be" of the land.

Site Analysis

Now that we have selected the location, what is our next concern? At the same time that the program requirements are being studied and refined we must gain a thorough understanding of the site and its surroundings—not only the specific area contained within the property boundaries, but the total site, which includes the environs to the horizon and beyond.

The feel of the land

Graphic survey information and supporting reference data are essential, but they must be supplemented by at least one, and preferably repeated, visits to the site. Only by actual site observation can we get the feel of the property, sense its relationship to the surrounding areas, and become fully aware of the lay of the land. Only in the field can we gain an understanding of the site's bounding road, the lines of pedestrian approach, the arc of the sun, the prevailing breeze, the good views, the ugly views, the sculptural landforms, the springs, the trees, the usable areas, those features to be preserved if possible, and those to be eliminated. In short, only on the ground can we come to know the site and its

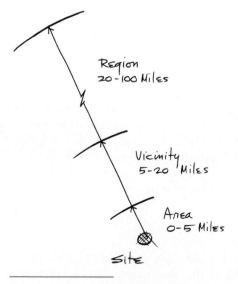

The site and its extensional environs.

character. We must climb from hollow to hill, kick at the sod, dig into the soil. We must look and listen and fully sense those qualities that are peculiar to this specific landscape area.

Whatever we can see along the lines of approach is an extensional aspect of the site. Whatever we can see from the site (or will see in the probable future) is part of the site. Anything that can be heard, smelled, or felt from the property is part of the property. Any topographical feature, natural or built, that has any effect on the property or its use must be considered a planning factor.

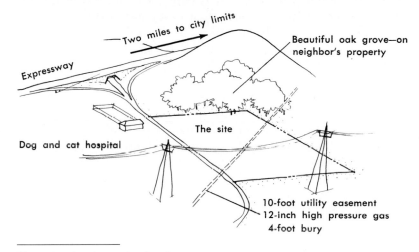

The extensional aspects of a site.

In our present power–happy and schedule–conscious era, this vitally important aspect of developing a simpatico feeling for the land and the total project site is too often overlooked. And too often our completed work gives evidence of our neglect and haste.

In Japan, historically, this keen awareness of the site has been of great significance in landscape planning. Each structure has seemed a natural outgrowth of its site, preserving and accentuating its best features. Studying in Japan, the author was struck by this consistent quality and once asked an architect how he achieved it in his work.

"Quite simply," said the architect. "If designing, say, a residence, I go each day to the piece of land on which it is to be constructed. Sometimes for long hours with a mat and tea. Sometimes in the quiet of evening when the shadows are long. Sometimes in the busy part of the day when the streets are abustle and the sun is clear and bright. Sometimes in the snow and even in the rain, for much can be learned of a piece of ground by watching the rainfall play across it and the runoff take its course in rivulets along the natural drainageways.

"I go to the land, and stay, until I have come to know it. I learn to know its bad features—the jangling friction of the passing street, the awkward angles of a windblown pine, an unpleasant sector of the mountain view, the lack of moisture in the soil, the nearness of a neighbor's house to an angle of the property.

"I learn to know its good features—a glorious clump of maple trees, a broad ledge perching high in space above a gushing waterfall that spills into the deep ravine below. I come to know the cool and pleasant summer airs that rise from the falls and move across an open draw of the land. I sense, perhaps the deliciously pungent fragrance of the deeply layered cedar fronds as the warm sun plays across them. This patch I know must be left undisturbed.

"I know where the sun will appear in the early morning, when its warmth will be most welcome. I have learned which areas will be struck by its harshly blinding light as it burns hot and penetrating in the late afternoon, and from which spots the sunset seems to glow the richest in the dusky peace of evening. I have marveled at the changing dappled light and soft, fresh colors of the bamboo thicket and watched for hours the lemon-crested warblers that have built their nests and feed there.

"I come to sense with great pleasure the subtle relationship of a jutting granite boulder to the jutting granite profile of the mountainside across the way. Little things, one may think, but they tell one, 'Here is the essence of this fragment of land; here is its very spirit. Preserve this spirit, and it will pervade your gardens, your home, and your every day.'

"And so I come to understand this bit of land, its moods, its limitations, its possibilities. Only now can I take my ink and brush in hand and start to draw my plans. But in my mind the structure by now is fully visualized. It has taken its form and character from the site and the passing street and the fragment of rock and the wafting breeze and the arching sun and the sound of the falls and the distant view.

"Knowing the owner and his family and the things they like, I have found for them here a living environment that brings them into the best relationship with the landscape that surrounds them. This structure, this house that I have conceived, is no more than an arrangement of spaces, open and closed, accommodating and expressing in stone, timber, tile, and rice paper a delightful, fulfilling way of life. How else can one come to design the best home for this site?"

There can be no other way! This, in Japan as elsewhere, is in simplest terms the planning process—for the home, the community, the city, the highway, or the national park.

In America, we planners approach our problems in a less contemplative frame of mind. We are "less sensitive" (of which fact we are proud) and "more practical" (a pathetic misnomer). We are rushed by the pressures of time, economics, and public temperament. The planning process is accelerated, sometimes to the point of frenzy. But the principle remains the same: to realize a project on a site effectively, we must fully understand the program, and we must be fully aware of the physical properties of the site and of the total environs. Our planning then becomes the science and art of arranging the most fitting relationships.

Comprehensive Land Planning

Traditionally, most land and landscape planning has been done on a limited scale and with only limited objectives. Given a proposed project description, the planner has been expected to fit it onto a given site to the maximum advantage of the owner. Sometimes the effects on the neighboring lands and waters were considered. Sometimes they were not. In our emerging environmental and land use ethic it is believed that they should and *must* be.

In building cabins in the forest the native instincts of the pioneers as they felled the trees and cleared the land may have been

Therefore, let us build houses that restore to man the life-giving, life-enhancing elements of nature. This means an architecture that begins with the nature of the site. Which means taking the first great step toward assuring a worthy architecture, for in the rightness of a house on the land we sense a fitness we call beauty.
Frank Lloyd Wright

Thus we seek two values in every landscape: one, the expression of the native quality of the landscape, the other, the development of maximum human livability. . . .

Site planning must be thought of as the organization of the total land area and air space of the site for best use by the people who will occupy it. This means an integrated concept in which buildings, engineering construction, open space and natural materials are planned together at one time. . . .
Garrett Eckbo

The comprehensive planning process is a systematic means of determining

where you are,

where you want to be,

and how best to get there.

There is little mystery to the art and science of site planning. Those whose professional work it is have developed it into a systematic process. Its purpose is to best arrange the elements of any planned development in relation to the natural and constructed features of a site and its environs. Whether for a home garden, university campus, or military installation, the approach is essentially the same.

The site–planning procedure normally involves the following ten steps, several of which may take place concurrently:

1. Definition of intent (scope, goal, and objectives)
2. Procurement of topographic survey
3. Program development
4. Data gathering and analysis
5. Site reconnaissance
6. Organization of reference plan set and file
7. Preparation of exploratory studies
8. Comparative analysis and revision of studies, leading to an approved conceptual plan
9. Development of preliminary development plans and estimate of costs
10. Preparation of construction plans, specifications, and bidding documents

good enough. In contemporary times, however, with land reserves receding so rapidly and with building sites under such stress, every development is subject to new planning factors. The larger and more intensive the project, the greater the consequences and the need for care and concern. This has led to a process known as *comprehensive land planning*. It is a systematic approach especially suited to developments of greater scope or sensitivity.

Even in single–home construction it is incumbent upon the planner to organize a file of background information. This will include the governing zoning maps, codes, and other pertinent regulations. City plans and street maps will show the location of community schools, parks, shopping, and other amenities to which the residence will relate. Needed also is a thorough investigation of all that transpires on, contiguous to, or beneath the building site—including such potential subsurface surprises as mine workings, high–pressure fuel transmission lines, or buried cables.

Comprehensive land planning is usually initiated with an investigation of the region embracing the project site. The immediate vicinity and its interrelationships with the property to be developed are given more thorough study. Finally, the project site itself is analyzed to gain the full understanding so essential to landscape planning.

Guideline

The following procedure is suggested as a guide to systematic site analysis.

Regional influences. The site analysis process most often begins with the location of the project site on a regional map and a cursory investigation of regional, vicinity, and area planning factors. From such documents as U.S. Geological Survey maps, road maps, various planning reports, and the Internet, much useful insight can be gained as to the surrounding topographic features, land uses, roadway and transportation network, recreational opportunities, and employment, commercial, and cultural centers. Together these establish the extensional setting to which the proposed project will relate.

The project site. Before design studies can be initiated, the planner must be fully conversant with the specific nature of the site— its constraints and its possibilities. This knowledge is obtained mainly by means of a topographic survey and site visitation.

Topographic survey. The basic topographic survey is customarily prepared by a registered surveyor at an engineering scale (as 1 inch = 20 feet, 50 feet, or 100 feet, etc.) This scale is to be predetermined as that being best for the planning studies. A survey *specification* describing the information to be provided by the surveyor and the form of presentation is the responsibility of the planner. (For example specification, see page 108.)

Site analysis map. One of the most effective means of developing a keen appreciation of the property and its nature is the preparation of a *site analysis map*. A print of the topographic survey fur-

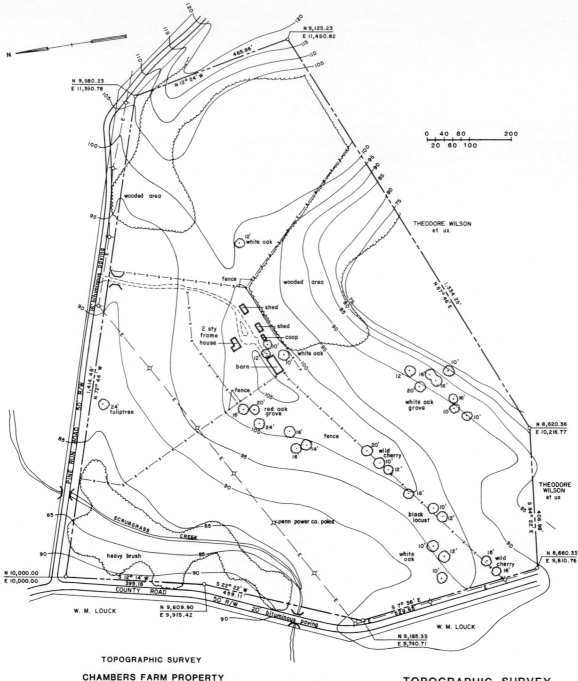

TOPOGRAPHIC SURVEY

CHAMBERS FARM PROPERTY

WESTLAND TOWNSHIP, PA.

**TOPOGRAPHIC SURVEY
(HYPOTHETICAL)**

nished by the surveyor is taken into the field, and from actual site observation additional notes are jotted down upon it in the planner's own symbols. These amplify the survey notations and describe all conditions on or related to the site that are pertinent in its planning. Such supplementary information might describe or note:

- Outstanding natural features such as springs, ponds, streams, rock ledges, specimen trees, contributing shrub masses, and established ground covers, all to be preserved insofar as possible
- Tentative outlines of proposed PCD (preservation, conservation, and development) areas

The best source of design criteria is *field observation.*

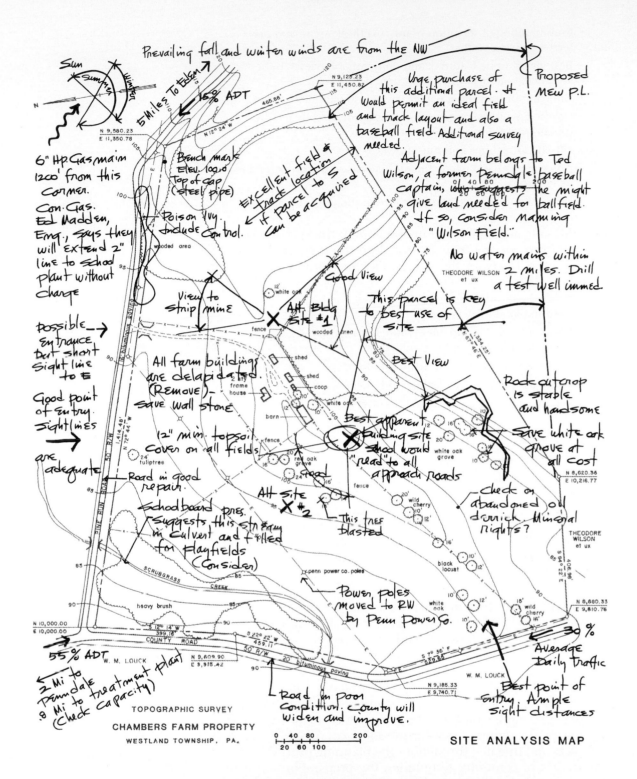

TOPOGRAPHIC SURVEY

CHAMBERS FARM PROPERTY

WESTLAND TOWNSHIP, PA.

0 40 80   200
20 60 100

SITE ANALYSIS MAP

- Negative site features or hazards such as obsolete structures or deleterious materials to be removed, dead or diseased vegetation, noxious weed infestation, lack of topsoil, or evidence of landslides, subsidence, or flooding

- Directions and relative volumes of vehicular traffic flow on approach roads; points of connection to pedestrian routes, bikeways, and riding trails

- Logical points of site ingress or egress

- Potential building locations, use areas, or routes of movement

- Commanding observation points, overlook areas, and preferred viewing sectors
- Best views, to be featured, and objectionable views, to be screened, together with a brief note describing each
- Direction of prevailing winter winds and summer breezes
- Exposed, windswept areas and those protected by nearby topographical forms, groves, or structures
- Off-site attractions and nuisances
- An ecological and microclimatic analysis of the property and its environs
- Other factors of special significance in the project planning

In addition to such information observed in the field, further data gleaned from research may be noted on the site analysis map or included separately in the survey file. Such information might include:

- Abutting land ownerships
- Names of utility companies whose lines are shown, company addresses, phone numbers, engineers
- Routes and data on projected utility lines
- Approach patterns of existing roads, drives, and walks
- Relative abutting roadway traffic counts
- Zoning restrictions, building code, and building setback lines
- Mineral rights, depth of coal, mined-out areas
- Water quality and supply
- Core-boring logs and data

Base map.   It is helpful early in the planning process to prepare a base map which sets the format for all sheets to follow. Drawn on drafting film or stable translucent paper to give clear reproduction, it sets the trim lines and title block with project name and location, owner's and planner's identification, north point, scale, and dateline. Aside from the property lines and coordinates, it will show only that information to be carried forward to all derivative sheets. Most site and architectural studies, conceptual plans, and working drawings will be prepared on reproducible prints of this base map.

Plan set and reference file.   As the surveys, base sheets, overlays, site analysis map, and other background data are developed, they are assembled as a coordinated reference file—together with supporting plans, reports, and correspondence. All are to be kept complete and updated throughout the planning process. With the application of computer techniques, the preparation of, maintenance of, and access to the reference files can be streamlined and expedited. (See "Computer Technology," page 127.)

The material in the reference file will vary for each project, depending upon its size and complexity. For more extensive planning—as for a hospital, stadium, or new community—the file may include such background data as:

- Regional and local master plans
- Zoning and subdivision regulations
- Projected highway network

66 *Perhaps the planning process can best be explained as a series of subconscious conversations . . . —the question posed, the factors weighed, and then the recorded conclusion. The more lucid the thinking, the more coherent the powers of idea communication . . . the better is the plan.*

B. Kenneth Johnstone

There is an area of the conceptual and forming process that is common to the four major physical planning disciplines and often to others as well. This is the formulation of the basic *plan concept* by which, in sketch or diagram, the use areas and plan forms are conceived in harmony with the natural and constructed forms, forces, and features of the total project site. Usually the plan concept is best arrived at through a collaborative effort in which all participants contribute freely of their experience and ideas.

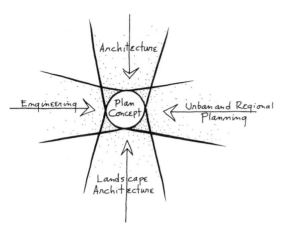

- Regional water management program
- Airfields and flight zones
- Transmission lines and stations
- Utility systems
- Fire, police, and ambulance services
- Flood and storm records
- Air and water pollution sources and controls
- Demographic data and user profiles
- Schools
- Recreation facilities
- Cultural amenities
- Economic statistics and trends
- Tax rates and assessments
- Governance

On larger commissions the landscape architect often serves as a member of a closely coordinated professional team, which includes architects, engineers, planners, and scientist–advisers. A generalist, the landscape architect brings to the planning–design process specialized training in the physical sciences—such as physiography, geology, hydrology, biology, and ecology—and a feeling for the land, human relationships, and design.

The Conceptual Plan

A seed of use—a cell of function—wisely applied to a receptive site, will be allowed to develop organically, in harmonious adaptation to the natural and the planned environment.

We have by now developed a comprehensive program defining the proposed nature of our project. We have begun to sense its resonance within the total environs. Up to this point, the planning effort has been one of research and analysis. It has been painstaking and perhaps tedious, but this phase is of vital importance because it is the only means by which we can achieve full command of the data on which our design will be based. From this point on, the planning process becomes one of integration of proposed uses, structures, and site.

Plan concepts

If structure and landscape development are contemplated, it is impossible to conceive one without the other, for it is the relationship of structure to site and site to structure that gives meaning to each and to both.

This point perhaps raises the question of who on the planning team—architect, landscape architect, engineer, or others—is to do the "conceiving." Strangely, this problem, which might seemingly lead to warm debate, seldom arises, for an effective collaboration brings together experts in various fields of knowledge who, in a free interchange of ideas, develop a climate of perceptive awareness and know–how. In such a climate, plan concepts usually evolve more or less spontaneously. Since the collaboration is arranged and administered by one of the principals (who presumably holds the commission), it is usually this team leader who coordinates the planning in all its aspects and gives it expressive unity. It is the work of the collaborators to advance their assigned planning tasks and to aid in the articulation of the main design idea in all ways possible.

Site-structure diagram

When planning a project or a structure in relation to a land area, we first consider all the various uses to be fitted together and

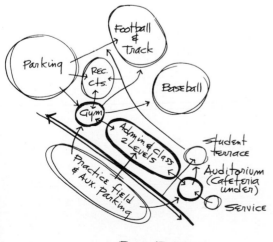

FLOW DIAGRAM

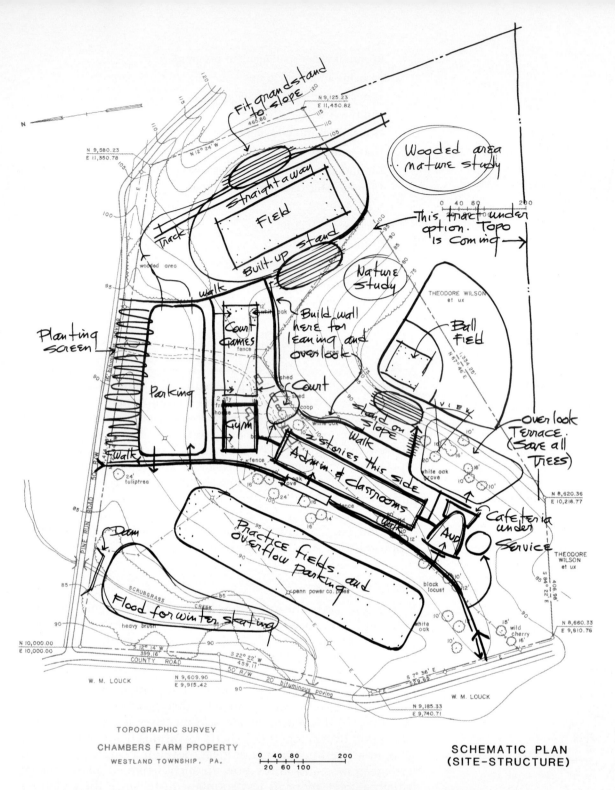

Fit grandstand to slope

N 9,125.23
E 11,450.82

Wooded area nature study

Straightaway

Field

Track

Built-up stand

This tract under option. Topo is coming

N 9,580.23
E 11,350.78

wooded area

Nature Study

THEODORE WILSON et ux

Planting screen

walk

Court Games fence

Build wall here for leaning and overlook

Ball Field

Parking

Court

shed

2 sty frame house

Gym

Stand on slope

white oak grove

VIEW

Overlook Terrace (Save all Trees)

Walk

coop

Admin & classrooms

2 stories this side

Walk

N 8,620.36
E 10,218.77

Dam

Practice fields and overflow Parking

Aud

Cafeteria under Service

THEODORE WILSON et ux

penn power co. poles

black locust

Flood for winter skating

SCRUBGRASS

CREEK

heavy brush

white oak

wild cherry

N 8,660.33
E 9,810.76

N 10,000.00
E 10,000.00

S 12° 14' W
399.16

COUNTY ROAD

S 22° 22' W
459.11

50 R/W

20 bituminous paving

W. M. LOUCK

N 9,609.90
E 9,915.42

S 7° 36' E

W. M. LOUCK

N 9,185.33
E 9,740.71

TOPOGRAPHIC SURVEY

CHAMBERS FARM PROPERTY

WESTLAND TOWNSHIP, PA.

0 40 80   200
  20 60 100

SCHEMATIC PLAN
(SITE-STRUCTURE)

accommodated. For a high school, for instance, we would determine the approximate architectural plan areas and their shapes—the general plan areas required for service, parking, outdoor classrooms, gardens, game courts, football fields, track, bleachers, and perhaps future school expansion. Over a print of the topographic survey (or site analysis map) we would then indicate, in freehand line, use areas of logical size and shape in studied relation to each other and to the natural and built landscape features. Having thus roughed in the site use areas, we may at last block in the architectural elements of the project. The result is the *site-structure diagram.*

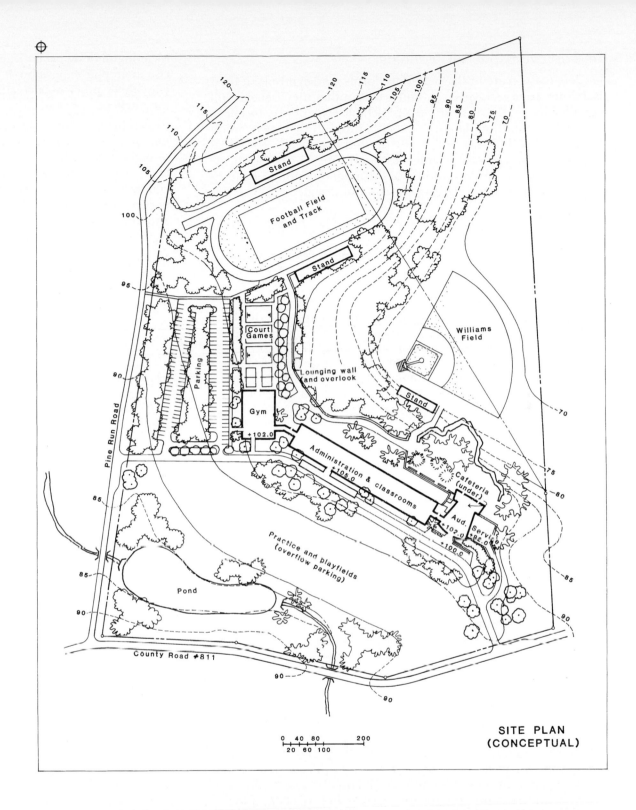

Labels within the site plan:

120
120
115
110
105
100
95
90
85
80
75
70

110
115
105
100
95
90
85

Stand

Football Field and Track

Stand

Williams Field

Court Games

Lounging wall and overlook

Parking

Pine Run Road

Gym

+102.0

Stand

Administration & classrooms
+105.0

Cafeteria (under)

Aud. Service
+102.0 +96.0
+100.0

Practice and playfields
(overflow parking)

Pond

85
90
90

County Road #811

90

90

90

80

85

90

75

70

80

85

90

**SITE PLAN
(CONCEPTUAL)**

0 40 80   200
20 60 100

Conceptual site plan

The balance of the planning process is a matter of comparative analysis and refinement of detail—a process of creative synthesis. A good plan, reduced to essentials, is no more than a record of logical thought. A dull plan is a record of ineffectual thinking or of very little thinking at all. A brilliant plan gives evidence of response to all site factors, a clear perception of needs and relationships, and a sensitive expression of all components working well together.

The creative aspect of planning

Planners may create in the materials, forms, and symbols of their disciplines an object, space, or construction that they believe will engender in the users a certain predictable experience. In effect, users will *re-create* the planned elements through their perception of them and will thus be led to the desired experience. For when we perceive, we actually retrace through our senses the form-giving process. An understanding of this phenomenon leads us to a clearer concept of the creative function of design.

The planning attitude

In his admirable treatise, *On the Laws of Japanese Painting*, Henry P. Bowie has written:

> One of the most important principles in the art of Japanese painting—indeed, a fundamental and entirely distinctive characteristic—is that of living movement, *sei do* ... it being, so to say, the transfusion into the work of the felt nature of the thing to be painted by the artist. Whatever the subject to be translated—whether river or tree, rock or mountain, bird or flower, fish or animal—the artist at the moment of painting it must feel its very nature, which, by the magic of art, he transfers into his work to remain forever, affecting all who see it with the same sensations he experienced when executing it.

And again:

> Indeed, nothing is more constantly urged upon his attention than this great underlying principle, that it is impossible to express in art what one does not feel.

And so it is with planning. We can create only that for which we have first developed an empathic understanding. A shopping mall? As designers, we must *feel* the quickening tempo, the pull and attraction, the bustle, the excitement of the place. We must sense the chic boutique displays, the mouthwatering sights and smells of the bakery shop; we must see in our minds the jam-packed counter of the hardware store and the drugstore with its pyramids of mouthwash, perfume, nail polish, hot-water bottles, and jelly beans. We must see in the market the heaps of grapefruit, oranges, rhubarb, brussels sprouts, bananas; whiff the heady fragrance of the flower stalls; picture the shelf on shelf of bargain books, the bolts of cotton prints, the sloping trays of peppermints and chocolate creams. We must feel the brightness of the sunshine on the sidewalks and the coolness and protection of shaded doorways and arcades. We must feel crowds and traffic and benches and trees and perhaps the sparkle and splash of a fountain or two. And then we can start planning.

A children's zoo? If we would design one, we must first feel like one of the flocking children, the gawking, clapping, squealing kids; we must appreciate the delight, the laughter, the chatter, the confusion, and the rollicking thrill of the place. We must feel the diminutive, squeaky "cuteness" of the mouse town, the bulk and immensity and cavelike hollowness of the spouting whale with its dimly illumined interior. We must know the preening strut of the

Meaningful design is far from an exercise in graphic exposition. It is an empathetic process—a creative act of the intellect.

Design begins with a conceptual determination of the desired nature of space or object. This "what shall it be" aspect may be focalized by a flash of intuitive genius, by a methodical analysis of possibilities, or by logical extension and improvement upon past examples.

The visual aspects of superior design are marked by a clear and direct expression of idea, time, place, materials, and technology, coupled with a fine instinct for three-dimensional form.

66 *It is not the thing done or made which is beautiful, but the doing. If we appreciate the thing, it is because we relive the heady freedom of making it. Beauty is the byproduct of interest and pleasure in the choice of action.*

Jacob Bronowski

elegantly wandering peacocks, the quack, quack, quacking of the waddling ducks, the soft furry whiteness of the lop–eared rabbits, and the clop, clop, clopping and creaking harness and the awed delight of the pony ride. We must, in our minds, be at the children's zoo, and we must see it, hear it, feel it, and love it as a child would love it as we make our plans.

Are we to design a parkway, hotel plaza, terminal, or bathing beach? If we would create them, we must first have a feeling for their nature. This self–induced sensitivity we might call the *planning attitude*. Before we mature as planners, it will be intuitive.

Impact assessment

It has been proposed that no development should be permitted if, all things considered, it were to do more harm than good. But how is this to be ascertained?

Until recently this might well be a matter of hotly debated opinion. With the advent of the federally invented *Environmental Impact Statement* (EIS), however, there is now the means of making a fairly rational appraisal.

The chart on page 130 provides a checklist of environmental and performance factors to be considered in large–scale, comprehensive planning.

An official Environmental Impact Statement, as is required on most federally aided projects, is governed by a pro forma set of instructions. Essentially, the statement is to describe:

- All significant *negative* impacts to be expected from the proposed development, and the means by which the planners have ameliorated them as far as feasible.
- All *positive* values created by the project, and the means by which they have been enhanced in the planning process.
- The rationale for proceeding with construction. Only with rare exceptions is approval justified unless the long–term negative factors are outweighed by the benefits.

When such environmental considerations are defined and explored early, they become not only a useful *test* but also a sound *basis* for the evolving studies and resulting plan solution. The negative impacts of the project can thus be reduced and the attributes significantly increased during the planning process. The many benefits of such a systematic approach cannot be overemphasized.

Computer Technology

The advent of the computer, the Internet, cyberspace, et al., has advanced the planning/design process immensely—yet fundamentally has changed it not at all. The goals and procedural steps of planning remain the same. As a means of attaining the goals, however, the computer has opened up an intriguing range of possibilities. Together with its accouterments it has provided a whole new array of bright and radiant *tools*. It is important that in our fascination with the tools we are not distracted from the task to be accomplished.

The Planning-Design Process

Architecture, landscape architecture, engineering

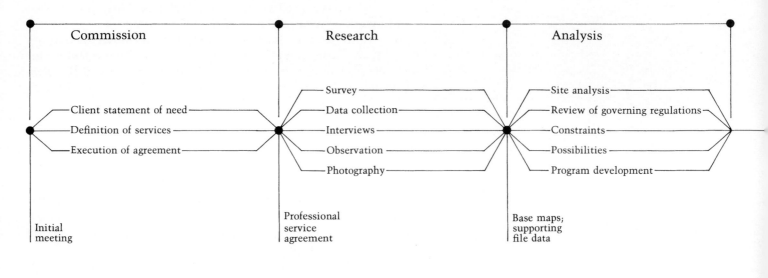

Commission	Research	Analysis

Client statement of need
Definition of services
Execution of agreement

Survey
Data collection
Interviews
Observation
Photography

Site analysis
Review of governing regulations
Constraints
Possibilities
Program development

Initial meeting

Professional service agreement

Base maps; supporting file data

Commission

Most planning-design interviews and commission awards are based upon experience and reputation.

Experience is gained by education and training, acceptance of increasingly demanding assignments, engaging consultants as required, and doing all necessary research.

Reputation is gained by full, prompt, and excellent performance. The successful professional has a widening coterie of pleased and vocal clients.

Effective professional service agreements embody a clear, simple statement of intent—who does what, how, when, and for how much compensation.

Remuneration for services is usually arranged in one of the following forms:

Lump sum, with phased payments

Time, plus reimbursement for travel, materials, and related expenses

A percentage fee based on construction costs

Consultation is normally provided on a per diem plus reimbursement basis.

Form of agreement.

A verbal agreement is often enough.

A letter of confirmation is better.

A standard professional agreement is better yet.

With large, complex, or long-term projects, as with many public agencies, a detailed legal instrument of agreement is prescribed.

Research

(an exercise in gaining awareness)

The basic tool in land planning is a topographic survey, meeting a specification to provide all, and only, the information needed.

Data collection begins with a listing of all materials required together with a notation of the most likely source.

Maps, reports, and other useful data are available in public agencies and planning offices, often without charge.

Interviews with potential users, agency staff members, and public officials not only yield helpful information but also build in an understanding of the project and a sense of contribution.

Research includes the study of past and present examples and a knowledge of innovative trends. It is a continuing process of travel, observation, reading, and experimentation.

Visits to the site are essential. A photographic record keyed to a location map is always beneficial.

Surveys, base maps, and all related information are to be organized into a convenient project reference file kept complete and updated.

Analysis

Supplementary planning information, observations, and notes can be recorded on prints of the topographical survey and overlays.

Constraints such as land use and density limitations, easements, areas of ecological sensitivity, hazards, and difficult terrain or subsurface conditions are noted.

Favorable site aspects and features are also described.

Governmental regulations, standards, and requirements are reviewed and underlined.

Finally, in the analysis phase, a comprehensive development program is formulated. This will respond to the stated intent as modified in the light of the survey information and data obtained. It will include:

A statement of goals and objectives*

A summary of preliminary findings

A description of the project components and their interrelationship

Proposals as to conceptual alternatives

An outline of performance standards

---

* A *goal* is a generalized statement of the result to be achieved. An *objective* is a means of attaining the desired result.

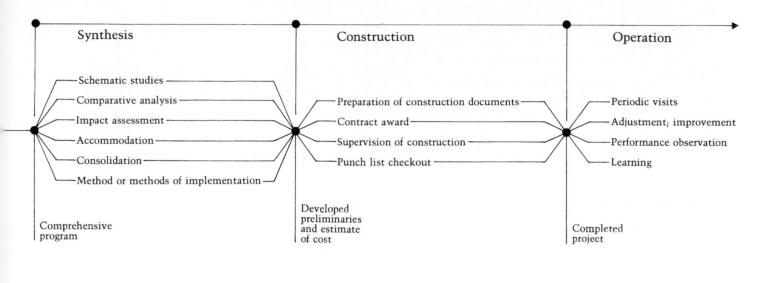

Synthesis   Construction   Operation

Schematic studies
Comparative analysis
Impact assessment
Accommodation
Consolidation
Method or methods of implementation

Preparation of construction documents
Contract award
Supervision of construction
Punch list checkout

Periodic visits
Adjustment; improvement
Performance observation
Learning

Comprehensive
program

Developed
preliminaries
and estimate
of cost

Completed
project

Synthesis

Schematic studies are prepared to explore the plan alternatives. These are kept simple and diagrammatic to explain as directly as possible the conceptual idea as it relates to the givens of the site.

As the schematics evolve, they are subjected to a comparative analysis of their positive and negative values and net yields.

Unsuitable schemes are rejected or modified, promising concepts are improved, and other schematic approaches suggested by the reviews are added to the array of contenders.

Insofar as feasible, all constructive ideas and recommendations are accommodated, negative environmental impacts ameliorated, and benefits increased.

When the most likely plan approaches have been delineated and compared, the best is selected for conversion into a *developed preliminary plan* and an *estimate of cost*.

Construction

Upon approval of the developed preliminary plan and estimate, detailed construction documents are prepared. These comprise plans, details, specifications, and bidding forms to be issued as a package. A final estimate of cost and a cash-flow analysis are also in order.

In form, bids are invited on the basis of either a *cost-plus proposal* (when top quality is a prerequisite and when conditions are uncertain or changes anticipated) or the *lowest responsible bid* (when economy and budget limitations are the decisive factors).

Professional services normally include supervision, "observation," or consultation during the bidding, contract award, and construction process.

Supervision is to be firm, fair, and expeditious. Field adjustments are to be welcomed if the project is thereby improved and if all parties have a clear understanding of the nature of the change and its cost implications.

During construction it is well to have the ongoing maintenance superintendent present to gain an understanding of the project installation and conditions.

In advance of construction completion a *punch list* is provided by the supervisor as the basis for final inspection and acceptance.

Operation

Prior to project completion the thoughtful planner will provide the owner with a sheet of instructions or, on larger projects, a concise manual to govern continuing operation and maintenance.

Many professional service agreements provide for continuing consultation. In any event, the conscientious planner will return for periodic visits to observe, learn, and advise as to suggested improvements.

There is no better lead to future commissions than a demonstration of continued interest in the project's success and the client's satisfaction.

Excel, and exceed expectations.

Environmental impact assessment checklist

1. Identify all proposed uses or actions that would have a significant impact upon the environment.
2. In the appropriate frame of the matrix place a square for a negative impact and a circle for one that is seen to be beneficial.
3. Within each square or circle place a number, from 1 to 10, to represent the magnitude and importance (local to regional) of each impact: 10 represents the greatest effect, 1 the least. While the arithmetic sum is not to be considered an absolute indication of the project's worth, it is a telling decision factor.
4. In text to accompany the completed chart discuss any unusual, potent, hazardous, or lasting impact or impacts inherent in the project.
5. In separate sections describe those means by which in the project planning and design the negative consequences have been mitigated and the benefits increased.

Proposed land use, project, or action

1. Destruction of habitat
2. Modification of habitat
3. Alteration of surface drainage
4. Change in stream or river flow
5. Effect on freshwater reserves
6. Excavation, filling, or grading
7. Dredging
8. Mining or extraction
9. Forestry
10. Agricultural uses
11. Home and garden
12. Residential communities
13. Recreational uses
14. Institutional uses
15. Commercial uses
16. Industrial uses
17. Urbanization
18. Transportation; transit
19. Transmission
20. Utilities
21. Impoundments
22. Harbors, piers, or marinas
23. Blasting, drilling, and explosions
24. Energy generation
25. Other (list)

Earth
- Landform
- Soils
- Mineral resources
- Geologic features

Water
- Surface conformation
- Visual appeal
- Quality
- Supply

Atmosphere
- Quality (gases; particulates)
- Climate (macro; micro)
- Temperature

Processes
- Flooding
- Erosion
- Sedimentation
- Stability (slides and slumps)
- Air movement
- Solar penetration (sunlight; cast shadow)

Flora
- Ecological systems
- Visual continuity
- Trees
- Shrubs
- Ground covers
- Crops
- Habitat
- Rare plant species

Fauna
- Birds
- Land animals and reptiles
- Fish and shellfish
- Rare or endangered species
- Food chains

Land use
- Wilderness
- Wetlands
- Forestry; grazing or agricultural uses
- Recreational uses
- Residential uses
- Institutional uses
- Commercial uses
- Industrial uses
- Urbanization
- Open-space preserve

Visual and human interest
- Scenic quality
- Landscape character
- Views and vistas
- Parks and recreation
- Conservation areas
- Archaeological or historical interest
- Unique physical features
- Inappropriate uses
- Pollution

Social factors
- Health
- Safety
- Cultural patterns (lifestyle)
- Employment
- Population density and distribution
- Public services
- Cultural amenities

Built environment
- Buildings
- Engineering structures
- Landscape development
- Community integrity
- Urbanization patterns
- Transportation network
- Utility systems
- Waste disposal facilities

Other
- List

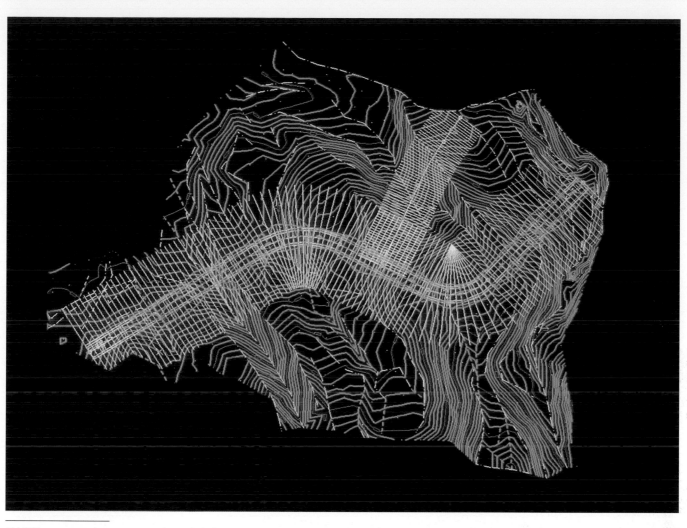

CADD-generated contours and road design.

Capability

The function of computer technology is to access, store, manage (manipulate), and display information. As to access, once the planner has developed the project program and decided upon the background material needed, the computer can search out the vast Internet storehouse of facts and graphic examples and put them on file for easy reference. Even surveys, plans, and photographs can be scanned and computerized—to be recalled on the screen and enlarged, reduced, or edited at will.

As schematic studies progress they too can be recorded for comparative analysis and optimization. The evolving schemes and resulting conceptual plan can be projected three-dimensionally for viewing from various angles. If so desired, the images may be modified by the planner to effect improvement. Or they may be supplemented with overlays showing perspective views of the actual project site and environs—and such design features as walls, paving, lighting standards, ancillary structures, or planting.

Concurrently with the visual comparison, the computer can provide running data on land and building coverage, area of various types of paving or ground covers, cubic yardage of masonry, soil, etc.—and thus the basis for comparative costs.

Application

The advantages of computer use are manyfold. Not only in time-cost savings but as well in the scope of research material made available and the ability to organize and store it for rapid retrieval. Not only in the ability to project, compare, and modify the schematic studies, but to test them for relative cost. Not only to display the various proposals by screen, but to select the viewing points and to visualize the plans and spaces by sequential movement through them.

In the recording of survey information and in the dimensioning of construction drawings, the use of coordinates for property corners, outlines, and locations saves endless hours of calculation and drafting. Computer imagery precludes the need for slide preparation and projection—and makes obsolete the clumsy presentation boards and easels set up at public meetings. The printout of plans and text in various sizes and forms, with ease of revision, is another obvious advantage. As if these advantages weren't enough, new capabilities and refinements are constantly coming on-line.

Limitations

What then are the limits to design by computer? The fact is that the valued computer cannot "design" at all. It is incapable of either *perception* or *deduction*. It cannot discern the personality of the client, cannot sense the character of the site, cannot know the feel of stone, wood, or water, or the wonder of a view. It cannot learn from experience, or apply to the planning process the lessons of travel and observation.

Some would-be planners have become enslaved by computer technology. For them, to sit before screen or keyboard is to go into a rapturous trance. It is to be hoped that with time they will recognize the computer's role for what it is—the esteemed and highly efficient servant, but never the intuitive master.

> The skill of drawing, that beautiful coordination between the hand, eye, and mind, is as crucial to making good use of computer graphics as it has always been to the design professions.
>
> William J. Johnson

COMPUTER TECHNOLOGY
(ENHANCED COMPUTER IMAGES)

Harmon Arena Proposal, PWWJ Associates

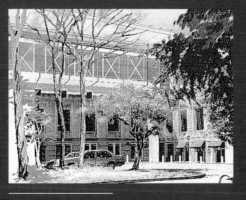

Printout with a "paint screen." Used to diminish the prominence of the details and highlight the basic landscape issues. "Simply a different button on the computer."

The printing process can produce numerous variations on the original sketch to meet different discussion needs in search for the most effective color hue. *Example 1.*

Example 2. Such manipulation is not possible in hand-drawn images with comparable speed.

Matte finish ink-jet printing is economical and provides a receptive surface for prisma-color highlights.

New cars, bollards, and foreground planting sketched in.

Base photo. Need to remove unwanted elements and add new elements.

Unwanted images removed and architectural elements added.

Examples and comments by William J. Johnston, ASLA, pioneer in enhanced computer imaging.

新しい駅とその周辺

鉄道の高架化により、旭川駅は高架の下におさまり、駅前に広い空間が生まれます。新しい駅は、旭川の玄関として水準の高いものとしていきます。駅前広場は、緑豊かな空間とし、川から駅、駅から広場へと自然環境が入り込んでくる空間を創出していきます。

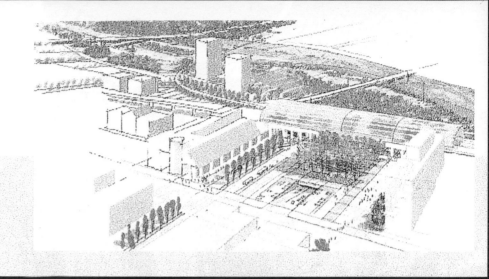

These computer sketches are often used in early project descriptions.
Though quick, they show a freshness that is elusive in computer drawings.

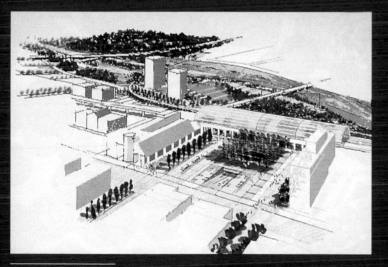

Hand-drawn additions to computer image.

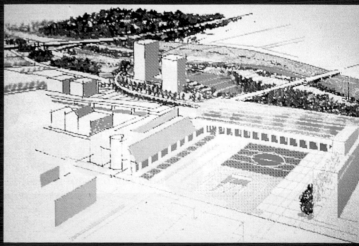

Direct print of "sketch" done in the computer from wire-frame 3-D.

Courtyard gardens.

Rural site

Land area is plentiful. The plan is more open, free, and "exploded." Although the specific site may be circumscribed by property boundaries, the visual limits may include extensive sweeps of the landscape far beyond. The scope of planning considerations is increased, since fence line geometry, orchards, paddocks, even a mountaintop miles away may become design factors and elements. Our scheme must be planned to the horizon.

Freedom, with open view of fields, woods, and sky, is the essential landscape quality. We may logically orient our plan outward to embrace the total site's best features and to command the best views.

The choice of a rural site would indicate a desire to be at one with nature. Make nature appreciation a design aim and theme. Insofar as possible, the natural environment will be disturbed or modified only to improve it.

The major landscape features are established. Build to them, feature the best, screen out and de-emphasize those that are less desirable, and contrive structural forms in best relation to the natural forms. Site use areas, sympathetically fitted to topographical features, may well dictate the architectural plan arrangement.

The landscape is dominant (in character and mood). Presumably the site was selected because of its qualities. If the existing landscape character is desirable, it may be preserved and accentuated by the site-structure diagram. If alterations are required, we may modify or completely change the site aspect, but only in such a way as to take fullest possible advantage of the existing features.

Earth and ground forms are strong visual elements. A structure conceived in studied relation to ground forms gains in architectural strength and in harmony with the topographical features.

The pleasant landscape is one of agreeable transitions. In the planning of transitions between structure and site, intermediate areas relating structure to the land are of key importance.

Structures become elements imposed on the landscape. Either structure or site must dominate. Either the site is considered basically a

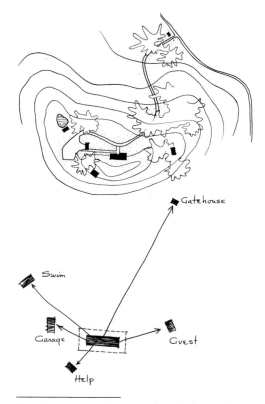

Ample area permits an exploded plan, each element being related to the most compatible topographic features.

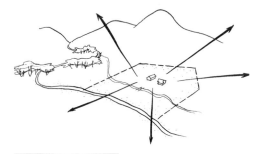

Rural property has an expansive feel. Streams, groves, distant hills, all features of the landscape that can be seen or sensed, are a part of the extensional site.

Major landscape features are established; build to, around, and among them.

Structural forms conceived in sympathy with ground forms borrow power from and return power to the landscape.

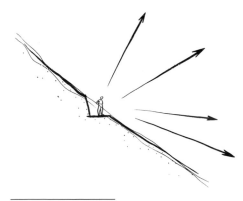

On the sloping plane, orientation is outward.

setting for a dominant structure, or the structure is conceived as subordinate to the landscape and designed to complement the natural contours and forms.

The rural landscape is a landscape of subtleties—of foliage shadings, sky tints, and cloud shadows. Our planning must recognize these qualities and treat them sympathetically, or they will be wasted.

In a rural site, one is more exposed to the elements and weather—rain, storms, sun, wind, snow, frost, winter cold, and summer heat. The site-structure diagram and architecture should reflect a thorough understanding of adaptation to the climate.

A rural site implies increased land area and greater maneuverability. The automobile and pedestrian approaches, important elements in our design, may often be aligned within the property boundaries to reveal the best site and architectural features.

The indigenous materials of a rural site—ledge rock, fieldstone, slate, gravels, and timbers—contribute much to its landscape character. The use of such natural materials in buildings, fences, bridges, and walls helps relate structures to their surroundings.

The essential quality of the landscape is the natural and the unrefined. Our structural materials may well reflect this naturalness and forego high refinement.

Site sympatico.

Steeply sloping site (unobstructed inclined plane)

Contours are major plan factors. Contour planning (the alignment of plan elements parallel with the contours) is generally indicated.

The areas of relatively equal elevation are narrow bands lying perpendicular to the axis of the slope. Narrow plan forms such as bars or ribbons are suggested.

Sizable level areas are nonexistent. Where required, they must be carved out of or projected from the slope. If they are shaped of earth, the earth must be retained by a wall or by a slope of increased inclination.

The essence of slope is rise and fall. A terraced scheme is suggested. Levels may separate functions, as in split-level or multideck structures.

vicariously through the senses of those who will see and use it. At any stage in the creative process, from rough sketches to final drawings or model, we can by our imagination lift ourselves up and look down at the project with a fresh perspective. We can bring it alive in our mind's eye. We can say, in effect, as we look down at the plans for a church:

"I am the minister. As I drive by my church or approach it, does it express those inspirational qualities to which I have dedicated my life? As I enter my study, do I sense that this space is remote enough to give me privacy for study and meditation, yet accessible enough to attract to its doors those who need help or counsel or those who come on church business? As an office is it so located that I can direct and oversee church activities? Does this church that I am to administer have an efficiently organized plan?"

"I am the janitor. As I come to work in the morning, where do I park my car? How do the barrels of cleaning compound get moved from the service dock to the storage area? Where do I store my ladders and snow removal equipment? Did someone in their planning think about me and my work?"

"I am a Boy Scout homing in to troop meeting. Are the walks planned to take me where I am going, or do I cut across the lawn? Some friends of mine are waiting outside. Do we have a place where we can rip around and blow off steam and maybe shoot a few baskets? Where do we put our bikes? Where do we set up practice tents? Where do we...?"

"I am a member of this church, and I am coming to worship. Does my church invite me in? Am I able to drive close to the entry on a cold, rainy day? Where do I park? Is there ample room? After service is there a pleasant space adjacent to the doors where we may linger and greet our friends and welcome visitors?"

All these things are a part of church life and are to be arranged for in its planning.

The function of any project and the relationship of building to site may thus be tested by an imaginary introduction to and, through it, of people typical of those who will see, service, or use it.

The process of site-structure plan development is a search for logical progressions and best relationships.

Site-Structure Unity

We have discussed the importance of developing responsive site-project relationships. Let us now consider other means by which we may achieve site-structure unity.

We may design the structural elements so as to utilize and accentuate landforms. A lighthouse, for example, is an extension of the jutting promontory. The ancient fort or castle extended, architecturally, the craggy top of a hill or mountain. Our modern municipal water tanks and transmission or relay towers rise from and extend the height of a topographical eminence. These applications are obvious. Not so obvious is the location of a community swimming pool to utilize and accentuate the natural bowl configuration of a landscape basin or valley. More subtle yet may be the conscious planning of a yacht club to utilize and emphasize the structural protective shoulders of a point or the soft receptive forms of a quiet bay.

A terraced restaurant stepping down the naturally terraced banks of a river, floating structures on water, light, airy structures

Land forms accentuated. (Harbour Town. Sea Pines Plantation, Hilton Head Island, South Carolina)

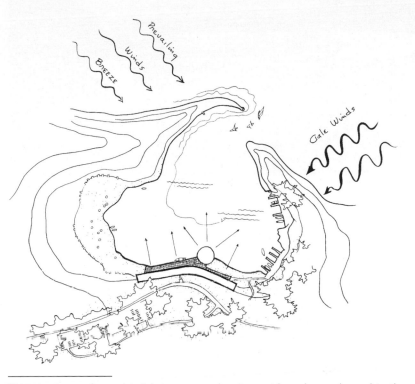

Site-structure unity: yacht club, terrace, and restaurant have been planned to the natural ground forms, which overhang and command the bay. Boat slips are fitted to the protective ridge. The beach area extends the soft receptive wash of the harbor. Cabanas follow the natural bowl. The breakwater and light extend the existing rocky shoulders of the point. The parking areas are "hidden" in the shade of the existing grove. Such a simpatico feeling for the existing topography ensures a plan development of fitness and pleasant harmonies of aesthetics and function.

fixed against the sky, massive structures rooted in rock—each draws from its site a native power and returns to the site this power magnified. Whole cities have been imbued with this dynamic quality—Saigon overhanging its dark river and slow-flowing tributaries, Lhasa braced proudly against its mountain wall, Darjeeling extending its timbered mountain peaks and towers into the clouds.

A structure and its site may be strongly related by the architectural treatment of site areas or elements. Clipped allées and hedges, water panels, precise embankments and terraces, all extend the limits of design control. Many of the French and Italian villas of the Renaissance were so architectural in their treatment that the entire property from wall to wall became one grand composition of palatial indoor and outdoor rooms. These grandiose garden halls were demarcated by great planes or arches of sheared beech, of masonry and mosaic, rows of plinths, and elaborate balustraded walls. They embraced monumental sculptured fountains and parterre gardens of rich pattern or mazes of sharply trimmed box hedges. The integration of architecture and site thus became complete.

Unfortunately, the results were often vacuous: a meaningless exercise in applied geometry—the control of nature for no more reason than for the sake of exerting control. Many such villas, on the other hand, were and still remain notable for their great symphonic beauty. In these, without exception, the highest inherent

Masonic Home, Elizabethtown, Pennsylvania. Just as the new structures are related by a repetition of the existing rooflines, so are the rectilinear plan forms reflected in the new site design.

This handsome residence is fitted into the natural forest, around the existing boulder, and to the view of the sea.

Dispersion of plan elements.

qualities of the natural elements of the site—plants, topography, water—were fully appreciated by the planner and given design expression. Seldom, for instance, has water as a landscape element been treated with more imaginative control than at Villa d'Este in Tivoli, where a mountain torrent was diverted to spill down the steep villa slopes through the gardens, rushing, pouring, gushing, foaming, spurting, spewing, surging, gurgling, dripping, riffling, and finally shining deep and still in the stone reflecting basins. Here at Villa d'Este, water, slopes, and plant materials were handled architecturally to enhance both the structure and the site and superbly unite the two.

Alternatively, the landscape features of the site may be embraced by the dispersion of structural or other planned elements into the landscape. The *satellite* plan, the *buckshot* plan, the *finger* plan, the *checkerboard* plan, the *ribbon* plan, and the *exploded* plan are typical examples.

Just as the early French and English explorers in North America controlled vast tracts of land by the strategic placement of a few forts, so can the well-placed elements of a scheme control a given landscape. Such is true of our national parks with their trails, lodges, and campgrounds so sited as to unfold to the user the most interesting features of the park. Such is true, in *linear* plan expression, of any well-planned scenic drive or highway extended into the countryside. Our military installations are often, in plan, scattered over extensive land areas, each function— be it rifle range, officers' quarters, tank proving ground, tent sites, or artillery range—relating to those topographical features that seem most suitable. For this same purpose, many of our newer schools are exploded in plan. Unlike the old three-story monumental school set *on* the land, the newer schools of which we speak are planned *to* the landscape, embracing and revealing its more pleasant qualities with such success that school and landscape are one.

The site and the structure may be further related by the interlocking of common areas—patios, terraces, and courts, for example. A landscape feature displayed from or in such a court takes on a new aspect. It seems singled out. It becomes a specimen held up to close and frequent observation under varying conditions of position, weather, and light. A simple fragment of rock so featured acquires a modeling and a beauty of form and detail that would not be realized if it were seen in its natural state. As we watch it from day to day—streaming with rain, sparkling with hoarfrost or soft snow, glistening in the sharp sun and incised with shadow, or glowing in subdued evening light—we come to a fuller under-

Villa d'Este at Tivoli, Italy.

standing of this landscape object and thus of the nature of the landscape from which it came.

The landscape may be even more strongly related to structure by the orientation of a room or an area to some feature of the landscape, as by a vista or a view. A view of a garden may be treated as a mural, a mural of constant change and variety of interest, extending the room area visually to the limits of the garden (or to infinity for a distant view). It can be seen that, to be pleasant, the scale, mood, and character of the landscape feature viewed must be suited to the function of the area from which it is observed.

To the foreign visitor in a traditional Japanese home, one of the most appealing features of many is the use of smoothly sliding screens of wood and paper by which the entire side of a room may be opened at will to bring into the space a cloudlike flowering plum tree, a vigorous composition of sand, stone, and sunlit pine, a view through tiered maple branches to the tiered roof of a distant pagoda, or a quiet pool edged with moss and rippled by lazily fanning goldfish. Each feature viewed is treated with impeccable artistry as part of the room, to extend and unite it with the garden or landscape. The Japanese would tell us that they have a deeper purpose, that what they are really trying to do is to relate people and nature completely and make nature appreciation a part of their daily lives.

To this end they introduce into their dwellings the best of those objects of nature that they can find or afford. The posts and lintels of their rooms, for instance, are not squared and finished lumber but rather a trunk or limb of a favorite wood shaped, tooled, and finished to bring out its inherent form and pattern of grain and knotting. Each foundation stone, each section of bamboo, each tatami (woven grass mat) is so fashioned by the artisan as to discover, and reveal in the finished object, the highest natural quality of the material that is being used. In the Japanese home one finds plants and arrangements of twigs, leaves, and grasses that are startling in their beauty. Even in their art forms the Japanese consciously, almost reverently, bring nature into their homes.

In such ways we, too, may relate our projects and structures to their natural setting. We may use large areas of fenestration. We may so devise our approaches and paths of circulation as to achieve the most desirable relationships. We may recall and adapt from the landscape colors, shapes, and materials. We may make further ties by projecting into the landscape certain areas of interior paving and by extending structural walls or overhead planes. We may break down or vignette our structures from high refinement to a more rustic quality as we move from the interior outward. This is a reverse application of the quality *wabi* mentioned before. This controlled transition from the refined to the natural is a matter of great design significance. It is a matter of such high art that only rarely can outstanding examples be found. One such example is the temple of Tofukuji in Kyoto.

If a building or plan area of any predetermined character is to be imposed on a landscape of another character, transition from the one to the other will play an important role. If, for example, a civic plaza and art museum are to be built at the edge of a city park, all plan elements will become more "civic" and sophisticated as one leaves the park to approach the plaza. Lines will become more precise. Forms will become refined and architectural. Materials, colors, textures, and details will become richer. The natural park character will give way gradually, subtly, to an intensified urbane character consonant with the planned expression of the museum. Conversely, if a rolling wooded public garden is to be built in a highly developed urban district, plan forms will relax and be freer and more "natural" as one approaches the garden preserve. Such controlled intensification, relaxation, or conversion of plan expression is a mark of skilled physical planning.

Yin and yang

The well-conceived plan involves far more than the application of a program to a plot of land: the fitting of the required use areas within the property boundaries. Planning that disregards the full array of landscape problems and possibilities can realize but a fraction of a site potential. Worse, it generates needless frictions. Often one or more of these frictions may become so insistent as to preclude the very uses for which the plans were made. Such a project fails.

Nor does a plan of excellence result often from the passive *adaptation* of designed components to the site as it exists. Such abject submission or attempt to blend into the scene usually produces an innocuous compromise.

The well-conceived project results instead from a design process of *integration* in which a new landscape is created. Components and site are consciously related and interrelated to yield the best that each can offer in dynamic interaction. Such unity is typified by the Chinese symbol yin and yang, evolved in the misty beginnings of time and representing the complete and balanced oneness of two opposing yet complementary elements—woman and man, earth and sea, and, in planning terms, the functions of the program and the functions of the site.

Site Systems

As a logical extension of the principles of site–project unification, the concept of *site systems* deserves special attention. The term implies simply that all site improvements are conceived to be constructed and function in a systematic way.

Natural systems

As a starter with such an approach, the natural systems are preserved insofar as feasible. It has been previously noted that every parcel of land is directly related to the surrounding landscape and may help to provide protection from the winds, storms, and erosion. It may contribute its share of surface and subsurface water. It may help to ensure the continuity of vegetative growth and wildlife habitat. Its ground forms and cover may also give a visual continuity to the landscape. The evident continuation of these relationships helps to ensure for the planned development a strong and satisfying tie to the environs.

Drainage

With few exceptions the natural site provides for storm runoff across its surface without causing erosion. The ground-stabilizing

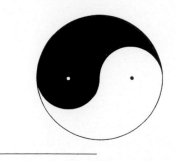

Yin and yang. Unity with diversity.

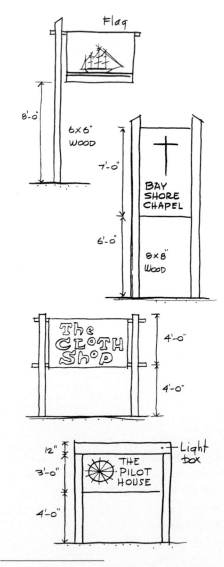

Unity with diversity is the key to identification signs. Shapes, sizes, and letter forms may vary with the information to be conveyed. Materials, mountings, and colors are usually standardized.

Coordinated informational signage.

roots and tendrils of living plants knit the soils and absorb precipitation. The fallen twigs and leaves also form an absorptive mat to keep the soil moist and cool the air. The natural swales, streambeds, and river gorges of the undisturbed landscape provide for the most efficient storm-water flow, while marshes, ponds, and lakes provide the ultimate storage and recharge basins. Any alteration to this established network is both disruptive and costly. The movement of materials is required, new storm drainageways must be shaped, and, often, extensive artificial storm-sewer systems must be constructed. Usually, with the installation of roofs, paved areas, and sewer pipe, the amount and rate of runoff is increased, to the detriment of the project site and downstream landowners.

Experience would suggest that artificial drainage devices be minimized and that the natural drainageways be preserved and utilitzed to the utmost.

Movement

Planned paths of pedestrian and vehicular movement that oppose the existing ground forms generate the problems and costs of earthwork, slope retention, interception gutters, storm-sewer connections, and the establishment of new ground covers. When such routes are aligned instead to rise and fall with the natural grades, to follow the ridge lines and ravines, or to trace a cross-slope gradient that requires no heavy cuts or fills, they not only are more economical to build but are also better to look at and more pleasant to use.

Well-designed walks, bicycle trails, and roadways also provide interconnecting networks of movement that assure regional continuity, are particularly suited to the type of traffic to be accommodated, and take into account all such factors as safety, efficiency, and landscape integrity. Materials, sections, profiles, lighting, signing, and planting are coordinated and designed as an integrated *system*.

Lighting

Site illumination does many good things. It provides safety in traffic movement and crossings, it gives warning of hazards, and it serves to increase security and reduce vandalism. It interprets the plan arrangement by giving emphasis to focal points, gathering places, and building entrances. It demarcates and illumines paths of interconnection, serving as a guide-on. With accent lighting, fine architecture or site areas of exceptional significance or beauty can be brought into visual prominence.

Well-conceived lighting gives clarity and unity to the overall site and to each subarea within it.

Signs

Graphic informational systems are closely allied with site illumination, since the two are usually interdependent and complementary. Street and route lighting obviously must be planned together with the positioning of related directional signs. Often, light standards provide support for signs and informational symbols. Signs, like lighting, are best developed as a hierarchy, each sign being designed in terms of its size, color, and placement to best serve its particular purpose and all existing together as a related family. When the system is kept simple and standardized, the signing gives its own sense of order and clarity to the trafficway pattern and the landscape plan.

Planting

Planting of excellence is also systematic. It articulates and strengthens the site layout. It develops an interrelated pattern of open, closed, or semienclosed spaces, each shaped to suit its planned function. Planting extends topographical forms, enframes views and vistas, anchors freestanding buildings, and provides visual transitions from object to object and place to place. It serves as backdrop, windscreen, and sunshield. It checks winter winds. It catches and channels the summer breeze. It casts shadow and provides shade. It absorbs precipitation, freshens the air, and modifies climatic extremes.

Aside from serving these "practical" functions, plants in their many forms and varieties are also pleasing to the eye. But even their beauty is increased if there is an evident reason behind their selection and use.

Fine plantings, like any other fine work of design, have a fundamental simplicity and discernible order. Many experienced landscape designers limit their plant lists to a *primary* tree, shrub, and ground cover and one to three *secondary* trees, shrubs, and supplementary ground cover—grasses, herbs, or vines, with all other supporting and accent plants constituting no more than a small fraction of the total.

Except in urban settings, the large majority of all plants used will be native to the region and will therefore fit and thrive without special care.

Essentially, each plant used should serve a purpose, and all together should contribute to the function and expressiveness of the plan.

Materials

Just as the palette of plant materials is limited in the main to those which are indigenous, so is it also with the materials of construction. Wall stone from local quarries seems most appropriate. Crushed stone and gravels exposed as aggregate, bricks made of local clays, lumber from trees that grow in the vicinity, and mulches made of their chipped or shredded bark all seem right in the local scene. Even the architectural adaptation of the natural earth, foliage, and sky colors relates the constructions to the regional setting.

The reduction of the number of materials used to a small and selective list lends simplicity and unity to the planned development.

Operations

All projects must be planned to work and work efficiently. Each building and each use area of the site must operate well as an entity, and all, together, as a well-organized complex. This can be achieved only if all components are planned together as an integrated *system.*

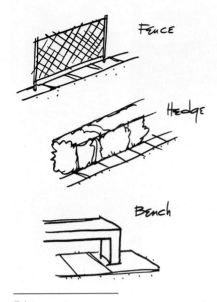

Edging strips
Paved mowing strips of concrete, set brick, or stone at lawn edges carry the wheel of an edger and eliminate hand trimming.

From small-home grounds to campus, to park, to large industrial complex, site installation and maintenance costs can be reduced and performance improved by the standardization of all possible components, materials, and equipment.

Use only the affordable best; therein lies quality and economy.

Maintenance

To be effective, maintenance must be a consideration from the earliest planning stages. This presupposes that all maintenance operations have been programmed. It also assumes that storage for the required materials and equipment is provided, that access points and ways are strategically located, that convenient hydrants and electrical outlets are installed, and that maintenance needs are reduced insofar as practical.

It also means that the number of construction materials and components and thus the replacement inventory of items that must be kept stocked are reduced to a workable minimum. This requires standardization of light globes, bench slats, anchor bolts, sign blanks, curb templates, paint colors, and everything else. Usually a reduction in the quantity of items stocked can result in improved quality at significant savings. This is possible only if the maintenance operation is planned from the start as, or converted to, an efficient *system*.

SITE DEVELOPMENT GUIDELINES

A Checklist of Helpful Considerations

These may vary in some instances with site or climatic conditions.

Excavation and grading

Keep to an absolute minimum.

Balance the on-site cut and fill. Off-site borrow or disposition is expensive.

Protect trees and established ground covers.

Remove and stockpile the topsoil.

Avoid working the soil when it is wet, powder-dry, or frozen.

Provide positive surface drainage away from buildings to swales, gutters, drain inlets, or outfalls.

Reestablish ground covers without delay. Unprotected soils cause erosion and siltation.

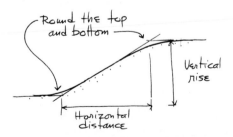

Most slopes are best blended into the natural landforms.

Slopes (earth cut or fill)

Do not exceed the *angle of repose* of the soils being graded or placed (the steepest angle at which the slope remains stable).

A slope of 1 on 2 maximum (1 foot vertical rise for 2 feet of horizontal distance) is recommended for mulched or planted embankments.

A slope of 1 on 3 maximum is preferred for lawn areas to facilitate mowing.

Place fill material in uniform layers of 6 to 8 inches of loose material.

Allow for soil shrinkage (or swelling in some instances); 3 to 5 percent shrinkage is normal in compacted fills.

Provide mechanical compaction. Natural compaction by the eventual settlement of loosely placed soils is seldom uniform or complete.

All fills should be *compacted fills*, placed on prepared benches cut through topsoil and overburden.

Thrust benches and positive drainage must be provided at the base of major fills.

Steps

Avoid steps, if possible, except when they are used as a landscape feature.

Always consider the disadvantaged and provide alternative access ramps.

Avoid use of single steps. They are hazardous.

The risers in architectural flights of steps should be of uniform height. In free-form or naturalized flights of steps (where consistency is not anticipated), riser and tread dimensions may vary widely within a given flight.

Good footing is essential. On concrete steps a wood float or light broom finish or the use of abrasive granules is suggested.

In rough terrain particularly, perrons (as in a stepped ramp) may be desirable on slopes ranging in grade from 16 to 25 percent.

Lawn and seeded areas

Provide a 1 percent minimum gradient for lawn areas (a fall of 1 foot for each 100 feet). A slope of 1½ to 2 percent is preferred to ensure more positive surface drainage.

Swales should have a gradient of 1 percent minimum, 4 percent maximum. (On steeper grades a loose stone or paved gutter is required to prevent erosion.)

Provide a 6-inch fall away from buildings in the first 20 feet.

A 4-inch compacted topsoil section is considered the minimum for new lawn construction. A 6- to 8-inch section (or deeper) is recommended when soils are impervious or overly porous, or when topsoil is abundant.

Walk paving

Provide a 1 percent minimum longitudinal or cross slope.

A slope of 1½ percent is recommended for terraces.

A pitch of 8 percent is considered maximum for walks if no handrail is provided. With a handrail, the walk pitch can be steepened to 15 percent (for a short ramp distance only).

Width: A confined walkway requires a minimum width of 2 feet per person for comfortable passing. In the open, where people's shoulders can overhang the walk edge, the outer pedestrian lanes can be reduced by up to 6 inches.

A width of 5 feet 0 inches for a typical low-volume community walk will allow three persons or one person and a baby carriage to pass.

If bicycle use is anticipated (such a joint use is not generally recommended), a walk width of 6 feet 0 inches is required for a bicycle and two persons or for two bicycles to pass.

Capacity: Each 2 feet of width will accommodate between *50 and 60 persons per minute*, or an average of *3300 persons per hour*. This holds as well for shuffling crowds, strolling window-shoppers, or students walking briskly across a campus, since as the rate of movement increases, the person-to-person spacing increases accordingly. Rates and capacities vary with climatic conditions, surface textures, and gradients. They are to be adjusted for intermittent movement as at crossings, constrictions, and counter pedestrian flow, which can reduce capacities by up to 50 percent.

Roads and driveways

In planning the approach drive or roadway consider:

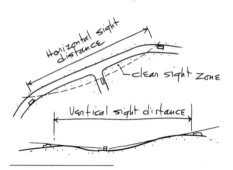

Sight distance: provide sufficient horizontal and vertical sight distance to give 10-second minimum observation time at permitted approach speeds.

    Adequate sight distances at intersections

    An attractive introduction and portal

    Sequential revealment of views, site features, and buildings

    All-weather and nighttime drivability, demarcation, and safety

    Recognition of topography, sun angles, and storms

    Economical length and minimum landscape disruption

    A pleasurable driving experience

Align roads and drives (and walkways) so that adjacent swales, gutters, and/or sewers will have continuous gravity flow, with minimum grading or depth of trenching.

A longitudinal gradient of at least 1½ percent is preferred; 1 percent is considered minimum.

When flatter grades are necessary, the road must be crowned or cross-sloped to drain, as:

    Concrete, ¼ inch per foot

    Bituminous, ⅜ inch per foot

    Gravel, ½ inch per foot

Use a dished (concave) section only in narrow lanes or minor service drives.

All road and drive intersections should be approximately perpendicular (90 degrees).

Horizontal and vertical curvature is subject to design speed and topography.

Horizontal curves are normally true arcs. Radii vary from 30 feet at the entrance to public roads to 600 feet or more on private drives.

Vertical curves are parabolic.

On private drives and in natural areas, both the horizontal and the vertical curvature may follow the topography freely without need for geometric computation. In such cases the grading equipment is guided by prelocated field stakes or flags and responds with a light touch to the existing landforms.

Recommended private local street widths (on-street parking prohibited)

Dwellings served	Paving width
1–5	12 feet, single lane optional to 500 feet
1–30	16 feet, two lanes
21–50	18 feet, two lanes
51 plus	20 feet, two lanes

For public roads, see local requirements:

    18 feet minimum for two lanes

    10 to 12 feet per lane normal

Parking

Allow a normal stall width of 8 feet 6 inches minimum to 12 feet maximum; 10 feet 0 inches is a comfortable average.

Stall marking: While a single divider stripe will suffice, two 3-inch lines, 12 to 16 inches on center with a half circle at the aisle end, is recommended.

For an approximate parking compound capacity calculation, allow 300 square feet of paved parking area per standard car, plus approach ramps, distributor loops, planting medians, turnabouts, collector walks, and buffer areas.

Site drainage

Preserve the natural drainageways insofar as feasible.

Preclude concentrated surface runoff to downgrade properties.

Avoid trapped water pockets.

Provide underdrains at road edges and low points.

Conduct surface water by swale, gutter, or buried pipe to storm-sewer mains or outfall.

If storm inlets and lateral sewers are needed, compute the required capacity and then use the next larger size.

Keep the site drainage system unobtrusive.

Site furnishings

In the selection and placement of lighting standards and fixtures, recreational equipment, informational signs, benches, movable tables, seating, etc., consider:

Functional suitability

Compatibility of form, material, and finish

Durability

Long-term cost; a higher initial expense that yields longer life with less required maintenance is usually a good investment.

Durability is to be stressed. Site equipment and furniture must be designed to withstand the effects of the elements, including sun, expansion-contraction, wind stress, moisture, and sometimes salt spray, frost, or ice.

Plan a coordinated *family* of shapes, materials, and finishes.

Generally, use strong, simple shapes, native materials, and natural finishes. Black, grays, and earth tones are basic, with bright colors reserved for accent.

Standardize components such as lighting globes, signposts and blanks, bench slats, bolts, and stains.

Invest in the best.

Landscape planting

Strive always for utmost simplicity.

Stress quality, not quantity. One well-selected, well-placed plant can be more effective than 100 plants scattered about at random.

When budgets are limited, economize on the extent of the lawn and planted areas, but invest in soil quality and depth, larger plant pits, soil preparation, and provision for drainage and irrigation.

Lawn areas are best given a well-defined and pleasant shape and (in an architectural context particularly) edged with paving, curb, or mowing strip.

Install no lawn area or plant without a predetermined purpose.

Select each plant to best serve the purpose intended.

In the use of plant materials consider:

    Need

    Suitability

    Appearance in all seasons

    Appearance in all stages of growth

    Compatibility of form, texture, color, and association in the total building and site composition

    Hardiness, cultural requirements, and degree of maintenance needed

As a rule, use only indigenous or naturalized materials except for bedding plants and container-grown exotics.

Plants used for backdrop, screening, shade, or space definition are generally selected for strength and cleanliness of form, richness of texture, and subtlety of color.

Plants to be featured are selected for their sculptural qualities and for ornamental twigging, budding, foliage, flowers, and fruit. They are to be placed strategically for optimum display.

Ground covers and mulches do much to enrich a fine planting.

In landscape planting of excellence, *restraint* is the key.

THE SITE PLANNING–DEVELOPMENT PROCESS

Recognizing that effective site planning is best achieved as the result of an orderly and systematic design approach, the U.S. Department of the Army prepared a guideline manual* describing the interdisciplinary process to be applied in the design of outdoor recreation facilities at military installations worldwide. In the illustrative examples which follow, a *conceptual plan* (Figure 1) was prepared for a hypothetical site. It followed the recommended procedure of:

- Program development
- Schematic study
- Comparative analysis
- Refinement to point of conceptual plan approval

From the start, the method of site plan development followed the steps illustrated in Figures 2 through 14, namely:

- Topographical survey
- Site analysis
- Area impact analysis
- Site area allocation
- Dimensioned plan layout
- Graphic presentation

Upon approval of the preliminary documents by the decision makers, detailed construction drawings and specifications for each project are then to be prepared.

---

* *Outdoor Recreation Facilities.* Illustrative examples by EPD, The Environmental Planning and Design Partnership, consultants.

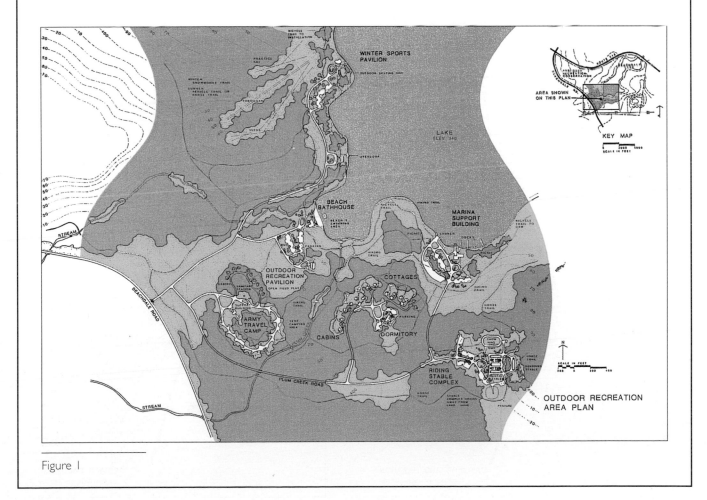

Figure 1

THE SITE PLANNING–DEVELOPMENT PROCESS

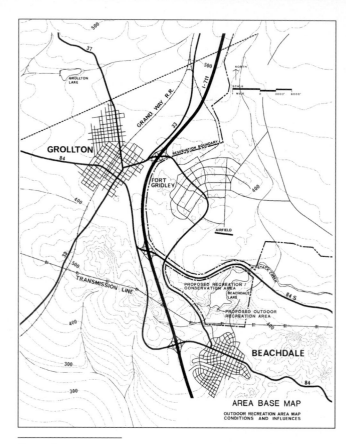

Figure 2

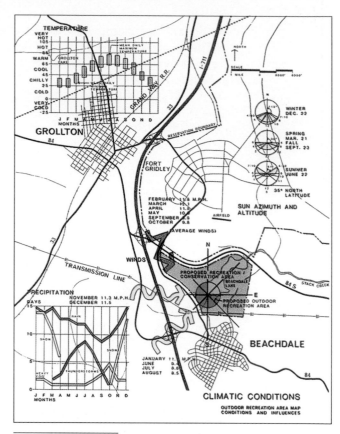

Figure 3

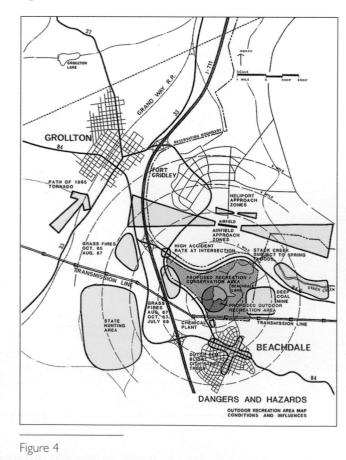

Figure 4

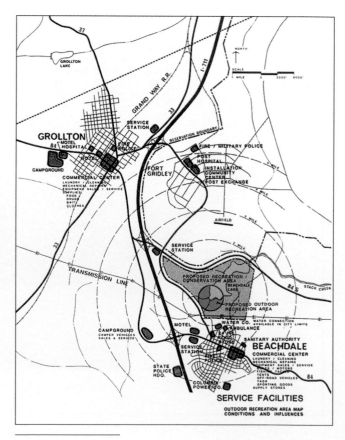

Figure 5

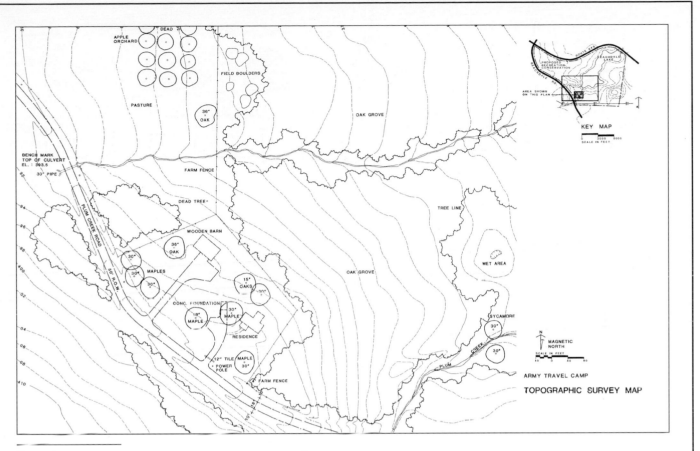

Figure 6

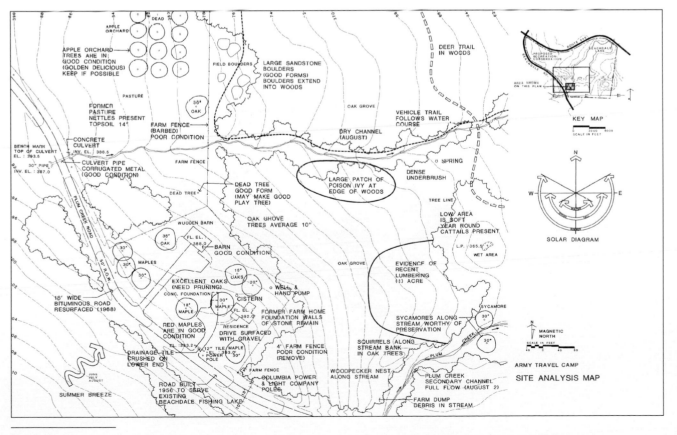

Figure 7

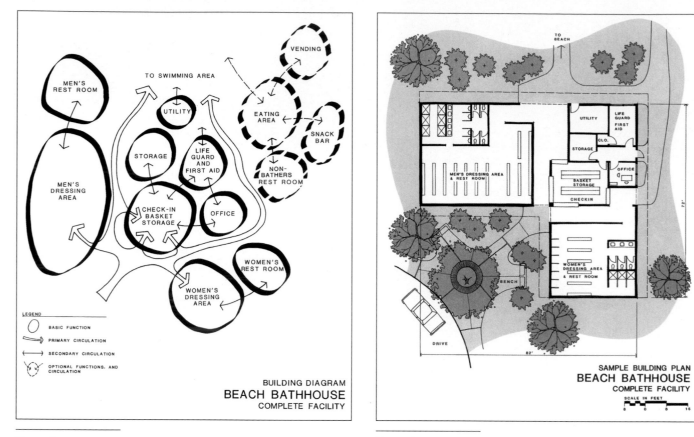

BUILDING DIAGRAM
BEACH BATHHOUSE
COMPLETE FACILITY

Figure 8

SAMPLE BUILDING PLAN
BEACH BATHHOUSE
COMPLETE FACILITY

Figure 9

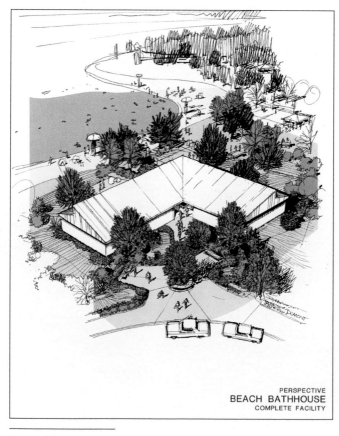

PERSPECTIVE
BEACH BATHHOUSE
COMPLETE FACILITY

Figure 10

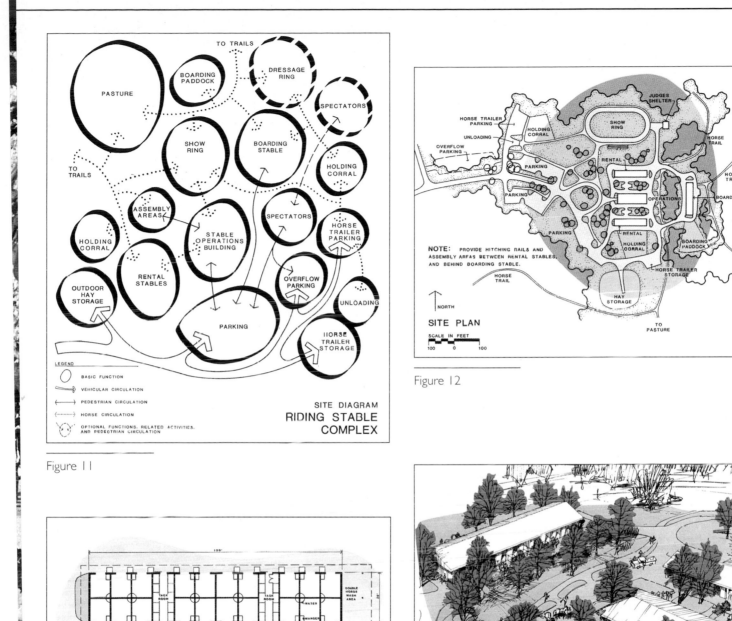

LEGEND

◯ BASIC FUNCTION

◁ VEHICULAR CIRCULATION

⟵ PEDESTRIAN CIRCULATION

⟵⟵ HORSE CIRCULATION

⟡ OPTIONAL FUNCTIONS, RELATED ACTIVITIES, AND PEDESTRIAN CIRCULATION

SITE DIAGRAM
RIDING STABLE COMPLEX

Figure 11

NOTE: PROVIDE HITCHING RAILS AND ASSEMBLY AREAS BETWEEN RENTAL STABLES, AND BEHIND BOARDING STABLE.

SITE PLAN

SCALE IN FEET
100 0 100

Figure 12

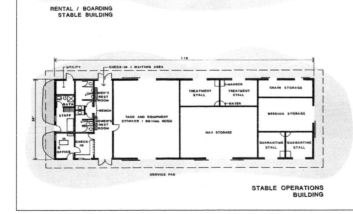

RENTAL / BOARDING STABLE BUILDING

STABLE OPERATIONS BUILDING

Figure 13

PERSPECTIVE
RIDING STABLE COMPLEX

Figure 14

SITE VOLUMES

Limitless space. (Virginia)

Discernible site volumes. (Virginia)

Natural space enclosure. (Virginia)

Architectural spatial enclosure. (Kentucky)

Our outdoor living environment is experienced as a sequence of interrelated volumes or spaces. These range in size from the vast to the minute, from the open and free to the more controlled, from the natural to the highly refined.

For each human activity, we seek out or construct a space or spaces suited to our purpose.

Rural. (Los Alamitos Trail, San Jose, California)

Domestic.

Hospital. (Lucile Salter Packard Children's Hospital, Palo Alto, California)

Campus. (Bechtel Engineering Library, University of California, Berkeley)

Civic. (Virginia State Capitol Grounds, Richmond)

liant, blazing, dazzling, or blinding. Light has motion—as shoot-ing, piercing, quivering, dancing, scintillating, creeping, flooding, or streaming light. It has distinctive character—as dappled, splotched, or mottled light; as subdued, harsh, or glaring light; as searching, glinting, shadowy, gleaming, or glowing light. Light has mood—as gloomy, haunting, or mysterious light; as cozy, inviting, or exciting light; as relaxing, refreshing, or cheering light. These are but a few of its qualities and effects that have design applica-tion. The solid overhead plane may serve as a shield or modifier of natural light, or it may act as a source of direct or reflected illu-mination.

If pierced or partially open, the overhead cover may not be in itself as important visually as are the shade and shadows it casts. We may consider such a plane as a disk or patterned screen held up between the sweeping orbit of the sun and the textured sur-faces upon which its shadows fall and over which they move. Generally, the spatial ceiling is kept simple because it is to be sensed more often than seen.

The Verticals

The vertical elements are the space dividers, screens, baffles, and backdrops. Of the three volumetric planes, the vertical is the most apparent and the easiest to control. It also has the most important function in the creation of outdoor spaces. The verticals contain and articulate the use areas and may tightly control and enclose them, as with masonry walls, or more loosely define them, as with vegetation.

By plan manipulation, the vertical elements may extend and expand the use areas to apparent infinity, by screening out the near or obtrusive features of the landscape and by revealing such receding or expansive features as the distant view, the horizon, or the limitless spaciousness of the open sky.

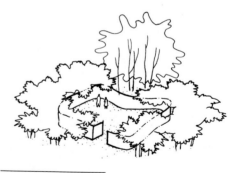

Site volumes: degrees of vertical enclosure.

A pleasant outdoor volume that provides both shelter and privacy.

By native vegetation, wrought metal panels,

wood, glass,

Enclosure for privacy

Neither enclosure nor openness is of value in itself. The degree and quality of enclosure have meaning only in relation to the function of a given space. Enclosure is desirable when privacy is desired. In Asian cultures, some people seem to have a faculty for creating their own privacy by mentally blocking out those things they find to be distracting or disturbing. They seem able to bring into sensed focus a volume suited to their pleasure or their needs. This ability enables them to enjoy a degree of privacy even in a crowded marketplace. For western minds, this can be more diffi-cult, and such privacy as we may require must usually be sought out or achieved by design.

It has been said that, in our contemporary civilization, pri-vacy is at once one of the most valuable and rarest of commodi-ties. We may readily observe this lack of privacy by walking down almost any city street.

We are only now beginning to realize again the advantages of private living and working areas that are screened from the pub-lic view and focused upon the enclosed court or garden. In Egypt, Pompeii, Spain, Japan, and all mature cultures, such walled resi-dences, palace courts, and temple grounds were, and still are, the most functional and pleasurable of all planned spaces. Privacy has long been recognized as essential to the cultivation and appreciation of those things of highest human value.

Enclosure for privacy need not be complete. It may be achieved by no more than a strategically placed screen or by the dispersed arrangement of standing elements.

Qualities of enclosure

Again, vertical enclosure may be as rugged as the rocky face of a cliff or a wall of piled-up fieldstone. It may be as sophisticated as a panel of etched glass—or light as a tracery of blossom or foliage. The range of form and materials is limitless. But whether the enclosure is massive or delicate, crude or refined, the essential business is to suit the enclosure to the use of the space or the use of the space to the predetermined enclosure.

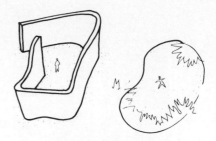

Enclosure may be light to solid.

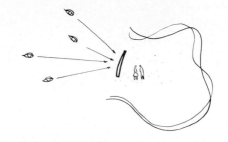

An arc of enframement may give adequate privacy.

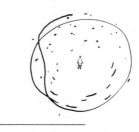

Enclosure by dispersed plan elements.

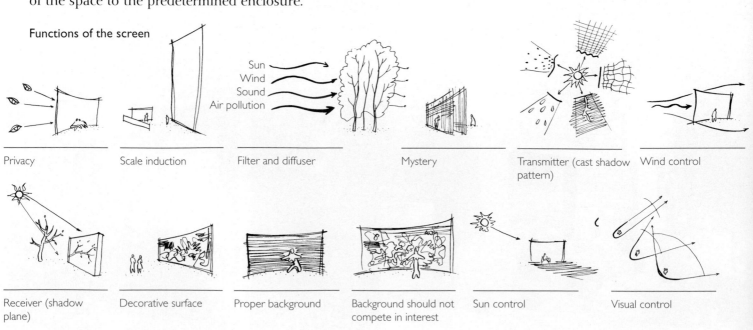

Functions of the screen

Privacy

Scale induction

Sun
Wind
Sound
Air pollution

Filter and diffuser

Mystery

Transmitter (cast shadow pattern)

Wind control

Receiver (shadow plane)

Decorative surface

Proper background

Background should not compete in interest

Sun control

Visual control

Vertical definition

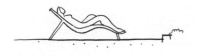

Edging.

Stand.

Seat.

Safety barrier.

Enclosure for privacy. Wall height is determined by function.

Visual control

All things seen from a space are a visual function of the space. Not only the extent and nature of the enclosure but also the nature of the revealment must be in keeping with the use. Anything that can be seen from a space is visually *in* the space and must be taken into account. Often an object far removed may be introduced to the space by opening to, enframing, and focusing on the object. A far-off mountain peak or a nearby tree may thus be "brought into" a garden. The bustle and clamor of a sprawling city and its harbor may, for its interest and therapeutic value, be brought into the convalescent spaces of a military hospital grounds. A distant cathedral campanile may thus be "transported" to a churchyard, or a quiet pond to a garden terrace.

Enclosure is desirable for those spaces in which an internal object is to be featured. It is evident in such cases that distractions should be eliminated and interest concentrated on the object to be viewed. It would be difficult, for instance, in viewing a piece of sculpture to appreciate those subtle nuances of light and shade that reveal the modeling of a torso if the sculpture were to be seen against a line of flapping laundry or a stream of moving traffic. Even against a vista of regal magnificence, much of the loveliness of an individual rose, for instance, would be lost to the observer. The backdrop of anything to be observed in detail

(Missouri Botanical Garden, St. Louis, Missouri)

Vertical space definers.

should rarely compete in interest. Spatial enclosure, when doubling as a backdrop, should be so devised as to bring out the highest qualities of the object seen against it.

In general, it may be stated that when interest is to be directed to an object within a given area, the elements of containment must focus attention inward. When interest is to be directed outward to object or view, the enclosure is pierced or opened to accentuate and frame that which is to hold our attention.

Elements within a space

Vertical planes provide not only containment, screen, and backdrop but often become the dominant spatial feature as well. Other vertical elements may include furniture set about on the base plane, a specimen magnolia of striking branching habits and

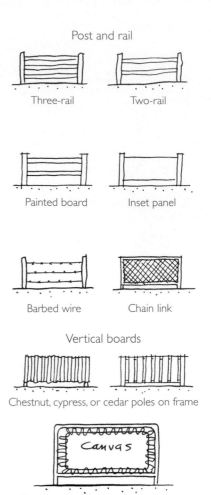

Post and rail

Three-rail   Two-rail

Painted board   Inset panel

Barbed wire   Chain link

Vertical boards

Chestnut, cypress, or cedar poles on frame

Canvas

Pipe frame with canvas and grommets

Fences.

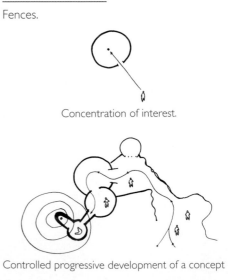

Concentration of interest.

Controlled progressive development of a concept

Visual control.

Functions of enclosure.

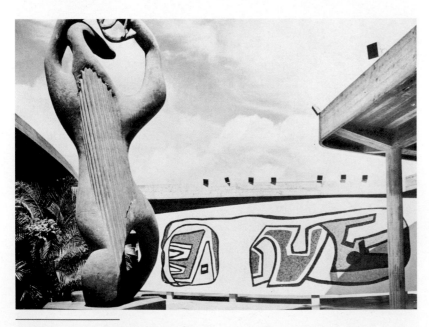

A vertical element as the focal point of a volume. The spirit of the figure and the spirit of the space are one. Note how the heavy structuring and deep shadows of the volume give emphasis to the airy, luminous quality of the moving sky.

Precise control of form, materials, light, acoustics, temperature.

Elimination of distractions.

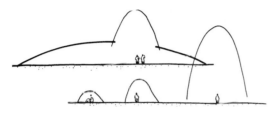

Emotional implications of varying spatial volumes.

No spatial variety—static.   Variety—dynamic

Increased spatial variety and interest.

Form clarity lost by improper enframement.

Complex form interest heightened by simple enframement.

Several objects placed in a volume relate to the enclosure not only singly but also as a group.

flower, a cool jet of rising and falling water, or a children's slide or climbing structure of welded metal tubing. Such freestanding objects assume a sculptural quality. In scale and form they must satisfy the hollowness of the volume, enrich it, and pick up and accentuate its character. The shape and color of freestanding objects may counterplay with the shape and color of the space, may "read" against the backdrop. If the object is to dominate, the backdrop plane is subdued to serve as a foil. If the spatial plane is to dominate, as in a mural or a building facade, the standing object is so placed or designed as to heighten the visual impact.

When an object is placed within a space, the object *and* enclosure may be perceived as an entity, but often more important is the expanding, contracting, evolving relationship of the spaces between the two. As an example, the roundness or squareness of an object may best be accentuated by placing it off-center in a variformed volume, so as to develop dynamic spatial relationships between it and the enclosing planes.

An object that of itself has complex form or intricate lines is usually best displayed in a volume of simple shape so that the spatial relationships enhance the object rather than confuse or detract.

When several objects are placed in a volume, the interacting spaces between objects, as well as between objects and the enclosing planes, are of design importance.

Structures as vertical elements

Often buildings are the dominant features within or surrounding a space. If within, they may be treated as sculptural elements to be experienced in the round. Within or without, the space is so developed as to focalize attention on the major facades or components and to impel movement toward the entrances.

The external spaces may be designed to serve as foreground or setting, as an anteroom, or as an external building compartment. The function of the building may even be concentrated in the exterior space and the building itself be incidental. Such

The vertical elements of the house are used to define, enframe, and interplay with the richly composed interior-exterior volumes.

War memorial within an urban open space. (Hyde Park, Sydney, Australia)

structures may serve primarily as spatial enclosers, dividers, and backdrops.

Public squares, courts, or plazas flanked by structures pose a complex problem in design, for they and the people who use them must all be in scale. Which has priority? St. Peter's clearly dominates its piazza and the assembled crowds. New York's Central Park rules as verdant queen over the edifices at her sides. The tiny town squares of Capri, Italy, and Taxco, Mexico, on the other hand, are, in effect, no more than charming stage sets for the lounging, dining, parading townsfolk and tourists who gather there from early sunup to the late, cool hours of the evening. People, spaces, or structures—which? There is no rule except that each, in turn and together, must be taken into full account and all relationships made pleasant through a sense of fitness.

The vertical as a point of reference

In planning an area for any purpose, except when mystery, bewilderment, or confusion might be intended, it is well to set up enough visual guide-ons to give orientation to the users. Often such points of reference serve also to provide the theme for their related spaces. A revolving ferris wheel, for example, draws one to, and becomes the symbol of, the amusement park. A venerable beech tree on a rise, the library campanile, or the ceremonial flagstaff of the parade ground may so "explain" and guide one through a campus, just as one is led around the golf course from green to numbered green.

In the treatment of sizable areas, the author has discovered an intriguing planning phenomenon that has many useful applications. He has found that a freestanding vertical element or panel brought near a small use area within the larger space may have such a strong visual relationship to the user that it imparts its

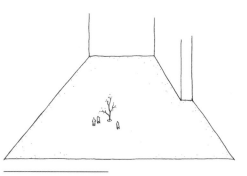

An object introduced within a large space may impart, within the area of its influence, its own lesser scale.

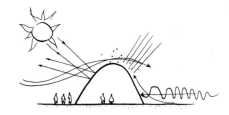

Privacy, shelter, protection.

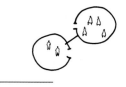

Classification of interest.

This village center at Reston is a favorite gathering place.

Human scale by design. (Dallas Arts District Master Plan and Improvements, Dallas, Texas)

own scale. A great plaza, for example, may be overwhelming to a person who enters or wanders through. If, say, a small bench were to be placed within the space, the volume by contrast would seem even more overpowering. A person seated on the bench would sense only the relationship to the total plaza. If, however, near the bench, we were to place a honey locust tree, a stone fountain, or a decorative screen, our intimidated friend would first sense being seated under the tree, beside the fountain, or near the screen and only incidentally would sense the dimensions of the greater volume. One would relate oneself to the scale of the introduced objects.

Within a large space, many such human reference points may be placed, and, indeed, these *must* be furnished if ease and pleasure are intended. (We recognize, of course, that historically the primary objective of many great public spaces has been to humble and sometimes even humiliate the crowds that mill about within them.) When awe, wonder, or humility is to be instilled by spatial impact, the human reference points are removed or distorted. When comfort and assurance are desirable, a human scale must be made evident. Generally, the steps, doorways, or windows of adjacent buildings suffice to establish a sense of scale; if not, such human reference points are to be otherwise provided.

The vertical in relation to pix

In spatial design, the verticals generally have the greatest visual interest. Since, either moving about or seated within a volume, we are face to face with the verticals, we are usually more conscious of them than of either the base or the overhead plane. We may rightly assume, therefore, that such standing surfaces or objects present the most telling design possibilities. Features of greatest interest or refinement are normally placed or incorporated on the verticals and at eye height—*pix*. It would seem obvious that pix for a seated person is lower than pix for a person who is standing, but because this critical design factor is too often ignored, the point is emphasized.

One of the most distressing of all visual experiences is to have a vertical plane terminate at or near eye level, particularly in the case of a fence or a wall. The top of such a wall or screen seems to do violence to the eyes of those who pass or see it.

One of the most pleasant of visual treats, on the other hand, is to have the eye come comfortably to rest upon an object or plane so placed that it falls into pleasing perspective and focus. If, moreover, in the thing observed the viewer discovers subtle and fitting relationships to the space, the use, and the user, the pleasure is intensified. Such relationships may sometimes be accidental, but more often they must be consciously planned.

Verticals as articulators

Verticals reinforce and "explain" the traffic and use patterns of the base plane. Just as the gate piers of a driveway say "Enter," the sweeping curbline says "Follow me," and the entrance platform says "Come to rest and alight here," so must the verticals of any space elucidate the plan. They must attract, deflect, direct, detain, receive, and accommodate the planned use as the area demands.

Compatible fit at massive scale. (Deere & Company Administrative Center, Moline, Illinois)

The plan pattern of the base plane most often sets the theme of a space, and the verticals most often modulate this theme and produce those variations that develop the rich harmonies.

Verticals as controlling elements

The verticals, providing as they do the degree and kind of spatial enclosure, are important in the control of wind, breeze, sunlight, shadow, temperature, and sound. The wind may be diverted, checked, or blocked. Desirable breezes may be directed to play across moist, cooling surfaces or used to give motion and sound by activating flags, foliage, mobiles, or those delightful Asian divertissements, wind–flutes or wind–bells. Sunlight may be intercepted, filtered, diffused, or admitted in its full glorious, healing, life–giving splendor.

Like the overhead, the verticals may serve an important function in casting shadows to wash across a paving, dapple a wall, dance, creep, flicker, tremble, stretch, blank out a space in dim coolness, or incise a bold architectural pattern onto a receiving plane.

Plant materials

Much of the earth's land surface, as it were, is subdivided into variformed volumes by trees—freestanding, in rows, in clumps, or in masses. Often, proposed use areas may be sited to take advantage of spaces already tree–enframed. Again, partial tree or shrub enclosure may be supplemented by additional planting or by grading and construction. In such cases the native growth provides the ideal transition from development to the natural scene and ensures landscape continuity. If we cannot use existing trees for full or partial volume control, in most localities we may draw upon an extensive palette of plant materials that range from the wildly free to the stiffly architectonic in their native or manicured forms.

Effective enclosure

It must be remembered that the vertical space enframers are not usually seen alone from within the volume but in the round as well. They, together with the spaces they enclose, become in total a unified landscape element to be related to all other landscape features.

An axiom

Lack of effective enclosure is the key to most unsatisfactory spaces or places. We cannot stress too strongly the need for the proper type and degree of vertical definition. All good site development is marked by the organization of vertical (and overhead) planes to provide both optimum enclosure and optimum revealment. By such means, it can be seen, we must synthesize not only the microlandscape but the extensional landscape as well.

THE BASE PLANE

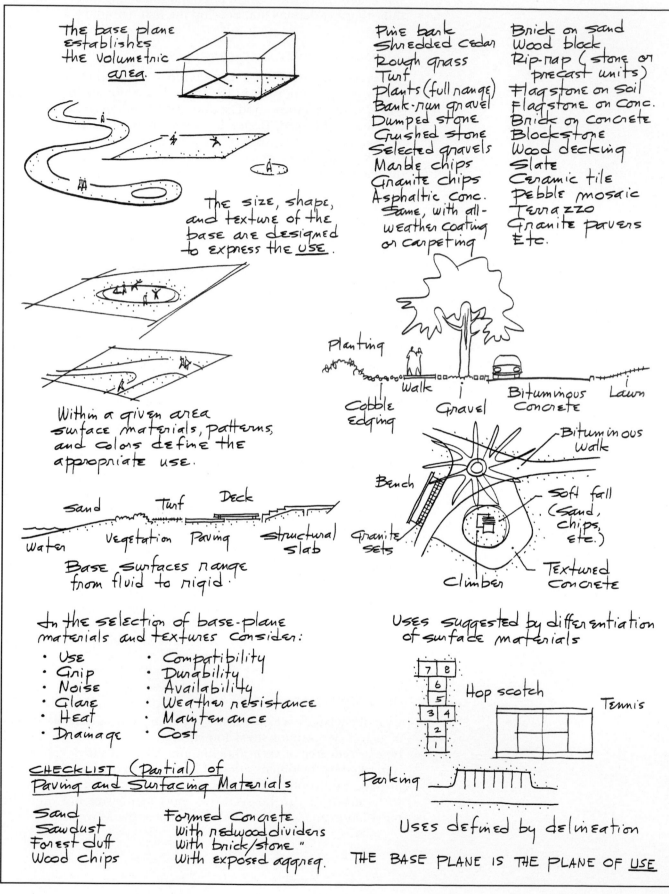

The base plane establishes the volumetric area.

The size, shape, and texture of the base are designed to express the USE.

Pine bark
Shredded cedar
Rough grass
Turf
Plants (full range)
Bank-run gravel
Dumped stone
Crushed stone
Selected gravels
Marble chips
Granite chips
Asphaltic Conc.
Same, with all-weather coating or carpeting

Brick on sand
Wood block
Rip-rap (stone or precast units)
Flagstone on soil
Flagstone on Conc.
Brick on concrete
Blockstone
Wood decking
Slate
Ceramic tile
Pebble mosaic
Terrazzo
Granite pavers
Etc.

Within a given area surface materials, patterns, and colors define the appropriate use.

Planting
Walk
Cobble Edging
Gravel
Bituminous Concrete
Lawn

Bituminous Walk
Bench
Soft fall (Sand, chips, etc.)
Granite Sets
Climber
Textured Concrete

Sand
Turf
Deck
Water
Vegetation
Paving
Structural Slab

Base surfaces range from fluid to rigid.

In the selection of base-plane materials and textures consider:

- Use
- Grip
- Noise
- Glare
- Heat
- Drainage

- Compatibility
- Durability
- Availability
- Weather resistance
- Maintenance
- Cost

Uses suggested by differentiation of surface materials

7 8
6
5
3 4
2
1

Hop scotch
Tennis

Parking

Uses defined by delineation

THE BASE PLANE IS THE PLANE OF USE

CHECKLIST (Partial) of Paving and Surfacing Materials

Sand
Sawdust
Forest duff
Wood chips

Formed Concrete
With redwood dividers
With brick/stone "
With exposed aggreg.

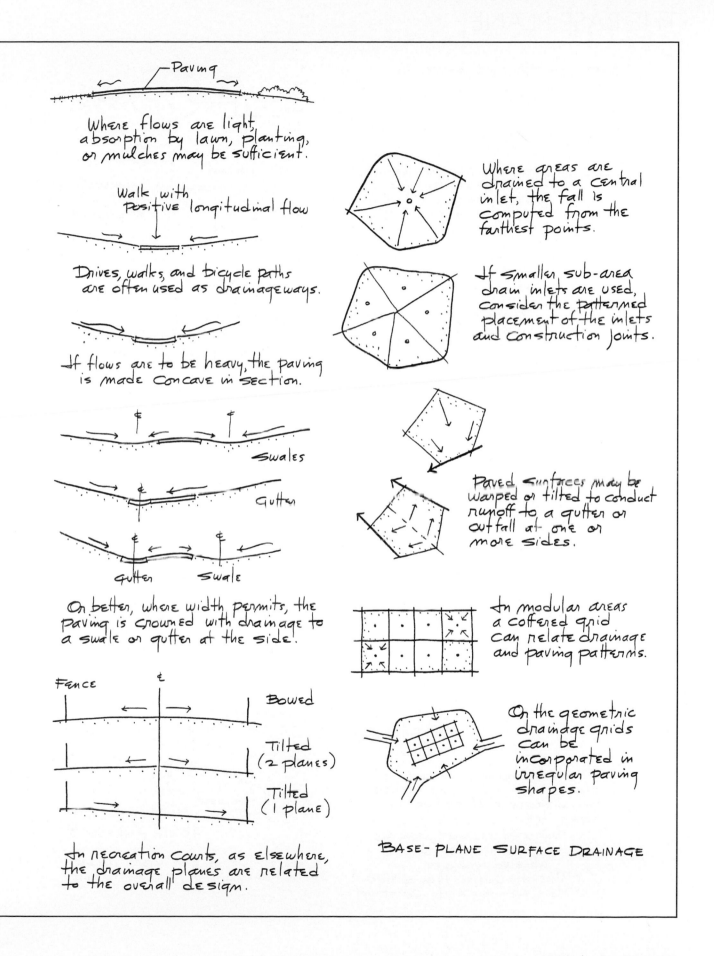

Where flows are light, absorption by lawn, planting, or mulches may be sufficient.

Walk with Positive longitudinal flow

Drives, walks, and bicycle paths are often used as drainageways.

If flows are to be heavy, the paving is made concave in section.

Swales

Gutter

Gutter   Swale

Or better, where width permits, the paving is crowned with drainage to a swale or gutter at the side.

Fence   ₵

Bowed

Tilted (2 planes)

Tilted (1 plane)

In recreation courts, as elsewhere, the drainage planes are related to the overall design.

Where areas are drained to a central inlet, the fall is computed from the farthest points.

If smaller sub-area drain inlets are used, consider the patterned placement of the inlets and construction joints.

Paved surfaces may be warped or tilted to conduct runoff to a gutter or outfall at one or more sides.

In modular areas a coffered grid can relate drainage and paving patterns.

Or the geometric drainage grids can be incorporated in irregular paving shapes.

BASE-PLANE SURFACE DRAINAGE

THE BASE PLANE

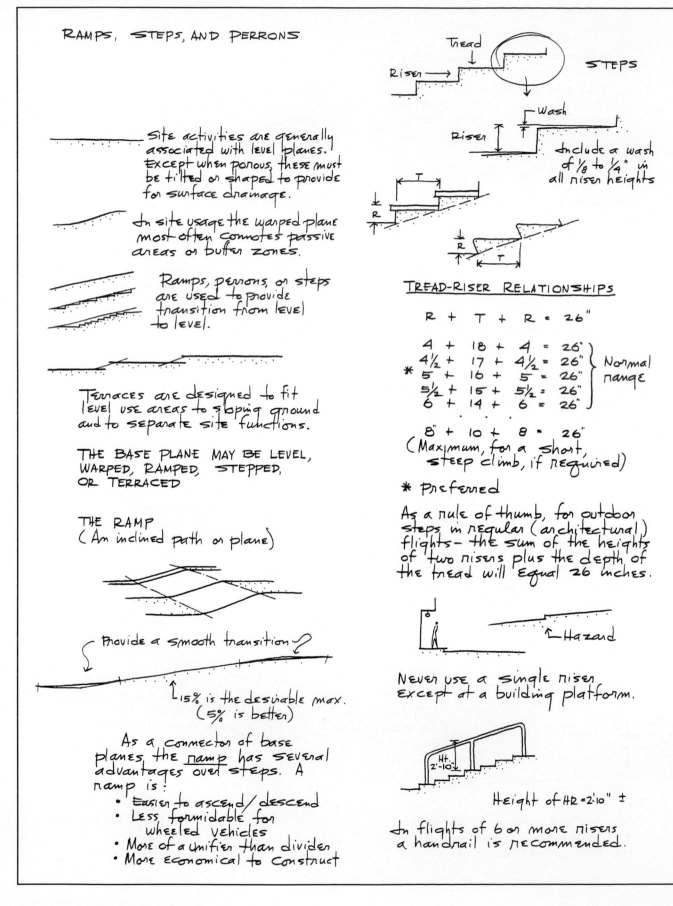

RAMPS, STEPS, AND PERRONS

Site activities are generally associated with level planes. Except when porous, these must be tilted or shaped to provide for surface drainage.

In site usage the warped plane most often connotes passive areas or buffer zones.

Ramps, perrons, or steps are used to provide transition from level to level.

Terraces are designed to fit level use areas to sloping ground and to separate site functions.

THE BASE PLANE MAY BE LEVEL, WARPED, RAMPED, STEPPED, OR TERRACED

THE RAMP
(An inclined path or plane)

Provide a smooth transition

15% is the desirable max.
(5% is better)

As a connector of base planes the ramp has several advantages over steps. A ramp is:
- Easier to ascend/descend
- Less formidable for wheeled vehicles
- More of a unifier than divider
- More economical to construct

Tread

Riser →

STEPS

Wash

Riser

Include a wash of ⅛ to ¼" in all riser heights

TREAD-RISER RELATIONSHIPS

R + T + R = 26"

4	+	18	+	4	=	26"	
4½	+	17	+	4½	=	26"	Normal
*5	+	16	+	5	=	26"	range
5½	+	15	+	5½	=	26"	
6	+	14	+	6	=	26"	

8 + 10 + 8 = 26"
(Maximum, for a short, steep climb, if required)

* Preferred

As a rule of thumb, for outdoor steps in regular (architectural) flights— the sum of the heights of two risers plus the depth of the tread will equal 26 inches.

Hazard

Never use a single riser except at a building platform.

Ht
2'-10"

Height of HR = 2'-10" ±

In flights of 6 or more risers a handrail is recommended.

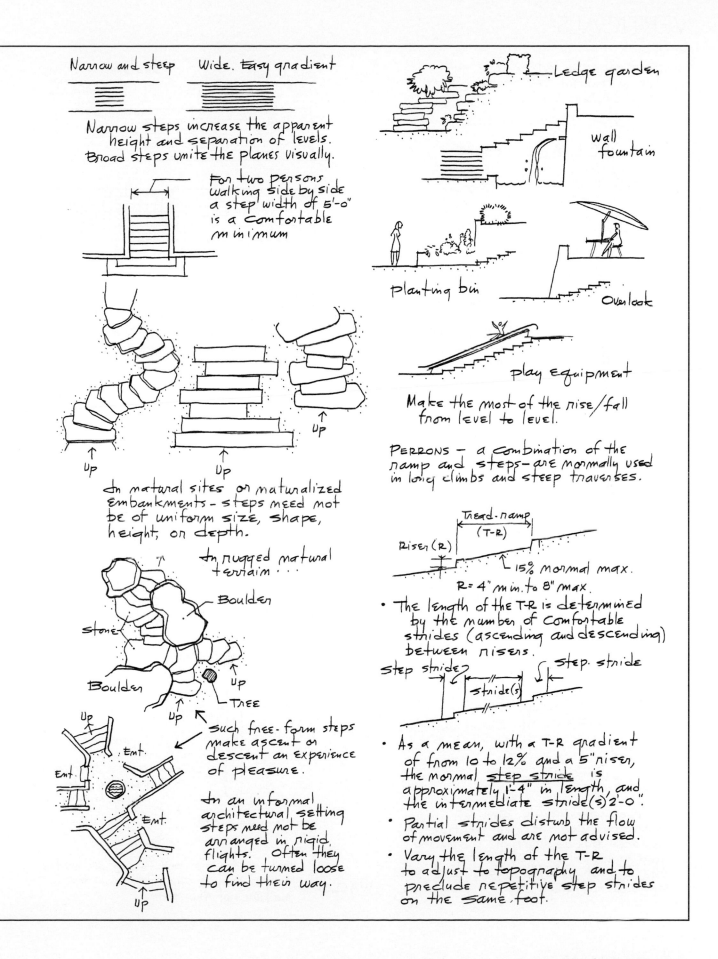

Narrow and steep   Wide. Easy gradient

Narrow steps increase the apparent
height and separation of levels.
Broad steps unite the planes visually.

For two persons
walking side by side
a step width of 5'-0"
is a comfortable
minimum

Up   Up   Up

In natural sites or naturalized
embankments - steps need not
be of uniform size, shape,
height, or depth.

In rugged natural
terrain...

Boulder
Stone
Boulder
Tree
Up   Up
Up

Such free-form steps
make ascent or
descent an experience
of pleasure.

Up   Ent.
Ent.   Ent.
Up

In an informal
architectural setting
steps need not be
arranged in rigid
flights.   Often they
can be turned loose
to find their way.

Ledge garden
wall
fountain
planting bin
Overlook

play equipment

Make the most of the rise/fall
from level to level.

PERRONS — a combination of the
ramp and steps — are normally used
in long climbs and steep traverses.

Tread-ramp
(T-R)
Riser (R)
15% normal max.
R = 4" min. to 8" max.

• The length of the T-R is determined
  by the number of comfortable
  strides (ascending and descending)
  between risers.

Step stride   Step. stride
Stride(s)

• As a mean, with a T-R gradient
  of from 10 to 12% and a 5" riser,
  the normal step stride is
  approximately 1'-4" in length, and
  the intermediate stride(s) 2'-0".

• Partial strides disturb the flow
  of movement and are not advised.

• Vary the length of the T-R
  to adjust to topography and to
  preclude repetitive step strides
  on the same foot.

VERTICALS

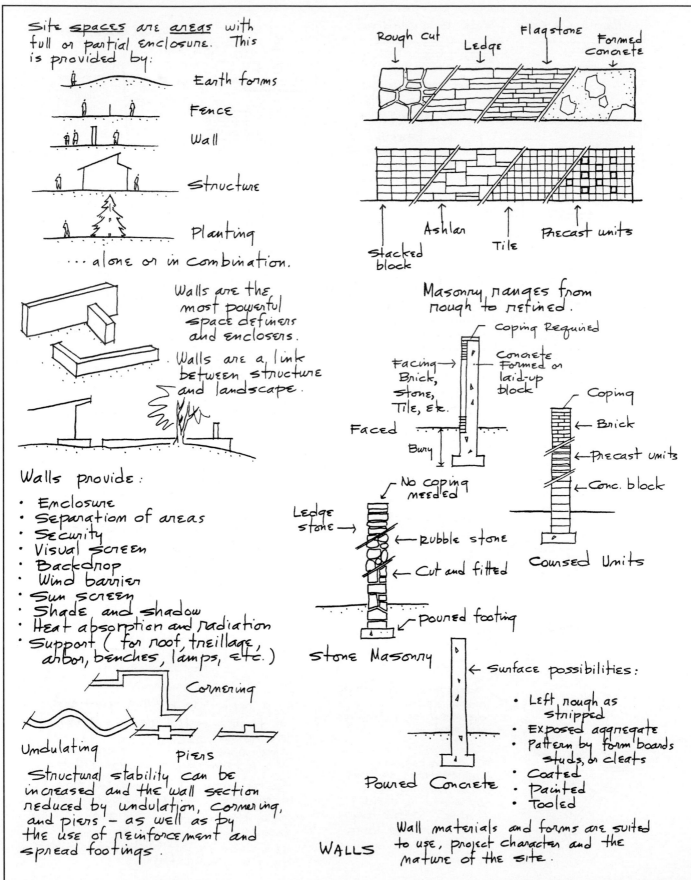

Site spaces are areas with full or partial enclosure. This is provided by:

Earth forms

Fence

Wall

Structure

Planting

...alone or in combination.

Walls are the most powerful space definers and enclosers.

Walls are a link between structure and landscape.

Walls provide:

- Enclosure
- Separation of areas
- Security
- Visual screen
- Backdrop
- Wind barrier
- Sun screen
- Shade and shadow
- Heat absorption and radiation
- Support (for roof, treillage, arbor, benches, lamps, etc.)

Cornering

Undulating   Piers

Structural stability can be increased and the wall section reduced by undulation, cornering, and piers — as well as by the use of reinforcement and spread footings.

Rough cut   Ledge   Flagstone   Formed Concrete

Stacked block   Ashlar   Tile   Precast units

Masonry ranges from rough to refined.

Coping Required

Facing Brick, Stone, Tile, etc.

Concrete Formed on laid-up block

Faced

Bury

Coping

Brick

Precast units

Conc. block

Coursed Units

No coping needed

Ledge stone →

← Rubble stone

← Cut and fitted

← Poured footing

Stone Masonry

Poured Concrete

← Surface possibilities:

- Left rough as stripped
- Exposed aggregate
- Pattern by form boards studs, or cleats
- Coated
- Painted
- Tooled

WALLS

Wall materials and forms are suited to use, project character and the nature of the site.

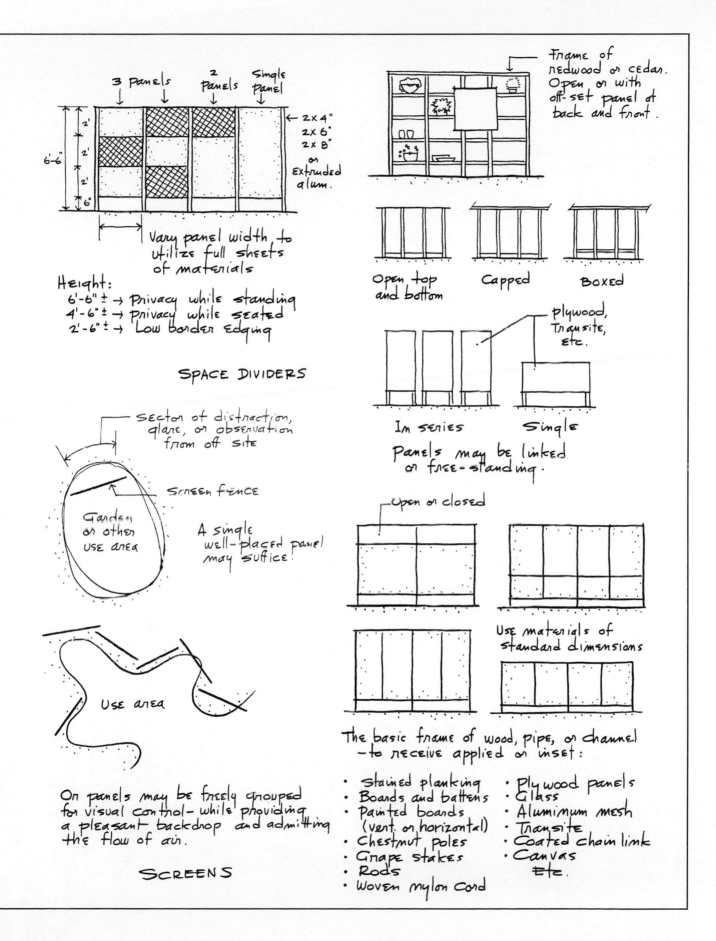

3 Panels 2 Panels Single Panel

6'-6" 2' 2' 2' 6"

2x4"
2x6"
2x8"
or
Extruded
alum.

Vary panel width to
utilize full sheets
of materials

Height:
6'-6"± → Privacy while standing
4'-6"± → Privacy while seated
2'-6"± → Low border edging

SPACE DIVIDERS

Sector of distraction,
glare, or observation
from off site

SCREEN FENCE

Garden
or other
use area

A single
well-placed panel
may suffice!

Use area

Or panels may be freely grouped
for visual control - while providing
a pleasant backdrop and admitting
the flow of air.

SCREENS

Frame of
redwood or cedar.
Open or with
off-set panel at
back and front.

Open top
and bottom   Capped   Boxed

Plywood,
Transite,
etc.

In series   Single

Panels may be linked
or free-standing.

Open or closed

Use materials of
standard dimensions

The basic frame of wood, pipe, or channel
— to receive applied or inset:

· Stained planking
· Boards and battens
· Painted boards
  (vert. or horizontal)
· Chestnut poles
· Grape stakes
· Rods
· Woven nylon cord

· Plywood panels
· Glass
· Aluminum mesh
· Transite
· Coated chain link
· Canvas
  Etc.

12
VISIBLE LANDSCAPE

The View

A view is a scene observed from a given vantage point. Often an outstanding view is reason enough for the selection of a property. Once the site has been attained, however, the view is seldom used to full advantage. Indeed, the proper treatment of a view is one of the least understood of all the visual arts. A view must be analyzed and composed with keenly perceptive artistry to utilize even a fraction of the full dramatic potential. Like other landscape features, the view, by its handling, may be preserved, neutralized, modified, or accentuated. But before we attempt to deal with the view, we must learn more of its nature.

A view is a picture to be framed, an evolving panorama of many blending facets.

A view is a theme. Its proper realization resembles the musical creation of variations on a theme.

A view is a constantly changing mood-inducer.

A view is a limit of visual space. It transcends the boundaries of the site. It has directional pull. It may evoke a sense of expansive freedom.

A view is a backdrop. It may serve as a wall of a garden or as a mural in a room.

A view is a setting for architecture.

Suitability as a factor

To be enjoyed, a view must be related to people and to those areas and spaces used by them. We must be sure, however, that the use and the view are compatible. A scene of great activity or excitement, for instance, should hardly be introduced visually

A view as a garden wall.

A view is a theme that may suggest and give added meaning to well-related functions.

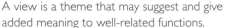
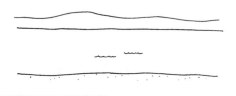

The best view is not always or often the full view.

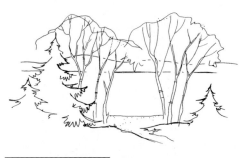

A view is usually better if enframed or seen through an appropriate screen.

into an area of quiet repose. How could the pupil concentrate in a classroom facing a ballpark or a river lock with its whistles, bells, shouting gatekeepers, straining tugs and tows? Or how, cajoled by such a view, could the artist keep eyes on drawing or the librarian thoughts on the work at hand? Again, a scene of gentle pastoral tranquility may negate the effectiveness of a space designed to exhort combatants to action or inspire one to lofty thought. For such a purpose, the view should be lofty and awe-inspiring, vast and grand, or there should be no view at all. The invigorating qualities of a rocky chasm scene with craggy fir and the thunderous roar of rushing, tumbling water might destroy the serenity or passive atmosphere intended for an introspective space. A dynamic industrial scene of belching smoke, leaping flame, and switching freight cars has its design applications and its limitations, too. Even a sweeping night scene of a sprawling river city with its jewel-like constellations and patterns of light, its cubes and prisms of shadow and illuminated surface, its luminous vapors of smoke and steam, its crawling, beetlelike traffic glows, its arching river wakes and shooting beams, its trembling cloud reflections—even such a wondrous view as this may be unsuited to a number of use areas, while for many others it would be ideal.

Design treatment of a view

A view has landscape character. This will, of course, determine those areas or functions with which it should be combined. If the view is a dominant landscape feature, the related use areas and spaces should be developed in harmony with the view as it exists or as it may be treated.

A view need not be seen full front or be approached from a fixed direction. It is a panorama or a segment of a panorama to be seen from any or all angles. It may be viewed on the oblique, on the sweep, or broadside.

A view is an impeller. A powerful magnet, it will draw one far, and from one position to another, for the opportunity of better commanding its limits or seeing some part in a new and intriguing way. The skilled planner will let a view develop as the viewer moves across it, just as a mountain climber experiences more and more of a view in the ascent until it is seen in total.

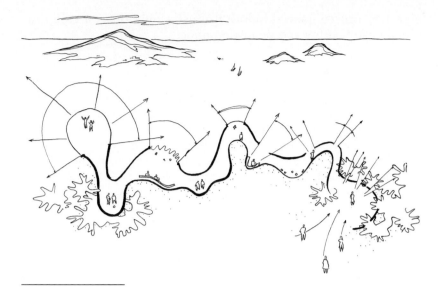

The modulation of a view. From a glimpse through loose foliage, to enframing slot, to wider sector, to reverse interest, to vista, to object seen against the view, to reverse interest, to objects placed against the view seen through a film of fabric, to concentration in a cavelike recess, to full, exuberant sweep.

A view may be subdivided. It may be appreciated facet by facet, with each bit treated as a separate picture and so displayed as to best capture its special qualities. By design, a view may be deftly modulated as one moves from area to area. Each area will, by direction, foreground, framing, or by the function of the space, relate one to some new aspect of the scene until, at last, it is fully revealed.

A view gains in effectiveness when certain plan areas are developed as a counterpoint or foil. If we stand for long at one vantage point, comprehending a view in its entirety, it begins to lose its first fresh appeal and strikes the senses with less impact. The interest of the open view may be sustained and much accentuated when certain plan areas are developed in balanced opposition. Such an area might be enclosed, with a narrow slot or a constructed aperture opening on some absorbing detail of the scenery. It might be a chaste volume kept simple and severe in form and neutral in tone, so that a colorful sector of view might glow more vividly. It might be a recessive area, leading one away from the view into some cavelike interior space for contrast, so that, emerging to the expansiveness of the view, one senses an emotional response of great release and freedom. A designed space may incorporate some feature subtly or powerfully related to the view: a ship relic related to a view of the ocean; hammered metal to a spectacle of blazing furnaces; a fruit bowl to an orchard view; a trout etching to a scene of splashing brook; a drawing of fox, grouse, or wild turkey or hunting accoutrements to a panorama of rolling game land; or a candle to a distant cathedral spire.

Some areas, to give respite, might best be planned without apparent relationship. For a heady view, like a heady drink, should be absorbed slowly and in moderation.

Split interest is a hazard in a treatment of a view. Light detail placed in front of a scene is usually lost or distracting—an element of annoyance. If the broad view is used as a backdrop, the

If the view is to serve as a backdrop, the object placed against it must be in character.

Light or incongruous detail placed against a view may result in split interest and annoyance.

object or objects placed before it must, singly or as a compositional group, either recede or dominate.

The power of suggestion

If a view or an object in the landscape is, by design, suggested only, the mind will multiply the possibilities of perception and thus expand the scope and richness of the suggested experience. The silhouette or shadow of a pine branch seen through a translucent panel or screen, or projected upon it, is often more effective than a direct view of the branch itself. The dim outline of a form seen at a distance or in half-light is thus often of more interest than the same form seen fully and in detail. And so it is with the view.

It has long been the belief of the Zen Buddhists, writes Kakuzo Okakura in *A Book of Tea*, that "true beauty could be discovered only by one who mentally completed the incomplete. It was this love of the abstract that led the Zen to prefer black and white sketches to the elaborately colored paintings of the classic Buddhist School."

Concealment and revealment

A view should be totally revealed for fullest impact only from that position in the plan where this is most appropriate. It is not to be wasted in one first blast but conserved and displayed with perhaps more refinement, though certainly with no less feeling for suspense and timing, than shown by the striptease artist.

It has been told that, near the village of Tomo in Japan, a celebrated tea master planning to build a teahouse purchased, after much deliberation, a parcel of land with a startlingly beautiful view of the idyllic Inland Sea. His friends were most curious to learn how this great artist would exhibit his scenic prize, but during the time of construction they were, of course, too polite to investigate and waited to be invited.

On the day when the first guests arrived at the entrance gate, they could hardly contain their eagerness to see the fabulous ocean view as it must be so eloquently displayed. As they moved along the narrow stone pathway toward the teahouse, they were aware that the sea was teasingly hidden from sight by the alignment of the path through thin bamboo clumps. At the door of the teahouse, they reasoned, the view would be opened to them in some highly sensitive enframement. They were more than a little perplexed at finding the view there to be effectively *concealed* by a shoulder of lichened rock and a panel of woven straw fencing. As is the custom before entering a teahouse, they paused and bent over a stone basin brimming with water, to rinse their hands. As they raised their eyes from this bowed position they caught a glimpse, no more than a glimpse, between the great rock and a low, dark branch of ancient pine, of the shining sea below them. And as they looked, they sensed with tingling comprehension the relationship of the mother sea and the cool water at their fingertips.

Inside on the mats of the teahouse with the translucent screens closed around them they performed the simple ritual of the tea ceremony, still mindful of the lesson of the sea. Relaxed and refreshed at the ceremony's conclusion, the guests were half

Vista.

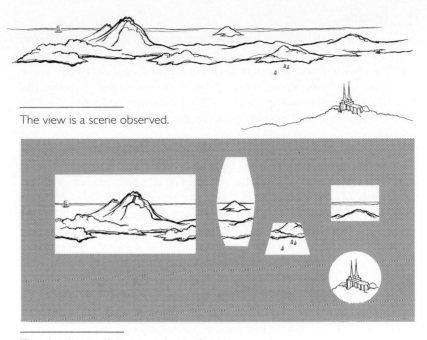

The view is a scene observed.

The vista is an enframed segment of a view.

surprised when their host rose quietly to slide back the screens at one side of the room, revealing in its perfect completeness the overwhelming beauty of a seascape that stretched from the edge of the grass floor mats to the farthest distant limits of the sky.

The Vista

A vista is a confined view, usually directed toward a terminal or dominant feature. It may be a natural vista, as an allée opened through a grove of Japanese maples to give a view of Fujiyama; or it may be architectural, as the majestic vista from the Palace of Versailles toward the lavish Neptune Fountain.

A vista, unlike most views, may be treated in its entirety and is therefore subject to precise control. Each vista has, in simplest terms, a viewing station, an object or objects to be seen, and intermediate ground. The three together should make a satisfactory visual unit and are usually conceived as an entity. If one or more of the elements already exist and are allowed to remain, then the others must, of course, be designed in conformity.

Again, vista and the allied places and spaces must be compatible. If the vista is planned as an extension of a use area or space, the relationships of character and scale are important. For example, from the boardroom of a powerful bank the vista, if there is to be one, should hardly terminate at the roller coaster of an amusement park or the gates of the state penitentiary. Commanded by such a rarefied viewing box of marble, gilt, and paneled rosewood, the vista and its terminus should be equally impressive and richly conservative. The vista toward a national monument should hardly commence at a service station, drugstore, or factory. It might well be observed from another monument, a civic building, or a public gathering space. It is fundamental to the fine vista that the end justifies the beginning and the beginning justifies the end.

Enframement and vista must be compatible.

The terminus

The terminal feature on which the vista is focused sets the theme to be developed. All other elements must fall into cadence, support the theme in harmony and counterpoint, and carry the work to a final satisfying crescendo. There is no room for discord, the superfluous, or the inappropriate. A well-conceived vista has the balance, rhythm, and polish of a symphony, or perhaps of a string quartet.

For vistas are not always grandiose in scale, not even those most memorable. The world is, in fact, laced and interlaced with beautiful vistas and with vistas within vistas, some no longer than the length of one's arm. And these are often the more delightful ones, not necessarily consciously designed but always the right thing seen from the right place with just the right enframement.

If it is planned that the terminal feature shall also become a viewing station, then the reverse vista should provide a new and rewarding visual experience as well. A terminal feature may serve as a focal point for several vistas. The vistas need not be identical; the viewing stations, middle-ground treatment, and enframement might well vary in each case.

A terminal feature may be seen in full or in part. It might be that a feature selected as a focal point is too large in mass or plan area for the suitable termination of the vista proposed. Some portion of the feature might in such a case be enframed because of its more suitable quality or scale. It is essential only that either the entire terminal feature or *a visually satisfying component* be brought into proper perspective.

The vista as an organizing element. (Proposal for Parque del Recuerdo, Santiago, Chile)

Enframement

A vista has three planes of enframement, all of which are usually best kept simple in form, texture, and color. The vertical planes may be natural or architectural—as loose as unclipped foliage or as solid as masonry. The base plane or planes may be sloping, level, or terraced; they may be of turf, water, paving, or other surfacing. Often the overhead plane is open, or it may be lightly defined by the foliage arch provided by overhanging trees, or it may be roofed. By the manipulation of overhead planes at the viewing stations or elsewhere, we may exercise control over the quality and scale of the vista. In all cases, distraction caused by interest in the form or the detail of the overhead enframement is to be precluded.

A monumental vista, particularly, is often reflected in a water panel. If so, the water basin must reflect from the viewing station or stations a visually pleasant unit of the terminal feature. "Of course," we say, "of course."

In this regard, the author recalls a shattering experience during a visit to our national capital. Wishing to view the Washington Monument across the full sweep of the Mall, he assumed that the handsomest vista would be enjoyed from the raised entrance platform of the Lincoln Memorial. As he mounted the grand stairway to the monument and the impressive seated figure of Lincoln, he was astonished to find the line of the top step rising higher and higher in perspective on the figure of Lincoln until it cut him off at his chin. Here was an unbelievable error in sightline design, a technique long ago perfected by the Egyptians and the Greeks. Flushed with embarrassment for the planner of this stairway, the author at last gained the main platform and turned to look back across the grand Mall to the towering shaft of marble at its far terminus. Surely, from here the viewing platform, reflecting panels, and shaft must have been coordinated into such a flawless vista as would be a marvel of civic art. Panels must have been thoughtfully shaped in materials and proportion to mirror the monumental image and hold it perfectly enframed in the long rectangle of water against the moving reflections of the background sky. But the image of the imposing shaft hardly reached the basin! From the platform at the base of the stairs the effect was equally disastrous. Crossing the avenue to the viewing stage at the basin's end, the author found the reflected image of the monument to be no more than an abortive stub projecting foolishly onto the far half of the panel's water surface. Nowhere along the Mall's entire length could viewer, panel, and terminus, let alone enframement, be brought into satisfying relationship. Shades of LeNôtre, Amon-Ra, and wise old Pericles!

Progressive realization

The terminal feature may be displayed in progressive stages. If a vista can be seen from several stations along the approaches, the section seen from each station is to be treated separately. Sometimes a terminus may be viewed along an entire approach. In such a case, it should be so revealed by its evolving spatial containment as to exact the full potential of its changing perspectives. If the approach is long, the vista becomes tiring and should be divided into segments by changing the level, by expanding or contracting the frame of reference, or by altering the character of the spaces through which and from which it is seen. Often, in moving toward a distant focal point, one can at first discern no more than the outline of the terminal feature. As one continues, the feature reveals itself progressively: the component masses, the subcomponents, and finally the details.

Any vista may be satisfyingly staged in an infinite number of ways. It is only necessary that, from all viewing stations or lines of approach, there be developed a pleasing visual entity.

A vista may induce motion or repose. Some vistas are static, to be enjoyed from one fixed viewing station, and are seen in their completeness from this point. Others, by the interest of their unfolding revelation or by the attraction of the terminus, draw one from point to point. All vistas subject the observer to a compelling *line* of sight. A vista is insistent, a directional attraction to the eye. As such, a vista is a function of the *axis*.

The Axis

Essentially, the axis is a linear plan element connecting two or more points. In use, it may be a court, a mall, or a drill field. It may be a path, a drive, a city street, or a monumental parkway. Always it is to be regarded as an element of connection.

In land planning, the axis has important applications. It has limitations also, for once an axis has been introduced, it generally becomes the dominant landscape feature. Established in a plan complex, it becomes so insistent that all other elements must be related to it directly or tacitly. Any area or structure impinging upon the axis, adjacent to the axis, or leading toward the axis must draw much of its use, form, and character from this relationship. Any planned experience of view or movement from a peripheral point of origin toward the axis must be regarded as an experience of transition, culminating at the area of juncture.

In the garden of Versailles, for example, when we wander through the shady groves and diverting spaces far to the side of the axial canal, we are always aware that the canal is there and somehow subconsciously adjust to this relationship. We sense that a certain path, for instance, leads *away* from the canal, and thus we expect it to relax its discipline of form and finish and dwindle into gradual rustication. Should the same path moving *toward* the great canal grow thin and less well defined, we would be perturbed; for we would know that just ahead we should soon be surveying the full grandeur of the great axial sweep, and we would expect the path to be preparing us for the experience. Even if surprise were intended by the planner, the relationship of path to axis would be as significant, for in such a case the planner would, by spatial manipulation, soothe viewers into a state of pleasant complacency and then suddenly, around a seemingly casual turn, confront them abruptly with an astonishing aspect of axial splendor.

Because it is a powerful landscape element, the axis tends to subjugate other landscape features. This can happen in more ways than one. It has been told that, in building the Palace of Versailles, King Louis XIV questioned the fact that the three approach avenues were unequally spaced on the drawings. When he was advised that the offending avenue was so aligned to miss a nearby village, Louis replied that he failed to understand the point. The plans were revised. To preserve a perfect symmetry, one axial approach was, of necessity, driven through the hapless village. Demolition crews set to work, and the hamlet was neutralized.

Almost as effective would be the driving of an axis through any established landscape area. Because the existing order of things would be disrupted, a new order would have to be devised, and this in relation to the intruding axial line, for there is little of polite gentility to the axis. It is forceful, it is demanding, and, as a result, things usually go its way.

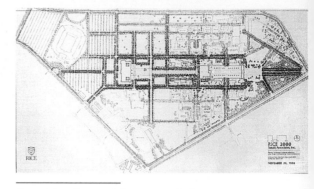

An axial and essentially symmetrical campus plan with its unifying advantages and inherent disadvantages. (Rice University Master Plan, Houston, Texas)

> An axis is directional.
> An axis is orderly.
> An axis is dominating.
> An axis is often monotonous.

This is not to say that the axis is always best avoided. It is only to suggest that none of these attributes are conducive to relaxation, pleasant confusion, nature appreciation, freedom of choice, or many other such experiences that we humans tend to enjoy.

Axial characteristics

From a given use area, an axis is a dynamic plan line leading out and thus orienting the area outward. Such an area, both as a viewing point and as a source of axial movement, might well express this outward flow. How can this be accomplished? By shaping the space to induce movement outward. By constructing,

The Arc de Triomphe on the Étoile, at the head of the Champs Élysées.

in effect, a viewing box with its aperture well focused. By fanning the paving lines out and away or by sighting them accurately down the axial center line. By concentrating interest at the forward edge of the staging area, inducing flow to and past it. By directional forms. By use of concentric arcs circling outward, as from pebbles tossed into a pond.

Often, in an axial plan, the viewing stations and termini are interchangeable. It can be seen that the forms and lines and details that dispatch us from one station would, if we approached from the opposite direction, seem to beckon and receive us. This is fortunate, because most axial treatments allow for looking both up and down the line of sight and for moving from one end to the other and back again. We find that each transmitting area thus becomes, in turn, a receiving area. We may correctly conclude that when viewing points and terminal features are interchangeable, each must express the characteristics of the source as well as the terminus of axial view and movement.

An axis, being a line of *movement* and *use* as well as *vision*, must satisfy all three functions. The axis, like the vista it creates, combines primary, intermediate, and terminal spaces in the same volume. It would seem only reasonable that all three need to be planned as integral parts of the whole. If the axial plan area is intended as a boulevard, it should, from start to finish, look like a boulevard and function as a boulevard. Every building at its flanks should "belong" to the boulevard. Every space projected or leading into its central volume should partake of the boulevard character.

Much lyrical praise has been heaped upon that prototype of all grand boulevards, the Champs Élysées of Paris. Much criticism has also been leveled at its social and economic impact on the city at the time of its construction, for it cleared out a wide swath of living urban tissue. But, for the moment, let us dismiss from our minds such weighty implications and let ourselves rise up in our imaginations until we can gaze down upon the whole stirring expanse of this magnificent axis.

Below us we see the grand Étoile, a wide traffic circle with forcefully radiating streets that disappear in the distance. The circle is massively defined by the stately trees and severe gray buildings at its sides. Its glistening pavement of clipped granite blocks is precise in pattern. The whole martial space has about it a stiffly proud and solemn air, as well it might, for there at its center looms the Arc de Triomphe, and at the arch's wreath–lined base the Tomb of the Unknown Soldier, with its eternally glowing flame of tribute. The Étoile is a volume remarkably suited to its uses. A focal point, the arch is seen fittingly framed for miles in all directions. The circle is a marshaling space and point of generation, for, as well as being the powerful terminus, the Étoile is also the head of the Champs Élysées, and its archway commandingly rallies attention to the start of the wide boulevard.

The axial boulevard marches on, out to the east, still crisply military, progressing firmly in measured cadence of structures and trees until, almost imperceptibly, we note less of a military and more of a regal character, less of the coldly regimented, more of the ornately monumental; for now we approach the palace group. Here the Grand and Petit palaces flank the Avenue Alexandre III as it moves in grandeur from the Esplanade des Invalides across the Seine to join the boulevard. The transition is from pala–

tial to civic as we continue along the Champs Élysées to the Place de la Concorde, with its pretentious ministries and secretariats.

In our journey eastward from the Étoile we have passed resplendent apartments with silver entablatures, elite shops with high velvet curtains, proud restaurants with glittering chandeliers, and, finally, small cafes with their trim green awnings and crowded sidewalk tables, between which bustle the white–aproned garçons with trays poised lightly on fingertips. Here the boulevard takes on a lively air. Colors are gay, spirits are light, the smile is quick, and the heart is glad on the boulevard in Paris.

Beyond the ordered spaces of the Place de la Concorde we come to the Tuileries, the magnificent public gardens and park. At the garden's end, and handsomely framed, we behold the Palace of the Louvre, with its warm stone walls and rich ornamentation. Fronting the majestic Louvre we see the espaliered allées of sycamore, the gardens rolling with color, the screeching traffic, trim nursemaids, perambulators, barking dogs, and dodging children, the white–bearded, pink–cheeked old men in blue berets drowsing on benches in the sun, the well–scrubbed jaunty sailors, and the *belles jeunes filles*. All that is in this whole exuberant space belongs to it—is of its very essence.

And where along the length of this great axis do we find the discrepancies in plan, the discordant notes? Some there must be, and many perhaps, but they are lost in the captivating and ringing experience of moving down through this evolving complex of boulevard volumes, the "elysian fields," from the hushed memorial solemnity of the arch at the Étoile to the palatial, then stately, governmental core, to the splendid apartments, the chic shops, the lively café district, and on through the carefree expanse of the public gardens, to the grandiose museum of fine arts. We feel ourselves to be, in turn, in one brief morning's stroll, the soldier, the courtier, the statesman, the man of wealth, the gay dilettante, the poet, the lover, the relaxed, free, and happy boulevardier, the stimulated observer, and finally the distinguished connoisseur.

If planned today, this Champs Élysées would have a different mien. And so it should, for since its conception times have changed and conditions have changed, and plan concepts and forms have changed with them. The new boulevard would have less of the old despotic formality, less unbending symmetry. Retaining its hallowed monuments, it would be less monumental. It would open out and free the teeming residential districts at its sides. It would be less of the classifier and more of the synthesizer. It would be more flexible and allow more flexibility. It would take its form from an empathetic understanding of individual Parisians and their emerging culture. It would express their new freedom, new ideas, and new aspirations. But let those who will change the present Champs Élysées first study it long and thoughtfully because, in light of the times and the society for which it was built and of its masterful handling of forms and space, there is no boulevard of its equal.

An axis has sometimes a negative, sometimes a positive effect on landscape elements within its field of influence. We have said that areas and objects adjacent to an axis are perforce related to it. Sometimes they suffer from the relationship, because interest is less in the things themselves than in the thing–axis relationship. A fine linden tree, for example, if standing alone, is observed in terms of trunk and limbing structure, twigging, burgeoning

Today, we are more honest, more practical, and quite functional, but it has been at the expense of grace and gentility....
Pietro Belluschi

Yes, we have forgotten the simple courtesy of pleasing. What is true of architecture is even more so of city planning where the chief object seems to be to get the driver from A to B sitting down.

Henry H. Reed, Jr.

What is the monumental? The word, by the way, in the architectural sense, is quite new. Ruskin a hundred years ago spoke only of power. Actually it is a recent borrowing from the French. "Monumental" they tell us is said of a building "qui a un caractère de grandeur et de majesté," for a monument is an "ouvrage d'architecture considérable par sa masse, son étendue, sa magnificence." Grandeur, majesty, magnificence!

Henry H. Reed, Jr.

The axis

An axis imposed on a free plan area demands a new and related order.

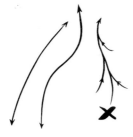

An axis may be bent or deflected but never divergent.

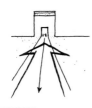

A powerful axis requires a powerful terminus.

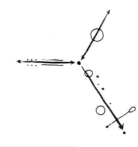

The axis is a unifying element.

foliage, sunlight and shadow patterns, and the beauty of its broad outline and delicate detail. If related to an insistent axis, however, the same tree is noticed primarily in that context. The subtle, the natural, and the unique are lost to the axial line.

Sometimes, by the fact of their relationship, axial elements may gain in interest and value. If as units they are dull, in pattern they may be striking. If by position they are inconspicuous, by axial frame of reference they may gain in significance.

The axis as a unifying element

A terminal or intermediate station of one axis may function also as the terminal or intermediate station of another. Thus two or more plan areas may be focalized on a common point. Washington, D.C., whose plan diagram exemplifies this principle, has thereby developed one of the most cohesive metropolitan plans yet devised. Its long, radial, tree-lined avenues, converging on park, circle, structure, or monument, enframe handsome vistas and bind the city's complex, extensive, and heterogeneous parts into coherent unity. If we distinguish in the plan arrangement the outline of monumentality, this seems preeminently fitting.

An aerial view of Washington, D.C. The imposition of radial axes upon a rectilinear street pattern creates many awkward slices and undesirable properties. The freer urban street and land patterns of the future will eliminate this difficulty. Yet in our future urban planning we would do well to learn from Washington its lesson of the radial axis to organize and unify a vast and sprawling city.

Additional characteristics

A powerful axis requires a fitting terminus. Conversely, powerful design features are often of such form or character as to require an axial approach. Such features are those best seen head on.

> Or those best situated at the hub of converging plan lines.
>
> Or those to be revealed in stages along a given line of approach.
>
> Or those requiring controlled enframement and established viewing points.

Or those that gain through a direct relationship to other lineal plan elements.

The axis presents the most imposing approach to a structure or other plan feature. The key word in this axiom is *imposing*, for the axis imposes a discipline upon spaces and forms as well as upon the viewer. The movement, attention, and interest of the viewer are imposed upon by axial composition and induced to alignment with the direction of its strong polarizing forces. An impressive, dogmatic design form, the axis expresses the supremacy of the human will over nature. It denotes authority, the military, the civic, the religious, the imperial, the classic, and the monumental.

To understand the significance of the axis when properly applied, we may well look to the ancient city of *Peking*,[1] the northern capital of the khans. Kublai Khan, its founder, and the great city builders who followed him understood the power of the axis as have few before or since. Centuries ago, in the building of their city, they scrupulously avoided the use of the axis in those areas where its insistent lines were unsuited. The refreshing parks, marketplaces, and winding residential streets were relaxed and free in their forms and spaces. In the whole fabulously delightful grounds of the Summer Palace, planned for sumptuous divertissement, there is scarcely a conscious axis to be found.

But where the imperial presence was to be made manifest or the people were to be subjected to the concept of supreme deity, omnipotence, or military might, the axis was employed with sensitive understanding, as witness the military roads that stretch in broad grandeur from the city gates to the entrance of the once golden-roofed Forbidden City of the emperor or the tree-lined axial boulevard that sweeps southward from the shrine atop Coal Hill at the north, through parks, past temple groups, through bustling city centers, to the Forbidden City's imperial gateways and on beyond through parade grounds, fields, and forests—dynamic lines of force, subjecting the whole city and countryside to the will and authority of the all-powerful emperor, who sat astride it on his royal throne of jade.

Axial planning also highlights the Temple of Heaven, which now lies in ruin on the plain to the south of the Imperial City. Here, each year at the time of the vernal equinox, the great khan rode in magnificent pomp and ceremony to welcome the coming of spring. The approach to this sublimely beautiful temple was by a wide causeway of white marble that commenced at the circular platform of noble proportions, rising in balustraded tiers. The spacious causeway, elevated above the level plain, extended to the gilded and deep-red-lacquered gates of the temple. Spaced out along the causeway sides, at regular intervals, were sockets to hold the standards of hundreds of waving banners, and between the standards were carved fire pits, in which pitch faggots were burned to illumine the long processions that moved past them in the night.

In the dark hours before the great annual event, the Khan's subjects flocked through the streets of their city and out through the gates toward the temple, where they massed along the wooded edges of the plain to stand in watchful, wide-eyed wonder and respect. Then, through the gates, the foot soldiers came

[1] Present-day Beijing.

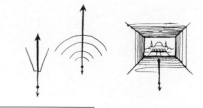

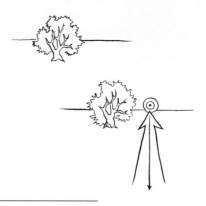

Terminus as a generator of axial movement.

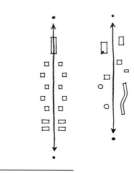

Often objects adjacent to a strong axis suffer in the relationship.

An axis may be symmetrical. But usually it is not.

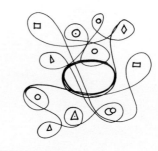

A small exhibit area may function well without a major vista or axis. Such a scheme permits a crowd to filter freely through the entire complex. In this case a powerful focal center is mandatory.

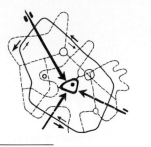

A diagrammatic and workable circulation plan for a large-scale exhibition area has the following features: main entrance, secondary entrances, major vista, minor vistas, strong focal point, major circulation loop, minor paths, and secondary focal areas and reference points for easy orientation.

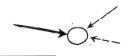

Major and minor vistas need not be perpendicular.

The terminus of a vista may be a space as well as an object.

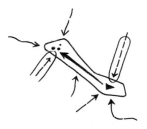

A major or a minor vista may be a function of an *area* or a *volume* as well as of a *line* of approach.

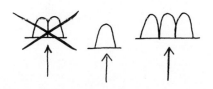

When the axis terminates in a structure that is to be entered, one or three openings are better than two since they provide a receptive element rather than an obstruction.

marching, division after bristling division of seasoned warriors, in dark helmets, chain breastplates, and padded felt boots, to mass in ordered formation along the causeway flanks. The courtiers and nobles followed in dazzling array, thousands upon thousands on horseback, each noble and mount in trappings of silk, gold, costly furs, and precious gems and each proudly taking his appointed place along the white marble pavement. The high priests, with smoldering incense pots, then moved in solemn procession, chanting, fur-capped, and in silken robes and gowns of unbelievable splendor. Slowly, with vast dignity, they took their august posts on the terraced platform, commanding the length of the ceremonial causeway.

Finally, as the first faint traces of light tinged the eastern sky with pink, the khan and his mounted retinue pranced through the golden gates of the Forbidden City and out through the throngs to the head of the causeway. There, to the cadenced booming of drums and the crashing of brass and silver gongs, the khan rode imperiously past the blazing fire pits, down the avenue of floating banners, on through the massed troops and kowtowing nobles, to the resplendent temple and the gleaming altar seen through its opened doors. Precisely at that hushed moment when he reached the high altar and bowed his head in grave salutation, the blazing red orb of the rising sun arched above the purple hills to the east, and every face and every eye and every thought in all Peking were focused down the length of that great axis to the sacred place where the exalted khan, their emperor, knelt to greet the spring.

The Symmetrical Plan

The use of the axis does not necessarily dictate the development of a symmetrical plan.

The elements of a symmetrical plan are the same and are in equilibrium about a central point or opposite sides of an axial line. The central point may be an object or an area, such as a fountain or the plaza that contains it.

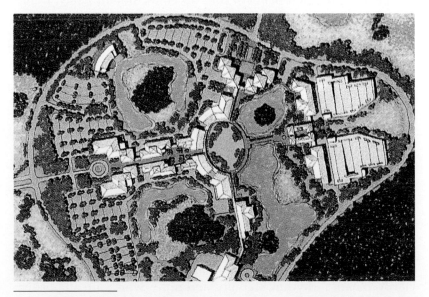

An asymmetrical axial plan. (Proposed campus plan, Florida Gulf Coast University, Fort Myers, Florida)

Court of the Lions, Alhambra Palace, Granada, Spain.

The symmetrical axis may be a line or plane of use, such as a path, a broad avenue, or a mall. It may be a powerfully induced line of sight or movement, as through a series of imposing arches or gates, or between rows of rhythmically spaced trees or pylons, or toward an object or space of high interest. It may be a quiet vista across an open panel of turf, on either side of which things appear to be equally balanced.

Symmetry may be absolute, as in the pillared and carved and polished perfection of the Alhambra's Court of the Lions. Or it may be as loose and casually implied as in the balanced order of fence rows and haycocks along a country road.

Growing things, including humans, are often symmetrical, for the seed or the cell may be by nature symmetrical, and thus also are the shapes evolved through their development or growth. But in the natural landscape, *plan symmetry* is a rarity. Where observed, therefore, symmetry generally indicates an imposed system of order.

It is revealing to note that in the western world the word *symmetrical* is often taken to be synonymous with *beautiful* and has the connotation of pleasant and handsome form. Perhaps this is because it implies an order to the scheme of things that is easily comprehended and thus enjoyed by humans. Perhaps it is because the word *symmetry* has come to be associated with plan clarity, balance, rhythm, stability, and unity, which are all positive qualities. Perhaps it is because we ourselves are symmetrical and take pleasure in the relationship.

Symmetry: plan elements in equilibrium

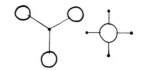

About a point or area

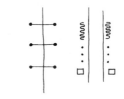

About an axis or plane

Bilateral—as the double wings of a maple seed

Trilateral—as the grappling hook

Multilateral—as the snowflake

Quadrilateral—as by geometry

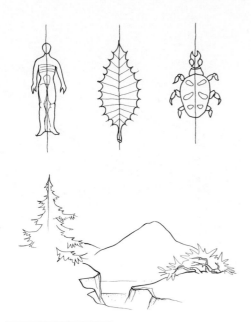

Symmetry in nature—growing objects in nature are often symmetrical because of the bilateral formation of their germ cell or seed; the natural landscape, a product of infinitely divergent forces, is rarely symmetrical.

The notion of identical figures to the right and left of an axis was not the basis of any theory in ancient [European] times.

Camillo Sitte

The Greeks used symmetry when appropriate, they did not use symmetry when not appropriate, and they never used symmetry in their (site) planning layouts.

Eliel Saarinen

Dynamic symmetry

When, by symmetry, two opposing elements or structures are seemingly held apart, an apparent attraction and tension develops between them. The two are strongly related, to the point at which the opposing elements read as one, together with the intervening space and all that it contains.

The symmetrical plan has a quality of stability. Each pole generates its own field of force, and between these two fields is a field of dynamic tension. Each element within this field is at once in tension and in repose. By definition, every symmetrical composition must be in balance and, therefore, in repose. But the repose of symmetry is the more compelling for the fact that it bespeaks the resolution of myriad opposing forces held in equilibrium.

Each object in a symmetrical plan creates a need for fulfillment—a fulfillment that can be achieved only by its opposite number. This becomes apparent when, in a symmetrical arrangement, even the smallest element is removed. The equilibrium is lost at once, and the entire composition seems to strain at the gap.

When, in perceiving a plan, the eye discovers a rhythm of objects and intervals, it develops an anticipation of the next object and interval, and one is surprised if this anticipation is not satisfied. If the break in rhythm reveals only a void, one senses a plan imperfection, and the reaction is disappointment. If, however, the experience of surprise coincides with the discovery of an interesting and appropriate plan feature, the reaction can be that of pleasure, and the feature is thus emphasized.

The despotism of symmetry

The symmetrical plan subjects plan elements to a rigid or formalized layout. Objects within a symmetrical frame of reference have meaning principally in their relation to the pattern of the whole. Each feature must always be considered, first and last, as a unit in the grand composition.

Sometimes a symmetrical plan may give added emphasis to objects. Such an object, for instance, might be featured as the terminus of a major or minor axis. Or it might be given greater importance through a progressively evolving sequence of approach or by its relationship to complimentary or complementary features. Usually, however, it may be said that the more powerful the total plan, the less potent the individual plan unit.

A symmetrical plan subjects a landscape to control. It systematizes the landscape. It organizes the landscape into rigid patterns. The natural environment is reduced to a setting or background for the plan composition.

A symmetrical plan subjects people to plan conformity. Not only are the landscape and all plan features subjugated to an organized plan of things, but so are we as well. We are held transfixed by a diagram of pattern. Our lines of movement are limited to the lines of the plan. The plan forms control our vision. We are consciously stirred or lulled by developing cadence, balanced repetitions, and the subjugation of all things to one concept. We are attuned subconsciously, as if by hypnosis, to the rhythmic symmetrical order of things and find ourselves in all ways conforming to the order of the plan. This conformity induces a sense of harmony, but if overworked it may often produce monotony and boredom.

It can be realized, however, that symmetrical plan forms, if skillfully handled, may be used to dramatize a concept and to evoke a sense of discipline, high order, and even divine perfection.

The nature of symmetry

Being precise and disciplined in plan, symmetry requires precision in detail.

Bold in concept, it demands bold forms.

The symmetrical plan becomes a structural framework, compartmentalizing site features and functions. To be successful, such an arrangement must be an expression of the logical relationship of the features or functions so grouped. The rhythmically recurring elements of a symmetrical scheme divide the plan field into units. Each such unit, complete in itself, must still be related as a segment to the total plan.

Usually the symmetrical plan has a strong relationship to adjacent structures. Often it is designed to extend such structures or to relate two or more of them. Such a plan is the familiar campus quad, an expanse of greensward crisscrossed with walks, flanked by dormitories and classrooms, and perhaps featuring on its long axis the library or chapel at one end and, on the other, the administrative center. College buildings symmetrically placed on their quadrangle may express a closely knit and well-balanced community of learning. Such a grouping is better suited to buildings of classic context and to areas where a sense of established order is to be engendered.

Symmetry is unsuccessful if it obviously forces unsymmetrical functions to a symmetrical plan arrangement. This is a common error in plan organization. It is painful to discover an important function balanced against the trivial. It is pathetic to find a plan area contorted beyond workability in order to achieve a visual balance with an area of dissimilar use. It seems dishonest to disguise a function or falsify a form to comply with the dictates of symmetry. If Keats was right in his observation that truth and beauty are one and the same, then such symmetry can never be beautiful, for not only must a plan be truthful to be beautiful, its truth must be evident.

Symmetry is a coordinator. It has application whenever it might be helpful in the comprehension of the whole of the plan or the relationship of the parts.

A symmetrical plan may be of crystalline form. This may be desirable if the function is by nature crystalline in its pattern of growth and expansion.

A symmetrical plan may be of geometric design. Such plan geometry may be excellent, but only if the function can be logically expressed in geometric line and form.

There are those who believe that geometry is the root of all beauty and that beauty of form and pattern can be consistently achieved by the application of mathematical formulas to the planning process. This thinking, they hold, gains support from the fact that people take pleasure in the comprehension of order. The writer contends, however, that the preference is generally for order over chaos rather than for symmetry over asymmetry.

A plan that imposes geometry without reason may destroy desirable landscape character or may neutralize the inherent qualities of the areas or objects affected.

The Louvre, Paris. Site and buildings are here combined in a grand plan of geometric symmetry. Such imperious and inhuman planning unfortunately characterized much of the work of the Renaissance.

❝ *There is no such thing as "beauty of symmetry," with the exception of those cases where, because of the nature of the problem and its logical solution, the "balance" line of design happens to coincide with the middle line of symmetry. Only in such cases is symmetry logical and thus beautiful.*

Eliel Saarinen

Occult balance

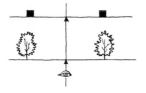

Symmetrical balance: equal and like masses balanced on either side of an optical axis or fulcrum.

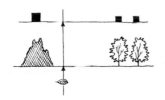

Asymmetrical occult balance: unequal and unlike masses balanced on either side of an optical axis.

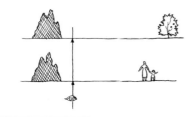

Asymmetrical occult balance: equilibrium achieved by mind–eye evaluation of form, mass, value, color, and association.

> We live in the midst of a whirlwind of light qualities. From this whirling confusion we build unified entities, those forms of experience called visual images. To perceive an image is to participate in a forming process; it is a creative act.
>
> *Gyorgy Kepes*

A geometric plan, direct and obvious, is quickly comprehended. It thus has the advantage of clarity. It has also the disadvantage of monotony if seen often or for long.

A geometric plan is not valid in the context of that which is natural or when it is intended that the human eye and mind and spirit be set free.

In far too many cases, symmetrical plans are conceived as a design expedient, a sort of geometric doodling. Such plans are repetitive and dreary, as uninspired as their authors. When geometric layouts are truly fitting, it is found that their symmetry is derived through clear logic and a conscious synthesis of all plan forms into symmetrical plan arrangement as the highest and best expression of the function. When appropriate and when intelligently applied in limited areas, symmetry is a plan form of compelling power.

The Asymmetrical Plan

In nature, we can seldom find the elements of a landscape symmetrically balanced on either side of a line of sight. Yet visual balance is fundamental to all satisfactory composition and to all art. It is generally conceded that any design, any picture, or any view or vista that lacks such balance is disturbing and unpleasant. Because we usually think of natural landscapes as being pleasant to look at, we might conclude that visual balance must somehow be inherent. This brings to mind two intriguing questions.

First, until an observer wanders along, how could there be visual balance? And then, does it not seem highly improbable that, from any given point of observation, the landscape should *happen* to balance visually on either side of a line of sight? Upon reflection it would seem, rather, that the eye must *find* or *define* in any landscape those vistas, views, or sight lines that *produce* a satisfactory visual balance. The trained eye is offended by the unbalanced and attracted to the balanced and tends constantly to seek out and bring into register those sections or portions of the visual landscape that provide a pleasant optical resolution of forces.

Visual balance

The human eye is constantly darting about, probing and exploring a vague and luminous flux of evolving visual impressions. These are sensed subconsciously. At intervals, the mind permits or directs the eye to bring out of optical limbo and into conscious focus certain visual images. This is a creative effort. For the mind demands that the eye "compose" a visual image that is complete and in equilibrium. This is a joint mind–eye effort, for the acceptable equilibrium is not one of form balance, value balance, or color balance alone, but one of associative balance as well. The mind–eye team may give little weight to a massive object that has no associative value, but it may give much weight to that which has strong associative value or immediate interest. A ripe apple swaying on a branch may thus outweigh the tree itself, or a chunk of rose quartz outweigh the mountain from which it was broken, or a solitary sunbather outweigh the immensity of a seascape.

Thus no two mind–eye combinations scanning a scene could ever bring into register an identical visual image or combination of images. For a scene has no limits, and the possibilities of selective composition are endless. But, by a vastly complicated series of instantaneous subconscious adjustments, each individual "creates" out of optical impressions visual images that, for that particular observer, are in equilibrium and, therefore, complete. The more sensitive and perceptive the mind–eye combination has become through instinct or training, the richer, the more delightful, and the more wondrous is the visual world that it reveals.

The child or the primitive perceives only *objects* in space. A more highly developed mind and a more selective eye perceive *relationships*.

It can be seen that only rarely in nature would a sensed composition be balanced symmetrically on either side of a visual axis, but because equilibrium is required of all visual images, it must be possible to have balance without bilateral symmetry. This is indeed the case. Such asymmetrical, or *occult*, balance is the norm. Except in those cases in which bilateral symmetry has for some reason been contrived, it is by occult balance that we compose and comprehend the world about us.

Asymmetric planning

Asymmetric planning brings us into closest harmony with nature. Freed of the rigidity of the symmetrical plan, each area may be developed with a fuller regard for its natural landscape qualities. Circulation is more free. Views are of infinite variety. Each object in the landscape may be seen and enjoyed for itself or its relationship to other landscape elements rather than for its relationship to a prescribed plan diagram. Such plan asymmetry is more subtle, casual, refreshing, interesting, and human. We are not led step by step along or through a rigid composition. We are, rather, set free to explore for ourselves and to discover in the landscape that which we may find to be beautiful, pleasant, or useful.

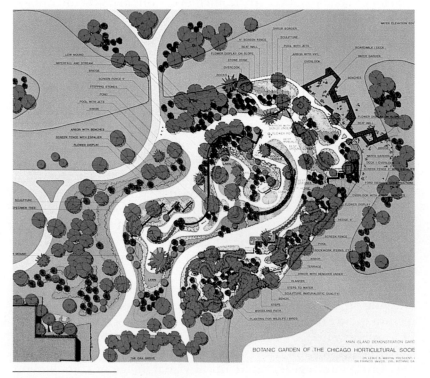

Area study, Chicago Botanic Garden.

> Balance may also consist in a disposition of objects not similar nor similarly placed, but still so chosen and arranged that the sum of the attractions on one side of the vertical axis is equalled by the sum of the attractions on the other side. This kind of balance is called unsymmetrical or occult balance.
>
> *Henry V. Hubbard*

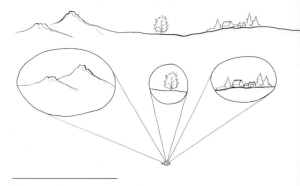

The mind-eye selection of visual images.

> The natural landscape is an indeterminate object; it almost always contains enough diversity to allow the eye a great liberty in selecting, emphasizing and grouping its elements, and it is furthermore rich in suggestion and in vague emotional stimulus. A landscape to be seen has to be composed. . . .
>
> *George Santayana*

> The eye, especially, demands completeness.
>
> *Johann Wolfgang von Goethe*

> When for any reason the eye is to be habitually directed to a single point—as to an altar, a throne, or a stage—there will be violence and distraction caused by the tendency to look aside in the recurring necessity of looking forward, if the object is not so arranged that the tensions of eye are balanced, and the center of gravity of vision lies in the point which one is obliged to keep in sight.
>
> *George Santayana*

> The term "organic design" need not be an empty platitude. Biology has many valuable hints to offer the designer. . . . Indeed, there is much that could be said in support of a biological approach to the entire process of design, mainly in the sense that one broad biological field, known as ecology, undertakes to investigate the dynamic relations of all the organisms—both fauna and flora—in natural association with each other and with the other forces of the total environment in a given area of the surface of the earth.
>
> Norman T. Newton

> Architecture is not an art, it is a natural function. It grows on the soil like animals and plants. It is a function of the social order. Don't forget that.
>
> Fernand Léger

> The basic law—in all fields of creation workers are striving today to find purely functional solutions of a technological-biological kind: that is, to build up each piece of work solely from the elements which are required for its function. But "function" means here not a pure mechanical service. It includes also the psychological, social, and economical conditions of a given period. It might be better to use the term "organic [functional] design."
>
> László Moholy-Nagy

> Let me remind you of a famous passage in which Samuel Taylor Coleridge defined organic form. In a lecture on Shakespeare, given in 1818, he made a distinction between what he called mechanic form and organic form. "Form is mechanic," he said "when on any given material we impress a predetermined form, not necessarily arising out of the properties of the material." Organic form, on the other hand, is innate; shaping itself from within, as it develops, so that "the fullness of its development is one and the same with the perfection of its outward form."
>
> Jacob Bronowski

> I detest everything that is cold and academic. Only where the living purpose exists will new things be formed.
>
> Eric Mendelsohn

Asymmetric planning requires less disturbance of the natural or built landscape. Because it is developed in sympathy with the site, it normally requires less grading, screening, and construction. It is therefore more economical.

Organic growth

The jack pine growing on the mountain slope sends out its probing roots in search of soil pockets and moisture. Its trunk and limbs are braced against the winds, its needle clusters are held up and extended as a living mesh, to best soak in the cool, drifting morning fogs and to absorb the utmost vitality from the light and warmth of the sun. It shapes itself to the patch of ground—the furrow and ridge, the rivulet, the stump, the fallen log, the boulder. It responds to the encroachment and to the protection of its neighbors. When a tip is bent or broken, a new tip is formed. When a branch is smashed or torn away, the wound is healed and the gaping void is filled with new wood or with fresh twigs and needles. All positive qualities of the environment are utilized. All negative factors are overcome to the limits of possibility. The form of the pine is expressive of its development in harmony with its environment. This age-old process we know to be the process of *organic growth*.

Organic planning

Organic planning, so widely touted and so seldom practiced, is fundamentally neither more nor less than the organic development of plan areas, volumes, and forms in response to all environmental constraints and opportunities.

Symmetrical plan form can never be organic in this sense, except in those rare instances in which the essential quality of the use is such that, given unrestrained freedom and developmental conditions, its most logical plan expression would be symmetrical. It can be seen that even in such a case the impact of natural landscape features would tend to disrupt the symmetry.

It is abundantly apparent that, in the great preponderance of cases, the logical site-structure or site-project diagram will be asymmetrical. If the diagram expresses a use or a complex of uses well suited to a site, and if, in plan refinement, each function is developed in best relationship to other functions and to all positive and negative factors of the site, then such planning is truly organic.

Most things in nature, as well as most structures, are best appreciated when seen in the round. The asymmetric plan best provides such viewing. The approach of the observer to each plan element is meandering rather than fixed, giving a sense of modeling and third dimension. This plastic (sculptural) quality of an object, revealing its nature, shape, and detail, can be appreciated only if the observer moves around or past the object. Even the pictorial quality of a landscape is imbued with greater interest when observed from a constantly changing line of observation.

An axis may be developed asymmetrically. Such a treatment preserves the positive features of the axis while allowing greater plan flexibility. It does preclude the controlled, measured cadence and hypnotic induction of bilateral symmetry—qualities which, we have found, are in some few cases highly desirable. But the asymmetrically treated axis has much more universal application.

The use of asymmetry

Asymmetry is well suited to large-scale urban planning. The most pleasant squares of Europe are asymmetrical. What a sad day it would be for San Marco in Venice if the piazza were to be reconstructed in rigid symmetry. The wonder and charm of such towns as Siena, Verona, and Florence would be lost to a symmetrical handling of their streets and buildings and spaces.

The most magnificent garden of history, the Yuan Ming Yuan, or Garden of Perfect Brightness, which today lies in ruin to the west of Beijing, was scrupulously asymmetric in plan, as attested to by Jean–Denis Attiret, a French priest who many years ago found his way to the court of Emperor Ch'ien–lung. In 1743, he wrote to a friend in France describing its wonders:

> One quits a valley, not by fine straight allées as in Europe, but by zigzag and circuitous routes—and on leaving one finds oneself in a second valley entirely different from the first as regards the form of the land and the structure of the buildings. All the mountains and hills are covered with trees, especially with flowering trees, which are very common here. It is a veritable paradise on earth.
>
> Each valley…has its pleasance, small in comparison with the whole enclosure, but in itself large enough to house the greatest of our European lords with all his retinue. But how many of these palaces would you think there are in the different valleys of this vast enclosure? There are more than two hundred.
>
> In Europe, uniformity and symmetry are desired everywhere. We wish that there should be nothing odd, nothing misplaced, that one part should correspond exactly with the part facing it; in China also they love this symmetry, this fine order. The palace in Peking…is in this style…but in the pleasances there reigns a graceful disorder, an anti–symmetry is desired almost everywhere. Everything is based on this principle. When one hears this, one would think it to be ridiculous, that it must strike the eye disagreeably; but when one sees them one thinks differently and admires the art with which the irregularity is planned.
>
> I am tempted to believe that we [in eighteenth–century France] are poor and sterile in comparison.[2]

The rash of symmetrical planning that marked the Renaissance in Europe had little reasonable basis. Far too often, it was symmetry solely for symmetry's sake, a senseless forcing of the natural and built landscape into geometric patterns. No wonder our friend Attiret, like many others to follow, found this planning, by comparison with the freedom and rich variety of asymmetry, to be but "poor and sterile."

Visual Resource Management

Visual resource management is a relatively new term being applied by several of the public agencies to the technique of preserving and enhancing the nation's scenery. Innovative approaches are outlined in a number of well–prepared manuals, which demonstrate a promising new concern.

---

[2] As quoted by Hope Danby in *The Garden of Perfect Brightness*.

> *In seeking now a reasonably solid grasp on the value of the word, organic, we should at the beginning fix in the mind the values of the correlated words, organism, structure, function, growth, development, form. All of these words imply the initiating pressure of a living force and a resultant structure or mechanism whereby such invisible force is made manifest and operative. The pressure, we call function—the resultant, form. Hence the law of form discernible throughout nature.*
>
> *Louis H. Sullivan*

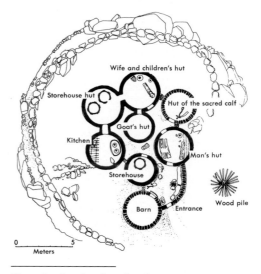

Organic planning: functional room arrangement of family dwelling. Cameroon.

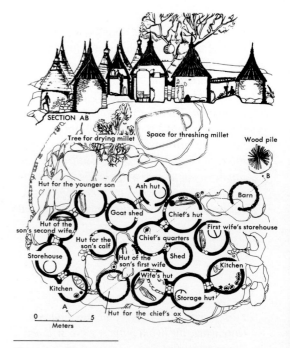

Organic cell cluster arrangement of rooms: residence of Cameroon chief.

Asymmetry prevails through the whole of this beautiful town on the Inland Sea, except at the central temple, where discipline, ceremony, and the implied presence of the supreme being demand symmetrical order.

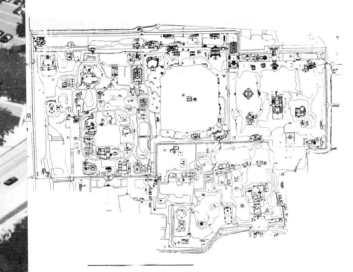

The Garden of Perfect Brightness

Eighty-five percent of perception is based on sight.

Essentially, for any area or corridor of proposed development or rehabilitation, both the scenic and the blighting landscape features are inventoried and recorded by various graphic means and given a rating as to their visual significance. Alternative proposals (for timber cutting, highway construction, extraction pits, reservoirs, or military installations, as examples) are then analyzed and evaluated as to their relative benefits and negative visual impacts upon existing conditions. In the decision as to the preferred route or course of action, the scenic considerations are shown to be telling and often deciding factors.

The procedures developed by the U.S. Forest Service are particularly sound, easy to understand, and effective. They are based on the premise that visitors to the national forests have an image of what they expect to see and that, insofar as possible, this expectation should be fulfilled. They recognize and consider the numbers and types of viewers, the duration of viewing time, and the relative quality and intensity of the viewing experience. They assume that all lands are to be viewed on the ground, from passing roads or transitways, and from the air. They build upon the principle that all landscapes have a definable character and that those with the greatest dramatic power and/or variety have the greatest scenic value. They assess each potential view in terms of its foreground, midground, and background contribution. They give priority, in each scene, to the dominant elements in terms of line, form, color, and imagery. They consider the capacity of each landscape area to absorb alteration without loss of its visual character. Finally, they outline a systematic, step-by-step process of evaluation that makes good sense. Often, in the recommended procedures of some agencies, far too much emphasis is given to the numerical weighting and tabular mathematical rating of the various scenic elements. (How many points should be assigned, for instance, for a view of a historic church, an acre of mountain laurel, or a plummeting waterfall?)

It is suggested that in the assessment of scenic or any other values, all *quantifiable* costs and benefits be computed and tabulated. The relative weight of these can be established with a fair degree of accuracy. *Unquantifiable* values, such as those of aesthetic, historical, or educational significance, can be reasonably evaluated only on a broad relative scale or on the basis of expert testimony in the presence of those who are to decide upon the merits of the alternatives.

The recent manuals on visual resource management are especially helpful as aids to untrained technicians and decision makers. Some provide the trained professional with welcome new insights and advanced approaches to the design of the visible landscape and have wide application.

Space modulation

It is an established planning fact that we seek in an area that quality of harmony, oneness, or unity that is the mark of any well-conceived work of science or art. We are attracted to such places and rebel at the intrusion of the incongruous element, for example, a claptrap hotdog stand in a beautiful natural gorge.

In addition, we seek a harmonious sequence of transition from one space to another. In going from club terrace to the swimming pool below, a detour through the parking lot would be disturbing. When driving the family from home to a picnic spot, we would avoid the business districts and prefer a parkway route, river road, or country lane, to sustain or heighten the anticipated mood and provide a pleasantly evolving transition. We seek, in all such cases, a unified sequential experience of *space modulation.*

People in motion take great pleasure in the sensation of change—change of texture, light quality, temperature, scent, visual patterns, expanding or contracting vistas, and the fluid visual impressions of objects, spaces, and views.

We take pleasure in an area arranged in shape, line, color, and texture to accommodate and express the use for which it was intended. We have learned also that our pleasure is increased when the area is further developed into a volume or series of volumes that, by degree and type of enclosure, further articulate the planned use. We enjoy moving to and through a space and around or past an object. We also enjoy moving from one space to another, the experience of sequential space-to-space transition.

Sometimes the transition is subtle. One may be led through a sequence of varying spaces that provide a complete change in use and mood in such a way that the transition is almost imperceptible. Sometimes the transition is powerful. One may, by planned intent, be so compressed into a low, tight, dark space that release into a lofty, dazzling, free space is startling and dramatic. But, in any event, the skilled planner, by spatial manipulation, can play upon human emotions, reflexes, and responses as surely as does the skilled musician with the harp or flute or drum.

In one of the Summer Palace groups near the Jade Fountain to the west of Beijing, there once existed a walled enclosure known as the Court of the Concubine. Here, many years ago, lived the favorite concubine of one of the imperial princes. At one end of the courtyard stood her handsome residence of lacquered wood, tile, soft mats, and woven screens, and at the other end a light, airy pavilion, where she and her maids whiled away the summer afternoons. By legend, she had been brought from the open plains of Szechwan (Sichuan) Province, and she longed for its lakes, woods, meadows, and far mountains and for the wide spaces and the freedoms she had known there. And here, in the Summer Palace, this confining courtyard had now become her world.

The prince and his planners, wishing to please her, set out to create, within the limits of this space, an expansive paradise of freedom and delight. From her residence, to give the illusion of distance, the walls of the courtyard were stepped both inward and down to increase the apparent distance to the facing pavilion. Furthermore, to reduce the effect of rigid enclosure, the far plantings extended on either side of, and beyond, the lines of the converging walls. Even the size of the paving slabs was reduced from near to far. Moving outward, all textures changed imperceptibly

Space modulation. Lakeside park. (Deere and Company Administrative Headquarters, Moline, Illinois)

from the rough to the refined, and colors varied from the warm scarlets, reds, oranges, and yellows to the soft, cool, muted greens and lavenders and evanescent grays. Trees and plants in the foreground were bold in outline and foliage; those near the fragile pavilion were dwarfed and delicate. Water in the near fountain gurgled and splashed, while in the far ponds it lay mirrorlike and still. By such manipulations of perspective alone, the views from the concubine's quarters were made to seem expansive and the pavilion remote.

As the mistress left the terrace of her residence, to move out in the courtyard, she passed through a pungently aromatic clump of twisted junipers to come upon a curiously contorted "mountain stone" that rose serenely from a bed of moss. On the stone wall behind it was incised a pattern of stylized cloud forms with the poetic inscription "Above the plains of Szechwan the clouds rest lightly on the lofty mountain peaks." Here, ten steps from her terrace, yet hidden from view, she could be, in her thoughts, again among her mountains.

Just beyond, and angling temptingly out of sight, was a wall of emerald tile with an embossed tile dragon that seemed to writhe in splendid fury toward an open gateway. Inside the gate was a low stone bin spilling over with blooming peonies that laced the sunlit space with their pastel colors and delicious spicy fragrance. The sound of trickling water was meant to lead her eye to a cool and shadowy recess where a teakwood bench was placed near the light spray of a waterfall. From overhead, the branches of weeping willow cascaded down until the tips dipped into the water, where gold and silver fantails drifted languidly among the floating willow leaves. A meandering line of stepping stones led across the pond to disappear into the tracery of a bamboo grove where swaying finches trilled and filled the light air with soft and tremulous melody. The thin pathway led out beyond to a ferny opening beside the farthermost lobe of the pool, which here lay deep and silent. At its edge, a carved soapstone table and cushioned seats were arranged in the shade of a feathery smoke pine near the steps of the pavilion.

From the raised pavilion platform, looking back, a surprising new vista met the eye. For, by forced perspective, the residence seemed startlingly near. The path that led from it was ingeniously concealed, and another route of return invited one to new garden features and spaces.

This masterful courtyard was designed as an evolving complex of spaces, each complete in itself. And each transition, space to space and element to element, was contrived, with a deft assurance born of long centuries of practice, as a harmonious progression.

Space modulation! We in America have yet to learn the meaning of the words. But we *will* learn it in the crowded years ahead, for indeed we *must*; and we will develop it, without a doubt, to new heights of artistry.

Conditioned perception

Experience has taught us that what a thing is, is often of less importance than how we relate to it. The tree unseen or unremembered for us does not exist. The tree on the distant hilltop may be for the moment only an object that marks our path. As we approach, we see it to be a pear tree with many pleasant connotations. Coming close, we may be tempted to pick its fruit. Or perhaps in the noontime heat of an August day we may welcome the chance to lie in its shade, hang a child's swing from one of the lower branches, or spread a picnic at its base. In every case the tree is the same, but our impression of it changes with our sensed relationship. This being so, it would seem that should we place a tree or any other object in a space, we must consider not only the relationship of the object to the space but also the relationship of the object to all who will use the space. We must program the user's perception of the object by a sequence of planned relationships that will reveal its most appealing qualities.

Our impressions of an object or a space are conditioned by those we have already experienced or those anticipated. A bright, sunlit court is the more pleasant because we have just left the leafy coolness of an arbor. The splash and spray of a fountain are the more appreciated when we have approached it by way of the hot, dry sunbaked court. The birch clumps have more meaning when we sense that the river lies just ahead. The wide, free space is wider and freer to us when we realize that behind or beyond it we have known or will know the compression of confined spaces.

An evolving sequential experience.

We plan, then, not a single experience alone but rather a series of conditioned experiences that will heighten the interacting pleasurable impact of each. The Chinese epicure would understand this procedure, for to him or her the well-conceived banquet is a balanced succession of sensory delights. The thin, bland shark-fin soup, the brittle wafer of salt seaweed, the glutinous pungency of jellied egg, mealy water chestnuts with almond bits, the sweet astringent bite of crab-apple preserves, light, fluffy fried rice, steaming sweet-sour fish in persimmon sauce, bitter tea, crisp vegetables braised in light peanut oil, tender chewy bits of mushroom and meat, soft noodles in broth with pigeon eggs, the rich custard of ripe durian, mouth-cleansing tea, the cool acidulous mango and more tea, and finally the lightest and driest of wines. Each such meal is designed as an artistically balanced sequence of gustatory, tactile, visual, and intellectual experiences. Should we be satisfied with less artistry in planning the places and spaces of our living environment?

Experience, we may see, is compounded of that which we have perceived, that which we are perceiving, and that which we expect to perceive.

As we move through a space or a complex of spaces, we subconsciously remember that which we have passed or sensed. We thus orient backward in time and space, as well as forward, and find that each orientation gives meaning to the other and to all.

Sequence

Sequence in terms of planning, may be defined as a succession of perceptions having continuity. Sequences have no meaning except as we experience them. Conversely, all experience is sequential.

In nature, sequences are casual and free. Sometimes, but not always, they are progressive. Such a progression may be one of ascent, as in the experience of climbing from lowland to mountain peak; or one of direction, as westward from the central plains across the desert, over the mountains, through the valleys, and to the ocean; or one moving inward, from the sunlit edges of a forest to its deep, shadowy interior; or a progression of enclosure, complexity, intensity, convenience, or comprehension.

Sometimes the sequences of nature are revealed with no more order than in the haphazard impressions of an adult or a child wandering lackadaisically through the landscape, along a lonely stretch of seashore, or among the shallow pools of a tidal flat.

The planned sequence may be casual or disciplined. It may be rambling and intentionally devil-may-care, or it may, to achieve a purpose, be contrived with a high degree of order. The planned sequence is an extremely effective design device. It may induce motion, give direction, create cadence, instill a mood, reveal or "explain" an object or a series of objects in space, or even develop a philosophical concept.

Stepping-stones in the Kiyozumi Garden, Tokyo, Japan: a planned sequence of high design quality.

A planned sequence is a conscious organization of elements in space. It has a beginning and an end that is usually, but not always, the climax. Indeed, there may be several or many subclimaxes, each of which must satisfy its supporting sequence. Through its suggestion of motion and momentum, one feels compelled to move from the start of a sequence to its completion. Once initiated, sequence and induced movement must be brought to a logical, or at least a satisfying, conclusion.

It can be seen that all planned spaces are experienced by a progressive order of perceptions or events. It can also be appreciated that such sequences are subject to design control. A well-conceived plan determines not only the nature of climaxes but also their timing, their intensity, and the transitions by which they are evolved.

A sequence may be simple, compound, or complicated. It may be sustained, interrupted, varied, or modulated. It may be focalizing or diversifying, minute or extensive; and it may be subtle or powerful.

A sequence in its abstract beat or meter may, like the varied rhythms of a jungle drum, instill a feeling of excitement, warning,

> In Japanese art space assumed a dominant role and their attitude toward it was strengthened by two important Zen concepts. Zen affirmed the reality of immediate experience and yet declared its indivisibility from a present defined as "The moving infinity"—its oneness with life in eternal flux. Space was felt to be the only true essential, for only in space was movement possible. Space was the universal medium through which life moved in constant transformation, in which place and time were only relative states.
>
> Norman F. Carver, Jr.

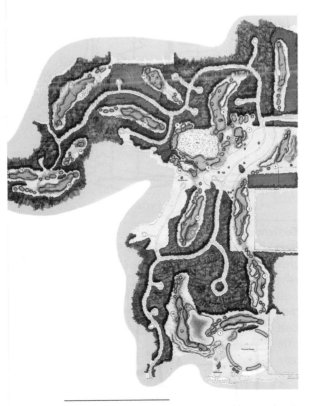

In this golf course plan, an exemplary work of landscape architecture, the cart paths are the *ways;* the fairways, rough, and greens are the *places.* (Boyne Highlands, Harbor Springs, Michigan)

PEDESTRIAN WAYS AND PLACES

Exploring the village of Ios, Greece

Steps are for more than up and down, they are a means of experiencing space and movement from one plane to another.

vegetation. Selective thinning is usually needed to articulate the road edges, enframe the views, and create a pleasantly modulated volumetric enclosure. Supplementary seeding and planting are, in the main, installed for slope protection and erosion control.

In the open, uncultivated countryside, a highly effective procedure is to seed all disturbed roadside areas to a hardy strain of wild grass. An undulating border is then mowed with a sickle bar, while the naturalized area beyond is left uncut to receive a crop of windblown seeds from the adjacent meadows and woodlands. Trees, shrubs, vines, weeds, and wildflowers combine in time to produce a maintenance-free roadside of great indigenous beauty.

Maximize the landscape values.   In every case, a well-designed roadway will be aligned through the landscape in such a way and be so constructed as to preserve and display the best features and views while attaining a harmonious fit. A good roadway provides comfort, interest, and pleasure to the traveler. A good roadway is also a good neighbor.

The approach drive

In the selection of a proposed site for any project, the off-site approaches are to be considered. What one experiences in coming or going may be a decisive factor. If, for example, the approach to an office center or residential community required passage through a freight yard or deteriorating neighborhood, one would look for other choices. Conversely, if the traveled route led through a forest preserve or past an attractive shopping court, this would be an incentive.

In locating a project on any site, the line of approach will influence or dictate not only the position of the structural elements but will probably also determine the relationships of the site use areas as well. Assuming that an approach drive is to be developed between an existing circulation drive or street and a proposed building, let us consider the design requirements. All else being equal, it should:

Announce itself at the passing roadway.   The driveway entrance is best located where it *wants* to be. This is at the point of the most logical penetration or highest visual interest along the fronting property line. The driveway should be well-identified by street number or appropriate entrance sign. It should be considered in relationship to adjacent driveway entrances and nearby landscape features. It will invite one in with recessive forms, as in a cove or harbor. In plan layout and site treatment it will set the theme for all that lies ahead. Often it will introduce at the gateway the materials and architectural theme that will be used throughout the site development.

Provide safe access and egress.   The driveway entrance is set at a point which will assure safe sighting distance up and down the passing street or roadway. It is not to be located just below a steep crest or around a sharp curve. Abrupt turning movements are avoided, and where possible, a glide-in entry with a generous turning radius is planned. On larger projects a deceleration lane is often provided if traffic volumes are heavy. A right-angle roadway entrance connection is best for two-way sighting.

Develop a pleasant transition.   We design an attractive space and theme modulation from driveway throat to building entrance,

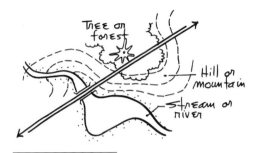

Whenever a roadway transects a natural landscape form, disruption and/or costly construction is the result:

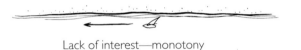

Lack of interest—monotony

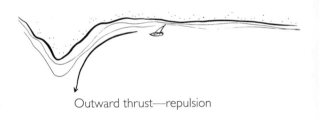

Outward thrust—repulsion

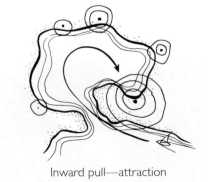

Inward pull—attraction

The pull of the harbor
The successful drive approach and forecourt will suggest a receptive cove. Usually the most attractive point on the cove periphery will be the entrance door or gate.

to parking court, and return. The drive width may vary, swelling at the drive entry, at the curves, and at the forecourt, always suggesting traffic *flow*.

We devise a transition from the character of the highway to the character of the project and structure, be it a residence, an apartment tower, a business office, a shopping mall, or a school. We move from the scale of the passing road to the scale of the building entrance court, from high velocity to repose. At one instant, for example, a person may be whisking along the trafficway at whistling speed; two minutes later the same person may be standing contemplatively at the building entrance. Between the two conditions are telling changes in mental attitude that must somehow be agreeably resolved. By the design of the driveway, the visitor must be prepared for the experience of arrival.

Be logical. The approach should present the driver with a minimum number of decisions. It is to be remembered that traffic tends to the right but also to the easier fork and to the easier grade. The pathway should be obvious but restrained. This is to say that it must read clearly to the driver while intruding as little as possible on the natural landscape.

Take full advantage of the site. The alignment of the driveway presents an excellent opportunity to plan for the visual unfolding or realization of the site—its topography, cover, vistas, views, and better landscape features. It should be so aligned as to reveal the pleasantly undulating edge of a woodlot or planting, the modeling of ground forms, and the counterplay of tree trunk against tree trunk, mass against mass, texture against texture, and color against color as one moves along.

Move with the contours. To preclude unnecessary disruption, the drive should flow with or angle easily across the contours. Often it may follow a broad ridgeline. Again, it may move up a drainageway to the side of and preserving the natural flow line, thus gaining positive drainage at one side while enjoying a degree of protection and concealment. Because a driveway and its gutters often provide for the storm-water flow from large areas of the property, the grades should be such as to permit surface flow without undue erosion. It should also provide for the gravity flow of any contiguous storm or sanitary sewers.

Avoid splitting the property. The driveway alignment will be such as to reserve as much land as possible in an undisturbed condition. The planner will strive to retain the best landscape features while defining cohesive use areas.

Be economical in layout. The driveway will be kept short for economy of construction and ease of maintenance. Other considerations include the relative ease of excavation, a balance of cut-and-fill materials, and the alternative costs of drainage structures or bridges.

Be safe. Avoid the crossing of other drives, walks, bicycle trails, or active use areas.

Be consistent. Keep the quality of the approach drive consonant with that of the site, the proposed project uses, and the structures.

Reveal the structures gradually. Design the approach road to make the first impression of the property and buildings attractive. A building is usually more interesting if seen from a curving drive approach, to show its form and extent before attention is centered on detail. Much of the nature of a structure is thus revealed by a planned exposition of its sculptural qualities

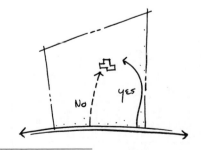

The approach loop Turn (*at left*) is contrary to normal flow. Approach from the center or right induces the correct turning movement.

Avoid splitting the property in locating the entrance drive.

from a drive that leads past or around it. Open successive views to the structure, each from the optimum distance and position and with the best attainable enframement.

The entrance court

The entrance court is an integral part of both the approach drive and the building. It terminates the one, introduces the other, and unifies the two.

The driveway should never appear to collide with a building but should rather sweep toward and past it.

Approach from the right.   Since in the United States a car moves in the right lane of traffic, we have developed taxicab and private car conditioning that tells us, as we near a destination, to chart a course that will bring the right side of the vehicle toward the building entrance. This right–curb approach is valid mainly because of two–way streets, which make pulling to the left curb inconvenient, illegal, or dangerous and usually all three.

Where possible, plan a one-way loop.   One-way traffic at a building entrance is always preferable. It is safer. There is also a psychological advantage, for a driver with right wheels to the curb feels superior and, for some reason, very clever.

Accommodate the left-hand approach where necessary.   On some sites an approach from the left is the only way possible. If this is planned, we try to arrange sufficient depth to permit the drive to swing past the entrance and circle back to achieve the favored position. If, perforce, the drive must lead in from the left, we do what we can to make this feasible by making the point of discharge obvious, by providing a landing platform opposite the building entrance, or by planning for discharge within a paved forecourt.

Consider the climatic conditions.   The approach court and building entry are planned for all conditions of weather, darkness, and light. Visitors are to be protected from storm winds, rain, and glaring sun. Since paving is hot in the summer and cold in the winter, the building is not to be planned as an island in a sea of paving. We avoid the long walk or the long view across paving toward the building entrance.

Avoid the need for backing.   The backing of vehicles near entranceways, especially in areas where children may be congregated or playing, is to be scrupulously avoided.

Parking compounds

Parking compounds provide an essential link between vehicular circulation ways, approach drives, and their termini. They are designed for the safe and efficient storage of cars. When space and site conditions permit, they are usually located beyond the building entrance as one approaches by car. Sometimes, however, they may serve in themselves as the approach court to one or more buildings. Whatever the planned function, it is to be accommodated and clearly expressed.

Test all plan possibilities.   The siting of parking areas is best achieved by the study of alternative shapes and flow lines in relation to the building and topographical features. The most prevalent parking layouts are easily diagrammed for adaptation and testing.

> *The psychology of arrival is more important than you think. If it is not obvious where to park, if there is no room to park when you get there, if you stumble into the back door looking for the front entrance, or if the entrance is badly lighted, you will have subjected your guests to a series of annoyances which will linger long in their subconscious. No matter how warm your hearth or how beautiful your view, the overall effect will be dimmed by these first irritations.*
>
> Thomas D. Church

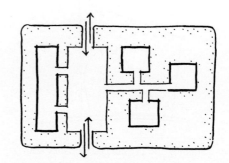

Provide off-street parking
Single and clustered buildings are benefited by the provision of internal parking courts.

Approach, pass, and park. Ideally, a driver will approach with the building to his or her right, discharge the passengers, continue to the parking space, and return on foot by a pleasant and convenient route to the doorway. Ideally, too, upon departing the driver would be able to pick up the car and circle back to passengers at the building entrance.

Screen the parking areas. A direct view from the entrance court into the parking area is not usually desirable. Except for commercial or business office projects, a well-placed parking or service compound is convenient but incidental to and secluded from the building.

Consider multiple use. A parking compound may be located for shared use by several buildings or activity areas concurrently. Or it may serve one purpose in daytime and another for evening or off-peak hours. Parking areas, when not in use for their primary purpose, may also serve other functions such as recreation, assembly, or temporary storage.

Accommodate the vehicle. Since the parking court is planned for the efficient storage of automobiles, it must be designed with full understanding of the maneuvering requirements of the car. These dictate gradients, turning radii, aisle and stall widths, and paving textures, which may well vary to differentiate lanes of movement and areas for parking storage.

Consider the disabled. The parking compound with its backings and turnings is an area of special hazard for pedestrians with impaired vision, hearing, mobility, or other handicap. For them, bays with widened stalls are to be reserved near building entrances. Moreover, as an added safety precaution and to preclude the random movement of vehicles, the traffic flow pattern is to be kept simple and well-defined, with the entire area illuminated. Those with parcels to carry, strollers to wheel, or children in tow will be among the grateful.

Segregate service traffic. Service vehicles range in size from small motorized carts and pickups to larger delivery and refuse trucks. They require convenient access to building entrances, collection stations, mechanical rooms, utility vaults, and similar locations. When practical, service vehicle circulation and parking areas are separated from passenger automobiles and are designed to accommodate the larger turning radii, maneuvering space, and holding patterns required.

Plan for emergency access. Fire trucks, ambulances, police cars, and utility service vans require building access. The site plan must ensure that these vehicles can get where they need to go. If direct road access cannot be provided, walks and other paved areas may be utilized, provided they are designed with this purpose in mind.

Travel by Rail, Air, and Water

Aside from the automobile, the traditional means of transporting people and goods have been trains, planes, and waterborne vessels. Their routes, crossings, and points of convergence have set the locations of our towns and cities and provided their outlying regions with the essential outlets for agricultural products and manufactured goods.

The railroads, ships, and airlines have served their purpose well. Recently, however, they have experienced increasing problems in their stubborn insistence, and sometimes forced requirement, that they maintain their original all-purpose role of moving

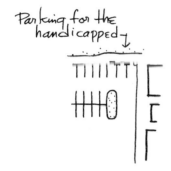

Consider the handicapped
Reserve stalls of extra width, with depressed curb, near the destination.

goods and people concurrently. The two functions are incompatible. As new forms of conveyance by rail, water, and air emerge, the carriers will be highly specialized, as will be their routes, equipment, and terminals. Improved means of transit, transportation, and distribution will change established concepts of *land use*, *community*, and *city* and require a whole new planning approach.

Travel by rail

Passenger travel by rail in its most recent forms is known as *rapid transit*. Some types are streamlined versions of the old interurban or commuter trains. They move on fixed rails on grade, underground, or elevated. Some vehicles are equipped with steel wheels, some with wheels that are coated. All are highly automated and can be computer-controlled. Other types use linked cars which are suspended from or propelled along a single or multiple glideway. All systems have been improved to a point at which they are light, bright, environmentally sound, and highly efficient. They can move people in groups from point to point within a region far more rapidly and at less cost per mile than the passenger car or bus. Why then hasn't rapid transit been more widely accepted?

First, it does carry many more people to more places each day than is generally realized. The advanced systems of San Francisco, Toronto, Montreal, and Washington, D.C., are promising examples, as are the guided systems of Disneyland and Disney World. Where rapid transit has not succeeded or has failed to realize its full potential, there are common causes at the root of the failure. As for instance:

Elevated transitway.

The dwellings within the communities served are too widely dispersed.   In the typical single-family-home suburb, it often takes longer to drive to or be driven to the station than to ride from station to destination.

The transit connections are not direct.   At the downtown end of the line the station is often blocks away from the office, shopping, or cultural centers.

The stations are inadequate.   They are often grim. Old railway stations or other obsolete structures are sometimes converted to the new use without remodeling or thought for the convenience, comfort, or pleasant relaxation of the waiting passengers.

The passing scenery is ugly.   Some routes, using the old railroad trackage or right-of-way, provide the most extensive slumming excursions extant. By established railroad custom, the public must ride the same route as the tank cars, flatcars, crated chickens, and bawling calves, past the rear doors of the soap factory, junkyard, and slaughterhouse. It is not a good way to attract or hold would-be commuters.

In 1950, in a typical metropolitan region, 30 percent of the workers commuted to work for an average travel time of 13 minutes.

40 years later, in 1990, 90 percent of workers commuted to work for an average time of 35 minutes.

Community transit stations should have direct vertical access to the central convenience plaza around which shops and multifamily apartments are clustered.

The transit potential

The mass movement of people at high velocities between areas of residential concentration and regional activity centers has manifest advantages. Among these are predictability, safety, and savings in time, land area, and energy. The era of transit is at hand, perhaps as much by necessity as by reason. It will come into its own as a flourishing travel mode when, but only when:

Regional rapid transit

Energy conservation (economic necessity) may soon force us to do what reason so far has not.

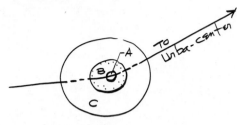

Transit node community   A—Station with minicar storage and recharge. Multifamily dwellings and convenience center. B—Dwellings within walking distance. C— Minitransit access by all-weather golf carts or electric bus.

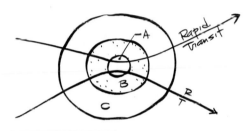

Urba-center   A—Multilevel transit terminal. B—Primary urban activity zone. Terraced pedestrian domain. Movement by elevators, escalators, and moving walks. C—Supporting urban activities. Movement by minibus or mini-rail. Decked parking but no surface automobile traffic. Goods distributed by tubes and belt-ways from peripheral transport terminals.

The solution to public transit is the planning of activity *centers* to which people can ride together.

- The transitway is planned as a means by which to structure or restructure the region and new types of residential communities and urban activity cores.
- The experience of travel by rapid transit is conceived in terms of safe, efficient, and pleasurable movement from center to center.
- The transit facility is programmed and planned as a complete and interrelated whole. In other words, communities, stations, vehicles, routes, and termini are planned together as a smoothly operating *system.*

The fleeting landscape

From the transit cars, as from the automobile, the passing scene is observed as a continuing flow of impressions. Just as in a static composition we take pleasure in harmonious relationships, so it is that in the blending compositions of the passing scene we seek harmonious transitions. That which is abrupt, chaotic, or inappropriate we find to be displeasing. That which is fitting and orderly and "evolves" we find agreeable.

Nearby objects streaking past have little meaning in themselves. They may serve effectively as screening, either as a blur of loose foliage or as a solid wall, earth bank, or building. They develop cadences, sometimes pleasurable, sometimes annoying. They may distract and disturb by their flicker and by the fact that one strains to distinguish and identify them. By their jittery insistence they often destroy the scenic qualities inherent in the landscape. Viewing in such cases would be made more pleasant if the foreground objects were removed or simplified.

As from the moving automobile, visual interest from a moving transit car is centered in the middle distance or on the distant view. The far view changes slowly and soon becomes monotonous unless given variety by things observed in the middle ground. To be enjoyable to the viewer, the midground interest or action must be consistent with the background and with the modulating foreground enframement.

Travel by water

When we think of a boat in motion, we think of a smoothly gliding hull, a curving wake of tumbling water, and dancing light. The course of a boat, like the water through which it moves, is fluid and undulating. Having no fixed track or roadway, it curves in wide arcs and must be given ample space for maneuvering. Even at rest at its mooring, a boat seems mobile. All plan lines relating to boats at rest or in motion should suggest this streamlined fluid mobility. In every way possible, smooth flow should be encouraged and obstructions eliminated. The heavy, the rough, the jagged, the sharp are out of place. They are destructive and impeding in fact and disturbing by connotation. Travel by boat seems almost frictionless. All things and places are left, passed, and approached on the glide. Movement is relatively slow. Except for the tacking sailboat, change of direction is seldom abrupt. The middle and far distances become, visually, a panoramic background for the objects and details to be seen more closely at hand. With the sky for the overhead plane and water for the base, interest is centered on the vertical.

Being exposed to the elements and the tides, a boat requires for its mooring a sheltered harbor or a protective pier. Harbor and pier provide such shelter by topography, structure, or a combination of both. They are points of transition between the water and the land, where the mobile and free meet the static. The fact of this meeting might well be developed and expressed in all plan forms. Indeed, no great stretch of the imagination is required to understand that *any* structure related to water and boatways gains when the full drama of the relationship is exploited.

A summer cottage on a lake or bay, for example, is best conceived as a planned transition from land to water. It relates the solid to the fluid, the mineral to the aqueous, the confined to the expansive, and strong cast shadow to shimmering light. Often it provides also a transition from car to yacht, yawl, or rowboat. It is terraced down; it overhangs, overlooks; it screens off and then subtly or dramatically reveals; it embraces, ramps, or steps into, invites view or movement from land to water and water to land. It accentuates, by lucid structural relationships, the highest qualities of land and water. At the land approach, it is of the land; at the water's edge, it is of the water.

A riverside restaurant, if worthy of its site, will orient to the river and its traffic and display it in all its motion and color. On the landward side, it will take its form from the features of the land and from the passing walk or street or highway. On the riverside, it will be shaped to the line of the river's flow and to the curve of approaching craft. It is a rewarding experience to dine in such a waterside restaurant, with its glass–walled dining room projected and elevated to catch the flowing river view, or at shaded tables set on a terrace or deck beside the river wall, or at tables spaced out on the pier beside the bobbing boats and lapping water. In the same way, with the seaside hotel, the waterfront park, the bridge, the pier, the harbor, and the lighthouse, our site plans and structures will express the land–and–water meeting.

Boatways and waterways, when well conceived, have few detrimental characteristics and many attractive features. Large bodies of water ameliorate the climate, enliven the landscape, and provide a direct and inexpensive means of travel and transportation. Rivers follow the valley floors. Usually their easy gradient encourages travel along their banks as well as upon their surface. They, together with their feeding streams and rivulets, promote a lush growth of vegetation and the most pleasing landscape environment of the regions through which they pass. All waterways attract industrial, commercial, and residential development. How can they all be accommodated? Which should have preference? The solution here is not usually one of blanket prohibition, for such prohibitions tend to dam up overriding pressures, but is rather one of planned relationships. Lucky the region or city that is empathically related to its rivers, lakes, canals, or waterfront.

Travel by air

The view from a plane unfolds a modeled and checkered landscape of towns, hills, lakes, rivers, valleys, farmland, field, and forest moving slowly under the wings. We are impressed with the continuity of the landscape. We sense, perhaps for the first time, that every object in the landscape is related to the whole. Sight distances are great. Visible areas are enormous. Objects, to be seen,

Proposal for a boating park.

Riverside restaurant. (Pittsburgh, Pennsylvania)

must be simple, bold, and contrasting in colors or textures. They are most often read from the air by their shadows. All essential plan forms or objects requiring recognition from the air, and especially at the airports and their approaches, must be so emphasized.

Travel by plane is *flight* and is seemingly effortless while one is airborne. This smooth, flashing speed accentuates the frictions and delays of the airport and cross-country travel beyond it. The frictions of port transfer and of port-to-city distance must be drastically reduced by improved land and transportation planning. The competitive port of the future will have fast and easy access to other transportation centers and to central discharge points. There are other problems to be overcome. Among them, the deafening din at the airport aprons is mounting, decibel by decibel, to a point at which it will soon become unbearable. Sometime before that critical point or very shortly after, the pressure of economics and the advance of science will have reduced the ear-shattering roar to a pleasant whistling hum.

An airport should rightly be planned as a *port*. Here, again, in this *air* harbor the land meets an opposite. This meeting and all induced transitions are to be analyzed and expressed. All current or foreseeable requirements and characteristics of planes, at rest or in flight, are to be accommodated. Further, the joint use of airfields by cargo and passenger planes with their varying speeds, needs, and capabilities will no longer be tolerable. Transport planes will be related to industrial and distribution centers. Passenger planes and ports will be linked to centers of population and urban activity. From the surrounding towns and cities new exclusive or classified approach roads will be necessary, as will a system of strategically placed air taxi stations. In this light, we can consider an airport primarily in terms of a continuing and ultimate experience of travel in which passengers can arrive by car, park, check baggage, and enplane or arrive by plane, pick up baggage, and leave by car, limousine, or tramway in one swift, pleasant, uninterrupted swoop. There are, of course, many other considerations in the planning of an airport.

Airports require large areas of flat topography or land that can be readily modified to give long, level runways. Because such areas are often of necessity remote, the tendency of airports is to bring to the spot as many port facilities as possible. Hotel, theaters, conference rooms, libraries, and even recreation, amusement, and shopping centers have been planned into the airports as revenue producers. In the interest of increased efficiency all extraneous uses must be limited in the future.

A municipal airport is no longer a landing strip, a dollysock, and a ticket booth. The modern airport is an extremely intricate complex of myriad related functions. These must be studied as to their optimum relationship to the cities and the region that the airport serves. Like all projects planned in the landscape, the airport must be studied in terms of minimizing its negative impacts and increasing its benefits.

People Movers

The need for increasing numbers of persons to get from here to there, usually in a hurry, has given rise to a whole array of vehicles and devices that have been grouped together in the category of transportation and circulation systems. Without them, many of our newer governmental, business office, and commercial centers and even zoos and botanic gardens could no longer function. In type and size they vary according to the distance and height to be traveled, the number of passengers to be carried, and the rate of speed required.

Moving walkways, chairways, and escalators. These are a low-speed, step-on-and-off means of movement that can be used alone or in combination, indoors or out.

Automated cars. Electronically controlled automated cars that move on rails or guideways are, in effect, horizontal elevators. Used singly or linked, they can transport groups of people at moderate speeds for distances ranging from several hundred yards to several miles. They are smaller campus and in-town adaptations of the longer-range and faster subway, glideway, and monorail transit vehicles.

Small bus trains. Jeeps with trailers may be open to the sky or provided with full, all-weather protection. Bus trains are used frequently in recreation or exhibition areas and are often equipped with public address systems.

Minibuses. Small buses of all sizes and shapes have longer ranges, higher speeds, and greater maneuverability than bus trains. Some minibuses, used to link airport waiting rooms with distant plane pods, are of "maxi" proportions, carrying many dozens of passengers and hoisting them by hydraulic lifts to the level of the plane door.

Long-range buses. Long-range buses on separate busway routes are an increasingly popular form of suburban-urban trans-

The bikeway as a lineal park.

portation. They make stops at strategically located community waiting shelters or at one or more peripheral parking fields and then provide express linkage on reserved lanes to downtown centers.

Cable cars.　Traversing steep slopes or mountainsides (as in Bogotá and Caracas) or skimming high overhead on suspended aerial cables (as at Cologne in Germany), cable cars can leap chasms, rivers, and ranges with safety and ease.

Bicycles, tricycles, and mopeds.　While self-propelled, these vehicles are not to be overlooked as people movers. It is only recently that, for the first time in many decades, the annual sale of bicycles in the United States has exceeded that of automobiles. Where off-road, off-sidewalk paths and trails are provided, especially as lineal parklike connectors to community and regional centers of attraction, bicycles and electric carts blossom into use.

The electric cart.　The modified golf cart on three to four wheels, with all-weather provision and carrying from one to a dozen passengers, is becoming popular. It will provide the ideal future link between home and transit station, where it can be easily stored and recharged while awaiting the transit rider's return. The use of such carts together with cycles for intra-community travel would reduce the need for internal roads and reliance on the more costly, more space-demanding automobile.

Integrated Systems

It might be thought that the proliferating assortment of people conveyers would lead to utter chaos in their weaving in and out, up and down, and back and forth on crisscrossing routes and trajectories. Far from it. These vehicles provide, at last, the components needed to fit together a rational *system* of multimodal transportation. They provide the key to the structuring or restructuring of the regions and metropolitan areas around intensive multilevel transit-transportation hubs. These concentrated activity centers, freed of automobile traffic and the divisive interchanges, streets, and parking lots, can become again urbane and delightful pedestrian domains.

The sterile vehicular trafficways and parking lots will be replaced by terraced plazas, garden courts and malls, and refreshing in-city parks through which people can move about on foot or be transported from level to level and center to center in year-round comfort.

Automobiles will swish through the open countryside on controlled-access parkways, freed of trucks and buses. They will provide safe and pleasant alternative means of connection between the urban and regional nodes, where they will be "stabled" at the periphery.

New integrated *systems* of circulation give promise of innovative and vastly superior concepts of land and community planning.

RESIDENTIAL STREETS

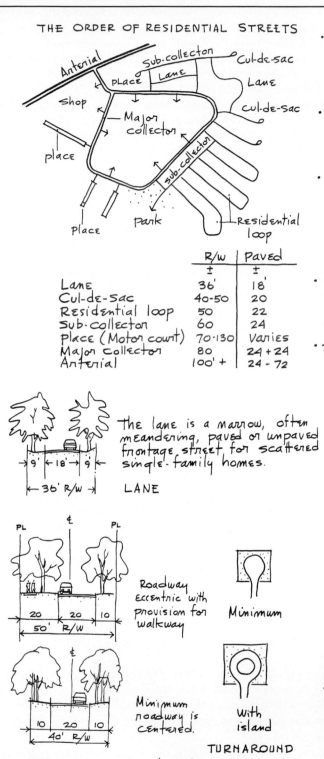

THE ORDER OF RESIDENTIAL STREETS

Arterial · Sub-collector · Cul-de-sac · Place · Lane · Shop · Major collector · place · place · Park · Residential loop · sub-collector · Lane · Cul-de-sac

	R/W ±	Paved ±
Lane	36'	18'
Cul-de-sac	40-50	20
Residential loop	50	22
Sub-collector	60	24
Place (Motor court)	70-130	Varies
Major collector	80	24 + 24
Arterial	100' +	24 - 72

- Low-speed traffic on neighborhood loop and cul-de-sac streets and in residential motor courts (places) often permits sharing the paved way with bicycles and pedestrians.

- Sidewalks and/or bikeways are usually provided on one or both sides of sub-collector drives where required for pathway linkage.

- Separate walks and bicycle paths may also be prescribed along major collector streets, arterial parkways, and boulevards— except where pedestrians or bicycles are to be accommodated by paths through internal community greenways.

- Direct building frontage and/or driveway connections are best prohibited on arterials, collectors, and some sub-collectors.

- Parking is not to be permitted on any community street.

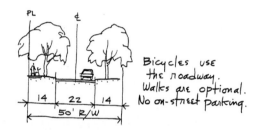

The lane is a narrow, often meandering, paved or unpaved frontage street for scattered single-family homes.

9 ← 18 → 9
← 36' R/W →

LANE

14 | 22 | 14
← 50' R/W →

Bicycles use the roadway. Walks are optional. No on-street parking.

Along these frontage streets are grouped the single-family homes and residential clusters of most neighborhoods. Low traffic volumes, low speeds, and good visibility are the essentials.

RESIDENTIAL LOOP STREET

20 | 20 | 10
← 50' R/W →

Roadway eccentric with provision for walkway

Minimum

10 | 20 | 10
← 40' R/W →

Minimum roadway is centered.

With island

TURNAROUND

The cul-de-sac provides desirable residential frontage on a low-speed lineal accessway, with a sense of neighborhood. It should not exceed 1000'± without intermediate turn-arounds.

THE CUL-DE-SAC

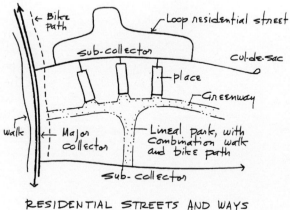

Bike Path · Loop residential street · sub-collector · Cul-de-sac · place · Greenway · Walk · Major collector · Lineal park, with combination walk and bike path · sub-collector

RESIDENTIAL STREETS AND WAYS

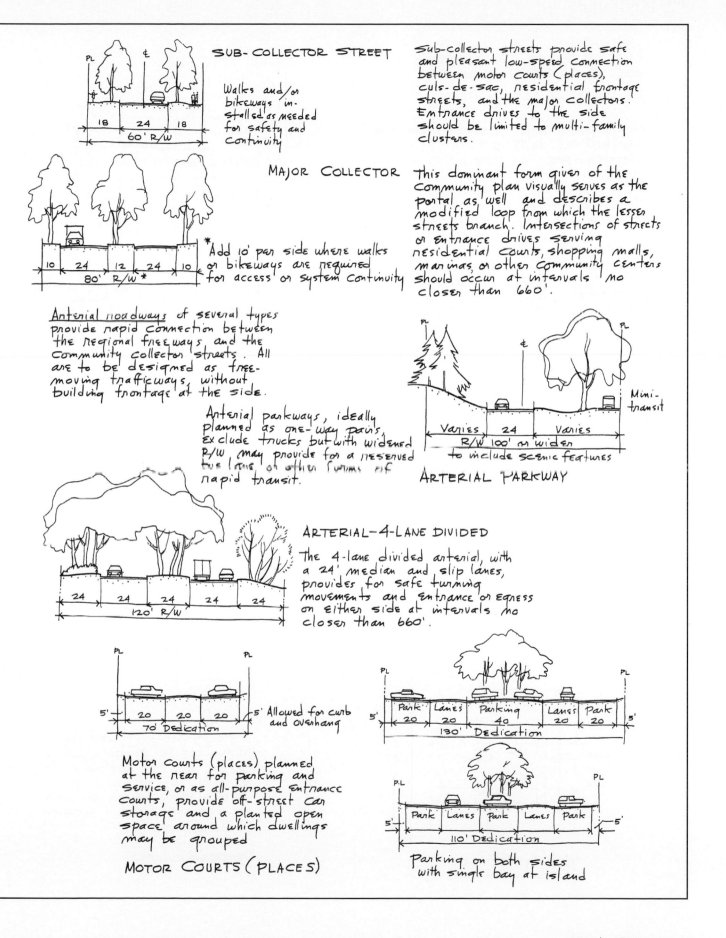

SUB-COLLECTOR STREET

Walks and/or bikeways installed as needed for safety and continuity

18 | 24 | 18
60' R/W

Sub-collector streets provide safe and pleasant low-speed connection between motor courts (places), culs-de-sac, residential frontage streets, and the major collectors. Entrance drives to the side should be limited to multi-family clusters.

MAJOR COLLECTOR

10 | 24 | 12 | 24 | 10
80' R/W *

*Add 10' per side where walks or bikeways are required for access or system continuity

This dominant form giver of the community plan visually serves as the portal as well and describes a modified loop from which the lesser streets branch. Intersections of streets or entrance drives serving residential courts, shopping malls, marinas, or other community centers should occur at intervals no closer than 660'.

Arterial roadways of several types provide rapid connection between the regional freeways and the community collector streets. All are to be designed as free-moving trafficways, without building frontage at the side.

Arterial parkways, ideally planned as one-way pairs, exclude trucks but with widened R/W, may provide for a reserved bus lane or other forms of rapid transit.

Varies | 24 | Varies
R/W 100' or wider
to include scenic features

Mini-transit

ARTERIAL PARKWAY

ARTERIAL-4-LANE DIVIDED

The 4-lane divided arterial, with a 24' median and slip lanes, provides for safe turning movements and entrance or egress on either side at intervals no closer than 660'.

24 | 24 | 24 | 24 | 24
120' R/W

5' | 20 | 20 | 20 | 5' Allowed for curb and overhang
70' Dedication

Motor courts (places) planned at the rear for parking and service, or as all-purpose entrance courts, provide off-street car storage and a planted open space around which dwellings may be grouped

MOTOR COURTS (PLACES)

5' | Park 20 | Lanes 20 | Parking 40 | Lanes 20 | Park 20 | 5'
130' Dedication

5' | Park | Lanes | Park | Lanes | Park | 5'
110' Dedication

Parking on both sides with single bay at island

PARKING

First determine the number and type of spaces required. (1)

As a rule of thumb: (2)

Single-family home	2 spaces/dwelling
Attached res. units	2 " "
Garden apts.	1.75 " "
Mid-rise "	1.5+ " "
High-rise "	1.5 " "
Hotels and motels	1 space/room
Restaurants	1 space/50 s.f. of patron area
Convenience shopping	1 space/250 s.f. of gross fl. area
Other commercial dept. stores, banks	1 space/300 g.f.a.
Bus. and prof. off.	1 space/400 g.f.a.
Churches, theatres, auditorium, etc.	1 space ±/3 seats
Schools (Jr.-Sr.)	1 space/200 g.fl.a. excluding gym.
Hospitals	1 space/bed
Industrial	1 space/2 employ
Parks/recreation	Varies

---

(1) Consider the parking of buses, service vehicles, compact cars, and cycles.

(2) To be modified to meet local zoning or other requirements. Staff parking is additional.

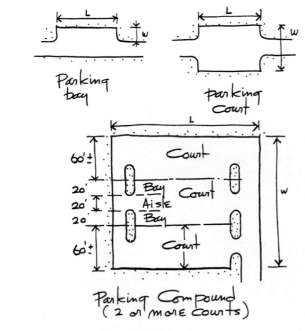

Parking bay

Parking Court

Parking Compound
(2 or more courts)

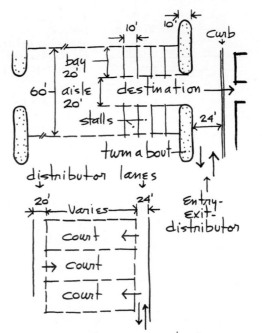

distributor lanes

In the trial layout of large parking areas these approximate (rounded) dimensions are useful. Actual dimensions are later adjusted in the construction drawings.

Learn the components.

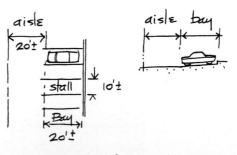

Perpendicular parking is standard for parking areas having two-way traffic in the aisles. It requires more space than angle parking and more difficult turning movements.

Perpendicular

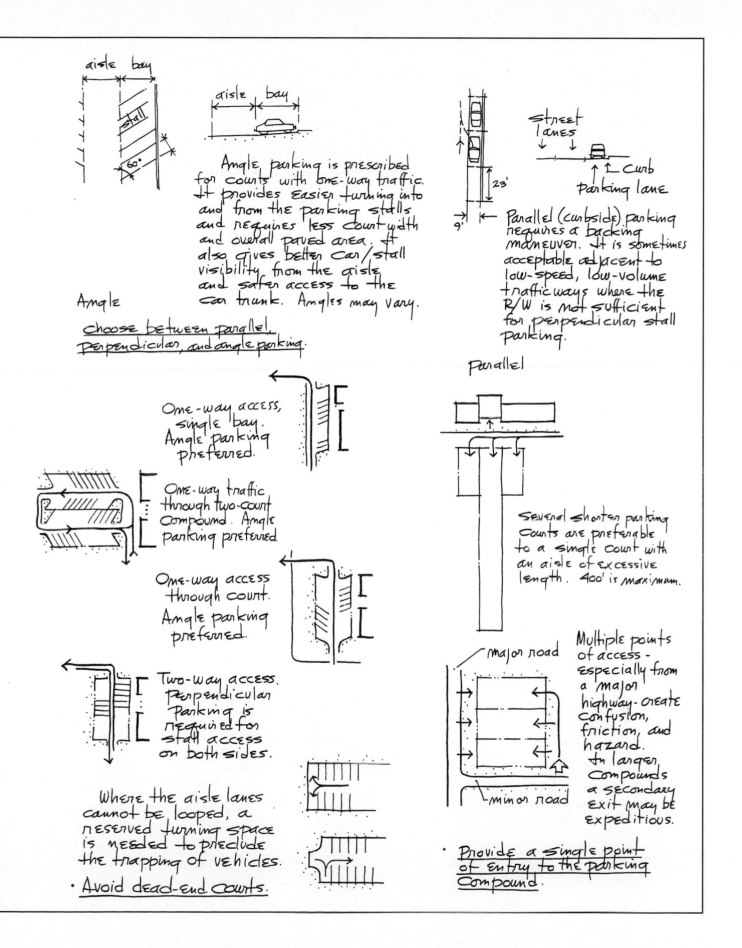

aisle bay

stall

60°

Angle parking is prescribed for courts with one-way traffic. It provides easier turning into and from the parking stalls and requires less court width and overall paved area. It also gives better car/stall visibility from the aisle and safer access to the car trunk. Angles may vary.

aisle bay

Angle

Choose between parallel, perpendicular, and angle parking.

street lanes

23'

9'

curb

Parking lane

Parallel (curbside) parking requires a backing maneuver. It is sometimes acceptable adjacent to low-speed, low-volume trafficways where the R/W is not sufficient for perpendicular stall parking.

Parallel

One-way access, single bay. Angle parking preferred.

One-way traffic through two-court compound. Angle parking preferred.

One-way access through court. Angle parking preferred.

Two-way access. Perpendicular parking is required for stall access on both sides.

Several shorter parking courts are preferable to a single court with an aisle of excessive length. 400' is maximum.

major road

minor road

Multiple points of access - especially from a major highway - create confusion, friction, and hazard. In larger compounds a secondary exit may be expeditious.

Where the aisle lanes cannot be looped, a reserved turning space is needed to preclude the trapping of vehicles.

· Avoid dead-end courts.

· Provide a single point of entry to the parking compound.

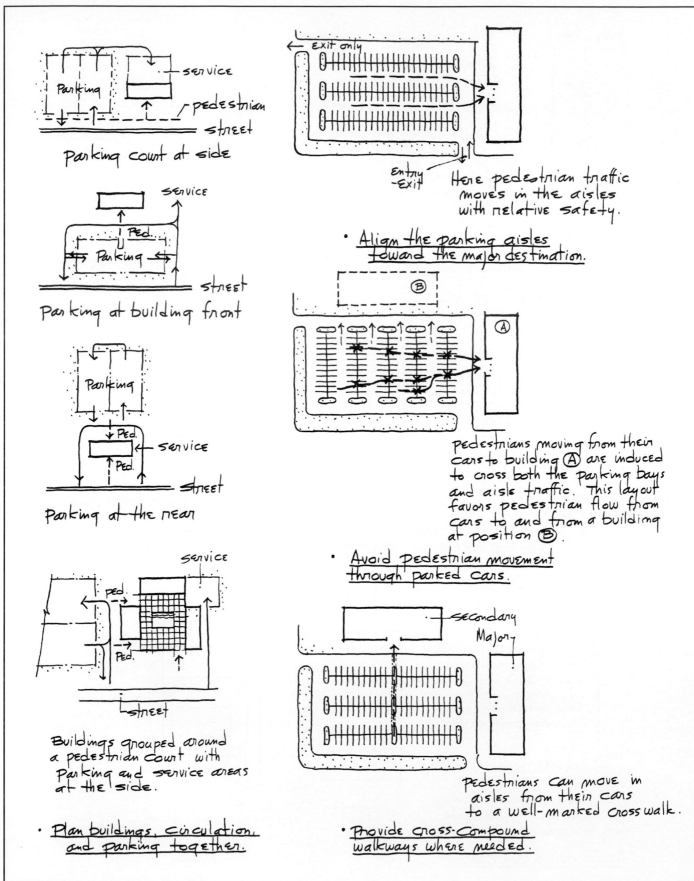

Parking court at side

Parking at building front

Parking at the rear

Buildings grouped around
a pedestrian court with
parking and service areas
at the side.

- Plan buildings, circulation,
and parking together.

Here pedestrian traffic
moves in the aisles
with relative safety.

- Align the parking aisles
toward the major destination.

Pedestrians moving from their
cars to building A are induced
to cross both the parking bays
and aisle traffic. This layout
favors pedestrian flow from
cars to and from a building
at position B.

- Avoid pedestrian movement
through parked cars.

Pedestrians can move in
aisles from their cars
to a well-marked crosswalk.

- Provide cross-compound
walkways where needed.

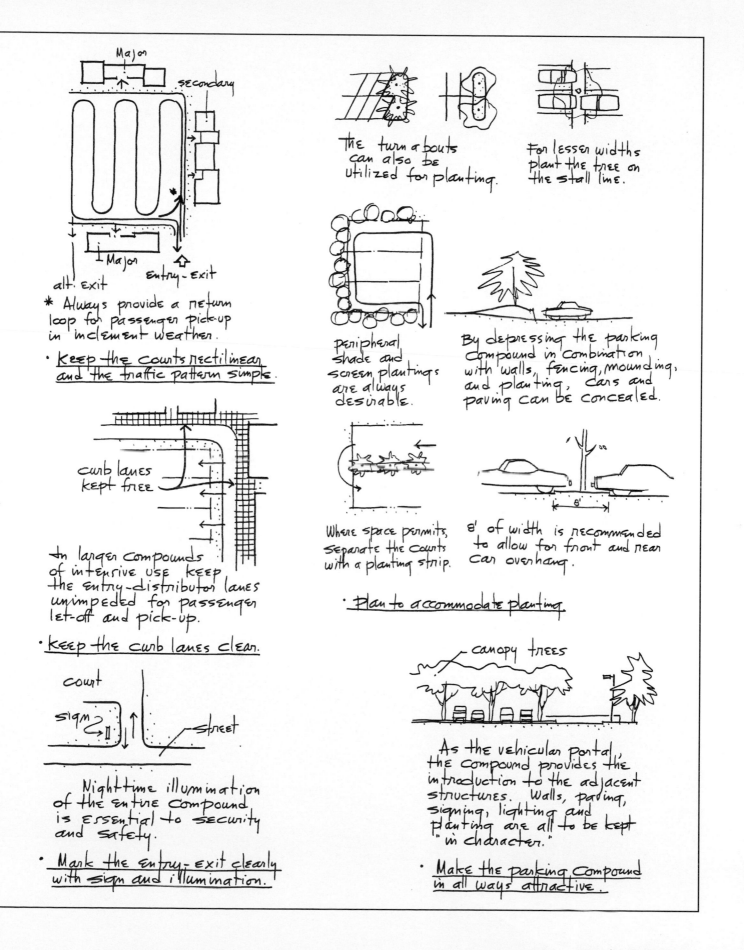

Major

secondary

Major

alt. exit

Entry-Exit

* Always provide a return loop for passenger pick-up in inclement weather.

· Keep the courts rectilinear and the traffic pattern simple.

curb lanes kept free

In larger compounds of intensive use keep the entry-distributor lanes unimpeded for passenger let-off and pick-up.

· Keep the curb lanes clear.

court

sign

street

Nighttime illumination of the entire compound is essential to security and safety.

· Mark the entry-exit clearly with sign and illumination.

The turnabouts can also be utilized for planting.

For lesser widths plant the tree on the stall line.

Peripheral shade and screen plantings are always desirable.

By depressing the parking compound in combination with walls, fencing, mounding, and planting, cars and paving can be concealed.

Where space permits, separate the courts with a planting strip.

8' of width is recommended to allow for front and rear car overhang.

· Plan to accommodate planting.

canopy trees

As the vehicular portal, the compound provides the introduction to the adjacent structures. Walls, paving, signing, lighting and planting are all to be kept "in character."

· Make the parking compound in all ways attractive.

14
STRUCTURES

I*N THEORY*, architectural and engineering structures are conceived by their designers as the ideal resolution of purpose, time, and place. When this is achieved, the resulting structure—be it a cabin or cathedral, an aqueduct or amphitheatre, a windmill, barn, or suspension bridge—is memorable for its artistry. The cities and landscapes of history are studded with such masterworks, many surviving as cherished cultural landmarks. It is fortunate that in contemporary times we may travel to study and learn from them —to understand their admirable traits and qualities.

What qualities, then, are common to the great examples?

Common Denominators

It can be observed that, with few exceptions, at the time of their building, these notable structures:

- Fulfilled and expressed their purpose—directly and with clarity.
- Reflected the cultural mores of their time, location, and users.
- Responded to the climate, the weather, and the dictates of seasons.
- Applied or extended the state of the art and current technology.
- Fitted compatibly into the built environs and the living land-scape.

Purpose

We have proposed that the adage, "Form follows function," is valid only when it is understood that the term *function* transcends the

Facing page: Pavilion, The Crosby Arboretum, Picayune, Mississippi

delimiting connotation of the "utilitarian." The term *function* in the context of expressive design is comprehensive and includes such considerations as traditional values, ethics, aesthetic quality, feasibility, acceptability, and fitness. Only if all such requisites are satisfied can it be said of a structure or form that it truly fulfills its intended function or purpose.

Culture

The culture of a community or nation is an evolving state of being or communal mind-set. It implies, although sometimes overkindly, a certain level of civilization. As such, it is at any given time the manifestation of a people's beliefs and aspirations—those ideas or things that are acceptable and those that are not. This cultural litmus test is by custom applied not only to dress, foods, and works of music, literature, and art, but perhaps most particularly to buildings and other structures.

Cultural approbation allows for obvious improvement and some innovation, but rejects vociferously, and sometimes violently, that which seems out of place or offensive. This being so, it would follow that the architect, engineer, or landscape architect in the planning stage might well take pains to ensure, insofar as possible, public approval and acceptance.

Successful structures and planned landscapes not only conform to discerning public taste, they serve to upgrade and refine it.

Locality

A masterful structure is an expression of *place*. It responds to and "grows out of" its site. It accentuates its positive qualities. At best, the design of structures is a highly developed exercise in creative synergy.

Sensitive design reflects, distills, and often makes more dramatic the indigenous landscape character. It utilizes every favorable aspect of the topography. It is aware of and braces for the directional winds and storm. It opens out to the breeze and favorable views. It traces the orbit of the sun. It designs into and composes with the adjacent built environment.

The mark of a well-conceived structure is that it enhances rather than degrades its site and surroundings.

Technology

Architecture, engineering, and landscape architecture are at the same time an *art* and a *science*. The art has to do mainly with visual qualities—craftsmanship, composition, and the appearance of things. Science entails the organization of structural and mechanical systems, and the satisfaction of human needs, all in accordance with the timeless laws and principles of nature.

Technology in recent years has advanced with astounding rapidity. In the design of structures, for example, it was not long ago that prestressed concrete was unknown, as was steel reinforcing, electronics—or even electricity for that matter. Now, with a broad range of new materials and construction techniques the possibilities have expanded manyfold. With the emergence of computer technology the design of physical structures has taken on new dimensions.

We contemporaries proceed in blithe disregard of the truths and lessons of history. If we, proud spirits that we are, must learn our truth firsthand, there need be no problem, for we are surrounded by examples of the good and the bad and need only develop a discerning eye to distinguish art from error.

> *A building is a thing in itself. It has a right to be there, as it is, and together with nature. I see it not as an isolated composition, but a composition related to nature, a composition of contrasts.*
> Marcel Breuer

> *Architecture subtly and eloquently inserts itself into the site, absorbing its power to move us and in return offering to it the symphonic elements of human geometry.*
> Le Corbusier

Each structure expressive of its use, site relationships, and the climate. (Study. Resort complex, Broward County, Florida)

> *We need desperately to relearn the art of disposing of buildings to create different kinds of space: the quiet, enclosed, isolated, shaded space; the hustling, bustling space pungent with vitality; the paved, dignified, vast, sumptuous, even awe-inspiring space; the mysterious space; the transition space which defines, separates and yet joins juxtaposed spaces of contrasting character.*
>
> *We need sequences of space which arouse one's curiosity, give a sense of anticipation, which beckon and impel us to rush forward to find that releasing space which dominates, which climaxes and acts as a magnet, and gives direction.*
>
> *Paul Rudolph*

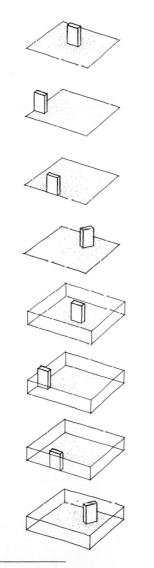

Composition of structures

When a structure is to be related to a given area or space, both the shape and the character of the area or space will be affected by the positioning of the structure.

Environs

What have these advances contributed to the betterment of our environment? Not much that is evident. Not yet at least. We can get around faster, build higher, and communicate with the speed of light. But many would hold that the net results of our building in this age of mechanical marvels has been to trash and grievously pollute not only our immediate living environment, but as well the greater continental land masses, the depths of the seas that surround them, and the atmosphere. Clearly, our technical and structural capabilities have outstripped our ability to envision and realize a world in which structures are conceived and built in full awareness of nature's forms and forces—and in harmony with the living earth.

A critical change of course is the challenge of our times.

Composition

We physical planners like to think of ourselves as masters of space organization, yet in truth we are often baffled by the simplest problems of spatial arrangement and structural composition. What, for instance, are the design considerations in relating a building to its surrounding sea of space, or a building to its fronting approaches, or two buildings facing each other across an intervening mall, or a group of structures to each other and the spaces they enclose? Let us start from the beginning.

Buildings and spaces

If we were to place a building on a ground plane, for instance, how much space should we allow around it? First, we will want to see it well from its approaches. The spaces about it should not only be large enough or *small enough* but also of the right shape and spatial quality to compose with the structure and best display it. We want to be sure that enough room is allowed to accommodate all the building's exterior functions, including approaches, parking and service areas, courts, patios, terraces, recreation areas, or gardens. Such spaces are volumetric expressions of the site-structure diagram. We want to be certain that the structure and its surrounding spaces are in toto a complete and balanced composition. Just as all buildings have purpose, so should the open spaces that they define or enclose. Such spaces must be clearly related to the character, mass, and purpose of the structures.

Often the form of a building itself is not as important as the nature of the exterior space or spaces that it creates. The portrait painter knows that the outline of a figure or the profile of a head is sometimes secondary to the shape of the spaces created between figure or head and the surrounding pictorial enframement; it is the relationship of the figure to the surrounding shapes that gives the figure its essential meaning. So it is with buildings. Our buildings are to be spaced out in the landscape in such a way as to permit full and meaningful integration with other structures and spaces and with the landscape itself.

Groups of structures

When two or more buildings are related, the buildings together with the interrelated spaces become an architectural entity. In such a situation, each structure, aside from its primary function, has many secondary functions in relation to the assemblage.

The buildings are arranged to shape and define exterior volumes in the best way possible. They may be placed:

As enclosing elements

As screening elements

As backdrop elements

To dominate the landscape

To organize the landscape

To command the landscape

To embrace the landscape

To enframe the landscape

To create a new and controlled landscape

To orient the new landscape outward or inward

To dramatize the enclosing structures

To dramatize the enclosed space or spaces

To dramatize some feature or features within the space

They are placed, in short, to develop closed or semienclosed spaces that best express and accommodate their function, that best reveal the structural form, facade, or other features of the surrounding structures, and that best relate the group as a whole to the total extensional landscape.

We have seen too often in our day a building rising on its site in proud and utter disdain of its neighbors or its position. We search in vain for any of those relationships of form, material, or treatment that would compose it with the existing elements of the local scene. Such insensitive planning would have been incomprehensible to the ancient Greeks or Romans, who conceived each new structure as a compositional element of the street, forum, or square. They did not simply erect a new temple, a new fountain, or even a new lantern; they consciously redesigned the street or square. Each new structure and each new space were contrived as integral and balanced parts of the immediate and extensional environment. These planners knew no other way. And in truth, there can be no other way if our buildings and our cities are again to please and satisfy us.

Each building or structure as a solid requires for its fullest expression a satisfying counterbalance of negative open space. This truth, of all planning truths, is perhaps the most difficult to comprehend. It has been comprehended and mastered in many periods and places—by the builders of the Karnak Temple, Kyoto's Katsura Palace, or the gardens of Soochow (Suzhou), for example. We still find their groupings of buildings and interrelated spaces to be of supremely satisfying harmony and balance; each solid has its void, each building has its satisfying measure of space, and each interior function has its exterior extension, generation, or resolution of the function.

What do we contemporary planners know of this art or its principles, which have been evolved through centuries of trial and error, modification, reappraisal, and patient refinement? Asian peoples have a highly developed planning discipline that deals with such matters in terms of *tension and repose*. Though its tenets are veiled in religious mysticism, its plan applications are clear. It

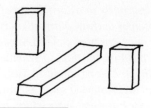

Composition of structures

Often the form of the structures themselves is not as important as that of the spaces they enclose. A single structure is perceived as an object in space. Two or more structures are perceived not alone as objects but also as related objects, and they gain or lose much of their significance in the relationship.

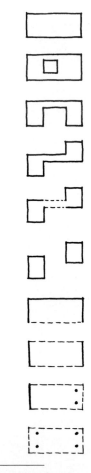

Spatial penetration of structure

This rage for isolating everything is truly a modern sickness.
Camillo Sitte

This handsome cluster of street lights was designed, in the best tradition, as an integral part of the city and square.

Static

Dynamic

Opposing structures generate a field of dynamic tension.

is a conscious effort in all systems of composition to attain a sense of repose through the occult balance of all plan elements, whether viewed as in a pictorial composition or experienced in three dimensions:

> The near balanced against the far
> The solid against the void
> The light against the dark
> The bright against the dull
> The familiar against the strange
> The dominant against the recessive
> The active against the passive
> The fluid against the fixed

In each instance, the most telling dynamic tensions are sought out or arranged to give maximum meaning to all opposing elements and the total scheme. Though repose through equilibrium must be the end result, it is the *relationship* of the plan elements through which repose is achieved that is of utmost interest. It is the contrived opposition of elements, the studied interplay of tensions, and the sensed resolution of these tensions that, when fully comprehended, are most keenly enjoyed.

A group of structures may be planned in opposition both to each other and to the landscape in which they rise, so that as one moves through or about them, one experiences an evolving composition of opposing elements, a resolution of tensions, and a sense of dynamic repose. A single tree may be so placed and trained as to hold a distant forest or group of smaller trees in balanced opposition and give them richer meaning. A lake shining deep and still in the natural bowl of a valley may, by its area, conformation, and other qualities, real or associative, hold in balanced repose the opposing hills that surround it. A plume of falling water at the lake's far end may balance the undulations of its points and bays.

Walter Beck, long a student of Asian art and composition, has said of the superb gardens that he planned at Innisfree: "On a wall, at the lake edge, is a rock which I call the dragon rock; it is the key in a grouping of stones whose function is to hold in balance the lake and nearby hills; whose function is to cope with the energies of the sky and the distant landscape."[1] It can be seen that tremendous compositional interest and power can be concentrated in such key objects—rocks, sculpture, structures, or whatever you will—that by design may hold a great system of elements in balanced tension and thus in dynamic repose.

It would seem, from a comparison of the European and Asian systems of planning, that the western mind is traditionally concerned primarily with the object or structure as it appears in space, while the eastern mind tends to think of structure primarily as a means of defining and articulating a space or a complex of spaces.

In this light, Steen Rasmussen, in his book *Towns and Buildings*, has made a revealing graphic comparison of two imperial parks, that of King Louis XIV at Versailles and the Sea Palace Gardens in Beijing (Peking). Both were completed in the early 1700s, both made use of huge artificial bodies of water, and both were immense; but there the similarity ends. A close study of these two diametrically opposed planning approaches, illustrated here, will lead one to a fuller understanding of the philosophy of both western and eastern planning in this period of history.

Too often when placing or composing structures in space we revert to cold geometry. Our architectural libraries are bulging with building plans and diagrams laid out in crisp, abstract patterns of black and white that have little meaning except in the flat. It is small wonder that buildings that take their substance from such plans are destined to failure, for they were never conceived in terms of form in space or of spaces within form. The world is cluttered with such unfortunate travesties. The intelligent planning of buildings, parks, and cities is a far cry from such geometric doodling. A logical plan in two dimensions is a record of logical thinking in three dimensions. The enlightened planner is thinking always of space–structure composition. His or her concern is not with the plan forms and spaces as they appear on the drawings but rather with these forms and spaces as they will be experienced in actuality.

Many Renaissance squares, parks, and palaces are little more than dull geometry seen in the round. One clear, strong voice crying out against such puerile design was that of Camillo Sitte, a Viennese architect whose writings on city building first appeared in 1889 and whose ideas are still valid and compelling today.

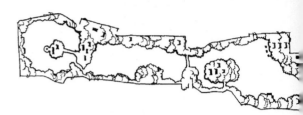

Peking, Sea Palace gardens

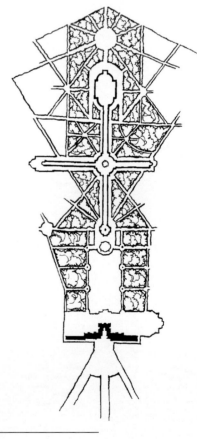

Versailles Park

---

[1] From *Painting with Starch* by Walter Beck (Van Nostrand, Princeton, N.J., 1956).

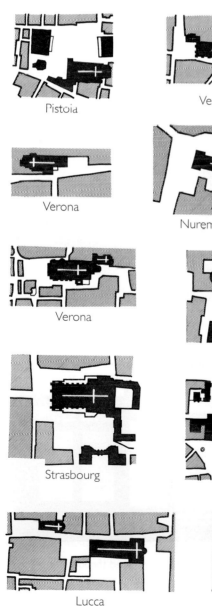

> *The location of the equestrian statue of Gattamelata by Donatello in front of Saint Anthony of Padua is most instructive. First we may be astonished at its great variance from our rigid modern system, but it is quickly and strikingly seen that the monument in this place produces a majestic effect. Finally we become convinced that removed to the center of the square its effect would be greatly diminished. We cease to wonder at its orientation and other locational advantages once this principle becomes familiar.*
>
> *The ancient Egyptians understood this principle, for as Gattamelata and the little column stand beside the entrance to the Cathedral of Padua, the obelisks and the statues of the Pharaohs are aligned beside the temple doors. There is the entire secret that we refuse to decipher today.*
>
> *Camillo Sitte*

It was Sitte who pointed out that pre–Renaissance people *used* their public spaces and that these spaces and the buildings around them were planned together to satisfy the use. There were market squares, religious squares, ducal squares, civic squares, and others of many varieties; and each, from inception through the numerous changes of time, maintained its own distinctive quality. These public places were never symmetrical, nor were they entered by wide, axial streets that would have destroyed their essential attribute of enclosure. Rather, they were asymmetrical; they were entered by narrow, winding ways. Each building or object within the space was planned *to* and *for* the space and the streams of pedestrian traffic that would converge and merge there. The centers of such spaces were left open; the monuments, fountains, and sculpture that were so much a part of them were placed on islands in the traffic pattern, off building corners, against blank walls, and beside the entryways, each positioned with infinite care in relation to surfaces, masses, and *space*. Seldom were such objects set on axis with the approach to a building or its entrance, for it was felt that they would detract from the full appreciation of the architecture. Conversely, it was felt that the axis of a building was seldom a proper background for a work of art.

Sitte discovered that such important buildings as cathedrals were rarely placed at the center of an open space, as we almost invariably place them today. Instead, they were set back against other buildings or off to the side to give a better view of facade, spires, or portals and to give the best impression from within the square or from its meandering approaches.

Rules of composition

Down through the centuries, much thought has been given to the establishment of fixed formulas or rules that might govern building proportions, or the relationship of one building to another, or the relationship of a building to its surrounding volumetric enclosure.

Pistoia

Verona

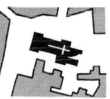

Verona

Nuremberg

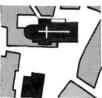

Verona

Perugia

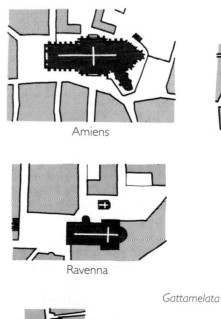

Amiens

Salzburg

Strasbourg

Cologne

Ravenna

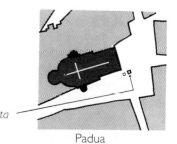

Gattamelata

Padua

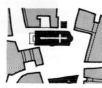

Lucca

Modena

Geneva

15
HABITATIONS

W*HAT DOES A DWELLING* want to be? Shelter? Family activity center? Base of operations? All three, no doubt, and each of these functions is to be expressed and facilitated. But in its fullest sense a *habitation* is much more. It is our human fix on the planet Earth, our earthly abode. Once accepted, this simple philosophic concept has far-reaching implications.

In the planning of their homes and gardens, people of Asian cultures not only adapt them with great artistry to the natural landscape but also consciously root them in nature. Constructed of materials derived from the earth (with varying degrees of tooling and refinement), these homes and gardens are humanized extensions of earth form and structure and are fully attuned to the natural processes. Like the nest of the bird or the beaver's lodge, they are nature particularized.

Dwelling-Nature Relationships

It is proposed that each human habitation is best conceived as an integral component of the natural site and landscape environs. The extent to which this can be accomplished is a measure of the dwelling's success and the occupant's sense of fitness and well-being.

This integration of habitation with nature is an exacting enterprise. How is it to be achieved? As a beginning:

Explore and analyze the site. Just as the bird or the animal scouts the territory for the optimum situation, just as the farmer surveys the holding and lays out fields and buildings to conform to the lay of the land, just so must the planner of each home and garden come to know and respond to the unique and compelling conditions of the selected site.

Adapt to the geological structure.   The conformation of every land area is determined largely by its geologic formation—the convolutions, layering, upheavals, erosion, and weathering of the underlying strata. These establish the stability and load-bearing capacity of the various site areas and the ease or difficulty of excavation and grading. They determine as well the structure, porosity, and fertility of the subsoil and topsoil, the presence of groundwater, and the availability of freshwater reserves. Only with the knowledge of subsurface conditions, gained by test holes or drilling, or the keen eye of experience, can one plan to the site with assurance.

Preserve the natural systems.   Topography, drainageways, waterways, vegetative covers, bird and wildlife trails and habitat, all have continuity. One test of good land planning is that it minimizes disruption of established patterns and flows.

Adjust the plan to fit the land.   In the recomposition of solids and voids the structural elements are usually designed to extend the hill or ridge and overlook the valley. Well-conceived plan forms honor and articulate the basic land contours and water edges. The prominence is made more dominant; the hollow and cove, more recessive.

Reflect the climatic condition.   Cold, temperate, hot–dry, or warm–humid, each broad climatic range brings to mind at once planning problems and possibilities. Within each range, however, there are many subarea variations of climate or site-specific microclimate that have direct planning implications.

Design in response to the elements.   Protect from the wind. Invite the breeze. Accommodate the rain or snow. Avoid the flood. Brace for the storm. Trace and respond to the arcing sun.

Consider the human factors.   On– and off–site structures, trafficways, utility installations, easements, and even such givens as social characteristics, political jurisdictions, zoning, covenants, restrictions, and regulations may have a telling influence.

Eliminate the negatives.   Insofar as possible, all undesirable features are to be removed or their impacts abated. The undesirables include pollution in its many aspects, hazards, and visual detractions. When they cannot be eliminated, they are mitigated by ground forms, vegetation, distance or by visual screening.

Accentuate the best features.   Fit the paths of movement, use areas, and structures around and between the landscape superlatives. Protect them, face toward them, focus upon them, enframe them, and enjoy them in all conditions of light and in all seasons.

Let the native character set the theme.   Every landscape area has its own mood and character. Presumably these were among the chief reasons for the site selection. Only if the indigenous quality is not desirable or suited to the project use should it be significantly altered. Otherwise, design in harmony with the theme, devising pleasant modulations, light counterpoint, and resonant overtones.

Integrate.   Bring all the elements together in the best possible dynamic relationships. This is the lesson of nature. This is the primary objective of all planning and design.

Whatever the type of dwelling, be it a single-family home, a town-house unit with garden court, or a tower apartment...

All landscape design of distinction embodies to some extent an abstract and idealized representation of nature.

When the area to be developed is small, the design will take into account all positive qualities of the site—the ground forms, cover, exposures, views, and all other natural or architectural features—and bring them into harmony.

When the area to be considered is large or complex, each *segment* is to be developed as an entity and all segments brought together into a unified whole.

Whatever the location, be the site urban or rural, mountain or plain, desert or lakeside...

The planning approach is the same.

Human Needs and Habitat

What would the ideal garden home be like? As a clue, observation will teach us that at least the following requirements of most home dwellers should be satisfied.

Shelter

The contemporary home, like all before it, is first of all a refuge from the storm. With the advent of sophisticated heating devices, climate controls, diversified construction materials, and ingenious structural systems, the concept of shelter had been brought to a new high level of refinement. But architecturally this basic function of shelter is to be served and given clear expression.

Protection

This implies safety from all forms of danger, not only from the elements but from fire, flood, and intruders as well. Although the nature of potential threats has changed through the centuries, our instincts have not. Safety must be implicit.

Today an ever-present hazard is that of the moving vehicle with its backings and turnings. It does not belong within our living areas and should not be admitted. The automobile should be stabled within its own service area or compound.

Utility

Each dwelling should be a lucid statement of the various purposes to be served. Not only is each use to be accommodated, it is to be conveniently related to all others. And what are these uses? They are those of food preparation, dining, entertaining, sleeping, and (perhaps) child rearing. These uses are supplemented by the library, correspondence corner, workshop, laundry... and supported by storage spaces, mechanical equipment, and waste disposal systems. Often, much of the home entertainment and relaxation takes place on the balcony, lawn, or terrace. The outdoor spaces also provide healthful exercise and satisfy our agricultural yearnings. Even the pot of chives or the parsley bed has its important symbolic meaning.

Utility connotes "a place for everything, and everything in its place," all working well together. While a home is far more than a machine for living, it must function efficiently.

In the gloaming. So nice to come home to.

Amenity

It is not enough that a dwelling works well. It must also be attractive and pleasant. It must satisfy the human bent for display and our love of beautiful objects. Beauty is not, however, to be confused with decoration, ornamentation, or the elaborate. True beauty is most often discerned in that which is utterly simple and unpretentious—a well-formed clay pot, a simple carpet of blended wools, handsomely fitted and finished wood, cut slate, hand–crafted silver—always just the right form, material, and finish to serve the specific purpose; always the understatement, for *less* is truly *more*.

In considering dwellings and display, mention should be made of the *tokonoma* of the traditional Japanese home. Constructed of natural materials of elegant simplicity, the tokonoma is a place reserved for the sharing of beautiful objects. These objets d'art are selected from storage cabinets or gathered from the garden or site and brought out, a few at most at one time, to mark the season or a special occasion. They may include hangings, paintings, a bowl, sculpture, or a vase or tray to receive a floral arrangement. Our western homes and gardens and their displays could well be distinguished by such artistry and restraint.

Privacy

In a world of hustle and hassle we all need, sometimes desperately, a place of quiet retreat. It need not be large—a space in the home or garden set apart from normal activities, where one can share the enjoyment of reading, music, or conversation or turn for quiet introspection. It is very human to feel the need for one's own private space.

A sense of spaciousness

Just as we feel the need to retreat, we feel also upon occasion the need for expansive freedom. With dwellings and neighborhoods becoming more and more constricted, such spaciousness inside property limits is almost a rarity. But we can learn from those cultures in which people have lived for centuries in forced compression that space can be "borrowed."

Living spaces may be so arranged and interrelated that common areas may be shared to make each component space seem larger. Apparent spatial size may be increased also by the subtle use of forced perspective and by miniaturization. Again, by the studied arrangement of walls and openings, views can be designed to include attractive features of the site or neighboring properties or extended to the distant hill or horizon. Even within the walled garden or court the ultimate spaciousness can be experienced by the featured viewing of the sky and clouds and the evening constellations. It is no happenstance that in crowded Japan a favorite spot on the garden terrace is that reserved for the viewing of the moon.

Nature appreciation

Deeply ingrained in all of us is an instinctive feeling for the outdoors—for soil, stone, water, and the living things of the earth. We need to be near them, to observe and to touch them. We need to maintain a close relationship with nature, to dwell amid natural features and surroundings, and to bring nature into our homes and into our lives.

A distinguishing mark of the recent American dwelling is the trend toward indoor–outdoor living. Most interior use areas now have their outdoor extensions—entryway to entrance court, kitchen to service area, dining space to patio, living space to terrace, bedroom to spa, game room to recreation court, and sun

Elegant simplicity.

Spring rides no horses
down the hill
But comes on foot
a goosegirl still
And all the loveliest
things that be
Come simply,
so it seems to me.
Edna St. Vincent Millay

The spirit of a garden is its power to charm the heart.
Kanto Shigemori

Evolution of a way of life

Primitive
Shelter is main consideration.

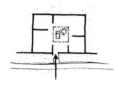

Greco-Roman
Protection and privacy are of prime value.

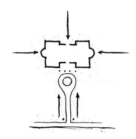

Renaissance
Each structure is an idealized object in space.

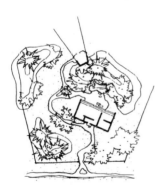

Oriental
Nature is revered, privacy is demanded; structures are related to lot and total landscape.

Borrowed scenery (an Asian term for visual volumetric expansion) is accomplished by the inclusion of objects, spaces, or views from beyond the site or garden wall. We in America have much to learn about such spatial expansion techniques, long applied in the diminutive living spaces of Europe and the orient.

Indoor-outdoor living space.

room to garden. In the well-planned habitation, especially in milder climes, it is often difficult to differentiate between indoors and out.

It has been theorized that, ideally, each home and garden should be conceived as the universe in microcosm. If this idea seems abstruse, let it pass. Perhaps in time, upon further reflection, you may find it to have deep meaning.

Residential Components

Existing site features

Often a residential site is selected because of some outstanding attribute. It may be a majestic oak or an aspen grove. It may be a spring, a pond, or a ledge of rock. Again it may be an outstanding view. All too often those things most admired when the site was acquired are ignored or lost in construction. It only makes sense that such distinctive features be preserved and dramatized in the homestead planning.

Area allocation

By custom in the United States, and almost uniquely among worldwide homesteads, the area fronting on the passing street has usurped a large part of each residential property for the sole purpose of home display. Traditionally, the foreground of open lawn has been bordered by shrubs, the house garnished with foundation planting for public approbation. Side yards too have been treated mostly as unused separation space—leaving only the backyard for family use and enjoyment. It is only recently that the unified house–garden concept has gained popularity and indoor-outdoor living has come into its own.

Some costly sweeps of irrigated and manicured lawn will long be with us, as will many "dollhouse" and "castle" homes designed primarily for display. Increasingly, however, the greenswards are being reduced in size, homes opened up to patios, courtyards, and open recreation space. More of the natural ground forms and vegetation are being preserved and family life is more outwardly oriented.

The dwelling

The residence is the centerpiece of the homestead—within which and around which everything happens. What happens depends upon the type of residence selected and the kinds of home life planned for. If there is truth to the saying that in time dog owners come to resemble their canine pets, then it can likewise be observed that much of what home owners are and do can be judged by their choice of dwellings.

The dwelling itself is a structural framework for living the good, full life. In some cases the good life may be confined to the walled enclosure of a residence standing proud, aloof, and self-contained. Again, other homes may open outward, serving as multifaceted viewing boxes and staging bases for a host of outdoor activities.

Be it an urban apartment, suburban residence, farm homestead, or wilderness retreat, each has its limitations and possibilities in terms of indoor–outdoor relationships.

In the city high-rise, the outdoor experience may be provided by no more than a sunny window ledge with potted plants or a balcony with seating, a view, and perhaps a hanging basket or two. With good fortune there might even be a private or shared roof garden. An on-grade town house may have its doorstep planting and a rear courtyard with expanded opportunities—as for dining space under a tree or arbor, a pool, a fountain, or a patch of herbs or flowers. The suburban home or farmstead, with more area, can open out to a wider array of outdoor living and working spaces. So too with the remote cabin or cottage whose owners may choose to leave the natural woodland surrounds unchanged.

Outdoor activity spaces

Every outdoor activity needs its measure of usable space. These may be as small as that required for a child's sandbox or kitchen herb garden—or as large as for a tennis court, swimming pool, vegetable garden, orchard, or even a putting green. No matter what the anticipated uses, if they are to be realized and enjoyed they must be designed into the plans.

The patio or terrace, embraced by the dwelling, extends its interior spaces and relates them to all outdoors. The area between home and garage, open or enclosed, may serve as an entrance court or outdoor living room—with paving and planting, and perhaps a wall fountain or other water feature.

Bordering the patio or terrace may be the game court or lawn, cultivated garden, or natural vegetation. The cultivated garden may be no more than a scattering of selected shrubs, clumps of

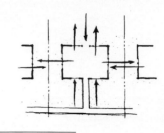

Present American showcase (vestigial renaissance)
Nature ignored. Outward orientation. Privacy is lost. Little use of property. A product of side-yard, setback, and no-fence restrictions.

Future American-trend home
Total use of site as living space. Privacy regained. Indoor-outdoor integration. Natural elements introduced. Compact home-garden units grouped amid open park and recreation areas which preserve natural-landscape features.

The earth is our home and the ways of nature our paths to understanding.

“ *The most obvious place to put the house is not always the right one. If there is only a small area of flat land, you'll be tempted to use it for the house. It probably should be saved for arrival, parking or garden....*

Is there one particular spot on the property that seems just right in every way? Have you picnicked there and found it idyllic? Have you spent long winter evenings planning a house there? Has it occurred to you that if you build your house there the spot will be gone? Maybe that's where your garden should be.

Thomas D. Church

iris, a swath of crocus and narcissus, a bed of lilies, or a patch of native grasses. It may consist of a specimen evergreen or a flowering crab apple tree in a planter with an edging of myrtle or ivy. It could be no more than a square of tulips within an area of paving or a raised bed of peonies surrounded by gravel mulch. A tubbed fig tree. A cactus garden. Or again, it could be an extensive outlay of well-tended borders and beds.

A single pot of geraniums on the table is a garden in itself, as is a poolside grouping of containers spilling over with blossoms. Some of the most beautiful garden spaces remembered could be encompassed by the outreach of one's arms.

The service area—open, walled, or partially screened—is most often associated with the garage and parking court. Here space is to be provided for deliveries, car storage, and turnabout. Here too will be provision for the temporary storage of refuse and recyclable materials waiting for collection and for the compost station.

As an adjunct there may be an offset storage shed for equipment and supplies. It may serve as well to house the meters and valves of utility systems and to hang the hose reels.

The service court border is a convenient location for the kitchen garden and for the entryway to a possible greenhouse, potting shed, or vegetable garden. Here, if there are screen walls, arbor, or fencing, is an opportune place for the growing of flowering vines, or grapes, or such espaliered fruits as oranges, lemons, pears, figs, peaches, or apples.

A service court often doubles as a paved recreation area, with netpost sockets, line markings, and perhaps a basketball backboard. At one side there may be a gated entry to the children's play space, with swings and play equipment—overseen, if possible, from the adjacent kitchen windows.

Supplementary structures

As noted, many site-related spaces can be planned into the dwelling or attached thereto by extension. Again, a garage, guest house, or studio may be detached and designed as an architectural counterpoint. So too with the smaller work shed or tool house. Supplementary structures may be intentionally varied in character—more related to the site than to the domicile, and suited particularly to the intended use. Such might be poolside dressing rooms or an overlook shelter. Sometimes living quarters are incorporated in a recreation structure such as a weekend ski lodge or a boathouse with its related slips and dock.

Furnishings

No homestead is complete without its outdoor equipment and furnishings. A well-organized storage wall or shed, complete with maintenance machinery and tools, is a must. Recreation equipment—the nets, paddles, and racquets; the quoits, stakes, and hammock; the archery target and chest of toys are all to have their ordered place. Then too there will usually be benches, chairs, tables, and such outdoor equipage. Paving, ground covers, and planting—which may or may not be considered furnishings—are treated in other chapters of this book.

Beside the basics there may be as well such decorative accoutrements as planters, window boxes, and a variety of wooden or

Here a flying deck overlooking a view extends the indoor-outdoor space to infinity

Outdoor "activity" spaces may be active or passive.

Looking out.

Looking in.

Looking in.

Looking out.

Residential gardens
From the casual,
to the more highly refined

Container gardens
For carefree gardening it is hard to surpass a garden
in a tub, pot, planter, or raised planting bin.

Outd
an

- Pro
S
- Imf
t
- Fit
as
it

Imma
or

RES

Outd

- I

- E

- T

Cant

16
COMMUNITY PLANNING

THE WORD *community* has many connotations, most of them favorable. For people, like plants and animals, seem to flourish in shared and supportive groupings. What is the nature of such community groupings, and how are they best formed?

The Group Imperative

Historically, people have banded together for some compelling reason, as for protection within the gated walls of the medieval city or the palisade of the fort. They have formed communities to engage in farming, commerce, or industry or to pursue their religious beliefs. In the opening up of America, other settlements grew spontaneously around harbors and river landings, at the crossings of transportation routes, and wherever natural resources were concentrated or abundant.

Within communal aggregations friendships have been made mainly on the basis of propinquity. Dwellings were built in the most favorable and affordable locations, and then families moved in to make friends or sometimes to feud with the folks next door. Social groupings and working alliances were for the most part accidental. Homes were permanent, and neighborhoods were relatively stable. Towns and cities proliferated—too often in patterns of squared-off streets. Residential districts became impacted, often without schools, conveniences, or open-space relief. As densities and traffic increased, time-distances became greater, pollution often became intolerable, and surrounding fields and woodlands melted inexorably away.

With the coming of the twentieth century and the advent of the automobile, the farm-to-city movement was suddenly reversed.

Initially a few of the wealthy fled the industrial city to build romanticized farmsteads and rusticated villas such as those along the Hudson River. They were soon joined by many members of the middle class, to whom social reform was bringing an improving standard of living and newfound mobility. These families shared the beckoning dream of a better, more fulfilling life beyond the city outskirts, where they could live amid forest, fields, and gardens in communion with nature. As they surged outward in ever-increasing numbers, the new suburbia was born. It was to became an American phenomenon. New types of dwellings would be designed, and innovative community patterns were to be created. The subdivision tracts, planned communities, and new towns gradually evolved and are still evolving. If they fall somewhat short of the vision, it is because they have destroyed too much of the nature that they sought to embrace. It is because they have carried along with them from the city too many of the urban foibles—the bad habit of facing homes upon traffic-laden streets instead of pleasant courts or open-space preserves, of inexplicably lining schools, churches, and factories haunch to haunch along the roaring highways. It is because we have allowed the interconnecting roadways to become teeming thoroughfares along which has coalesced mile after mile of crass, traffic-clogging strip commercial development. It is because we still have much to learn about the basics and intricacies of group living, of land use, and of transportation planning.

Problems

Without controls, unsuitable uses infiltrate residential areas. Widened streets and highways draw to their sides strip commercial coagulations which reduce their carrying capacity and restrict the traffic flow. Deterioration and blight are rampant. Vacant structures are vandalized. Property values plummet, and the solid citizens of the original homes move out if they can. Sadly, wherever they go to start anew, without better planning and regulation, the cycle will be repeated. It need not be so.

Monotony

Too often in suburban development a well-wooded site is leveled, the trees and cover destroyed, the streams and drainageways encased in massive storm sewers or open culverts. Look-alike houses are then spaced out in rows along a geometric checkerboard of streets. A new flora of exotic plants is installed in the hard-packed ground. The native fauna—the furred and feathered creatures of the wood and meadow—take off to seek a more livable habitat.

Variety, the antithesis of monotony, can be preserved and attained by sensitive land and community planning, with far more resident appeal and at far less initial and continuing cost.

Inefficiency

The well-planned neighborhood or community—urban, suburban, or rural—should function as an efficient mechanism. This is to say that energy and materials are to be conserved and frictions eliminated. Energy conservation suggests that things and services

Any consideration of the future of open space, such as exists between our urban centers, requires a thoughtful appraisal of one of our most voracious consumers of land: housing. Man's preference in housing, especially in urban fringe areas, results in the sprawl of single detached units in an awesome continuum across the countryside.

What is the origin of the desire for this type of shelter expression—this compulsion to flee the city and to build cube on cube across the open land? Is it a desire for tax relief? Vested equity? Breathing space? Contact with the land? Or the poetics of "Home Sweet Home"? Regardless, is the solution largely that of better design within the acceptance of this preference? Or change from separated horizontal forms to unified collective density patterns? Perhaps as space between units decreases, space between our urban centers may be preserved, or may increase.

Walter D. Harris

The subdivision as we know it is a typical United States invention, with few counterparts in Europe or Asia.

Radburn, New Jersey, 1928. This revolutionary concept of community living was devised by its planners, Henry Wright and Clarence Stein, as an answer to living with the automobile. Homes were grouped in superblocks with automobile access from cul-de-sac streets precluding high speed through traffic. Pedestrian walkways, free of automobile crossings, provided access to large central park areas in which and around which were grouped the community social, recreational, and shopping centers.

In this plan concept were sown the seeds of ideas that have sprouted in most of the superior neighborhood and community plans of succeeding years.

needed—schools, shopping, and recreation—should be convenient—easy to reach and close at hand. Yet in some neighborhoods many blocks must be traveled and many streets crossed in order to buy a quart of milk or a loaf of bread. Playgrounds and even elementary schools can be reached only by braving a grid of rushing trafficways. As we know from reading the papers, some children, and adults, never make it.

In a planned community, by comparison, dwellings of all types are clustered around the activity centers. Access on foot, by bicycle, or by electric cart is via traffic-free greenways. Safer. More pleasant. Far more efficient.

The alignment of homes and apartment buildings along roadways and streets was for years the accepted procedure. It is no longer considered desirable. Few families would opt for a home that faced upon a busy trafficway if offered the alternative of off-street courtyard living. Offset residential groupings not only provide more salable and rentable housing, they do so more economically. Further, the efficiency of the passing street is increased by the elimination of curbcuts at every driveway, with the intrusions that these imply.

With clustered off-street housing, the high cost of street and highway construction with its trunkline sewers and utility mains can be shared by many more dwellings. Single- and double-loaded streets are not only uneconomical, they are fraught with all sorts of problems.

The common practice of constructing sewers, utility mains, and energy distribution systems within the street right-of-way is another source of recurrent difficulties. Power poles and overhead wires interfere with street tree plantings which must then be periodically mutilated to keep the lines clear. Beyond that, it is patently impractical to tear up a section of pavement and close a lane, if not the whole street, for the installation of each new service lateral—or for the seemingly endless repair of in-street water, gas, or sewer mains. Far better that a utility easement be reserved along rear property lines to leave the streetscape unscathed.

In many unplanned communities the greatest waste is in uncalled-for and destructive earthwork and unneeded storm sewer construction. These costs are incurred because the site layout runs counter to the topography. The natural covers protect and stabilize the soils and slopes. The natural drainageways and streams carry off the excess precipitation. But with the vegetation destroyed and the drainageways blocked, the heavy expense of resultant drainage structures and soil stabilization must be factored into the cost of each dwelling. Not to mention replacement plantings.

In the home-building and community development industries—profit motivated and highly competitive as they are—it is indeed fortuitous that the most successful entrepreneurs have learned that well-conceived and well-built projects are not only more efficient, they are more environmentally sound, they are more people-friendly, more salable or rentable—and more profitable.

Unhealthful conditions

Mens sana in corpore sano.

A sound mind in a sound body.

What has community planning to do with the state of one's health?

If we are, as it is said, largely the product of our heredity and our environment, then let us hope that we come of hardy stock, for living in neighborhoods that are obsolescent, polluted, and/or traffic-fraught is hardly conducive to health.

Mental well-being derives from rational order and behavior. When living conditions are clearly unreasonable, when the daily experience is one of frustration, anxiety, or disgust, it is hard to maintain a positive state of mind.

As to behavior, we live in a revved-up society that our parents could not have imagined. In our crowded lives everything is done at double speed and driven intensity. Between spates of whizzing about to keep up the pace we spend long hours in sedentary occupations. Much of the working day is spent hunched over the desk, counter, or machine—or staring into computers. We are detached from the wholesome reality of the field and furrow, the woodlot, the vineyard, the creatures of the barn and dooryard that kept our forebears sane and healthy. Can our planned communities of the future provide the antidote, the counterpoint, to such mechanistic living? Can we find in our new neighborhoods the opportunities for healthful outdoor exercise and recreation, for group activities and fulfilling communal life? It is believed so.

Danger

Who could deny that our present communities, as most of us experience them, pose danger to life and limb?

> The street crossings and trafficway intersections
> The mix of people and vehicles
> Overhead power lines
> Toxic levels of soil and water contamination
> The polluted air that we breathe...

Not to ignore the increasing threat posed by crime in our streets and alleys—the weekly muggings, break-ins, or drive-by shootings. These are endemic to obsolescence and vacancies, to unlighted lurking places—and as well to the lack of better places to be and better things to do.

All these potential and very real dangers are subject to planned improvement.

Possibilities

As we set out to plan the more salubrious neighborhoods of the future, wherein lie the possibilities? It is proposed that they will have:

> A better fit of construction to the land
> A better fit of homes to related trafficways
> A better fit of homes to homes and homes to activity centers
> A rich variety of things to see and do
> Freedom of individual expression and innovative improvement
> A shared sense of true *community*, of compatible living *together*

Building arrangements

Why do houses face upon streets? "Because," some might say, "they always have." Probably such respondents are right, for we humans are slow to accept any change, even when the advantage is obvious.

Until recently in the United States it was, uniformly, a legal requirement that all plotted homesites be dedicated with frontage upon a public right-of-way. As a consequence, homes sprouted row upon row along streets and highways across the countryside. This posed few serious problems as long as the roads were used by horses and horse-drawn carriages, wagons, and carts.

Then came the automobiles. They came, and came, and they keep on coming. The roadways are overwhelmed. They have been widened and lengthened until today the trafficway network covers most of the landscape like a coarsely woven mesh. Meanwhile, buildings continue to crowd alongside the pulsing motorways. Communities are thus cut apart—divided and subdivided again by lines of fast-moving traffic. This makes little sense—either for the residents or for the motorists.

In seeking solutions to the dilemma, land planners have sought to have the frontage requirement rescinded. Where this has been accomplished it has produced building-road relationships that hold much promise.

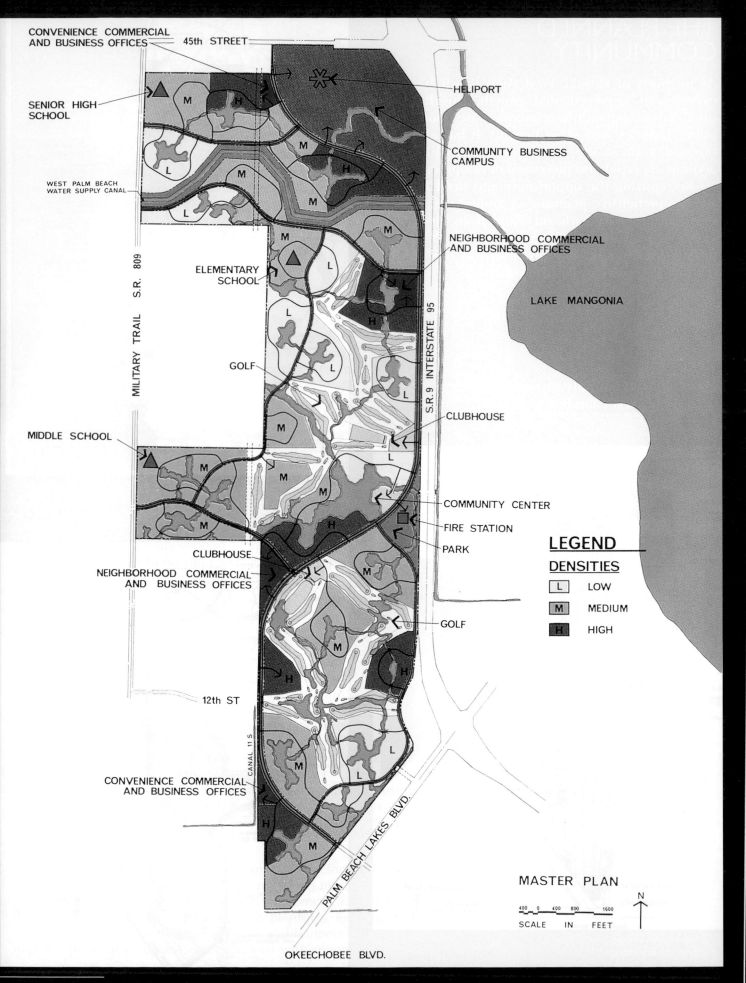

CONVENIENCE COMMERCIAL
AND BUSINESS OFFICES

45th STREET

HELIPORT

SENIOR HIGH
SCHOOL

COMMUNITY BUSINESS
CAMPUS

WEST PALM BEACH
WATER SUPPLY CANAL

NEIGHBORHOOD COMMERCIAL
AND BUSINESS OFFICES

LAKE MANGONIA

MILITARY TRAIL S.R. 809

ELEMENTARY
SCHOOL

GOLF

S.R. 9 INTERSTATE 95

CLUBHOUSE

MIDDLE SCHOOL

COMMUNITY CENTER

FIRE STATION

PARK

CLUBHOUSE

NEIGHBORHOOD COMMERCIAL
AND BUSINESS OFFICES

GOLF

LEGEND

DENSITIES

L	LOW
M	MEDIUM
H	HIGH

12th ST

CANAL 11 S

CONVENIENCE COMMERCIAL
AND BUSINESS OFFICES

MASTER PLAN

N

400 0 400 800   1600

SCALE   IN   FEET

PALM BEACH LAKES BLVD.

OKEECHOBEE BLVD.

Conceptual community plan.

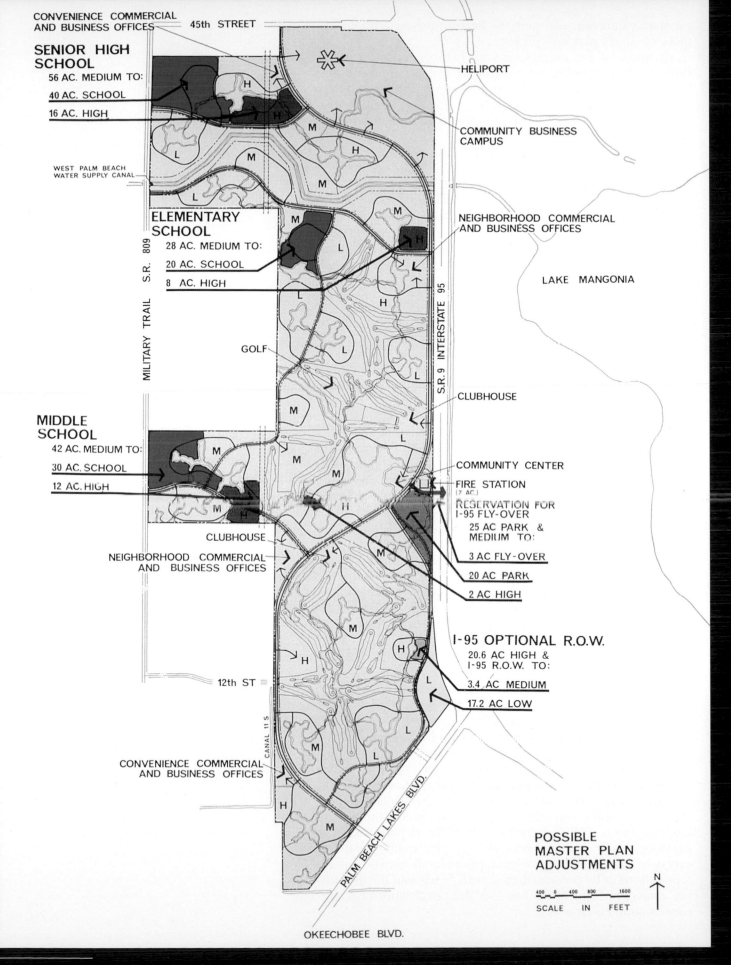

CONVENIENCE COMMERCIAL
AND BUSINESS OFFICES — 45th STREET

**SENIOR HIGH
SCHOOL**

56 AC. MEDIUM TO:

40 AC. SCHOOL

16 AC. HIGH

HELIPORT

COMMUNITY BUSINESS
CAMPUS

WEST PALM BEACH
WATER SUPPLY CANAL

H

H

M

M

M

L

L

L

**ELEMENTARY
SCHOOL**

28 AC. MEDIUM TO:

20 AC. SCHOOL

8 AC. HIGH

M

M

L

H

NEIGHBORHOOD COMMERCIAL
AND BUSINESS OFFICES

LAKE MANGONIA

S.R. 809

MILITARY TRAIL

GOLF

L

L

L

H

L

S.R. 9 INTERSTATE 95

CLUBHOUSE

**MIDDLE
SCHOOL**

42 AC. MEDIUM TO:

30 AC. SCHOOL

12 AC. HIGH

M

M

M

M

M

H

L

COMMUNITY CENTER

FIRE STATION
(2 AC.)

RESERVATION FOR
I-95 FLY-OVER

25 AC PARK &
MEDIUM TO:

3 AC FLY-OVER

20 AC PARK

2 AC HIGH

CLUBHOUSE

NEIGHBORHOOD COMMERCIAL
AND BUSINESS OFFICES

M

M

H

H

I-95 OPTIONAL R.O.W.

20.6 AC HIGH &
I-95 R.O.W. TO:

3.4 AC MEDIUM

17.2 AC LOW

12th ST

CANAL 11 S

CONVENIENCE COMMERCIAL
AND BUSINESS OFFICES

M

L

L

H

M

**POSSIBLE
MASTER PLAN
ADJUSTMENTS**

N

400 0   400 800   1600

SCALE   IN   FEET

PALM BEACH LAKES BLVD.

OKEECHOBEE BLVD.

for shade, benches, and perhaps here and there a bike rack or a piece of child's play equipment.

In most of the more successful planned unit developments, homes and apartments are arranged in compact groupings or clusters to squeeze out wasted separation space around and between the buildings. This is not only more land- and cost-efficient, but also, with the same overall densities, yields an increased measure of shared open space.

This compaction is evident also in the better activity centers. Both at the neighborhood and community levels, compatible uses are combined. Examples include the elementary school and park; the high school, game courts, and athletic field; the shopping, business, and professional office complex; the community building, church, library, and performing arts assemblage; or the museum and center for arts and crafts. In all such cases the intensification is beneficial. Moreover, the gathering together of once dispersed uses into more vibrant nuclei also provides, in the overall community plan, additional open area.

Open space

Why community open space? Because without it there can be little sense of *community*. It is mainly in the outdoor ways and places that communal living takes place.

Open space equates with many forms of recreation. Some, like lacrosse or field hockey, require expansive areas. Others need only a limited space. A child's slide or a basketball backboard, for instance, will fit almost anywhere. Baseball fields and basketball courts are among those needing precise orientation and construction, while more passive kinds of recreation—picnicking, kite flying, or playing catch—take little more than an open field. Lineal spaces, as for jogging paths, health trails, or bikeways, must be carefully woven into community plans to assure continuity.

Open space has other values, too. If it follows and envelops the drainageways and streams it serves to preserve the natural growth and define buildable areas with lobes of refreshing green. It also provides cover for birds and small animals that contribute much of delight to the local scene. Not only in the suburbs but in the inner city as well.

Where does such open space come from? As noted, it is a natural product of the PUD planning approach which, with fixed densities, features clustered building arrangements. Available open spaces include the unpaved areas of the street rights-of-way—or the whole of utility easements. They are acquired in part as segments of park and recreation systems. Unbuildable areas such as floodplains, marshes, steep slopes, and narrow ridges make their contributions, as do the open areas of business office parks, the university campus, and institutional grounds. Some highly desirable open space may be derived from the reclamation of extraction pits, landfills, strip-mining operations, cutover timberlands, or depleted farms. Public agencies such as the department of transportation, water management districts, or the military may transfer excess or vacated holdings. Again, prime lands may be donated by foundations or by private citizens, with or without the incentives of tax abatement. And there are, too, the possibilities of scenic and conservation easements.

> The latent longing . . . for a life in mutual appreciation should be brought to blossom and fruit by education; but the external conditions needed for its fulfillment must also be created. The architects must be given the task to build for human contact, to build an environment which invites meetings and centers which give these meetings meaning and render them productive.
>
> E. A. Gutkind

Piece by piece, parcel by parcel, an open-space system can in time be fitted together for the good of all concerned—provided that for each community there is a program and a plan.

The new ethic in community planning (P-C-D)

Preserve the best of the natural and historic features.

Conserve, with limited use, an interconnecting open-space framework.

Develop selected upland areas with site-responsive building clusters.

By this approach the project site is thoroughly analyzed by a team of qualified planning experts and scientific advisors. Then on the topographic surveys a line is drawn around those areas of high scenic, historic, or ecological value (P). These areas and features are to be *preserved* intact, without significant disturbance. Around them, as protective buffers, are then described *conservation* swaths of lesser landscape value. The *C* (for "conservation") areas may be devoted to such limited open space or recreational uses as will not harm their natural quality. *Development* (D) or construction areas are only then allocated on the receptive higher ground. Here the structures are usually clustered in more compact and efficient arrangements within the blue and green open-space framework. Here, without inflicting negative impacts, people can live and work at peace with their natural surroundings.

Planned communities are prime examples of *sound economic development coupled with conservation*. Yet even the most glowing examples have come into being only after long years of battle with outmoded codes, and with self-styled environmentalists, who by all

> Many conservationists who would protect and assure the best use of our lands and waters have yet to learn that cooperative, large-scale, long-range planning is more effective than the common no-growth tactic of "block and delay."

Flowing spring and natural environs preserved as central features of the planned community. (The Springs, Longwood, Florida)

reason should be the greatest advocates. For mile after mile of beachfront and thousands upon thousands of acres of prime forest and wetland have already been set aside and preserved intact, voluntarily, by comprehensive community planning.

Much can be accomplished when this process comes to be carried forward in full cooperation with local citizens, dynamic conservation groups, and contributing public agencies. It can be seen that such P–C–D planning applies not only to residential development but as well to every type of use and parcel—to whole regions and to the state.

New Directions

In appraising the better examples of recently planned communities we find many promising features. Some planning concepts, like the *transfer of development rights and flexibility zoning*, were unheard of even a few years ago. Some have met with immediate acceptance, others have not, and still others have yet to be adequately tested. While some approaches have failed in their initial application, they may have in them the seeds of ideas that will flower in the communities of the future.

With the transfer of development rights, owners of ecologically sensitive or productive agricultural land may negotiate with planning officials a trade–off by which the right to develop the prime landholding is forfeited in exchange for the right to develop a similar, or different, type of project at an alternative location. Often by such an arrangement a valuable community asset can be preserved—and extensive tracts of marginal or depleted property transformed into highly desirable real estate. Everyone thus benefits.

Fine communities seldom if ever just happen. They must be thoughtfully and painstakingly brought into being. Improved approaches are continually emerging and give new meaning to such words as *housing, health, education, recreation,* and *community.* In the shaping of our more advanced residential areas the following principles are being successfully applied.

> *Apply the PUD approach.* Planned community development, or planned unit development (PUD) as it is sometimes called, is a rational framework for the phased development of community plans. Essentially it establishes at the start the types of uses to be included, the total number of dwellings, and a conceptual plan diagram. The traditional restrictive regulations are waived, and each successive phase as it is brought on in detail is checked against the conceptual plan and judged solely on the basis of foreseeable performance.
>
> *Request flexibility zoning.* For larger tracts, this permits within the zone boundaries the free arrangement and progressive restudy of the land use and traffic–flow diagrams as long as the established caps are rebalanced and not exceeded and as long as the plan remains consistent with community goals.
>
> *Consider the transfer of development rights (TDR).* In recognition of the fact that, for reasons of their ecologic, scenic, or other values, certain areas of land and water should be preserved in their natural state, TDR provisions allow and encourage a developer to transfer from the sensitive area those uses originally permitted by zoning. Although the relocation of the uses or dwelling units to another property is sometimes provided,

> *All good planning must begin with a survey of actual resources: the landscape, the people, the work-a-day activities in a community. Good planning does not begin with an abstract and arbitrary scheme that it seeks to impose on a community; it begins with a knowledge of existing conditions and opportunities....*
>
> *The final test of an economic system is not the tons of iron, the tanks of oil, or the miles of textiles it produces: The final test lies in its ultimate products—the sort of men and women it nurtures and the order and beauty and sanity of their communities.*
>
> Lewis Mumford

Conversion of marginal farmland to a more usable landscape. The new town site at start of planning. (Miami Lakes, Dade County, Florida)

View of a completed residential neighborhood with excavated lakes, reshaped topography, and site development (Miami Lakes, Florida)

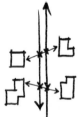

Home-to-home relationships across a busy street or highway...

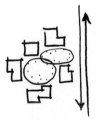

should give way to roadside clusters around a shared court.

TDR is most effective when the densities of contiguous building sites in the same ownership are increased to absorb the relocated units.

Relate all studies to water resource management. The fourfold purpose is to prevent flooding, protect water quality, replenish freshwater reserves, and provide for wastewater disposal.

Provide perimeter buffering. As supplementary or alternative open space, a band of land in its natural state may well be left around the borders of larger development sites. This provides a screen against adjacent trafficways or other abutting uses and a welcome backdrop for building construction.

Create a community portal. One of the best ways in which to engender a sense of neighborhood or community is by the provision of a cohesive circulation system and an attractive gateway.

Assure regional access. Thriving communities need connection to the shopping, cultural, and recreation centers and the open spaces of the regions which surround them. Aside from paths and controlled-access roadways, linkage may be attained by bikeways, by boat if on water, and by rapid transit in one or more of its many forms.

Preclude through-community trucking. Although local streets must be used on occasion by heavy trucks (by permit) and for daily deliveries by smaller vehicles, a direct truckway link to the community storage and distribution center has many advantages. Here heavy loads may be broken down for home or commercial delivery and bulk and private storage space provided for seasonal equipment, boats, and recreation vehicles.

Plan an open-space framework. As an alternative to facing homes and other development directly upon trafficways, many communities now wisely provide for the reservation of variformed swaths of land, in public or private ownership, as preferred building frontage. Vehicular approach to buildings, parking, and service areas is from the rear. The open-space system, which usually follows streams and drainageways, may also include walks, bicycle and jogging paths, and wider recreation areas.

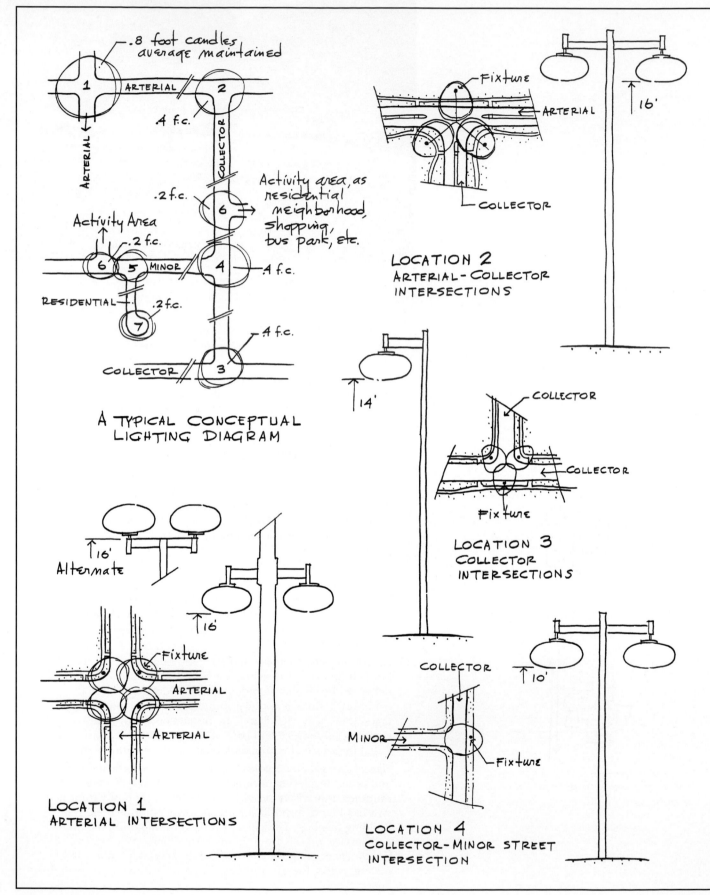

.8 foot candles average maintained

ARTERIAL

ARTERIAL

COLLECTOR

.4 f.c.

.2 f.c.

Activity Area

.2 f.c.

MINOR

RESIDENTIAL

.2 f.c.

Activity area, as residential neighborhood, shopping, bus park, etc.

.4 f.c.

.4 f.c.

COLLECTOR

A TYPICAL CONCEPTUAL LIGHTING DIAGRAM

Fixture

ARTERIAL

16'

COLLECTOR

LOCATION 2 ARTERIAL-COLLECTOR INTERSECTIONS

14'

COLLECTOR

COLLECTOR

Fixture

LOCATION 3 COLLECTOR INTERSECTIONS

16'

Alternate

16'

Fixture

ARTERIAL

ARTERIAL

LOCATION 1 ARTERIAL INTERSECTIONS

COLLECTOR

10'

MINOR

Fixture

LOCATION 4 COLLECTOR-MINOR STREET INTERSECTION

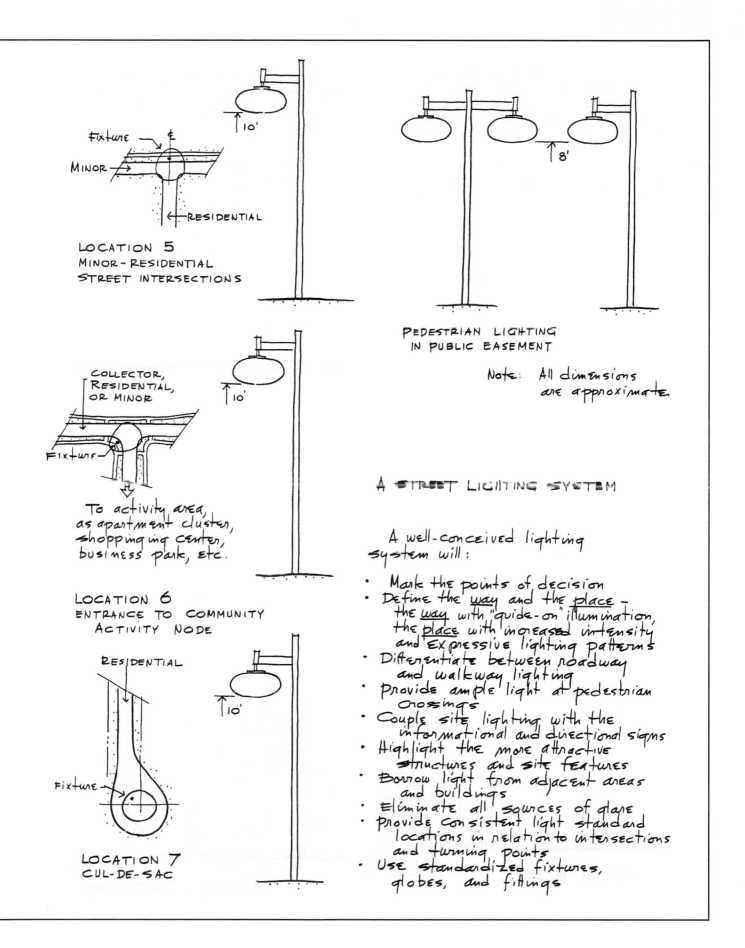

LOCATION 5
MINOR – RESIDENTIAL
STREET INTERSECTIONS

Fixture

MINOR

RESIDENTIAL

10'

LOCATION 6
ENTRANCE TO COMMUNITY
ACTIVITY NODE

COLLECTOR,
RESIDENTIAL,
OR MINOR

Fixture

10'

To activity area,
as apartment cluster,
shopping center,
business park, etc.

LOCATION 7
CUL-DE-SAC

RESIDENTIAL

Fixture

10'

PEDESTRIAN LIGHTING
IN PUBLIC EASEMENT

8'

Note: All dimensions
are approximate.

A STREET LIGHTING SYSTEM

A well-conceived lighting
system will:

- Mark the points of decision
- Define the _way_ and the _place_ –
  the _way_ with "guide-on" illumination,
  the _place_ with increased intensity
  and expressive lighting patterns
- Differentiate between roadway
  and walkway lighting
- Provide ample light at pedestrian
  crossings
- Couple site lighting with the
  informational and directional signs
- Highlight the more attractive
  structures and site features
- Borrow light from adjacent areas
  and buildings
- Eliminate all sources of glare
- Provide consistent light standard
  locations in relation to intersections
  and turning points
- Use standardized fixtures,
  globes, and fittings

Plan a hierarchy of trafficways.   Even in smaller communities a clear differentiation between arterial, circulation, and local-frontage streets ensures more efficient traffic movement and safer, more agreeable living areas.

Limit roadside frontage.   Insofar as possible, the facing of build-ings upon arterials and circulation streets is to be precluded, with intersections to local-frontage streets spaced no closer that 660 feet.

Make use of three-way ("T") street intersections.   They reduce through traffic, increase visibility, and make pedestrian crossing much safer.

Provide for rapid transit.   Sheltered bus and minitransit stops and attractive community rapid transit stations, where appropriate, do much to stimulate transit use and reduce vehicular traffic.

Integrate paths of movement.   Only when streets, walkways, bicy-cle trails, and other routes of movement are planned together can their full possibilities and optimum interrelationships be realized.

Vary the housing types.   A well-balanced community provides not only a variety of dwellings, from single-family to multifamily, but also accommodates residents of differing lifestyles and a broad income range.

Systematize the site installations.   All physical elements of a com-munity—buildings, roadways, walks, utilities, signage, and lighting—are best planned as interrelated *systems.*

Cluster the buildings.   The more compact grouping of individual dwellings and the inclusion of patio and zero-lotline homes yield welcome additional open space for neighborhood buffer-ing and recreation use.

Feature the school-park campus.   The combining of schools with neighborhood and community parks permits much fuller use of each at substantial savings.

Include convenience shopping.   While regional shopping centers fill the largest share of family marketing needs, they usually require travel by automobile. Neighborhood and community centers, with access by walks and bikeways, are needed to pro-vide for a lesser scale of convenience shopping and service.

Provide employment opportunities.   Bedroom communities—those planned for residential living only—require the expenditure of time, income, and energy just to get to and from work. Inte-gral or closely related employment centers add vitality and convenience.

Relate to the regional centers.   The larger business office campus, industrial park, or regional commercial mall is best kept out-side, but convenient to, the residential groupings. Such centers are logically located near the regional freeway interchanges and accessible to the interconnecting circulation roads.

Plan for transient accommodations.   When highway-related motel, hotel, or boatel accommodations do not otherwise fulfill the traveler's needs, a community inn is a welcome addition.

Consider a conference center.   In addition to the auditorium and meeting rooms of the school-park community centers, a con-ference facility related to the commercial mall, business office park, cultural core, marina, golf course, tennis club, or inn is a popular amenity and asset.

Make recreation a way of life.   Aside from private recreation opportunities and those provided at the neighborhood and community school parks, there is usually need for swimming, golf, and racquet clubs, a marina and beach club if the com-

The evolution in playground design is taking on ecological dimensions.

For many elementary schools the out-door play courts have become an extension of the indoor learning center. Here the students have not only their group games, but may also construct things out of loose components, paint murals on a wall, or plant a teaching garden. In effect, such innovative play-grounds have become outdoor class-rooms.

66 *In Great Britain a charitable organization called the* Learning through Landscapes Trust *has transformed nearly 10,000 school yards into imaginative learning gardens.* Landscape Architecture *magazine October 1994*

munity is on water, a youth center, and access to hiking, jog-ging, and bicycle trails. The broader the range of available recreation, the more fulfilling is community life.

Encourage community programs, activities, and events. Although many do not require special space or site areas, no development pro-gram could be complete without consideration of all those social activities that contribute so much to community living. These include worship, continuing education and health care pro-grams, children's day care, a craft center and workshop, a little theater, game and meeting rooms, a newspaper, service clubs, Little League, dances, contests, and parades. Some start sponta-neously, others may require encouragement and guidance.

Build out as you go. Scattered or partially finished building areas are uneconomical and disruptive. In the better communities, construction proceeds by the phased *extension* of trafficways, utilities, and development areas. They are *completed* as exam-ples. Construction materials and equipment are brought in from the rear, and the prearranged staging areas and access roads retreat as the work advances.

Assure a high level of maintenance. A maintenance center and enclosed yard, perhaps combined with a water storage or treat-ment plant, is best located inconspicuously at the periphery, with ready access to trucking and the areas to be served. It is to be well equipped and phased in advance of development to provide complete maintenance from the very start.

Honor the historic landmarks. When features of archaeological or historical significance exist, they are to be cherished. Their presence extends knowledge of the locality, its beginnings, and traditions and gives depth of meaning to life within the community.

Establish nature preserves. Every locality or site has in some degree its prized natural features. Be they subtle or dramatic, they add richness and interest and are to be protected, inter-preted, and admired.

Name a scientist advisory council. In both initial and ongoing planning much can be gained by the naming of a team of sci-entist advisers. Convened periodically to bring their expertise to bear on the evolving plans and proposals, they are espe-cially helpful in the study of large, complex, or ecologically sensitive holdings.

Appoint an environmental control officer. In the phased construc-tion of each new parcel the responsibility for environmental protection is best centralized in one trained person who is present during all phases of planning, design review, and field installation.

Form a design review board. The plans for all buildings and major site improvements are best subjected from the start to a panel of qualified designers for review and recommendation as to acceptance, rejection, or modification. An architect, a landscape architect, and the environmental control officer would be appropriate members.

Prepare a development guideline manual. As the basic reference document for all planning, design, and continuing operation of the community, an expanding loose-leaf manual is essential. As it evolves, it will contain:

> The community goals and objectives
>
> The conceptual community plan
>
> Each phased neighborhood or parcel plan as it is brought into detailed study

A section and flowchart describing plan review procedures

Plan submission requirements and forms

Architectural design guidelines

Site design guidelines

The master planting plan and policy and recommended plant lists

A section on environmental quality control

A section on energy conservation

A section on solid waste disposal and recycling

Home-owners association covenants

As the need arises or is foreseen, supplementary sections will be added and the manual kept updated and complete. To be fully effective, its provisions must be equitably and uniformly enforced.

Establish a means of governance. It is important from the start of planning to have in mind the type of political entity that the community is to be or to become a part of. This will be a key factor in the determination of the type and level of public services to be provided and of responsibilities for planning reviews and permitting, for the installation of utilities, streets, and other improvements, and for taxation and decision making.

Create a home-owners' association. The developer, builders, and final home owners all benefit by the early formation of a permanent organization in which the owner of each lot or home has a pro rata responsibility and vote and to which assessments are paid. The purpose of the association is to provide the mechanism for the formulation and implementation of continuing community maintenance and improvement policies.

Ensure flexibility with control. The most successful American communities have been guided in their development by policies that

- Established the broad outlines of compatible land use and routes of movement

- Provided the guidelines required to ensure flexibility, design quality, and environmental protection

- Encouraged individuality and creativity

COMMUNITY FOCAL POINTS

The character of a neighborhood or community is judged by the activity centers and focal points to which it is oriented.

Playlots.

Shops.

Public gardens.

Restaurants.

Recreation centers.

17
URBAN DESIGN

IT SOMETIMES SEEMS that our contemporary planning is an unholy game of piling as much structure or as much city as possible in one spot. The urban areas to which we point with pride are often merely the highest, widest, and densest piles of brick, stone, and mortar. Where, in these heaps and stacks of masonry, are the forgotten, stifled people? Are they refreshed, inspired, and stimulated by their urban environment? Hardly, for in our times, too often a city is a desert.

Cityscape

To be bluntly truthful, our burgeoning American cities, squared off and cut into uncompromising geometric blocks by unrelieved, unterminated trafficways, have had more of this arid desert quality than those of other cultures past or present.

If we compare a map of Rome as it was in 1748 with an aerial photograph of New York as it is today, we marvel at the infinite variety of pleasant spaces that occurred throughout the Eternal City. Of course, as Rasmussen has pointed out in *Towns and Buildings,* "Great artists formed the city, and the inhabitants, themselves, were artists enough to know how to live in it." We wonder why such spaces are for the most part missing in our contemporary city plans.

Traditionally, the urban spaces of America have been mainly corridors. Our streets, boulevards, and sidewalks have led past or through to something or somewhere beyond. Our cities, our suburbs, and our homesites are laced and interlaced with these corridors, and we often seek in vain to find those places or spaces that attract and hold us and satisfy. We do not like to live in corridors;

According to a recent poll, most Americans (56 percent), if given the choice, would now prefer a rural life; 25 percent would opt for the suburbs, and only 19 percent for an urban living environment.

The corridor-canyons that are New York City's streets stretch on interminably without relief, without focal point, or without the welcome interruption of useful or meaningful space.

we like to live in rooms. The cities of history are full of such rooms, planned and furnished with as much concern as were the surrounding structures. If we would have such appealing outdoor places, we must plan our corridors not as channels trying to be places as well but as free-flowing channelized trafficways. And we must plan our places for the use and enjoyment of people.

The city experienced

The old cities of Europe, Latin America, and Asia had, and still have to their credit and memorable charm, their plazas, piazzas, courts, squares, and fountains and their distinctive, undefinable, uplifting spirit of joie de vivre. These cities were conceived as three-dimensional civic art and in terms of meaningful patterns of form and open spaces. Our cities, with few exceptions, are oriented to our traffic-glutted streets.

Whom are we to blame for this? Aristotle, in his *Rhetoric*, states, "*Truth and justice are by their nature better than their opposites, and therefore if decisions are made wrongly, it must be the speakers who (through lack of effective powers of persuasion) are to blame for the defeat*." For our purpose, this passage might well be paraphrased: "*Facility, interest,*

Large cities seen from an altitude of several hundred feet do not present, as a whole, an orderly facade. Their vastness is their most striking feature; whatever quality they possess is lost in sheer quantity. Areas that give evidence of planning occupy but a small surface. Disorder predominates. Buildings are piled up near the center and scattered haphazardly toward the outskirts. The few green spots and other places of beauty known to the tourist, seem hidden in a maze of grey and shapeless masses that stretch toward the surrounding country in tentacular form. The very borders of the city are undefined, junk and refuse belts merging with the countryside. If on beholding this sight we pause to contemplate modern cities and consider what they could have been if planned, we must admit in the end that, in spite of their magnificent vitality, they represent one of man's greatest failures.

José Luis Sert

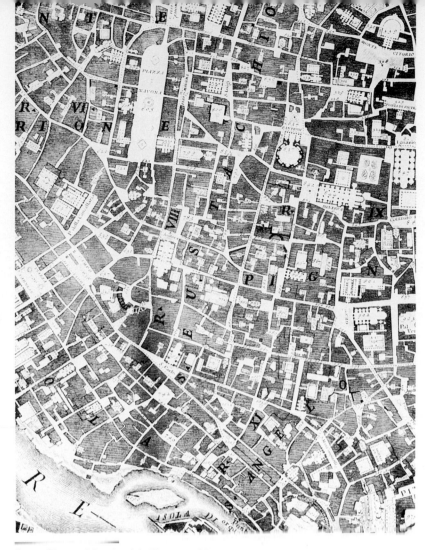

From Giovanni Battista Nolli's map of Rome.

> *The essential thing of both room and square is the quality of enclosed space.*
>
> *Camillo Sitte*

The basic tenet of urban design is disarmingly simple: the best city is that which provides the best experience of living.

For the most part, it is proposed that those cities have proven most agreeable that are the most expressive of and responsive to their time, place, and culture; that are functional; that afford convenience; and that are rational and complete.

and beauty are by nature better than chaos, the dull, and the ugly, and therefore if decisions are made wrongly, it must be we planners who, through lack of effective powers of persuasion (or more compelling concepts of urban living) are to blame."

In searching for a more enlightened approach to urban planning we must look back and reappraise the old values. While recognizing the fallacies of the "city beautiful" in its narrowest sense, we must rediscover the age-old art of building cities that inspire, satisfy, and work. And surely we will, for we are disturbed by the vapid nature of the cities we have planned or, worse, have allowed to grow unplanned in sporadic, senseless confusion.

Evident needs

We, in contemporary times, have lost the art of, and feeling for, overall plan organization. Our cities lack coherent relationships and plan continuity. With our automobiles as the symbol and most demanding planning factor of our times, we have found the meandering streets, places, and plan forms of the ancient cities to be unsuitable. We have rejected (with good reason) the synthesizing device of the inexorable "grand plan" but have found, for the most part, few substitutes save the mechanical grid and other patterns of uninspired geometry. The transit, the protractor, and the

CENTRAL PARK

Central Park is the first public park built in America. A competition for its design was held in 1858. the winners, Frederick Law Olmsted and Calvert Vaux, were the first American landscape architects.

This magnificent urban open space of 843 acres has attracted to its sides much of the prime residential, commercial and cultural construction of the city. Its effect on real estate values, its inestimable contribution to the city, its ineffable meaning to all who see and sense and use it—these lessons should never be forgotten by the urban planner.

View from north to south.

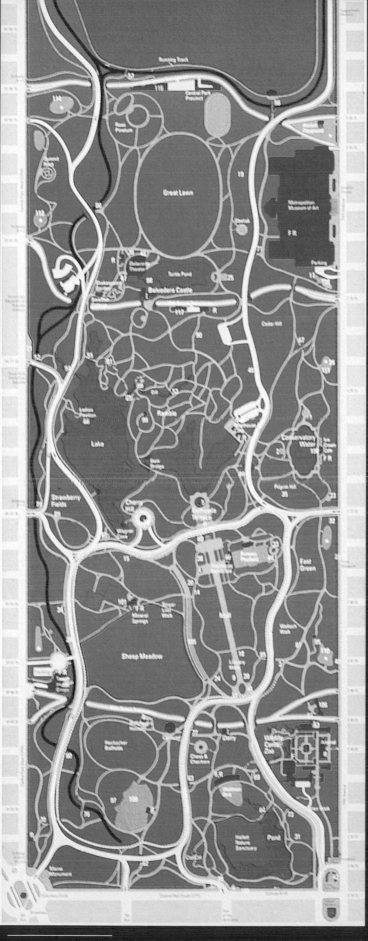
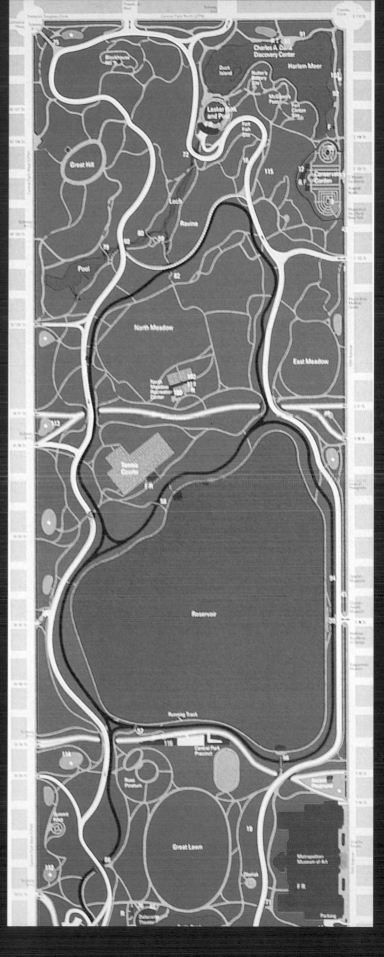

Plan, Central Park. From south (bottom left) to north (top right).

compass have delineated for us a wholly artificial pattern of living areas and spaces. We must and will develop new types of plan organization better suited to our way of life. In future urban planning considerations, the significant space is bound to return, and we will again have ways and places as important as the structures.

The desert character of our cities is concentrated in the downtown core. Here the average cityscape is a conglomeration of metal, glass, and masonry cubes set on a dreary base plane of oil-splattered concrete and asphalt. It is bleak, chill, and gusty in wintertime, and in summer it shimmers and weaves with its stored-up, radiating heat. Within view of its naked towers, the open countryside beyond is often many degrees warmer in winter and cooler in the summertime.

Such an oppressive and barren cityscape falls far short of the mark. Our cities must be opened up, refreshed, revitalized. Our straining traffic arteries must be realigned to bypass the city cores, to pass under or around the perimeter of unified pedestrian areas or levels in which offices, shops, and restaurants are planned together in close proximity and in which people may move about without on-grade crossings of trafficways. In contrast with the stark masonry canyons and roaring avenues, the new pedestrian domains will provide a gardenlike setting for freely composed groupings of towers and terraced structures, variformed courts, and walkways—providing the welcome relief of foliage, shade, splashing water, flowers, and bright color. Like oases, such intensified multiuse plazas will transform the city into a refreshing environment for vibrant urban life. Many exemplary prototypes are appearing in America and abroad.

The City Diagram

To understand how a city works (or why it doesn't work) and plan toward its improvement, it is helpful to dissect it into its various parts and to examine each part separately. Such an approach re-

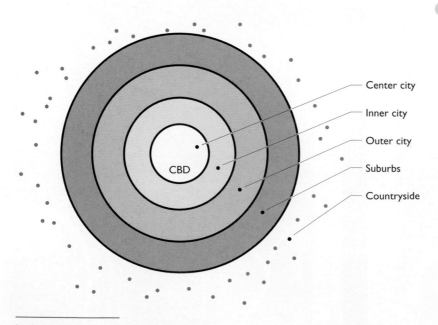

Center city

Inner city

Outer city

Suburbs

Countryside

CBD

In thriving cities, each component district is well-defined and fulfills its contributing functions.

> The unit of measurement for space in urban society is the individual. . . .
> Arthur B. Gallion

> A city plan is the expression of the collective purpose of the people who live in it, or it is nothing.
> Henry S. Churchill

> The first step in adequate planning is to make a fresh canvass of human ideals and human purposes.
> Lewis Mumford

> From cradle to grave, this problem of running order through chaos, direction through space, discipline through freedom, unity through multiplicity, has always been, and must always be, the task of education, as it is the moral of religious philosophy, science, art, politics and economy.
> Henry Adams

> Will the city reassert itself as a good place to live? It will not, unless there is a decided shift in the thinking of those who would remake it. The popular image of the city as it is now is bad enough—a place of decay, crime, of fouled streets, and of people who are poor or foreign or odd. But what is the image of the city of the future? In the plans for the huge redevelopment projects to come, we are being shown a new image of the city—and it is sterile and lifeless. Gone are the dirt and noise—and the variety and the excitement and the spirit. That it is an ideal makes it all the worse; these bleak new Utopias are not bleak because they have to be; they are the concrete manifestation—and how literally—of a deep and at times arrogant, misunderstanding of the function of the city.
> William H. Whyte, Jr.

Garden city center. (Pacific Place, Hong Kong)

There are, certainly, ample reasons for redoing downtown—falling retail sales, tax bases in jeopardy, stagnant real-estate values, impossible traffic and parking conditions, failing mass transit, encirclement by slums. But with no intent to minimize these serious matters, it is more to the point to consider what makes a city center magnetic, what can inject gaiety, the wonder, the cheerful hurly-burly that make people want to come into the city and to linger there. For magnetism is the crux of the problem. All downtown's values are its by-products. To create in it an atmosphere of urbanity and exuberance is not a frivolous aim.

Jane Jacobs

veals the surprising fact that in few cities have such components been planned, or even considered, as functioning entities. As to components, for the purpose of this examination it is proposed that we consider, first separately and then together, the *center city*, the *inner city*, the *outer city*, and the *suburbs*.

The center city, or central business district (CBD)

The center city serves a double purpose. It is not only the core of the urban metropolis, it is as well the polarizing and dynamic core of the whole surrounding region. Here one expects to find the centers of government, commerce, and trade; the principal financial institutions; and the corporate headquarters of industry, manufacturing, and communications. Here too are most often found the cultural superlatives—the cathedral, performing arts center, central library, museums, and galleries, and as well the theaters, stadium, and sports arenas.

With each complex a small empire in itself, there is reason to allocate for each its own distinctive segment of the center. Since all segments share the need for shopping, dining, and hotels, a centralized superplaza is suggested, around which the various building groupings can take form. With few exceptions, parking, storage, distribution, and mechanical systems are to be relegated to subsurface plaza levels.

Within the CBD, through streets will be eliminated—phased out in time and replaced by circulation loop drives around and between the traffic-free plaza islands. These surface drives, bridged at the plaza-to-plaza crossings, will provide for the free circulation of cabs, buses, emergency vehicles, and a limited number of private cars by special permit.

Rooftop gardens such as this may be the forerunners of terraced garden cities.

On the linked plaza islands of the revitalized center will rise a new urban architecture. The free-standing megaliths of the present will be replaced by interconnected complexes of high and low structures with flying terraces, roof gardens, inset patios, open courts, domed conservatories, and galleries. Aloft, boxed window ledges, balconies, and terraced setbacks will become the private gardens of the center city. Rooftop restaurants and illuminated recreation courts and pools will add sparkle and animation to the skyline. At pedestrian levels buildings will open out upon a labyrinth of landscaped courts and meandering walkways. Passageways from place to place and level to level will be weather-protected. They will be flanked with seasonal exhibits, displays, and plantings—with flower stalls and book marts; candy, nut, and pizza shops; pretzel, fruit, and popcorn stands...and provision for sidewalk bazaars with paintings, carvings, crafts, antique jewelry, mechanical toys, entertainers, and all those divertissements that add excitement and pleasure to shopping.

With surface traffic and parking restricted within the city center, rapid transit will flourish. (Such cities as Stockholm, Toronto, and Paris are telling examples.) Multilevel transit hubs, centrally located, are major regional destinations and points of transfer. Linked, computerized cars arrive and depart at swishing speeds through illuminated subsurface transitways or by aerial monorail.

It is proposed that the CBD of the future will be confined, and *constricted*, by a tight and inflexible *ring* to preclude its "leaking out"

The CBD, in compression, will grow upward instead of out; obsolescence will disappear, densities will increase, and the core will regain its dynamic intensity.

Our present troubled, largely obsolescent, and woefully inefficient urban centers are spilling out over their boundaries and messing up the countryside. Such uncontrolled sprawl can and must be stopped. Not only for the good of the cities, which are losing their focal dominance and vitality, but as well for the farmlands, forests, and rural American landscape, which are rapidly going to pot.

An arcade or mall of shops and restaurants that never close helps keep the streets safe and the downtown vital. Occupants of upper-story apartments in office and commercial buildings add to the evening street life, and round-the-clock surveillance.

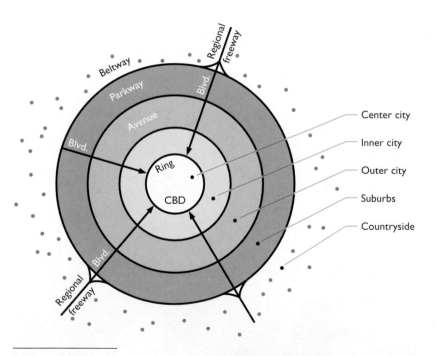

Center city

Inner city

Outer city

Suburbs

Countryside

The memorable cities of the world—London, Amsterdam, Paris, Copenhagen, Madrid, Athens, Rome, Montreal, New York, New Orleans, San Francisco—are those in which people live where they work. Civic and business centers are interspersed with townhouses, apartments, and cafés, with bakeries and boutiques, with wine, cheese, fruit, and florist shops, and with artists' studios.

Almost without exception, and for obvious reasons, metropolitan transportation authorities are coming to adopt a system of free-flowing concentric arterial freeways/parkways with radial access to the center city.

This system, adjusted to the topography and other existing conditions:

• Provides motorists with the opportunity to bypass the city entirely and rid it of unwanted through traffic.
• Allows drivers to home in on targeted sectors without multiple grid-block crossings.
• Helps define and delimit the various component city areas, while providing optimum ingress-egress.

The best way to promote security in a downtown area is to ensure that the streets are alive with responsible urban residents who come out to enjoy the evening sights and activities. In such an atmosphere, restaurants and theaters thrive, shops stay open, and people can linger or stroll about in relative safety.

Patterns of mix are important. The vibrant centers are those in which the old is intermixed with the new, the low with the high, the simple with the elaborate.

When rows of shops and homes are interrupted by blocks of stark office towers or by blank building walls, evening street life is diminished. To sustain street appeal and nighttime activity, office and apartment towers are best grouped around off-street plazas or courts. Business, residential, and commercial relationships are all thereby intensified.

The *layering* of shops, apartments, and offices is proving to be a successful means of keeping the evening streets alive, with people at hand to enjoy them.

Eminent domain is the authority by which a government or public agency can appropriate, with due recompense, private property for public use or benefit.

To make the exercise of eminent domain more acceptable, its application may be conditioned by such provisions as:

1. Use only after open negotiation has been tried and failed.
2. Use only for the final 10 percent of the land required when a holdout has blocked acquisition.
3. When long-range acquisition is in the public interest, grant the owner tenancy for a stated period or lifetime.
4. Purchase, with leaseback for conditional uses.

and ensure its intensity. Access by automobile via radial boulevards will be intercepted at the center-city perimeter by a decked distributor ring road within a spacious right-of-way. Vehicles arriving at the ring can either circumvent the CBD entirely if this is desired or enter by well-spaced ramps into the parking and transport levels of the plazas. The ring is more than a free-flowing trafficway. Its wide swath of space can accommodate ample open-air parking compounds as well as water management holding ponds and recreation areas. Here, too, available to center-city visitors can be located such attractions as elements of the zoo, botanic garden, and aviary. Or perhaps the annual art fair or ethnic festivals.

Housing? The more successful cities have proven the value of devoting the upper stories of buildings and towers to in-city apartments for executives and higher-salaried workers who then in the evenings throng into the pedestrian ways and places to keep them alive and thriving.

The inner city

Outward of the ring lies the area best described as the "inner city." It is the band containing the bulk of housing and service facilities that provide the necessary support of the CBD and adjacent urban satellite communities. Commonly, in its present form, it is mostly obsolescent—left behind in the exodus of the previous residents who followed the expanding trafficways into the lands beyond. In its dilapidated state it is pocked with abandoned structures and vacant properties. Here and there are the remnants of once-thriving neighborhoods. Here too one finds start-up businesses in reclaimed buildings and blocks of homes restored and renovated by enterprising newcomers.

Available opportunities

Here in the inner city with its frequent stretches of boarded-up buildings and rubble-strewn land, there is opportunity to acquire at affordable cost the sites for clustered housing enclaves or whole new communities. Until recently this was not possible because of absentee or "hold-out" parcel owners. Now, however, with innovative redevelopment techniques providing the powers of eminent domain, the sizable sites required can be assembled and cleared by a redevelopment authority.

In city after city such reclaimed tracts of inner-city wasteland are now sprouting with well-planned, mixed-use, residential developments. Dwellings range in type from single-family homes to multistory apartments. Residents, many of whom are employed nearby, may be workers of low to moderate income or high-salaried executives.

The inner city offers the greatest opportunity for urban renewal and redevelopment, for with overall planning and self-help incentives, it can provide not only the housing but also a wide spectrum of the service and supply facilities needed to support the adjacent CBD and outer city. With unemployment and the lack of housing two of the major urban problems, the inner city teems with latent solutions.

Housing

It is in the inner city that low to moderate income housing will make its most telling advances. While the tower apartments of the CBD (on costly land and with elevators required) will be designed mainly for residents with the higher incomes, the mixed-use neighborhoods outside the ring will include the full range of housing types for those of all income levels, including the displaced and presently homeless.

At the upper end of the housing scale will be zero-lotline homes, town houses, garden apartments, and low-rise multifamily apartments resembling horizontal condominiums. The separated single-family homes facing on local streets or culs-de-sac (with front yards devoted to display and side yards unused) will no doubt persist, but there will be a preponderance of dwellings with common walls and fenced or walled outdoor living areas.

Town houses are a long-standing tradition—from Boston and Philadelphia to San Francisco. Georgetown in Washington, D.C., surely one of the most delightful residential areas of our country, has narrow brick homes set wall to wall along its narrow, shaded streets. Its brick walk pavements, often extending from curb to facade, are opened here around the smooth trunk of a sycamore or punched out there to receive a holly, a boxwood, a flowering tree, or a bed of myrtle. In this compact community, where space is at such a premium, the open areas are artfully enclosed by fences, walls, or building wings to give privacy and to create a cool and pleasant well of garden space into which the dwelling opens.

Mid- to lower-scale dwellings will also be designed in compact arrangements within open-space surroundings—with schools, child care centers, and convenience shopping close at hand. Again, some residential buildings will resemble horizontal "habitats," with

There is a truism to the effect that in every problem and seeming disaster are to be found the seeds of opportunity. In many ways our present cities are little short of disasters. Where then do the opportunities lie?

The inner city, where the problems seem most hopeless, may become "the promised land." In this deteriorated band are to be found many sound homes and start-up business structures inviting rehabilitation. Here too are endless opportunities for employment in the demolition of obsolete structures, clearing of land, reconstruction of streets and utility lines, and for privately financed redevelopment and planned communities.

The best features of townhouse living are exemplified in this attractive residence.

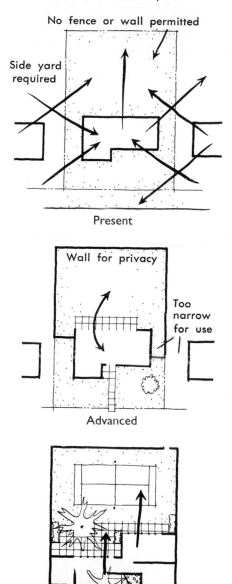

The house on the city lot

No fence or wall permitted

Side yard required

Present

Wall for privacy

Too narrow for use

Advanced

Ultimate

Relaxation of side-yard, setback, and enclosure restrictions will permit full use of lot, privacy, and indoor-outdoor transitions.

common laundries, storage spaces, gardens, and even kitchens. New concepts will be evident also in modular and prefab construction. While the construction framing members and panels will be of uniform dimensions, the room shapes and arrangements can be of infinite variety—as can panel materials and finishes. Fixtures, equipment, and furnishing will be standardized but freely arranged within the living spaces. (This will be a modernized version of the age–old, economical and delightfully varied Japanese modular approach to residential construction.)

With wide front– and side–yard setbacks consolidated into shared usable space, the building groupings can be diverse and compact, with things to see and do close at hand. For most home owners and tenants this will be a desirable feature.

The author, in working with urban renewal and model cities programs, has discovered that the openness of newer communities was at first the thing with greatest appeal to families relocated from older neighborhoods or from cramped and aching slums. But the residents soon became dissatisfied with the severe buildings, the wide grass areas, and the play equipment set out on flat sheets of pavement. One would hear the officials ask, "What's wrong with these people? Why aren't they happy? What did they expect? What more do they want?"

What they wanted, what they missed, what they unconsciously longed for, were such congregating places as the carved and whittled storefront bench, the rear–porch stoops, the packed–clay, sun–drenched boccie courts, the crates and boxes set in the cool shade of a propped–up grape arbor or in the spattered shadow of a spreading ailanthus tree. They missed the meandering alleys, dim and pungent, the leaking hydrants, the hot, bright places against the moist, dark places, the cellar doors, the leaning board fences, the sagging gates, the maze of rickety outside stairs. They missed the torn circus posters, the rusting enameled tobacco signs, the blatant billboards, the splotchy patches of weathered paint. They missed the bakery smells of hot raisin bread and warm, sugared lunch rolls, the fish market smells, the clean, raw smell of gasoline, the smell of vulcanizing rubber. They missed the strident neighborhood sounds, the intermittent calls and chatter, the baby squalls, the supper shouts, the whistles, the "allee, allee oxen," the pound of the stone hammer, the ring of the tire iron, the rumbling delivery truck, the huckster's cart, the dripping, creaking ice wagon. They missed the shape, the pattern, the smells, the sounds, and the pulsing feel of life.

What they missed, what they *need,* is the compression, the interest, the variety, the surprises, and the casual, indefinable charm of the neighborhood that they left behind. This, in essence, is the appeal of the Left Bank of Paris, of San Francisco's Chinatown, of Beacon Hill in Boston. This same charm of both tight and expansive spaces, of delightful variety, of delicious contrast, of the happy accident, is an essential quality of planning that we must constantly strive for. And one of the chief ingredients of charm, when we find it, is a sense of the diminutive, a feeling of pleasant compression. Private or community living spaces become a reality only if they and the life within them are kept within the scale of pleasurable human experience.

A further error of our planning has stemmed from the lingering compulsion to force our cities into lots and blocks of uniform size and use. Such "ideal" cities of monotonous conformity are gray in tone. If we examine most recent city plans, we find that one zone is designated for single-family homes, another zone for town houses, and another for high-rise apartments; an isolated district is set aside for commercial use; a green area will someday be a park. May we place in this residential area an artist's studio? It is not allowed! An office for an architect? A florist shop? A bookstall? A pastry shop? No! In a residential area such uses are usually not permitted, for that would be "spot zoning," the bureaucratic sin of all planning sins. These have too often been the rules, and thus the rich complexities that are the very essence of the most pleasant urban areas of the world are even now still being regulated out of our gray cities. London, after the blitz, was replanned and rebuilt substantially according to this antiseptic planning order. The first new London areas were spacious, clean, and orderly, and all would have seemed to be ideal except for one salient feature: they were incredibly dull. Nobody liked them. Our zoning ordinances, which to a large degree control our city patterns, are still rather new to us. They have great promise as an effective tool and a key to achieving cities of vitality, efficiency, and charm when we have learned to use them to ensure these qualities rather than preclude them.

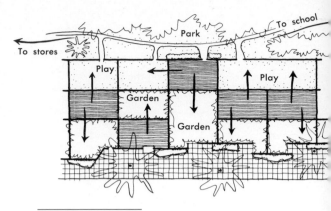

Minimum homes for maximum living.

The outer city

In the replanned, far more efficient city diagram, the limits of the revitalized inner city will be defined by a circumferential parkway that provides external vehicular access, as well, to the satellite centers of the outer city.

In the expanding rings of previous outward growth those districts farthest removed from the city center are usually newer, with many sound neighborhoods yet remaining. Without land regulation, however, most outer residential areas have been infiltrated by such incompatible uses as repair shops, used car lots, and truck stops, to name a few. These disparate uses are to be phased out—gathered into their own unified compounds where they can operate more efficiently without disrupting their neighbors or the landscape.

It is in the outer city also where new satellite centers—as for health, education, business offices, manufacturing, and recreation —can take form at receptive sites surrounded by the communities of their employees. Such satellites connected center to center with intercity rapid transit and at the peripheries by the regional freeway and parkway circumferentials will attract those enterprises seeking togetherness in more conducive surroundings. Thus will be achieved far more efficient activity centers, with the advantage of nearby housing and optimum regional access. Such "centering" is believed to be the *only* means of ending the all-American scourge of urban sprawl.

The suburbs and beyond

It would seem that suburban living has become the American dream. The early abandonment of the industrialized city in search of greener pastures gained momentum until it became a rout. The migration was given impetus by the coming of the automobile and the expansion of highway networks. Moreover, as families and businesses pulled up stakes, city taxes were raised to com-

> *Disastrous urban sprawl can be effectively pre-empted by investing in the fundamental systems that protect and nourish a healthy urban environment.*
>
> *Dylan Todd Simonds*

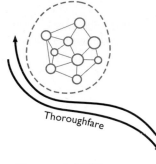

Central business district (CBD)

Thoroughfare

Compact vital CBD

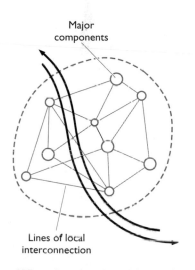

Major components

Lines of local interconnection

CBD weakened—split and dispersed

Within a theoretical central business district (CBD), the circles represent major destinations such as banks, department stores, civic centers, regional sports facilities, or entertainment districts. The lines represent paths of pedestrian circulation. A closely knit set of CBD elements is mutually sustaining. A compact center makes for easy connections in terms of time, distance, and friction. Dispersion of the CBD negates the advantages of "downtown."

pensate for the loss, while property values declined. The outward flight has continued until now many who work in the city and live in exurbia must spend hours a day in bucking traffic as they drive to and fro. It is only recently that the balance is beginning to tip. As suburban communities become commercialized and lose their appeal, and as revitalized cities become more attractive, there is an increasing back–to–the–city movement. As a result the agricultural lands and forest beyond are less threatened. With the stemming of scatteration and the emerging acceptance of regional planning and redevelopment we can in time have the best of all worlds—thriving cities, attractive suburbs, and a protected regional matrix of productive farmsteads, forest, and wilderness preserves.

The Ubiquitous Automobile

Even more than the industrial revolution, even more than our threatening population explosion, even more than electronic technology—the automobile has been the chief determinant in American land planning for the past many years. In the foreseeable future this will probably yet be the case. Without a drastic change in our thinking, the automobile will continue to dominate our cities, our communities, and our lives. The challenge is to segregate and improve our trafficways while at the same time devising the means by which cohesive living and working areas may be freed of through-traffic intrusions.

The drivers and passengers of motorized vehicles are safest and happiest when the travel experience is one of *flow* through pleasant and variformed corridors. Street crossings and on-grade intersections are anathema to fast-moving traffic. They are to be avoided. By realigning expressways and arterial highways *around*, not *through*, residential and activity centers, the major causes of interruptions and accidents can be eliminated.

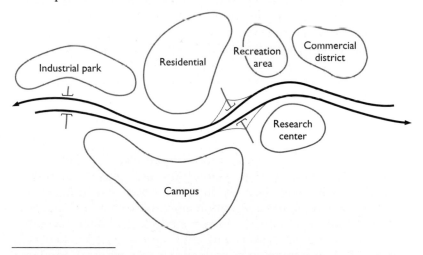

An expressway should respect established social, political, and economic districts, threading between, not through, them.

People Places

Where do city people like to be? Not where they feel intimidated by rushing traffic or the blank walls of massive office towers. Not where to get from here to there entails a long walk, wait, or tiresome climb. Not in a blazing or frigid, windswept expanse of paving. Not where there is little of interest to see or do. People prefer instead to be in or move through ways and places of comfort, interest, and delight. They enjoy the meandering walk through contracting and expanding spaces. They enjoy the charm of diminutive nooks and passageways—of places where they can rest, to talk or people-watch. Such experiences are seldom happenstance; they must be thoughtfully planned.

Well-designed ways and places, especially those intended for public use, accommodate *everyone*. Not only the fit, but, as well, all who by reason of age or disability have special needs or problems. All of us in our lifetimes—from stroller days to the times of crutches, the cane, the walker, or wheelchair—are "disadvantaged" to some degree in terms of mobility or cognizance.

Only in recent years have our public agencies and physical planners come to recognize the needs and possibilities, and take positive action. Now most building codes and regulations incorporate requirements designed to make life safer, more comfortable, and convenient.

With recent passage by Congress of the *Americans with Disabilities Act* (ADA), there is now a national mandate to shape and reshape our living environment with the disadvantaged in mind. All people will benefit from such sensitive planning.

Among the more helpful innovations are well-marked, well-lighted pedestrian street crossings. Curbs at street corners are depressed and tapered. Ramped platforms are provided at bus stops to allow for the loading and unloading of passengers at the conveyance floor level. In parking courts, stalls are reserved near the entranceways for the use of the handicapped. Steps to public buildings and areas are being eliminated or alternative ramps installed with easy slopes and with handrails. Often entrance gates and doors are fully automated. Since many persons cannot read or have language difficulties, the use of internationally standardized symbols has become a welcome feature of informational and directional signs.

In general it can be said that in reviewing the merits of any architectural or landscape architectural proposal it should be tested vicariously by the experience of *all* potential users.

The starkness of once hostile downtowns has been relieved with shade-tree plantings, parklets, seating, fountains, and floral displays. Gradually our evolving metropolitan areas are taking form around interconnected, traffic-free business, shopping, and residential centers. On these well-furnished islands the experience of getting about, or being, in safe, attractive, and refreshing surroundings gives new meaning to town and city.

Urban Green, Urban Blue

Few would deny that cities would be more pleasant if less bleak and more gardenlike. Is that asking too much of the system? Not when we can witness many examples of downtown transformation. Everywhere across the nation once-barren streets are now a-greening and a-blooming. Flower bedecked planters, window boxes, and hanging baskets enframe store windows. Recessed bays and setbacks are converted to miniparks with raised planting beds and seating. Concrete boulevard medians are converted to seasonal showpieces. Vacant lots in the inner city are cleared of trash by citizen groups and, with the help of civic groups or clubs, made neighborhood gardens and gathering places.

The local embellishments are heartening signs of new attitudes. At the larger citywide scale, publicized and aided tree-planting programs have clothed mile upon mile of streets and drives with

PEOPLE PLACES

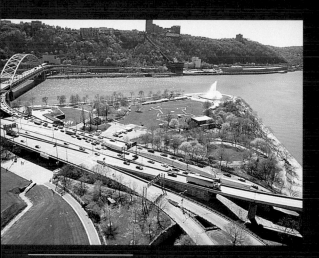

Here pedestrian traffic from the center city flows unimpeded under the highway approach and circumferential parkway. (Point State Park, Pittsburgh, Pennsylvania)

Where in-city towers and apartments are faced inward to traffic-free plazas with subsurface parking, everything works better. (Equitable Plaza, Pittsburgh, Pennsylvania)

The urban shopping–business office mall with peripheral access and parking has revised many downtowns. (Boulder Valley Mall, Boulder, Colorado)

City life is vibrant where pedestrian domains are provided in redevelopment plans. (Unknown)

burgeoning foliage. Polluted stream beds and riverbanks have been cleared of debris and restored to verdant waterways. Lakeshores and waterfronts have become a focus of public improvement and the focal points and pride of many cities.

Building upon such successes, sentiment is growing for open-space programs that will in time incorporate or consolidate large swaths and small bits and pieces of public land into integrated systems. Under the centralized guidance of expanded departments of parks, recreation, and open space, our contemporary cities might well in time come to approach the ideal of "an all-embracing garden-park within which buildings, travelled ways and gathering places are beautifully interspersed."[1]

But, one might ask, with urban real estate being sold by the square foot instead of the acre, how can such open space be afforded and assembled?

In the center city, the vacation of through and selected local streets would yield more than enough area for the ring-road by-pass with its buffering parkland. The elimination of the divisive existing parking lots and structures can free up another 10 percent of the average CBD, as can the razing of half-used obsolete buildings. Reclaimed vacant or tax-delinquent lands can be added to park and recreation holdings. If within the city there are cliffs, steep slopes, or arroyos, so much the better. Where there are in-city streams or a waterfront the possibilities are expanded.

Throughout the greater metropolitan confines, the evolving processes of reclamation, rehabilitation, and redevelopment will create extensive open-space reserves. To these can be added the gifts of property by public-spirited donors and the essential links and fill-in parcels acquired with bonds or budgeted capital improvement funds. The lands are there in various conditions ready to be put together into an open-space *system* and framework for ongoing development.

Waterfront park. (Toledo, Ohio)

The New Urbanity

The needs of the human beings who would work and live in our cities must come to have precedence over the insistent requirements of traffic, over the despoiling demands of industry, and over the callous public acceptance of rigid economy as the most consistent criterion for our street and utility layouts and for the development of our boulevards, plazas, parks, and other public works.

What are the human needs of which we speak? Some have been so long ignored or forgotten in terms of city planning and growth that they may now seem quaint or archaic. Yet they are *basic*. We human beings need and must have once again in our cities *a rich variety of spaces*, each planned with sensitivity to best express and accommodate its function; spaces through which we may move with safety and with pleasure and in which we may congregate. We must have *health, convenience,* and *mobility* on scales as yet undreamed of. We also must have *order*. Not an antiseptic, stilted, or grandiose order of contrived geometric dullness or sweeping emptiness but a functional order that will hold the city

It has become apparent that urban waterfronts, whether natural or artificial, are now prime pieces of real estate, essential ingredients in forming a community image, valuable stages for architectural display and great places for public recreation.

Grady Clay

---

[1] Kublai Khan, in outlining the plan for his new capital city, Tatu, the present-day Beijing.

BLUEWAYS/GREENWAYS

All trafficways can contribute their measure of
green or blue open space.

(Robson Square, Vancouver, British Columbia)

(Pelican Bay, Collier County, Florida)

(Minneapolis, Minnesota)

(Frito Lay Inc. Headquarters, Plano, Texas)

(Betty B. Marcus Park, Dallas, Texas)

(Riverside parkway)

(Nationwide Atrium, Columbus, Ohio)

(Greenacre Park, New York)

(The Pittsburgh Point and Riverfront, Pittsburgh, Pennsylvania)

together and make it work—an order as organic as that of the living cell, the leaf, and the tree. A sensed cohesive and satisfying order that permits of the happy accident, is flexible, and combines the best of the old with the best of the new. An order that is sympathetic to those structures, things, and activities that afford interest, variety, surprise, and contrast and that have the power to "charm the heart." We humans need in our cities *sources of inspiration, stimulation, refreshment, beauty, and delight.* We need and must have, in short, a *salubrious, pollution-free urban environment* conducive to the living of the whole, full life.

Such a city will not ignore nature. Rather, it will be integrated with nature. And it will invite nature back into its confines in the form of clean air, sunshine, water, foliage, breeze, wooded hills, rediscovered water edges, and interconnected garden parks.

Pittsburgh, Pennsylvania, circa 1930. From "Hell with the lid off" to modern metropolis. If it could happen in Pittsburgh it can happen anywhere.

Gradually, but with quickening tempo, the face of urban America is taking on a new look. It is a look of wholesome cleanliness, of mopping up, renovation, or tearing down and rebuilding. There is a sense of urgency, directness, nonpretense, and informality. There is a new group spirit of concerted actions and of people enjoying the experience of making things happen, of coming and being together in pleasant city surroundings. There is a freshness, sparkle, and spontaneity as American as apple pie.

The movement was born partly of desperation—of the need by property owners to "save the city" and protect their threatened investments. It responds to the need for energy conservation and the contraction of overextended development patterns. It stems from revulsion at pollution, filth, decay, and dilapidated structures. It is a strengthening compulsion to clean house, repair, and rebuild, mainly by private enterprise. There is a new vitality. There is a sense of competition, too, marked by inventiveness. Fresh winds are astir in our cities.

The Metropolis of the Future

- There will be no through vehicular thoroughfares within the city centers.

- All buildings will face inward upon pedestrian greenways, malls, and plazas.

- Optimum urban land use and roadway capacities will be predetermined and controlled.

- Activity centers of varying types will be dispersed throughout the metropolitan region as satellites of the urban nucleus.

- Interconnecting multimodal transit and transportation facilities will be planned and operated as balanced, integrated systems.

- All major roadways and transit lines will move through the regional open-space framework.

- All highways will be "classified" and designed to serve their specific purposes.

- A network of transit-transportation-transmission corridors will be acquired as public land and reserved for future uses. Leasing revenues will offset acquisition costs.

- An innovative array of trafficways and vehicles will provide unprecedented levels of mobility and service.

66 *There is only meager evidence that we Americans recognize the urgent task confronting us—to shift the emphasis from "bigger" to "better," from the quantitative to the qualitative, and to give significant form and beauty to our environment.*

Walter Gropius

66 *The time has come for American industry to be toilet trained . . . to cease and desist from voiding millions, perhaps billions, of tons and gallons of excrement into the environment.*

Ian McHarg

Pittsburgh Point circa 1990.

Pittsburgh Point circa 1940.

URBAN DESIGN

Courts and squares
City life is much enriched by such traffic-free spaces.

(Greenacre Park, Midtown Manhattan, New York)

(Buffalo Fountain Plaza, Buffalo, New York)

(Mellon Square, Pittsburgh, Pennsylvania)

Plazas
Urban plazas of various types are welcome crowd tractors.

(Marina del Rey, California)

(Equitable Plaza, Pittsburgh, Pennsylvania)

Urban plazas of various types are welcome crowd attractors.

(Jacobs Field, Cleveland, Ohio)

(Los Angeles, California)

Upper-level landscapes
The rooftops of urban America are largely undiscovered and unused.

In-city hanging gardens (Robson Square, The Law Courts, Vancouver, British Columbia)

Shangri-La Hotel, Bangkok, Thailand

18
THE REGIONAL LANDSCAPE

Rᴀᴛɪᴏɴᴀʟ ʟᴀɴᴅ ᴜsᴇ ᴘʟᴀɴɴɪɴɢ can stop at no property line or jurisdictional boundary. For streams flow, trafficways must interconnect, and polluted air, for example, is wafted wherever the winds may blow it.

Every land or water holding abuts other properties and should respect the relationship. Every downstream property is influenced by all that transpires in the watershed above. Each habitation, community, and municipality affects and is affected by conditions within its surrounding social, economic, political, and physical region. Since these are not synonymous, what should the regional boundaries be? They will vary, depending upon the nature of the study. This principle of flexible and appropriate study boundaries is fundamental to all sound regional planning.

Interrelationships

For too long the city has been considered a circumscribed entity. By tradition we have thought of the city *versus* the farmland, the city *versus* the suburbs, the city *versus* the townships or counties in which the city lies. Many serious and often needless conflicts have resulted from a lack of coordinated planning. There have been costly duplications of administration and facilities. Animosities have been generated that will for years preclude intelligent cooperation on even the simplest of interarea issues. There is, however, a wise and growing tendency to plan for the development of the city and its surrounding matrix as a unified *region*.

Concurrent with the trend to broaden the scope of planning from an urban to a regional basis is the drive to structure or

(Taipei Terminal Urban Design Plan, Taipei, Taiwan)

(Allegheny Center Redevelopment, Pittsburgh, Pennsylvania)

restructure residential districts into more self-sufficient neighbor-hoods. These, surrounded by greenbelts and connected by free-ways to the manufacturing complexes, the urban cores, and the outlying hinterlands, give promise of a more humanized living environment.

Our homes, neighborhoods, and cities are telltale physical expressions of the way we think and live. Their plan layout and form are in a state of continuous evolution to reflect our chang-ing ideas about living, as we constantly seek a better fit with our natural and built environment. With this in mind, it might be well to study the broad outlines of our present patterns of social and land use organization. Perhaps with better understanding we can improve the relationships and our way of life.

The family

In our democratic society, as in most cultures of the past, the fam-ily is the smallest and yet most significant social unit.

Family lifestyles as we know them today are far different from those of the log cabin, the working farm, or the plantation. The free and rigorous life of the pioneer has given way to the more ordered routine of the farmers on their acreage or the conformity

 The family

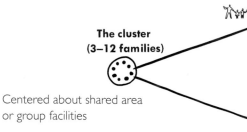
**The cluster
(3–12 families)**

Centered about shared area
or group facilities

The neighborhood

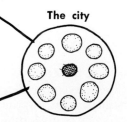

Centered about its ele-
mentary school, parks,
and shopping center

The community

Centered about its high school and
supporting junior high schools, parks,
churches, and shopping centers

The city

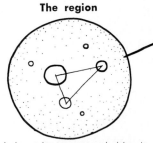

Centered about its communities, its central business district,
and its urban institutions

The region

Centered about its towns and cities, its
regional parks, its agricultural and industrial
centers and regional shopping centers

> *I would beg my fellow conservationists, as I would beg my fellow farmers, to realize that we must quit thinking of our countryside piecemeal, in terms of separate products or enterprises: tobacco, timber, livestock, vegeta-bles, feed grains, recreation, and so on. We must begin to think of the human use of each of our regions or localities as one economy, both rural and urban, involving all the local products.*
>
> *Wendell Berry*

> *The problem of the landscape architect—even as of the architect, the town planner, the engi-neer, and indeed all men of good will—is now, and will be more acutely every day, the develop-ment of ways and means for bridging the gap between town and country, the antithesis between urban and rural life—more specifi-cally between the masonry, the asphalt, and the dingbat construction of the town and the quiet greenery of meadow, forest, and shore. How to open up the town to the country, how to bring the town culturally to the country—that is our primary problem. . . .*
>
> *Garrett Eckbo*

> *To see the interdependence of city and country, . . . to appreciate that there is a just and a harmonious balance between the two—this capacity we have lacked. Before we can build well in any scale we shall, it seems to me, have to develop an art of regional plan-ning, an art which will relate city and country-side. . . .*
>
> *Lewis Mumford*

> *As long as man's activities are in sympathy with nature, or are on so small a scale that they do not interfere with nature's self-renewing cycle, the landscape survives, either in a predominantly natural form or as a bal-anced product of human partnership with nature. But as soon as the growth of the popu-lation or its urban activities are sufficient to upset nature's balance, the landscape suffers, and the only remedy is for man to take a con-scious part in the landscape's evolution.*
>
> *Sylvia Crowe*

of confined city dwellers. Parental attitudes have changed. The discipline of once paternal- or maternal-dominated family living has become more relaxed and casual. Salons, grand balls, and great dinners are almost a thing of the past, as are the chambermaid, the cook, and the well-trained staff of servants.

Life has become so automobile-oriented that many families have taken their cars into their homes or parked them at the front door. Homes and gardens are less pretentious, less ornate. They are mechanized, less cluttered, more open. Front and rear porches have disappeared along with the stable and alley. The wide front lawn has been replaced by the walled garden courts of patio homes and town houses. Exterior house walls have been opened up to let in more air and sunlight and to enframe the views of garden, sky, and landscape—to provide more contact with nature and with the stone, water, and plants of the earth. As concepts of family living have changed, the forms of our dwellings have changed to reflect them.

The cluster

It has been learned that from three to twelve families constitute the optimum interfamily social group. If their dwellings are clustered in a convenient plan arrangement, kaffeeklatsches, parties, children's play and games, and "get-togetherness" on a first-name basis are natural and spontaneous. Neighbors borrow cups of butter or sugar and exchange views and form friendships at the parking compound; children share toys and turf.

Ideally, the families in such a cluster would have the same general goals and standards but a diversity of individual status and interests.

As a group exceeds twelve to sixteen households in number, it becomes unwieldy, tends to lose its cohesion, and automatically breaks up into smaller social alliances.

The most desirable plan arrangements for the cluster will afford an off-street parking compound, freedom from the noise and danger of passing traffic, pedestrian interaccess, and a focal place or feature such as a central lawn panel or a children's play court. The grouping will have a harmonious site and architectural character and physical separation from adjacent clusters or structures. Compactness and the sharing of party walls are the mark of many successful clusters, where the normally unusable side-yard space is squeezed out and aggregated for group use and enjoyment.

The neighborhood

A neighborhood is at best a grouping of residential clusters around shared open space. It should be small enough to encourage participation of all families in group activities and large enough to contain a convenience-shopping center, playfields, and buffering. An enduring neighborhood plan and one that has accommodated changing concepts of social behavior and education is one formed around and providing safe walkway access to an elementary school. In size and population it is shaped to yield or contribute to the approximate number of students required for a balanced school facility. It is not essential, however, that either the school, shopping, or other shared amenities be centered

Any architect worth his salt knows that a building is not designed by putting together a series of rooms. Any building that is good has an underlying design concept that binds all the parts together into a whole. Without this it is not architecture. Nor does a designed neighborhood consist of a series of "projects" that are strung together. There must be an underlying design plan that binds together the pieces and makes the neighborhood an entity.

Edmund N. Bacon

The physical plan can seldom if ever, create a "neighborhood" except in the most abstract use of the word. It can, however, very materially assist other forces in fostering a true neighborhood feeling.

Henry S. Churchill

within the single neighborhood confines. It is often more desirable that they be placed outside or between subneighborhood enclaves of varying character and size and be laced together with interconnecting greenways, walks, and bicycle trails.

In the well-conceived neighborhood, peripheral roads will provide access and vehicular connection to free-flowing regional parkways. Through traffic will be precluded. Ideally, the neighborhood will be composed of planned tracts grouped around and between lobes of semiprivate park that open into the larger community school-park system. Each such tract, developed as an entity, would be freed of all arbitrary lot restrictions. Its proposed layout would be subject to review by the planning agencies solely on the basis of livability. Land use patterns and densities, as approved, would then be fixed by covenants between the landowners and the municipality.

The community

A *community*, as differentiated from the *neighborhood*, would at best comprise two or more neighborhoods separated by greenbelt spaces. It will be interconnected with controlled-access parkways and oriented to the more important communal features and nodes. It need not be contained within the limits of a city. Satellite communities, or the larger new towns, spaced out in the open countryside and served by freeways and rapid transit, have many advantages.

Being more self-sufficient, they reduce the number of external vehicular trips required and thereby conserve fuel and energy. They are less disruptive of neighboring trafficways, land uses, and established systems than if developed within or immediately contiguous to other residential areas. All planned communities, whether perforce impacted or formed more freely as satellites, have the great advantage of being brought on area by area and

Reston, one of the better-planned American communities of the twentieth century.

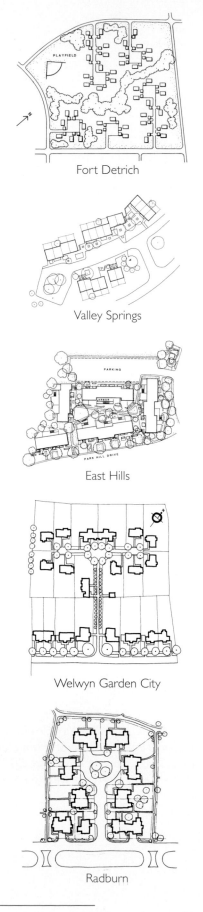

Fort Detrich

Valley Springs

East Hills

Welwyn Garden City

Radburn

Five cul-de-sac arrangements that provide a cluster of family dwellings.

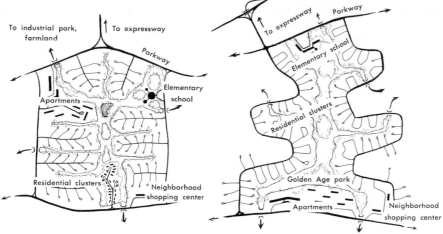

Neighborhood plan diagram number 1: approximately 1200 families (one-third in multifamily units).

Neighborhood plan diagram number 2: approximately 1200 families (one-third in multifamily units).

Neighborhood plan diagram number 3: approximately 1200 families (one-third in multifamily units).

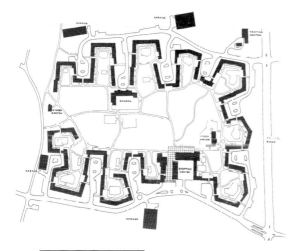

A neighborhood of apartment dwellings, each related to an exterior approach and an interior social court and to a large central park area. The relatively high density of the apartment groups yields large open space where it counts.

stage by stage in accordance with a balanced overall conceptual diagram. The ultimate capacities of roadways, schools, parks, and freshwater supply mains, for example, can be predetermined and facilities phased in without the need for costly periodic enlargement or reconstruction.

The land use patterns, traffic-flow diagrams, and population cap will be determined initially. There will be defined flexibility zones (the more extensive the better) within which the approved

A planned community (with the P-C-D approach).
Beach, dunes, and tidal estuary *preserved*. Wetlands, waterways and native vegetation protected (*conserved*). Clustered *development* on the upland, within an interconnected open-space frame. All working well together. (Pelican Bay, Collier County, Florida)

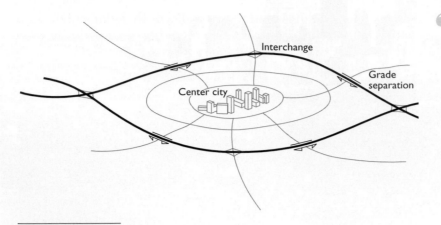

Freeways should surround rather than penetrate the center city, with collector-distributor highways providing interarea movement. The construction of freeways through an urban center where traffic is already at a saturation point can only result in chaos.

- Order, efficiency, beauty, and a milieu conducive to the development of the full human powers
- Clean and healthful surroundings
- A free-flowing and easy transition between urban, suburban, and rural areas

The region

A region is a large and generally unified, but loosely defined, geographical area that provides the supporting base for one or more centers of population concentration. To simplify the complex problems of regional planning almost to the point of naïveté, it might be proposed that each region should be analyzed and planned for its highest and best use in relation to the land and its resources.

Planning on a regional basis, whether in terms of geographic, political, social, or economic regions, provides a more comprehensive and effective frame of reference than the consideration of any community, town, city, or county alone.

Regional planning agencies are at best nonpolitical and service-oriented. They provide planning coordination, regional information, and technical assistance to the member jurisdictions. Their primary functions are:

- Data gathering, analysis, storage, and distribution
- The preparation and updating of a comprehensive regional plan
- The conduct of studies for various planning elements such as housing, transportation, and open space
- The provision of liaison with state, federal, and local jurisdictions
- The processing of state and federal grants-in-aid to local governments
- The recording and coordination of all proposals relating to the protection, alteration, or development of salient land and water areas
- Recommendations as to the significance of regional environmental impacts

In every historical epoch except our own, the cultivated and influential person, the civilized, polite and urbane citizen, inevitably lived within the city. . . . Indeed, the classical names for the city express these very virtues: civis—city, civilized, civilization; urbs—urbane; polis—polite and elegant.

Ian L. McHarg

Regional planning is the conscious direction and collective integration of all those activities which rest upon the use of earth as site, as resource, as structure. . . .

Lewis Mumford

The new regional pattern will be determined by the character of the landscape: its geographical and topographical features, its natural resources, by the use of land, the methods of agriculture and industry, their decentralization and integration; and by human activities, individual and social in all their diversity.

Ludwig K. Hilberseimer

A regional plan that pieces together the disparate plans of the various member jurisdictions and blankets the whole with a layer of further restrictions does more harm than good.

Worthy regional planning starts with an understanding of human needs and the landscape.

The goal of regional planning is to develop through intergovernmental cooperation the best possible *diagrammatic framework* of land uses and trafficways, to provide the evolving *performance standards* required to ensure environmental integrity, and then to *encourage the free and creative expression of private enterprise.*

Study. Proposed regional recreational center well-fitted to its site. (Marine World, Redwood City, California)

Regional planning agencies can be effective only if

- The state officially prescribes the boundaries of each region.
- Regions are defined along county lines, since socioeconomic data are normally acquired on a countywide basis.
- County membership in, and support of, the regional agency is mandated by the state.

Regional Form

The land use and trafficway patterns of each region, if well considered, will respond to the "want to be" of the land. They will preserve the scenic superlatives, protect areas of ecological sensitivity, and ensure the integrity of the natural systems. They will recognize and adjust to the natural land and water forms. They will avoid the delays and hazards of on–grade trafficway crossings. They will provide economies in travel time and distance and in construction, operation, and maintenance costs. They will provide a setting within which and around which development may take place freely and creatively as the direct expression of human needs.

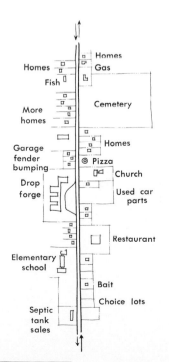

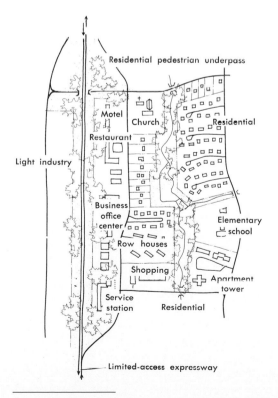

The highway and adjacent uses. A highway almost anywhere in almost any state: fifty driveway entrances per mile; unplanned, unzoned, unintelligent—a study in friction, confusion, inefficiency, and chaos.

Planned, zoned, intelligent: highway traffic flows freely; functions are grouped; homes orient to park; school, church, and shopping areas have access.

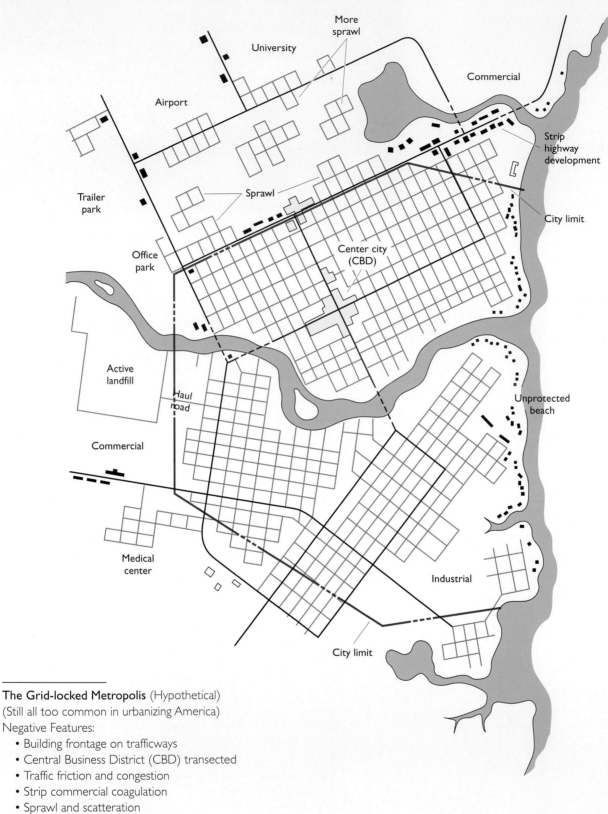

The Grid-locked Metropolis (Hypothetical)
(Still all too common in urbanizing America)
Negative Features:
- Building frontage on trafficways
- Central Business District (CBD) transected
- Traffic friction and congestion
- Strip commercial coagulation
- Sprawl and scatteration
- Resulting vacancies and obsolescence
- Lack of facile interconnection between activity centers
- Disorganization and inefficiency
- Unconsolidated land use districts
- No open-space system or preserves
- Lack of coastal and waterway protection
- Little response to topography

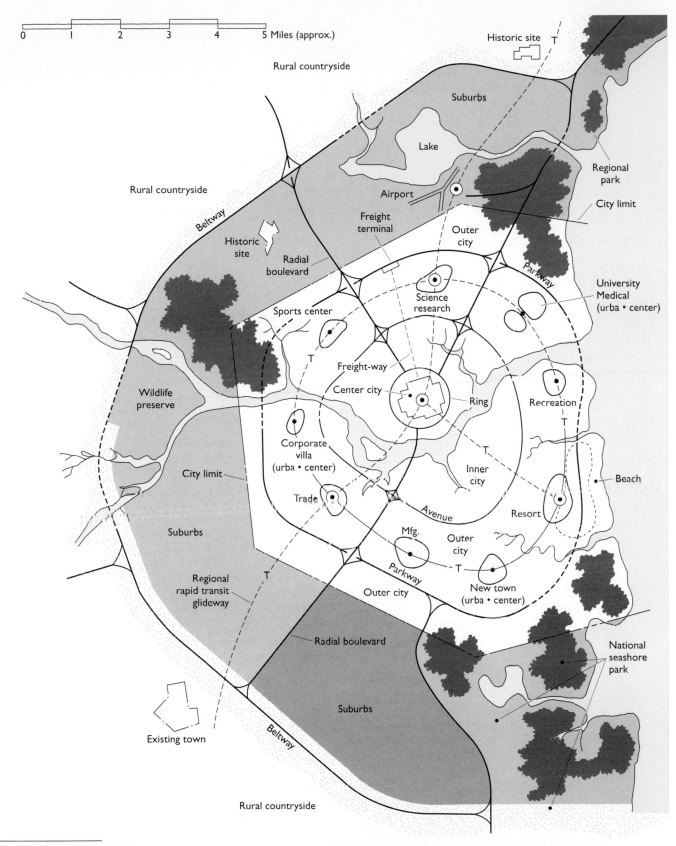

Scale: 0 1 2 3 4 5 Miles (approx.)

Rural countryside

Historic site

Suburbs

Lake

Regional park

City limit

Rural countryside

Beltway

Airport

Outer city

Freight terminal

Historic site

Radial boulevard

Science research

University Medical (urba • center)

Sports center

Parkway

Freight-way

Center city

Ring

Recreation

Wildlife preserve

Corporate villa (urba • center)

Inner city

Beach

City limit

Trade

Resort

Suburbs

Mfg.

Outer city

Avenue

Regional rapid transit glideway

Parkway

New town (urba • center)

Outer city

National seashore park

Radial boulevard

Existing town

Suburbs

Beltway

Rural countryside

A City for the 21st Century

A prototype conceptual plan for phased long-range development, redevelopment, and renewal. Shown is a conceptual plan, or model, for a typical urbanizing region. As can be seen, it preserves and conserves (protects) the best of the dominant topographic features. Development areas and routes of interconnection are fitted compatibly with the natural landscape enframement. (Hypothetical plan. Reproduced from page 216 of *Garden Cities 21*, by John Simonds, with permission of McGraw-Hill.)

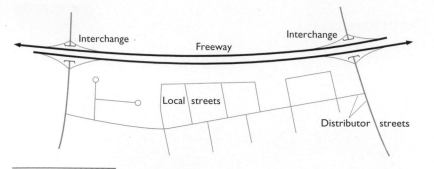

The limited access concept of freeway development should be extended where feasible to all through or distributor roads within the metropolitan region. While building frontage would not be permitted on these thoroughfares, connections to local streets would be encouraged and facilitated.

Desirable features of the region will include:

- Compact and thriving off-highway neighborhoods, communities, and cities within an open-space surrounding
- Phased development contours precluding the uncontrolled growth and sprawl of urbanizing areas
- The "land-banking," in public or tax-adjusted private ownership, of all holdings not foreseeably needed or desirably suited for development
- Wide, free, uninterrupted preserves allocated for farmsteads, forest, recreation, wildlife management, and conservation
- The location of all new activity centers in optimum relationship to land and water resources, topographical features, and other planned uses
- Nonfrontage expressways, circumferential and radial roadways with parkway characteristics providing free-flowing regional access to urban centers and satellites
- Direct rapid-transit interconnection of the regional hubs with subsurface or overhead approaches to the station plazas
- Separate, consolidated transmission-truckway corridors linking major production, processing, and distribution centers
- The programmed provision and *strategic allocation* of all basic service centers and amenities needed for living the good, full life
- A unified park, recreation, and open-space system
- Arterial parkways, with scenic-historic byway loops traversing areas of natural and historic significance
- A long-range land and water management program based upon ongoing ecological studies and a regional resource inventory
- Development based on the highest and best use of the land, and performance standards, rather than blind-sided conventional zoning

Open-space Frame

The regional open-space frame will embrace and separate the various land uses and activity nodes. It will provide background, base, and breathing room, and when so arranged as to preserve the best of the landscape features, it will give each region its unique landscape character.

Most municipalities and regions have zoned development land far in excess of foreseeable needs. Not only does this encourage scattered parcel-by-parcel construction, it results in tax assessments disproportionate to productivity and drives homeowners from their properties and farmers from their farms.

New construction would be better accommodated by the infill of existing centers until they were built out and unified. When additional land might then be needed for development, new cohesive communities could be defined through the process of comprehensive planning.

The open-space preserves of a region should be so designated and land-banked. Only those agricultural and recreational uses that would cause them no significant harm should be permitted, and land should be taxed accordingly.

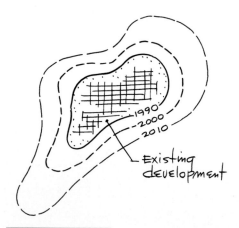

Urban service lines

As a device to ensure infill and protect open-space lands, some municipalities are including as an element of their comprehensive plans a map of *urban service lines* showing by year the limit to which public services are to be extended. Within the period noted, development will not be permitted beyond the designated line.

When and only when adequate public services can be assured through the economic *extension* of existing trafficways or mains (or by a centralized installation, in the case of satellite communities) should "preserve" land be rezoned and development be allowed to proceed.

As a counter-action to urban sprawl with its destruction of wildlife habitat—many landowners are establishing their own on-site habitats and wildlife preserves.

It is foolish to permit satellite shopping malls to be built if they reduce the vitality of existing commercial centers.

New regional shopping nodes should be permitted only as their need can be demonstrated.

A complete regional recreation system provides insofar as feasible the whole range of opportunities, from the child's play lot within the residential cluster to the state or national park.

On the ascending order of social groupings—i.e., home, cluster, neighborhoods, community, etc.—each may be expected to provide for its own particular recreation needs. Beyond these, two or more groups or jurisdictions may jointly provide additional facilities such as public swimming pools, tennis centers, or golfing that perhaps neither could provide alone.

Larger installations such as zoos, botanical gardens, or major marinas require areawide support, as do expansive regional parks and forest preserves.

On an even grander scale, state and national parks provide for recreation within the context of scenic or historic superlatives.

Perhaps the most important task of regional planners is to define and help to bring into being a spacious, interconnecting, and permanent open-space preserve as the framework for ongoing development.

Greenways and Blueways

Greenways are paths of movement for vehicles, pedestrians, and migrant wildlife. *Ways* because they are paths; *green* because they are enveloped in foliage. They may vary in scale from a woodland trail to a national parkway through mountainous terrain.

Blueways trace the flow of surface runoff—from rivulets to streams, to broad and sometimes raging rivers. Like the veins and arteries of the human body, they tend to serve as an interconnecting system. They transport nutrients from the uplands, and feed and drain the bottoms. Within the flow-ways are to be found the most verdant foliage and abundant bird and wildlife populations of each region. In all seasons they ameliorate the climate and add interest to the landscape. They are best preserved in their natural state.

By a single regulation, and without cost, the most rational of all open-space diagrams could be established by and for each region. To wit:

> From this date neither unauthorized construction of any type, nor the destruction of natural vegetation, shall be permitted within the 50-year flood limits of a stream or waterbody.

The result would be a protected flow-way of privately and/or publicly owned lands that would reduce the surface runoff of precipitation, reduce erosion and siltation, conserve water, moderate the extremes of climate, and enhance the landscape. As a border to tillable or buildable lands it would provide windscreen and flood control.

Residential parkway.
Freeflowing drives, walks, bicycle paths, and waterways can be planned together as a lineal park and attractive community feature. (Pelican Bay, Collier County, Florida)

When by reason of public ownership, or by easement, a greenway can be aligned through or contiguous to a blueway corridor, the benefits are manyfold.

The Essentials

It is believed that the evaluation of sound regional development can be reduced to four simple tests:

1. *Does it belong?* Is the proposed use of the land or water area consistent with federal, state, and regional plans and with community goals?

2. *Is it sustainable?* Can it be built without exceeding the carrying capacity of the land? The use should not be permitted if it would impose significant long-term stress on the natural ecological systems. Should there be question, the filing of an environmental impact assessment might well be required.

3. *Would it be a good neighbor?* Is the proposed use complementary and complimentary to the existing and proposed uses in the neighborhood? Or would it have harmful physical or visual effects? Would it reduce property values? Would it destroy, or preserve, cherished landmarks? A well-conceived, well-designed project should enhance, not harm, its environs.

4. *Are adequate levels of public service in place?* At all stages of project construction and use, the proposed improvement should have available all public services required, without overloading of trafficways, power or water supply systems, storm sewers, waste treatment plants, fire and police facilities, and (in the case of residential development) schools and recreation areas. Not only should all such facilities be on-line when needed, but the local government should also be assured that the developers and users will bear their fair share of the cost.

If these four conditions can be satisfied, there should be no cause to oppose the project, for it should become a welcome regional asset.

Regional Planning

There are three approaches to regional planning—four, really. The fourth is the "do-nothing" course of just letting things drift—to watch the landscape disintegrate area by area, until it comes apart at the seams. Scatteration, traffic glut, and loss to the many for the gain of the few are the inevitable consequences.

In a more rational approach, the regional jurisdictions form a voluntary association composed of selected local officials as representatives. With a small paid staff funded by contributions, they undertake studies and make recommendations to the various responsible agencies. Such an association has the advantage of political clout, but the disadvantage of political jousting.

A more effective advisory group is civic in nature. In form it may well be a citizen's committee or council initiated by one or more public-spirited individuals who, by invitation, assemble a team of nonpolitical but highly respected leaders in various aspects of regional life. Representatives of business, educational, financial, scientific, social, labor, and agricultural interests are

Zoning as commonly practiced is not workable.

❝ *In the creation of healthy environment nature's collaboration is not only important, but also indispensable.*
Eliel Saarinen

The *carrying capacity* of a land–water area or a natural ecological system is the limit of its ability to support a population without significant degradation or breakdown.

among the potential participants. Again, with a small but well-trained staff they define the goals and objectives and set about on a comprehensive course of phased studies. The council may meet as a body no more than once a year, but their consensus recommendations, when adopted, carry impressive weight with the officials and agencies concerned.

A third means of addressing regional issues is the formulation of an official regional planning commission with responsibility for certain metropolitan programs. Such a metro commission receives its charter from the state, with well-defined powers and provisions. The commission members are elected by the region-wide constituency. A professional director and staff are appointed. In the areas of assignment the focus is on coordinated planning, and construction and operation in the best interest of the entire metropolitan region and all of its citizens.

Governance

The citizens of each locality and jurisdiction like to handle their own affairs—and should, within reason. It is reasonable that they have their own school boards, committees, councils, and elected officials to keep an eye on things and respond to local needs and aspirations.

It is unreasonable, however, that within a cohesive metropolitan region such common and overriding concerns as transportation, transit and transmission, regional land use planning, resource management, law enforcement, and recycling should be handled in such a fragmented and inefficient manner as is usually the case. Most cities, towns, and boroughs now do their own independent thing—in disregard and often defiance of what goes on just across their borders. Those responsible for essential regional services are thus confounded by the need to patch together a host of disparate local programs rather than put into operation coherent, region-wide plans. It can be seen that the multitudinous duplications of staff, administrative overhead, and equipment—let alone the resolution of conflicts—is costly and wasteful in the extreme.

By all reason, most (though not all) regional planning, construction, and implementation procedures should be systematized and centrally controlled. This calls for a *metro* form of government. Where this has been most successful, several basics have applied:

- The metro government concept was voted into being by all citizens affected, after an educational campaign and series of public forums.

- The enabling legislation and charter delegate broad powers, but limit the initial responsibilities to a few well-defined programs that are clearly of regionwide scope. Responsibilities can be expanded from time to time on the basis of proven performance.

- Certain powers and tasks are reserved to the local jurisdictions and officials to ensure their independent authority and support.

- The metro council membership comprises elected leaders representing the various interests of the region.

Generally it can be stated as observable fact that *whatever is good for the region as a whole is good for the whole of its people.*

Town and country must be married and out of the union will spring a new life, a new hope, a new civilization.

Ebenezer Howard

19
THE PLANNED ENVIRONMENT

To PLAN FOR THE PEOPLE of any culture or even to understand their simplest life patterns and art forms, it is necessary first to have some comprehension of their underlying beliefs.

This may be seen in the culture of the Athenians. Philosophically, the Greeks understood and believed in the truth of utility and the beauty of function (which, from a close look at our cities, homes, automobiles, and other artifacts, most present-day Americans do not). And so, for their day-to-day living, they planned their streets, spaces, and structures in response to topography, for ease and directness of function, and for pleasurable convenience. Each form, each space, and each structure was designed to express and facilitate its use.

Philosophic Orientation

Philosophically, the Greeks believed that the family lay at the inward center of their world; and so, with absolute logic, their homes were faced inward. From the outside, they were unostentatious. The entrance, often no more than a simple aperture in the wall that faced the winding street, opened into a private world of serenity and delight—into private spaces where living, conversing, and learning were cultivated as high arts.

Philosophically, the Greeks conceived of their civic buildings and temples in different terms. These were symbols of all that was high and noble and, as symbols, were set back or held up to be seen in the round. They were planned to embody and connote the ideal and the highest degree of order. They were consciously created focal points to which a whole city was tacitly oriented. To

- Controlled-access highways that sweep around, not through, plant and animal communities and human settlements
- The logic of "carrying capacity" in land use management, rather than (superficial) area zoning
- Communities fitted to and around the best features of the landscape
- An end to urban sprawl and the scourge of scatteration
- More compact and efficient cities and towns spaced out within a protected open-space frame of productive farmland, forest, and nature preserves
- The fostering through education of a caring concern for the well-being of planet Earth

Much of what needs to be done in the way of environmental planning falls within the category of *growth management*. This goes beyond the obvious need to stabilize doubling, redoubling, overwhelming, and shifting populations. It deals essentially with bringing people, land, and other resources into balance. In this endeavor it can directly affect the future of every region.

There are some—yea, many—localities where a desirable equilibrium has already been attained. Where land is preserved, or "built out" to capacity in its "highest and best use." Where trafficways, utilities, schools, and other amenities are working well together and where further growth would be disruptive. Again there are areas of scenic splendor, ecologic sensitivity, or high agricultural productivity where the existing condition is best left largely undisturbed.

In every region, however, there can be found potential sites for well-planned communities or other enterprises if and when it can be established that they belong.

Unless or *until* our exploding population growth is checked, more and ever more construction is inevitable. We can no longer, however, allow the uncontrolled development of our prime remaining natural or agricultural lands. We must first explore and maximize the possibilities of renewal and redevelopment. We must reclaim, redefine, reuse, and often reshape our obsolescent or depleted urban, suburban, and rural properties. We can and must create a whole new re-formed landscape within the grand topographical framework of protected mountain slopes, river basins, shores, desert, forest, and farmland.

Implicit in long-range planning is the concept of sustainable development. For unless continuity is planned into the system the term "long-range" has little meaning. Ideally the supply of land, water, and other resources would be inexhaustible. Since this is not a fact of life, our planning must be the formulation of strategies for restraint, wise use, replenishment, and restoration.

It involves such broad and diverse concerns as growth management and the efficient use of energy. It deals with such finite matters as limitation on consumption, land use controls, and recycling. As to land and landscape planning, it soon leads to the realization that urban sprawl and scatteration *must* be curbed and reversed—replaced with concentrated and interconnected centers of human activity within a protected and productive open-space surround. It demands, in short, comprehensive *regional* planning.

In our *planning and replanning*, we must preserve intact such significant natural areas as are necessary to protect our water-

Growth management is a search for the best relationships of people to land, water, other resources, and to routes of travel.

Two key provisos of growth management policy are that entrepreneurs contribute their fair share of the funds needed for off-site improvements—and that all required services be in place before occupancy is permitted.

Growth management is not a door slamming shut, as some might think—as some might wish. It is more of a regulating valve by which flow and capacities are brought into optimum balance.

“ *At the dawn of civilization, say 5,000 years ago, the population of the world cannot have numbered much more than 20 million. Today the yearly increase in world population is nearly twice this amount. Self-multiplying, like money at compound interest, world population reached the billion mark in the 1850's and the 2 billion mark in the 1920's. Even more disquieting the rate of increase has also been steadily increasing. At the present rate, today's population will double itself in less than 50 years.*

Julian Huxley

The frontiers of waste management are yet to be explored. Beyond the exclusion of trash landfill mountains and off-shore refuse reefs are the possibilities of massive topsoil replenishment. A blend of salvaged wood fiber, pulverized plastic and glass mixed with processed sewage could in time restore to vast areas of eroded land a productive soil mantle.

Sustainability equates with *good husbandry* and, ultimately, with survival.

Preservation entails more than simply bypassing a landmark or "leaving it undisturbed." Meaningful preservation addresses the historic, scenic, ecologic, or cultural attribute in such a way as to bring it into context with the surrounding community while protecting its integrity.

sheds and maintain our water table, to conserve our forests and mineral reserves, to check erosion, to stabilize and ameliorate our climate, to provide sufficient areas for recreation and for wildlife sanctuary, and to protect sites of notable scenic or ecological value. Such holdings might best be purchased and administered by the appropriate federal, state, or local agencies or conservancy groups.

We must ensure the logical *development* of the existing landscape. Such thinking points to a national resource planning authority. Such an authority would be empowered to explore and determine, on a broad scale, the best conceivable use of all major land and water areas and natural resources. It would recommend the purchase of those that should be so conserved. It would encourage, through zoning, enabling legislation, and federal aid, the best and proper development of these and all remaining areas for the long-range good of the nation. It would constantly reassess and keep flexible its program and master plans and engage for this work the best of the trained physical planners, geographers, geologists, biologists, sociologists, and experts in other related disciplines. Regional, state, and federal environmental advisory boards composed of distinguished scientists and thinkers might well be constituted, with participants nominated to this post of high honor by their respective professional groups.

Further, we must consciously and astutely *continue the evolution* toward a new system of physical order. This may be one of improved relationships, as of people to people, people to their communities, and all to the living landscape. Since we have now become, in fact, world citizens, the new order may stem from a philosophic orientation that borrows from and incorporates the most positive driving forces of the preceding cultures.

While the Athenians, as has been noted, faced their homes inward to family domains of *privacy,* while the Egyptians expressed a compulsion for *lineal progression,* while the Chinese designed their homes and streets and temples as *incidents in nature,* and while the western predilection was for a *continuum of flowing space,* perhaps the new universal philosophic guidelines may be a felicitous blending.

The value of the secure, private contemplative space may come to be generally recognized. The appreciation of lineal attainment may be translated into the design for pleasurable and rewarding movement along transitways, parkways, and paths. Whole cities and regions may be harmoniously integrated with the natural landscape, in which interconnecting open space may provide a salubrious setting for our new architectural and engineering structures.

For the first time in the long sweep of history, environmental protection is becoming at last a world concern. The wise management of our land and water resources and the earthscape is becoming a common cause. Fortunately, when the problems are nearing crisis proportions, the essential technology is at hand. Perhaps we can pull it all together in time, and sooner than many might suppose, with enlightened, creative planning.

Significant environmental improvement does not necessarily require a monumental effort. It is sometimes achieved at a massive scale, as by effective and far-reaching flood control programs, clean air legislation, or the scientific management of regional farmlands, wetlands, or forest. For the most part, however, it is accomplished on a far lesser basis. It is the sum of an infinite number of smaller acts of landscape care and improvement. It is:

- The advent of a well-designed park or parklet
- The placing underground of power distribution and telephone cables in a new community
- The cleanup and water-edge installation of paths and planting along a forgotten stream
- Neighbors caring for their street
- A linden tree installed beside the entrance of an urban shop
- A vine on a factory wall
- A scrap of blowing paper picked up by a child in the schoolyard

Each act generates others; together they make the difference.

A Need for the Visionary

The world is fast changing, and the tempo of change is accelerating. We struggle to keep abreast of the times. Experience has taught us that we can no longer base our long-range planning on simple projection. New concepts burst upon us, disrupting all established criteria. Ideas that seemed implausible yesterday are accepted and applied today, and tomorrow will already be outmoded. As physical planners looking to and arranging the very framework for the future, we must be sensitive to the trends and alert to the signs that presage them. We must accept the fact that many revolutionary ideas, whether we now find them personally revolting or appealing, *may* become realities. Such ideas include:

- Interplanetary travel
- The colonization of outer space
- Antigravitational devices
- Selective, instantaneous, and unlimited audiovisual communication
- New sources and applications of vast power
- The tapping of the energies of the tides, the sun, and the earth's molten core
- Weather control
- Hydroponic culture of food and raw materials
- Large-scale mining and harvesting of the sea
- Compulsory birth control
- Euthanasia
- The mastery of our technology
- Low-cost, flexible shelters and vehicles, blown, woven, or fabricated of lightweight modular segments
- New, intensified forms of domed urbacenters of commercial, civic, and cultural activity at the regional transit hubs
- Clean and inspiring cities of pedestrian scale, on terraced decks above service levels, within a park and garden setting
- Satellite towns and communities dispersed throughout the open countryside, well defined and interconnected with innovative systems of transportation and transmission

A whole settlement (Plymouth Plantation), a whole region (Kentucky Bluegrass), or a whole state (Vermont) may qualify as a historic district deserving of protection.

Historic preservation can transcend the traditional protection of designated structures, artifacts, and sites. In a broader approach, whole cultural landscapes can be so treated and used as to maintain their authenticity.

❝ *We have begun to understand that designing our physical environment does not mean to apply a fixed set of esthetics, but embodies rather a continuous inner growth, a conviction which recreates truth continually in the service of mankind. . . .*
Walter Gropius

❝ *To build intelligently today is to lay the foundations for a new civilization.*
Lewis Mumford

❝ *The mistakes of planning are found in the overcautious concepts—not the bold.*
Paul Schweikher

❝ *Make no little plans; they have no magic to stir men's blood, and probably themselves will not be realized; make big plans, aim high in hope and work, remembering that a noble logical diagram, once recorded, will never die, but long after we are gone will be a living thing, asserting itself with ever growing insistency.*
Daniel Burnham

- A reconsolidated American landscape in which pollution has been eliminated, depleted and eroded lands have been restored to productivity, and our natural superlatives have been protected for the use and enjoyment of all people of all generations to come
- National resource planning

Lifting Our Sights

It is time now that we advance to a higher concept of life and living within our circumambient universe.

Such a new concept will evince a greater respect for the human being and will seek a deeper insight into our true nature and requirements. It will seek, perhaps for the first time, to satisfy *all* our needs—of body, mind, and spirit.

Such a new concept will instill in us a better understanding of nature's compelling powers. It will not seek to conquer or imitate nature but will rather engender a sense of belonging.

It will encourage us to relearn the old truths and discover new truths of nature's law. We will, in time, regain the old instincts, experience again the glowing animal vitality and spiritual vibrancy that comes from a way of living attuned to the natural world. We will find our own *Tao*, or way of life in harmony with nature.

Our new concepts of planning will look to the future to guide us into those areas of most promise and most meaning. Because we humans are the most highly developed organisms of which we so far know, the continuation of this development must surely be our purpose here. Our philosophers confirm this thinking when they tell us that our ultimate destiny is to realize our full potential.

> *Designing is an intricate task. It is the integration of technological, social and economic requirements, biological necessities, and the psychophysical effects of materials, shape, color, volume, and space: thinking in relationships.*
>
> László Moholy-Nagy

> *Man is a sun-roused dreamer, en route to tomorrow, a place he spins out of himself across the emptiness of time from gossamers of his imaginings.*
>
> John Lear

the Hall of Casts cleared of every vestige of the once sacred columns and pediment. The egg–and–dart frieze was carted away. The holy Corinthian capital was relegated to the cobwebs and mold of the basement. We half expected some sign of God's wrath. But the wrath did not come, and the enlightenment continued.

As the architects sought a new approach to the design of their structures, the landscape architects sought to escape the rigid plan form of the major and minor axis, which diagram, inherited from the Renaissance, had become the hallmark of all polite landscape planning. Inspired by the example of our architectural colleagues, we assiduously sought a new and parallel approach in the field of landscape design.

Through the resources of Harvard's great library of planning we peered into history. We pored over ancient charts and maps and descriptions. We scanned the classic works of Europe and Asia for guidance. We searched for inspiration in the related fields of painting, sculpture, and even music.

Our motives were good; our direction excellent. But, unknowingly, we had made a fatal error. In searching for a better design approach, we sought only to discover new *forms*. The immediate result was a weird new variety of plan geometry, a startling collection of novel clichés. We based plan diagrams on the sawtooth and the spiral, on stylized organisms such as the leafstalk, the wheat sheaf, the fern frond, and the overlapping scales of a fish. We sought geometric plan forms in quartz crystals. We adapted "free" plan forms from bacteria cultures magnified to the thousandth power. We sought to borrow and adapt the plan diagrams of ancient Persian courtyards and early Roman forts.

We soon came to realize that new forms in themselves weren't the answer. A form, we decided wisely, is not the essence of the plan; it is rather the shell or body that takes its shape and substance from the plan function. The nautilus shell, for instance, is, in the abstract, a form of great beauty, but its true intrinsic meaning can be comprehended only in terms of the living nautilus. To adapt the lyric lines of this chambered mollusk to a schematic plan parti came to seem to us as false as the recently highly respectable and generally touted practice of adapting the plan diagram of say, the Villa Medici of Florence to a Long Island country club.

We determined that it was not borrowed forms we must seek, but a creative planning *philosophy*. From such a philosophy, we reasoned, our plan forms would evolve spontaneously. The quest for a new philosophy is no mean quest. It proved as arduous as had been that for new and more meaningful forms. My particular path of endeavor led in a search through history for timeless planning *principles*. I would sift out the common denominators of all great landscape planning. At last, I felt sure, I was on the right track.

Findings

In retrospect, I believe this particular pilgrimage in search of the landscape architectural holy grail was not without its rewards, for along the way I met such stalwarts as LeNôtre, Humphrey Repton, Lao–tse, Kublai Khan, Pericles, and fiery Queen Hatshepsut. Many of their planning concepts so eagerly rediscovered (some to be set forth in this book) have served, if not as a planning philosophy, at least as a sound and useful guide.

Like good Christians who, in their day–by–day living are confronted with a moral problem and wonder, "What would Christ do if he were here?" I often find myself wondering at some obscure crossroads of planning theory, "What would Repton say to that?" or "Kublai Khan, old master, what would you do with this one?"

But back to our landscape classes and our student revolution. Sure that we had found a better way, we broke with the axis. According to Japanese mythology, when the sacred golden phoenix dies, a young phoenix rises full–blown from its ashes. We had killed the golden phoenix, with some attending ceremony, and confidently expected its young to rise strong–winged from the carnage. We had never checked the mythological timing. But we found that, in our own instance, the happening was not immediate.

In lieu of the disavowed symmetry we turned to asymmetrical diagrams. Our landscape planning in those months became a series of graphic debates. Our professors moved among our drafting tables with wagging heads and stares of incredulity. We had scholarly reasons for each line and form. We battled theory to theory and principle to axiom. But, truth to tell, our projects lacked the sound ring of reality, and we found little satisfaction in the end result of our efforts.

Upon graduation, after seven years' study in landscape architecture and a year of roaming abroad, and with a hard–earned master's degree, I seemed to share the tacit feeling of my fellows that while we had learned the working techniques and terms of our trade, the indefinable essence had somehow escaped us. The scope of our profession seemed sometimes as infinite as the best relating of all humankind to nature, sometimes as finite as the shaping of a brass tube to achieve varying spouting effects of water. We still sought the poles to which our profession was oriented. For somehow it seemed basic that we could best do the specific job only if we understood its relationship to the total work we were attempting. We sought a revealing comprehension of our purpose. In short, what were we, as landscape architects, really trying to do?

Like the old lama of Kipling's *Kim*, I set out once again to wander in search of fundamentals, this time with a fellow student.[2] Our journey took us through Japan, Korea, China, Burma, Bali, and India and up into Tibet. From harbor to palace to pagoda we explored, always attempting to reduce to planning basics the marvelous things we saw.

In the contemplative attitude of Buddhist monks, we would sit for hours absorbed in the qualities of a simple courtyard space and its relationship to a structure. We studied an infinite variety of treatments of water, wood, metal, plant material, sunlight, shadow, and stone. We analyzed the function and plan of gardens, national forests, and parks. We observed people in their movement through spaces, singly, in small groups, and in crowds. We watched them linger, intermingle, scatter, and congregate. We

---

[2] Lester A. Collins, later chairman of Harvard's department of landscape architecture.

noted and listed the factors that seemed to impel them to movement or affected the line of their course.

We talked with taper-fingered artists, with blunt-thumbed carpenters, with ring-bedecked princes, and with weathered gardeners whose calloused hands bore the stains and wear of working in the soil. We noted with fascination the relationship of sensitive landscape planning to the arc of the sun, the direction and force of the wind, and topographical modeling. We observed the development of river systems and the relation of riverside planning to the river character, its currents, its forests and clearings, and the varying slopes of its banks. We sketched simple village squares and attempted to reduce to diagram the plan of vast and magnificent cities. We tested each city, street, temple group, and marketplace with a series of searching questions. Why is it good? Where does it fail? What was the planner attempting? Did he achieve it? By what means? What can we learn here? Discovering some masterpiece of planning, we sought the root of its greatness. Discovering its overall order, we sought the basis of order. Noting unity in order, we sought the meaning of unity.

This consuming search for the central theme of all great planning was like that of the old lama in his search for truth. Always we felt its presence to some degree, but it was never clearly revealed. What were these planners really seeking to accomplish? How did they define their task? How did they go about it? Finally, wiser, humbled, but still unsatisfied, we returned to America to establish our small offices and be about our work.

Insight

Years later, one warm and bright October afternoon I was leaning comfortably in the smooth crotch of a fallen chestnut tree, hunting gray and fox squirrels, the timeless sport of the dreamer. My outpost commanded a lazy sunlit hollow of white oak and hemlock. The motionless air was soft and lightly fragrant with hay fern. Close by, beyond a clump of dogwood still purple with foliage and laced with scarlet seed pips, I could hear the squirrels searching for acorns in the dry, fallen leaves. An old familiar tingling went through me, a sense of supreme well-being and an indefinable something more.

I half recalled that the same sensation had swept through me years ago, when I first looked across the city of Peking (now Beijing), one dusky evening from the Drum Tower at the North Gate. In Japan it had come again in the gardens of the Katsura Detached Palace, overlooking the quiet water of its pine-clouded pond. And again I recalled this same sensation when I had moved along the wooden-slatted promenade above the courtyard garden of Ryōanji, with its beautifully spaced stone composition in a panel of raked gravel simulating the sea.

Now what could it be, I wondered, that was common to these far-off places and the woodlot where I sat? And all at once it came to me!

The soul-stirring secret of Ryōanji lay not in its plan composition but in what one *experienced* there. The idyllic charm of the Silver Pavilion was sensed without consciousness of contrived plan forms or shapes. The pleasurable impact of the place lay solely in the responses it evoked. The most exhilarating impacts of magnificent Peking came often in those places where no plan lay-out was evident.

What must count then is not primarily the designed shape, spaces, and forms. What counts is the *experience!*

The fact of this discovery was for me, in a flash, the key to understanding Le Corbusier's power as a planning theorist. For his ideas, often expressed in a few scrawled lines, dealt not so much with masses or form as with experience creation. Such planning is not *adapted* from the crystal. It is crystalline. It is not *adapted* from the organism. It is truly organic. To me, this simple revelation was like staring up a shaft of sunlight into the blinding incandescence of pure truth.

With time, this lesson of insight (perception and deduction) becomes increasingly clear. One plans not places, or spaces, or things; *one plans experiences*—first, the defined use or experience, then the conscious design of those forms and qualities conceived to achieve the desired results. The places, spaces, or objects are shaped with the utmost directness to best serve and express the function, to best yield the experience planned.

Evolution and Revolution

That was long ago. Now, with over 50 years of practice and teaching behind me, I look back with widened perspective to the days of the student rebellion, and the subsequent years of search and application. In that time there has been another revolt in the fields of architecture and landscape planning. This was a counter-revolutionary movement against the stark geometric forms and overutilitarianism of the Bauhaus, Gropius, and "Corbu" and their fervent disciples, myself among them.

The first mellowing phase of the raw post–Bauhaus evolution added a welcome warmth and richness. It produced what many believe to be the finest designs of the century. Not only in architecture, but in the related arts and sciences as well. While the direct fulfilling of need remained a given, and while "styles" and ornamentation were taboo, the hard lines were softened, textures and colors were given full play, and sculptors, weavers, and artists were welcomed back into the fold. Buildings were opened up to the sun, the breeze, and the view. Nature was rediscovered.

In landscape planning the trend veered abruptly away from the formalism of the European Renaissance—to one of respect for topographical form and features. The great expanses of leveled and patterned nothingness disappeared along with clipped parterres, the laboriously tended "knot garden," and the demanding axis. Hillocks, ravines, and wooded slopes were left intact to be admired—as were rock outcroppings, springs, streams, dunes, and tidal estuaries. It seemed a near return to Olmstedian times, with echoes of Thoreau. One could hear Aldo Leopold calling.

Then came *postmodernism*, the "full flowering" of the revolution. In the name of free expression, it elaborated. It distorted. It fantasized. In its heyday it created some of the most bizarre, flamboyant structures and artifacts yet foisted on the public. True—banks, office buildings, and private homes no longer resembled the Beaux Arts Greek temples, Tudor palaces, or Georgian countinghouses. Nor the sometimes brutal concrete and glass constructions of Bauhaus times. Instead, the postmodern "blossoming"

Architecture is again in transition. This time in a knee-jerk reaction to the bombastic excesses of later postmodernism to a time of searching introspection. A turning from buildings conceived principally as design objects to simpler, less pretentious and more humane structures. From those designed to dominate their sites to those fitted compatibly to ground forms, drainage patterns, vegetation, and the arc of the sun. From showpiece mechanisms to environment-friendly, indoor-outdoor habitations conducive to living the good, full life.

brought on a fantasyland of utter disfunctionalism. Office towers built in regions of blazing summer heat and winter chill, for example, were conceived as glittering Valhallas—with cooling and heating loads that sank their sponsors financially. No matter, the creations made a powerful statement. Too often, however, the only statement was, "Look at me. Look at me. Look at *me.*"

In the extreme, some landscape architects as well came to violate the natural sites to which, by rights, their projects should have responded. Self–conscious "landscape art" was "designed" for its shock value. Live trees were sprayed pink. Fountains spouted fresh water in rainbow hues. Exotic bedding plants by the acre replaced native covers of ground pine and trailing arbutus. Human needs, natural systems, and ecologic factors were blithely ignored, and by some, even ridiculed.

Some years ago Henry Elder, a brilliant architectural historian, shared with his students his concept of the cyclical nature of design. By a simple looping diagram, with examples, he traced through recent history the periods of creative innovation, the maturing toward the classic ideal, and then the decline into the fanciful and effete. Elder noted that well before the "bottoming out" there always appear the dissenters who, in revulsion, buck the system in protest and start the next upward loop. In their own rebellious ways they seek a new direction—a fresh start in which design, lean and clean, once again leads the way to expressive and meaningful form.

It may well be time for another revolt, this time with an environmental thrust and an ecological spin. A time when once again "form follows function," but in which the context of *function* is expanded to include the accommodation of *all* human needs and aspirations.

¡Viva la revolución!

Landscape art is not to be confused with landscape architecture. In the former context, natural elements such as water, stone, or plant materials are used to create a pictorial design or aesthetic experience.

Landscape architecture differs in that it is the art and science of preserving or creating compatible relationships between people and their activities and the natural world about them.

At every turn in the progressive development of our profession there is need for experimentation and innovation. There is need, too, for a constant infusion of new ideas from the world of art and from artists on the leading edge. It is essential, however, that we differentiate between the timely and welcome contributions of landscape artists and the timeless and far broader mission of the landscape architect.

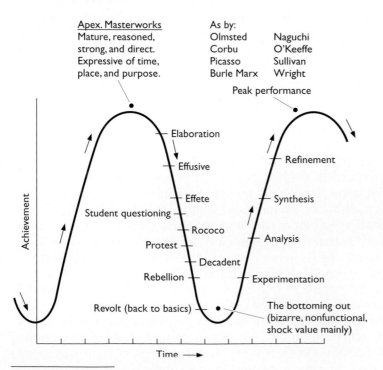

Apex. Masterworks
Mature, reasoned, strong, and direct. Expressive of time, place, and purpose.

As by:
Olmsted   Naguchi
Corbu   O'Keeffe
Picasso   Sullivan
Burle Marx   Wright

Peak performance

Elaboration
Effusive
Effete
Student questioning
Rococo
Protest
Decadent
Rebellion
Revolt (back to basics)

Refinement
Synthesis
Analysis
Experimentation
The bottoming out (bizarre, nonfunctional, shock value mainly)

Achievement

Time →

The Cycles of Design Expression
As in the arts, architecture, and landscape architecture

One plans not places, or spaces, or things . . . one plans experiences:
Mellon Square, Pittsburgh.

The Planned Experience

One plans not places, spaces, or things; one plans *experiences*.

By this criterion, a highway is not best designed as a strip of pavement of given section, alignment, and grade. A highway is properly conceived as an experience of movement. The successful highway is planned, in this light, to provide for the user a pleasant and convenient passage from point to point through well-modulated spaces with a maximum of satisfaction and a minimum of friction. Many of the serious failures of American roadways stem from the astounding fact that, in their planning, the actual experience of their use was never even considered.

The best community, by this test, is that which provides for its habitants the best experience of living.

A garden, by this standard, is not designed as an exercise in geometry; it is not a self-conscious construction of globes, cubes, prisms, and planes within which are contained the garden elements. In such a geometric framework the essential qualities of stone, water, and plant materials are usually lost. Their primary relationship is not to the observer but to the geometry of the plan. Final plan forms may be, in some rare cases, severely geometric,

Essentially the best living space, indoors and out, is that best suited to the needs and desires of the users.

but to have validity a form must be derived from a planned experience rather than the experience from the preconceived form.

A garden, perhaps the highest, most difficult art form, is best conceived as a series of planned relationships of human to human, human to structure, and human to some facet or facets of nature, such as the lichen–encrusted tree bole of an ancient ginkgo tree, a sprightly sun–flecked magnolia clump, a trickle of water, a foaming cascade, a pool, a collection of rare tree peonies, or a New Hampshire upland meadow view.

A *city*, also, is best conceived as an environment in which human life patterns may be ideally related to natural or constructed elements. The most pleasurable aspects of cities throughout history have not derived from their plan geometry. Rather, they have resulted from the essential fact that, in their planning and growth, the life functions and aspirations of the citizens were considered, accommodated, and expressed.

To the Athenian, Athens was infinitely more than a pattern of streets and structures. To the Athenian, Athens was first of all a glorious way of life. What was true of Athens should be no less true of our "enlightened" urban planning of today.

The design approach then is not essentially a search for form, not primarily an application of principles. The true design approach stems from the realization that a plan has meaning only to people for whom it is planned and only to the degree to which it brings facility, accommodation, and delight to their senses. It is a creation of optimum relationships resulting in a total experience.

We make much of this matter of relationships. What then is an optimum relationship between a person and a given thing? It is one that reveals the highest inherent qualities of that which is perceived.

> To understand life, and to conceive form to express this life, is the great art. . . . And I have learned to know that in order to understand both art and life one must go down to the source of all things: to nature. . . .
>
> Nature's laws—the laws of "beauty," if you will—are fundamental, and cannot be shaken by mere esthetic conceitedness. These laws might not be always consciously apprehended, but subconsciously one is always under their influence. . . .
>
> The more we study nature's form-world, the more clearly it becomes evident how rich in inventiveness, nuances, and shiftings nature's form-language is. And the more deeply we learn to realize, in nature's realm, expressiveness is "basic."
>
> Eliel Saarinen

Successful landscape planning and design brings all elements—land and water forms, structures, and paths of movement—into harmonious relationship. (Pelican Bay Planned Community, Naples, Florida)

> *For to live, wholly to live, is the manifest consummation of existence.*
>
> Louis H. Sullivan

Nautilus.

In the final analysis, in even the most highly developed areas or details one can never plan or control the transient nuances, the happy accidents, the minute variables of anything experienced; for most things sensed are unpredictable and often hold their very interest and value in this quality of unpredictability. In watching, for instance, an open fire, one senses the licking flame, the glowing coal, the evanescent ash, the spewing gas, the writhing smoke, the soft splutterings, the sharp crackle, and the dancing lights and shadows. One cannot control these innumerable perceptions that, in their composite, produce the total experience. One can only, for a given circumstance or for a given function, plan a pattern of harmonious relationships, the optimum framework, the maximum opportunity.

The perception of relationships produces an experience. If the relationships are unpleasant, the experience is unpleasant. If the relationships sensed are those of fitness, convenience, and order, the experience is one of pleasure, and the degree of pleasure is dependent on the degree of fitness, convenience, and order.

Fitness implies the use of the right material, the right shape, the right size, and the right volumetric enframement. *Convenience* implies facility of movement, lack of friction, comfort, safety, and reward. *Order* implies a logical sequence and a rational arrangement of the parts.

The perception of harmonious relationships, we learn, produces an experience of pleasure. It also produces an experience of *beauty*. What is this elusive and magical quality called *beauty?* By reasoning, it becomes evident that beauty is not in itself a thing primarily planned for. Beauty is a result. It is a phenomenon that occurs at a given moment or place when, and only when, all relationships are perceived to be harmonious. If this is so, then beauty as well as usefulness should be the end result of design.

All planning of and within the landscape should seek the optimum relationship between people and their living environment and thus, per se, the creation of a paradise on earth. Doubtless this will never be fully accomplished. Humans are, sadly, too human. Moreover, because the very nature of nature is change, such planning would be continuing, without possible completion, without end. And so it must be. But we may learn from history that the completion is not the ultimate goal. The goal for all physical planners is an enlightened planning *approach*. Again, for instruction on this point, we may turn to the wisdom of the east. Because of the dynamic nature of their philosophies, the Zen and Taoist conceptions of perfection lay more stress upon the process through which perfection is sought than upon perfection itself. The Zen and Taoist art of life lies in a constant and studied readjustment to nature and one's surroundings, the art of self-realization, the art of "being in the world."

Plan not in terms of meaningless pattern or cold form. Plan, rather, a human experience. The living, pulsing, vital experience, if conceived as a diagram of harmonious relationships, will develop its own expressive forms. And the forms evolved will be as organic as the shell of the nautilus; and perhaps, if the plan is successful, it may be as beautiful.

Dowden, C. James: *Community Associations: A Guide for Public Officials Published Jointly by the Urban Land Institute and the Community Associations Institute*, Washington, D.C., 1980.

Hall, Kenneth B.: *A Concise Guide to Community Planning*, McGraw–Hill, New York, 1994.

Harker, Donald, and Elizabeth Ungar Natter: *Where We Live: A Citizen's Guide to Conducting a Community Environmental Inventory*, Island Press, Washington, D.C., 1995.

Hester, Randolph T., Jr.: *Planning Neighborhood Space with People*, Van Nostrand Reinhold, New York, 1984.

Little, Charles E.: *Challenge of the Land: Open Space Preservation*, Pergamon Press, New York, 1969.

Moore, Colleen Grogan: *PUD's In Practice*, Urban Land Institute, Washington, D.C., 1985.

Smart, Eric: *Making Infill Projects Work*, Urban Land Institute and Lincoln Institute of Land Policy, Washington, D.C., 1985.

Terrene Institute (and U.S. EPA): *Local Ordinances: A User's Guide*, Terrene Institute, Washington, D.C., 1995.

Whyte, William H.: *Cluster Development*, American Conservation Association, New York, 1964.

4. Urban and Regional Form

Urban and regional patterns and form receive attention in these references on land use, transportation, recreation, and resource planning.

Arendt, Randall: *Rural By Design: Maintaining Small Town Character*, Planners' Press, Chicago, 1994.

Bacon, Edmund N.: *Design of Cities*, rev. ed., Viking Press, New York, 1974.

Breen, Ann, and Dick Rigby: *The New Waterfront: A Worldwide Urban Success Story*, McGraw–Hill, New York, 1996.

Calthorpe, Peter: *The Next American Metropolis: Ecology, Community, and the American Dream*, Princeton Architectural Press, New York, 1993.

Collins, Richard C., Elizabeth B. Waters, and A. Bruce Dotson: *America's Downtowns: Growth, Politics and Preservation*, Preservation Press, The National Trust for Historic Preservation, Washington, D.C., 1990.

Harr, Charles M.: *Land Use Planning: A Casebook on the Use, Misuse, and Reuse of Urban Land*, Little, Brown, Boston, 1976.

Jacobs, Jane: *The Death and Life of Great American Cities*, Modern Library, New York, 1993. (Originally published 1961.)

Katz, Peter: *The New Urbanism: Toward an Architecture of Community*, McGraw–Hill, New York, 1993.

Kunstler, James Howard: *The Geography of Nowhere: The Rise and Decline of America's Man-Made Landscape*, Simon & Schuster, New York, 1993.

Laurie, Ian C.: *Nature in Cities*, John Wiley & Sons, New York, 1979.

Little, Charles: *Greenways for America*, Johns Hopkins University Press, Baltimore, 1990.

MacKaye, Benton: *The New Exploration: A Philosophy of Regional Planning*, University of Illinois Press, Urbana, Ill., 1962.

Mertes, James D., and James R. Hall: *Park, Recreation Open Space, and Greenway Guidelines*, National Park and Recreation Association in cooperation with the American Academy for Park and Recreation Administration, Washington, D.C., 1996.

Simonds, John Ormsbee: *Garden Cities 21: Creating a Livable Urban Environment*, McGraw–Hill, New York, 1994.

Spirn, Anne Whiston: *The Granite Garden, Urban Nature and Human Design*, Basic Books, New York, 1984.

Spreiregen, Paul D.: *Urban Design: The Architecture of Town and Cities*, McGraw–Hill, New York, 1965.

Whittick, Arnold (ed.): *Encyclopedia of Urban Planning*, McGraw–Hill, New York, 1974.

Whyte, William H., Jr.: *Rediscovering the Center City*, Doubleday, New York, 1990.

5. Site Planning

Among the many excellent source books on site and landscape planning and design, the following provide a working introduction.

Brown, Karen M., and Curtis Charles: *Computers in the Professional Practice of Design*, McGraw–Hill, New York, 1995.

Church, Thomas D., et al.: *Gardens Are for People*, 3d ed., University of California Press, Berkeley, Calif., 1995.

Collins, Lester A.: *Innisfree, An American Garden*, Sagapress/Harry Abrams, New York, 1994.

Crowe, Sylvia: *Garden Design*, Antique Collectors Club, Wappingers Falls, N.Y., 1994.

Dattner, Richard: *Civil Architecture: The New Public Infrastructure*, McGraw–Hill, New York, 1994.

Eckbo, Garrett, *Philosophy of Landscape*, Process Architecture Co., Tokyo, 1995.

EDAW: *The Integrated World*, Process Architecture Co., Tokyo, 1994.

Harris, Charles W., and Nicholas T. Dines: *Time-Saver Standards for Landscape Architecture*, McGraw–Hill, New York, 1988.

Kiley, Dan: *In Step with Nature*, Process Architecture Co., Tokyo, 1993.

Lebovich, William L.: *Design for Dignity*, John Wiley & Sons, New York, 1993.

Oehme, Wolfgang, and James van Sweden: *Bold Romantic Gardens*, Acropolis Books, Reston, Va., 1990.

Robinette, Gary O.: *Water Conservation in Landscape Design and Management*, Van Nostrand Reinhold, New York, 1984.

Van Sweden, James: *Gardening With Water*, Random House, New York, 1995.

Walker, Peter, William Johnson, and Partners: *Art and Nature*, Process Architecture Co., Tokyo, 1994.

Zion, Robert: *Landscape Architecture*, Process Architecture Co., Tokyo, 1994.

Other Publications:

(Bookstore catalogs available)

American Institute of Architects
1735 New York Avenue, N.W.
Washington, DC 20006

American Planning Association
122 S. Michigan Ave.
Suite 1600
Chicago, IL 60603

American Society of Landscape Architects
4401 Connecticut Avenue, N.W.
Washington, DC 20008

Community Builders Handbook Series
Urban Land Institute
625 Indiana Avenue, N.W.
Washington, DC 20004–2930

Process Architecture Publications
Process Architecture Publishing Co., Ltd.
1–47–2–418 Sasazuka,
Shibuya-Ku
Tokyo, Japan

Sierra Club Books
2034 Fillmore St.
San Francisco, CA 94115

Sunset Magazine: Sunset Gardening and Outdoor Books publish an enduring series of excellent paperback publications relating particularly to residential landscape design.
Lane Publishing Company
Menlo Park, CA 94025

Quotation Sources (page)

Adams, Henry: *The Education of Henry Adams*, Houghton Mifflin, Boston, 1928 (336)

Ardrey, Robert: *African Genesis*, Dell, New York, 1961 (8)

Aristotle: *Rhetoric* (139)

Bacon, Edmund N.: *Planning*, The American Society of Planning Officials, Chicago, 1958 (361)

Beck, Walter: *Painting with Starch*, Van Nostrand, Princeton, N.J., 1956 (284)

Bel Geddes, Norman: *Magic Motorways*, Random House, New York, 1940 (256, 259)

Benét, Stephen Vincent: *Western Star*, Farrar & Rinehart, New York, 1943 (6)

Bergmann, Karen: *Landscape Architecture*, May 1990 (196)

Berry, Wendell: *Another Turn of the Crank*, Counterpoint, Washington, D.C., 1995 (360, 379)

———: *The Gift of Good Land*, North Point Press, San Francisco, 1981 (379)

Borissavliévitch, Miloutine: *The Golden Number*, Alec Tiranti, London, 1958 (286)

Bowie, Henry P.: *On the Laws of Japanese Painting*, Dover, New York, 1952 (republication of 1911 edition) (126)

Braun, Ernest, and David E. Cavagnaro, *Living Water*, The American West Publishing Company, Palo Alto, Calif., 1971 (11)

Breuer, Marcel: In conversation (280)

———: *Sun and Shadow*, Dodd, Mead, New York, 1955 (376)

Bronowski, Jacob: *Arts and Architecture*, February and December 1957 (3, 126, 235)

Carson, Rachel: *The Sea around Us*, Oxford University Press, New York, 1951 (17)

Carson, Rachel: *Silent Spring*, Buccaneer Books, New York, 1994 (6)

Carver, Norman F., Jr.: *Form and Space of Japanese Architecture*, Charles E. Tuttle, Rutland, Vt., 1956 (249)

Chase, Alston: *In a Dark Wood*, Houghton Mifflin, Boston, 1995 (16)

Church, Thomas D.: *Gardens Are for People*, Reinhold, New York, 1955 (264, 298)

———: Quoted in article by Dr. Joseph E. Howland in *Southern Florist and Nurseryman*, January 30; 1981 (300)

Churchill, Henry S.: *The City Is the People*, Harcourt, Brace, New York, 1945 (336, 361)

Clark, Kenneth: *Civilisation*, Harper & Row, New York, 1969 (5)

Clawson, Marion: *Man and Land in the United States*, University of Nebraska Press, Lincoln, 1964 (39)

Clay, Grady: *Water and the Landscape*, McGraw–Hill, New York, 1979 (93, 346)

Crowe, Sylvia: *Tomorrow's Landscape*, Architectural Press, London, 1956 (360)

Cullen, Gordon: *Townscape*, Reinhold, New York, 1961 (195)

Danby, Hope: *The Garden of Perfect Brightness*, Henry Regnery Company, Chicago, 1950 (236)

Eckbo, Garrett: *Landscape Architecture*, May 1990 (115)

———: *Landscape for Living*, McGraw–Hill Information Systems Company, McGraw–Hill, Inc., New York, 1950 (118, 178, 360)

Eiscley, Loren: *The Immense Journey*, Random House, New York, 1957 (52)

Gallion, Arthur B.: *The Urban Pattern*, Van Nostrand, New York, 1949 (336)

Gardner, James, and Caroline Heller: *Exhibition and Display*, McGraw–Hill Information Systems Company, McGraw–Hill, Inc., New York, 1960 (252)

Giedion, Siegfried: *Space, Time and Architecture*, Harvard University Press, Cambridge, Mass., 1941 (98, 114)

Goshorn, Warner S.: In correspondence with Harold S. Wagner (40)

Graham, Wade: "The Grassman," *The New Yorker*, August 19, 1996 (62)

Gropius, Walter: "The Curse of Conformity," *The Saturday Evening Post*, September 6, 1958 (380)

———: *Scope of Total Architecture*, Harper, New York, 1955 (350)

Gutkind, E. A.: *Community and Environment*, C. A. Watts & Co., London, 1953 (14, 318)

Hayakawa, S. I.: *Language in Thought and Action*, Harcourt, Brace, New York, 1939 (4, 240)

Hilberseimer, Ludwig K.: *The New Regional Pattern*, Paul Theobald, Chicago, 1949 (256, 366)

Hubbard, Henry V., and T. Kimball: *An Introduction to the Study of Landscape Design*, Macmillan, New York, 1917 (234)

Huxley, Julian: "Are There Too Many of Us?" *Horizon*, September 1958 (378)

Kennedy, John F.: Quoted in *Hydroscope*, publication of the Southwest Florida Water Management District, December 1979 (60)

Kepes, Gyorgy: *Language of Vision*, Paul Theobald, Chicago, 1944 (233, 240)

Landscape Architecture, October 1994 (326)

Lawrence, D. H.: *Etruscan Places*, Martin Secker, London, 1932 (5)

Le Corbusier: *The Radiant City*, republication, Orion Press, New York, 1964 (100, 282)

Leopold, Aldo: *A Sand County Almanac*, reprint, Oxford University Press, Fair Lawn, N.J., 1969 (43, 262)

Li, H. H.: Translation of Chinese manuscript (7)

McHarg, Ian L.: *Landscape Architecture* (quarterly magazine of the American Society of Landscape Architects), January 1958 (366)

McHarg, Ian: *A Quest for Life: An Autobiography*, John Wiley & Sons, New York, 1996 (16, 350)

McPhee, John: *Coming into the Country*, Bantam, New York, 1979 (39, 40)

Mendelsohn, Eric: *Perspecta* (the Yale architectural journal), 1957 (235)

Michener, James: *Return to Paradise*, Random House, New York, 1951 (6)

Millay, Edna St. Vincent: "The Goose-Girl," *Collected Lyrics of Edna St. Vincent Millay*, Harper and Brothers, New York, 1939 (296)

Moholy-Nagy, László: *The New Vision*, Wittenborn, Schultz, New York, 1928 (182, 235, 381)

Mumford, Lewis: *The Culture of Cities*, Harcourt, Brace, New York, 1938 (10, 336, 360, 364, 380)

———: *Faith for Living*, Harcourt, Brace, New York, 1940 (320, 376)

Neutra, Richard J.: *Survival through Design*, Oxford University Press, New York, 1954 (7, 188)

Newton, Norman T.: *An Approach to Design*, Addison–Wesley, Cambridge, Mass., 1941 (9, 235)

Niemeyer, Oscar: *Modulo* (286)

Ognibene, Peter J.: "Vanishing Farmlands," *Saturday Review*, May 1980 (42)

Okakura, Kakuzo: *The Book of Tea*, Charles E. Tuttle, Rutland, Vt., 1958 (153)

Phillips, Patricia C.: *Landscape Architecture*, December 1994 (332)

Pope, Alexander: *Of the Use of Riches* (7)

Rasmussen, Steen Eiler: *Towns and Buildings*, Harvard University Press, Cambridge, Mass., 1951 (284)

Read, Sir Herbert: *Arts and Architecture*, May 1954 (180)

Reed, Henry H., Jr.: *Perspecta* (the Yale architectural journal), 1952 (226)

Russell, Bertrand: "The Expanding Mental Universe," *The Saturday Evening Post*, July 18, 1959 (9)

Saarinen, Eliel: *Search for Form*, Reinhold, New York, 1948 (114, 231, 232, 288, 372, 390)

Santayana, George: *The Sense of Beauty*, Dover, New York, 1955 (234)

Sert, José Luis, and C.I.A.M.: *Can Our Cities Survive?* Harvard University Press, Cambridge, Mass., 1942 (283, 332)

Severud, Fred M.: "Turtles and Walnuts, Morning Glories and Grass," *Architectural Forum*, September 1945 (12)

Shigemori, Kanto: In conversation (296)

Simonds, Dylan Todd: In correspondence (342)

Simonds, John Todd: In conversation (3)

Sitte, Camillo: *The Art of Building Cities*, Reinhold, New York, 1945 (231, 282, 285, 333)

Spencer, Earl F.: As quoted by Wendell Berry in *The Gift of Good Land*, North Point Press, New York, 1981 (6)

Spengler, Oswald: *Decline of the West*, Alfred A. Knopf, New York, 1939 (189)

Sullivan, Louis H.: *Kindergarten Chats*, Wittenborn, Schultz, New York, 1947 (236, 391)

Sze, Mai–mai: *The Tao of Painting*, The Bollingen Foundation, New York, 1956 (17)

Taut, Bruno: *Fundamentals of Japanese Architecture*, Kokusai Bunka Shinkōkai, Tokyo, 1936 (188)

Tunnard, Christopher: *Gardens in the Modern Landscape*, Charles Scribner's, New York, 1948 (13, 99)

Van der Ryn, Sim, and Stuart Cowan: *Ecological Design*, Island Press, Washington, D.C., 1996 (6, 11, 38, 379)

Van Loon, Hendrik: *The Story of Mankind*, Boni and Liveright, New York, 1921 (9)

Veri, Albert R., et al.: *Environmental Quality by Design: South Florida*, University of Miami Press, Coral Gables, Fla., 1975 (15, 64)

White, Stanley: *A Primer of Landscape Architecture*, University of Illinois, Urbana, 1956 (12, 15, 102)

Whyte, Lancelot Law: "Some Thoughts on the Design of Nature and Their Implications for Education," *Arts and Architecture*, January 1956 (4)

Whyte, William H., Jr.: *The Exploding Metropolis*, Doubleday, New York, 1958 (336)

Wittkower, Rudolph: *Architectural Principles in the Age of Humanism*, University of London, Warburg Institute, 1949 (287)

The World's Great Religions, Time Inc., New York, 1957 (11)

Zevi, Bruno: *Architecture as Space*, Horizon Press, New York, 1957 (186)

Illustration Credits

Except for photos by the author, the images shown have been provided by courtesy of the following offices, firms, or professional photographers. Position on the page is indicated as follows: T = top; B = bottom; M = middle; L = left; R = right.

2, Grant Heilman; 5T, Arthur Rothstein; 5B, Grant Heilman; 6, Underwood and Underwood; 7, Grant Heilman; 8, Underwood and Underwood; 9, Ansel Adams; 10BL, 10BM, Harry Callahan; 10BR, 11, 12TL, 12TR, Carl Struwe; 12BL, BM, BR, 13B, Hermann Eisenbeiss, courtesy LIVING LEICA; 13T, Aero Service Corporation; 14TL, Siegfried Hartig, courtesy LIVING LEICA; 16, Belt Collins Hawaii; 17T, Courtesy Mount Wilson and Palomar Observatories; 17B, U.S. Atomic Energy Commission; 18-19, Grant Heilman; 21B, Courtesy Northstar-at-Tahoe; 22T, 22B, 24T, 24B, Grant Heilman; 26-27, Author; 28, Lloyd Bond; 32-33, 34, Grant Heilman; 36TL, 36TR, 36B, 37TL, The Department of Conservation and Recreation, Commonwealth of Virginia, and the Virginia Tourism Corporation; 37TR, The Department of Conservation and Recreation, Commonwealth of Virginia, and the Virginia Tourism Corporation. Photo: Tim Thompson; 37M, The Department of Conservation and Recreation, Commonwealth of Virginia, and the Virginia Tourism Corporation. Photo: Dwight Dyke; 37B, The Department of Conservation and Recreation, Commonwealth of Virginia, and the Virginia Tourism Corporation. Photo: Richard Gibbons; 38, 39, 41, 42, 50-51, Grant Heilman; 53T, The Department of Conservation and Recreation, Commonwealth of Virginia, and the Virginia Tourism Corporation; 53B, EPD (Environmental Planning and Design); 55TL, Author; 55TR, Sasaki Associates, Inc.; 55BL, 55BR, Author; 56TL, The Department of Conservation and Recreation, Commonwealth of Virginia, and the Virginia Tourism Corporation. Photo: Dwight Dyke; 56TR, Minneapolis Park and Recreation Board; 56B, The Department of Conservation and Recreation, Commonwealth of Virginia, and the Virginia Tourism Corporation; 57T, The Department of Conservation and Recreation, Commonwealth of Virginia, and the Virginia Tourism Corporation. Photo: Dwight Dyke; 57M, 57B, The Department of Conservation and Recreation, Commonwealth of Virginia, and the Virginia Tourism Corporation; 58M, 58B, Grant Heilman; 59, Author; 60, 61, Belt Collins Hawaii; 62, Oehme, van Sweden & Associates; 63, McFadden Air Photos, courtesy Sengra Development Corp.; 64T, Author; 64B, Courtesy The Springs, Longwood, Florida; 65, Sasaki Associates, Inc. Photo: Nick Wheeler; 66TL, EPD; 66TR, Minneapolis Park and Recreation Board; 66BL, Photo: Edward L. Blake, Jr.; 66BR, 67T, Sasaki Associates, Inc.; 67M, Theodore Osmundson & Associates; 67BL, EPD; 67BR, Sasaki Associates, Inc. Photo: Roy J. Wright; 69, Belt Collins Australia; 70, Royston, Hanamoto, Alley & Abey; 76TL, Oehme, van Sweden & Associates. Photo: James Anthony van Sweden; 76TR, Oehme, van Sweden & Associates; 76BL, 76BR, EPD; 77TL, Island Developers Ltd., Fisher Island, Florida; 77TR, Wallace Roberts & Todd; 77B, Island Developers Ltd., Fisher Island, Florida; 78T, Sasaki Associates, Inc. Photo: Alan Ward; 78B, Sasaki Associates, Inc. Photo: Susan Duca; 79TL, Oehme, van Sweden & Associates; 79TR, Courtland P. Paul, Peridian Group. Photo: Ronald Izumita; 79B, Sasaki Associates, Inc.; 80, 82, Author; 85, EPD; 87, Grant Heilman; 88-89, 90T, 90B, 91T, 91M, 91B, Author; 93, Courtesy Burnham Hoyt, Architect; 94, Underwood and Underwood; 95, Courtesy Italian State Tourist Office, New York City; 96, Cour-

tesy Miller, Wihry, Lee, Inc., Landscape Architects, Engineers, and Planners; 97, Norman F. Carver, Jr.; 98, Royston, Hanamoto, Alley & Abey; 98M, Underwood and Underwood; 99T, EPD; 99B, Belt Collins Hawaii; 100T, Michio Fujioka; 100B, Courtesy Dr. Siegfried Giedion and the Swiss National Tourist Office, New York City; 101, Rollie McKenna; 103, Author; 104-105, Arthur Hills and Associates; 109, U.S.G.S. Information Service, Denver Federal Center, Denver, CO 80225; 111, Arthur Hills and Associates and The Golf Club of Georgia; 112-113, Belt Collins International; 116T, Sengra Development Corp.; 116M, Oehme, van Sweden & Associates. Photo: James Anthony van Sweden; 131, Belt Collins Hawaii; 133-135, Courtesy William J. Johnston, FASLA; 136-137, 140TL, 140TM, 140TR, Falcon & Bueno; 141, Edward Pinckney; 143T, 143M, Pedro E. Guerrero; 144T, Hedrich-Blessing; 144B, EPD; 145, Photos: John E. Hoffman; 148TL, Belt Collins Hawaii—Golfscapes; 148ML, Edward Pinckney; 148BL, Oehme, van Sweden & Associates. Photo: James Anthony van Sweden; 148R, Belt Collins International; 149TL, Wallace Roberts & Todd; 149TM, Sasaki Associates, Inc.; 149TR, Belt Collins Hawaii; 149ML, Belt Collins Hong Kong; 149MR, 149BL, 149BR, 150, Sasaki Associates, Inc.; 151, Mitchell & Ritchey, Architects; 152T, Rollie McKenna; 152B, G. E. Kidder Smith; 155T, Clarke + Rapuano; 155B, Sasaki Associates, Inc. Photo: Susan Duca; 164-165, Oehme, van Sweden & Associates; 167, Arthur Hills and Associates, 168, EPD; 169, Oehme, van Sweden & Associates; 170L, Island Developers Ltd., Fisher Island, Florida. Landscape Architect: Taft Bradshaw, Golf Architect: P. B. Dye, Conceptual Community Planning: EPD; 170R, Author; 171, Royston, Hanamoto, Alley & Abey; 176-177, 178ML, 178TR, Royston, Hanamoto, Alley & Abey; 179TL, Soichi Sunami, courtesy Museum of Modern Art, New York City; 179TR, David E. Scherman, courtesy Museum of Modern Art, New York City; 180, Courtesy Museum of Modern Art, New York City; 181, EDAW Inc., Denver; 182T, © Courtesy Spacenet by Gametime, Inc., Fort Payne, Alabama; 182B, Julius Schulman; 183, Courtesy Museum of Modern Art, New York City; 184TL, The Department of Conservation and Recreation, Commonwealth of Virginia, and the Virginia Tourism Corporation. Photo: Carl Purcell; 184TR, The Department of Conservation and Recreation, Commonwealth of Virginia, and the Virginia Tourism Corporation; 184BL, The Department of Conservation and Recreation, Commonwealth of Virginia. Photo: Richard Gibbons; 184BR, Horst Schach; 185TL, Author; 185TR, Theodore Osmundson & Associates; 185MR, 185BL, Royston, Hanamoto, Alley & Abey; 185BR, The Department of Conservation and Recreation, Commonwealth of Virginia, and the Virginia Tourism Corporation; 186, Leonard Schugar; 187, Gateway Film Productions, Ltd.; 189, G. E. Kidder Smith; 190TL, Lloyd Bond; 190TR, Author; 190BL, Royston, Hanamoto, Alley & Abey; 190BR, Island Developers Ltd., Fisher Island, Florida; 191T, Sasaki Associates, Inc.; 191B, EPD; 194TL, Author; 194TR, Minneapolis Park and Recreation Board; 194B, Island Developers Ltd., Fisher Island, Florida; 195T, Theodore Osmundson & Associates; 195B, Ernest Braun; 196T, Author; 196B, Ezra Stoller; 197TL, Oehme, van Sweden & Associates. Photo: James Anthony van Sweden; 197TR, Author; 197ML, EPD; 197MR, Karen Kienholz Steeb. Photo: Don Normark; 197BL, Author; 197BR, EPD; 198T, Phil Palmer, courtesy California Redwood Association; 198M, Sasaki Associates, Inc.; 198B, Maggie Baylis; 199TL, Jeffrey Lindsay,